STEPHEN KOREIVO

Fifty Years of Tailgate Tales:

The Good, the Fun and the Ugly

First published by Platypus Publishing 2023

Copyright © 2023 by Stephen Koreivo

All rights reserved. No part of this publication may be reproduced, stored or transmitted in any form or by any means, electronic, mechanical, photocopying, recording, scanning, or otherwise without written permission from the publisher. It is illegal to copy this book, post it to a website, or distribute it by any other means without permission.

Stephen Koreivo has no responsibility for the persistence or accuracy of URLs for external or third-party Internet Websites referred to in this publication and does not guarantee that any content on such Websites is, or will remain, accurate or appropriate.

First edition

ISBN: 978-1-959555-83-4

This book was professionally typeset on Reedsy. Find out more at reedsy.com

Through these Tales, the names of many college football players tell this story. Many games reminisced within this journey celebrate victories determined in the final minutes of play. Great effort, dedication, heart, and teamwork came from all of these players – the winners and the defeated. I dedicate this book to all the players and coaches who played to win these games until time expired. Never give up! A most valuable life lesson taught playing the game of college football.

Contents

Foreword	v
Preface	x
Acknowledgement	xvi

I   Tales - mostly the Good and the Fun!

America's Teams - Forever	3
Turncoat and Burnout / Close encounters	9
Culture Shock! Dawg Days.	14
Stunners	21
The End of the Beginning to Nowhere	26
Ups and Downs in Happy Valley	30
College Football History 101 / From "Bear" to Saban	39
Not just Basketball	43
Prelude to a Championship / "The Fridge"	47
Bowling Cougars / Charlie's Corner	52
Of Feathers, Flame and Philadelphia History	56
Tigers from Guinea Pigs to Top Dogs	60
From Low-scoring Affairs to Travels with St. Laurie	63
Pitt Pride Pays Me Well	66
Sentimental Souvenirs /"And Almost Oh"	68
Orange Streak to Six Bowls /"Wild Horses" to the Fifth...	73
You Call This a Classic? / Husker – Power!	77
"How's the Corn …?" / Hawkeye Happenings	81
How about those Hurricanes? / Collective Caveat.	86
From Royal plan to "Dodge-ball" to Super-Conferences	91

Classic Lesson: Bring us your Quarterback! Strategic...	95
Against Gators, "No-Show Bo!" / Later, Best of Gators.	101
Down to the wire…and beyond! / OSU vs PSU Rivalry.	104
From Low-budget to New Heights	108
Welcome, "New Ball Coaches"	112
"♪Yogi Bear is smarter than the average bear…♪"	115
"Wunderbride" and "Wunderkind"	118
Battles for Bowls	125
Fumble-fest to a Miracle on Techwood Drive	129
King of the Commander-in-Chief's Trophy / Into the Wild Blue...	134
This Side of the Rainbow and Back / ...	140
Ten + one = Big Ten? / Game 600!	145
Rush hour in Un-Happy Valley / Cheerleader – Not!	151
Upset! Upset! Upset! And Avoiding Deacon Blues	157
Historic Doormat No More / Wildcat Leader	163
Rose-colored Frog / Oregon Trails	167
♪♪ Goin' to Carolina… ♪♪ / Easy Pickings …	171
Seeing Red! Now Orange, thanks to "Jersey Mike"	176
From the Ashes to the Rising Sun Belt	186
Greatest Game Ever! / Killing the Moment	192
Location! Location! Location!	199
Try this at your local super market! / Aggies look to Jerry...	201
Watch a Blow-out, Fix a Flat / At West Point, Who'll Stop...	206
Snatched from the Jaws of Defeat! / Memphis vs. Mids	209
Not your Father's Homecoming / ...	212
Rockets Sink Navy	216
Advance to the Big-time! / UConn's Man Dan / Portal traps	218
One Burnt Cookie / Greatest FBS Comeback	223
Eli's Comin'! So are reviewable plays / The Grove!	229
A Whole, New World	236
From Toys of Troy / To Transfer Portals	242
From Storrs to Logan to Tuscaloosa.	248

Now that's what I call service! / Blind-side Block	254
Time and Now Tide / The D-3...	264
Angel in the Desert / Why to Wyoming?	268
End runs and Enron / Record-setting trip	274
Shipshewanna, Indiana / Punt, Leach, Punt	280
Still Rockin' State Stifles Mike Leach	286
Am I really here? / Bowl Selections and Perceptions	290
Toe beats Heels by a Foot / ...	298
Dumped on!	301
Undefeated and BCS-bound - Not! / ♫♫Liberty! Liberty!...	304
Didn't get a good night's sleep? / ...	308
UNJ-Durham Fans? / My Two Utes Games	313
Out on the Nut Farm / Finding my Way to San Jose.	316
Mr. San Diego State! Aztec to the End / UTEP joins C-USA	322
Hey, Ralphie...Girl? /"Prime Time."	331
Honorary Pony on The Boulevard / Pony Express to...	342
Not so Green, and not that Mean / On to AAC	347
It's the Final Countdown!	350
Will-Call / Terrible Trio – CFP, Sooners and The Heisman	355
Shoot-out at OK State!	361
Perfect Ending! A Future Rivalry / A Step Back / Note: Sorry...	365
Hilltoppers rocky-topped! Whew!	371
Reason for this Season / USA - Full Speed Ahead	375
To be Big Time, or not Big-Time? / Back to the FCS?	381
Texas State – only a beginning / TXST...	384
These are the Good, Old Days / As the Tide Turns	389
Fight Fire with Fire, and "Ice" with "Ice"	394
Battle of the Interims / Legacy of Joe Moglia	400
Battle of Independents	405
It's not over! Fast forward to…	412

II   Essay I

Vision of the Future   419

III   Essay II

For the Love of the Game   449
Afterword   472
Bucket List   474
About the Author, Steve Koreivo   477
BIBLIOGRAPHY   479

Foreword

Initially, I started to write this book with only the idea to share a lot of my great experiences attending so many college football games over fifty years. But, beyond game action and history, even more I wanted to share more about friendships, travels, influences that guided me to games I attended, and how I meshed my crazy passion for college football with everyday life, my family, my career, and friendships forged over the course of a lifetime. With all this being said, the original title for this book could have been, "Fifty Years of Tailgate Tales: It's a Wonderful Life."

Eleven years prior, I self-published a book entitled Tales from the Tailgate: From the Fan who's seen 'em all! However, it lacked cohesion. I wrote some good, fun and interesting experiences about how I'd seen every Division-IA college football team play at least once. Copies were printed, the publisher advertised on its website, I was immersed back in my Purchasing career, had little time to promote the book or to re-strategize, and regretfully, did not sell many copies. Since that first publication, I still enjoyed going to games every fall weekend and now even some weekday nights. Through 2021 and headed into retirement, I still enjoyed chasing new adventures. Rather than seek part-time work or consult just to "keep busy," I decided instead to stay focused on my passion for college football and continue my original story line, but primarily to do it better now since I could dedicate more time to share my unique experience.

I signed up for a course about self-publishing to get some practical and professional guidance to help me seek input and strategies on how to present this unique story from a better perspective. I also knew the self-publishing industry had changed a lot since my original endeavor. A major message I took notice of from mentor Matt Rudnitsky of the

Platypus Publishing Team was that people preferred to read books to help improve their lives or to understand a subject better. They sought insight and direction regarding provocative issues. My initial story, happy to say, was unique, light-hearted and fun to share. What could I present so provocatively, however, regarding college football to interest and help potential readers to improve their lives or to better understand?

Well, college football started to undergo major changes impacting it the past few years threatening to change things, some for better, but some for worse, despite many fans enjoying it as is for so long. If you listen to talk show sports programs, they glance over things happening primarily from a positive point of view because they promote sports as their livelihood. However, like some of the benefits discussed regarding these topics, they present the short-term aspects, but don't dwell on long-term implications of our great game. Briefly, here are some of those topics which need to be analyzed further:

- In essence, players sought means to compensate themselves beyond expensive, free educations colleges offered to them. The development of social media they've grown up with allows them to have these opportunities now.
- As one who transferred from D-IA football school to a D-3 back in the '70s, I had to sit out a year of eligibility even though I didn't even play for the initial school's D-IA football program. Now, players can basically transfer to any other school without sitting out for one football season.
- Four years of playing eligibility under NCAA rules became five at most for red-shirt (injury or playing) purposes, and then all players were granted a sixth due to COVID-19 restrictions in 2020. Now the NCAA is even granting waivers for student athletes to play a seventh year of football.
- In the meantime, competition for a championship at the highest level of college football played for by more than 130 teams comes down to basically the same handful of teams annually. What gave them

such superior advantages? Why should this be limited to so few? Granted they may have the best coaches and players, but why always them? Among so many teams, shouldn't more be able from the start to compete as equally as possible to recruit and develop the same quality of coaches and players for the same goal?

Multiple provocative factors started steering college football in a direction to make the sport more competitive for fewer teams rather than for more. To incorporate these issues into my "It's a Wonderful Life" tale, I decided to present my lifetime adventures to share "the Good" and "the Fun" while also starting to address "the Ugly," the best way I could describe the negativity challenging competitiveness for all teams. Some of these issues combined could potentially change this great sports tradition for millions of dedicated fans. Understandably, more would like to see their teams and others challenge for the same success that only that small handful gets to compete for every year.

I took the original stories of games in Tales from the Tailgate and updated the chapters regarding most of the schools seen. I included highlights and adventures surrounding their best of the best games I saw each play in since. I touch on specific significant game action, but more than that, I intertwine this chronological history of how I did this successfully during the course of a lifetime. If anyone has a passion for something beyond family, career and just living everyday life, this is an example that this can be done, and that it can be enjoyed along with the ups and downs of everyday life. Many of the tales told I took directly from Game Reviews I recorded since 2011 on my website www.collegefootballfan.com. Aside from the editing this book to avoid making it too long, that was the easy part. Over the years of reporting on my site, I posted op-ed pieces under the title I call "Steveo's Salvos." I reported on current events taking place in college football. Some involved a particular program while others were more in general about the entire sport.

Since the end of the 2022 college season as I started to write Fifty Years of Tailgate Tales: The Good, the Fun, and the Ugly, a lot was already happening regarding changes to college football. Instead of writing more "Salvos" online, I started to work these more provocative issues into my life-long story. This was the tough part. The good thing was I continued to pull together resources and do my analysis. As the season approached, these issues became moving targets at a rapid pace. Things changed almost daily and rumors persisted – like schools changing conferences, players transferring, challenges by the NCAA to players' proposed transfers, state laws offsetting NCAA jurisdiction to maintain fairness within the Association's membership, and news about Name, Image, and Likeness (NILs) contracts influencing players to move about which wasn't the intent supposedly. The toughest part was nailing down and communicating these issues on the fly. Some changes I liked, some I didn't, and some I found hard to understand at all. I always wanted to share some of my own original ideas as well after so many years of following this sport avidly. More due diligence had to be done, more than I originally anticipated, while hoping to self-publish before the start of the upcoming season.

Writing this book took on a new additional meaning to me. I love this great game for all the great experiences I've enjoyed watching games in person and savoring all the experiences surrounding them over the last 50 years. I also admire the game for the lessons it teaches young men outside of the classroom - teamwork, loyalty, commitment, spirit and toughness. However, like other fans, as close as I consider myself to this great game, I envision the future, and I'm not sure where my favorite sport is headed. I observed many factions changing; I see how some changes could make this game better or even worse. However, as I analyzed the impacts of some of these together, I envisioned the world of college football becoming an entity something totally different from what it was intended to be for over the last century.

I think true college football fans may not anticipate how the game may be impacted due to some recent and pending changes. Will fans still embrace college football like they do now? Call me a Traditionalist or a Boomer, but I'm open to changes to improve the sport for players, schools and fans. On the other hand, if several changes forthcoming come to fruition holistically, I don't know if fans are still going to embrace this game as the wonderful, fun tradition we've known it to be.

Preface

"College football—what better way to spend an autumn afternoon?" That catchphrase of ABC's Chris Schenkel during the 1960s always stirs memories of growing up watching NCAA football on television every fall Saturday afternoon. As a kid, I would tune into the games to not only witness the exciting action on the field, but to experience emotions from the sights and sounds surrounding the games – fight songs, drumbeats, school colors, cheerleaders, card sections, chants, feisty mascots, and passionate crowds – and I wanted to experience all of that *in person* someday.

For more than fifty years, I have attended college football games in person and seen every Football Bowl Subdivision (FBS) football program play in person at least once. Great football, of course, but something more. This journey has provided me with a lifetime of rewarding experiences: sharing times with family and friends, visiting new places, making new friends, enjoying memorable travel adventures, and sharing lots of good times around the tailgate or with others while watching a game. In other words, for me, I share a lot of the wonderful moments and memories that make College Football the greatest spectator sport on earth. In this book, I share these good and fun times. However, I also want to reflect and react to how the game has and is starting to change – for better and worse – in recent years and beyond.

My journey began without a plan

After graduation from Juniata College in 1979, I embarked on this journey practically every fall weekend since. Without an actual plan in place, I'd eventually attend games seeing half the "big-time" teams play. Graduate school at non-football Seton Hall University forced me to cut back on my favorite pastime from 1987-1992, but during those years, I began to seek quality instead of quantity — in life as well as in football. In 1989, I married a beautiful, understanding, and forgiving woman (eventually referred to by others as "*St. Laurie*") who changed life as I had known it.

We settled into a typical and mostly happy, home life. Two wonderful kids came along who changed life even more during the 1990s. Through all of the typical, ongoing, lifestyle changes, I still managed, more often than not, and not only always with St. Laurie's blessings, to join up with friends or to bring the family along on a fall Saturday for "*what better way to spend an autumn afternoon?*"

Before the 2000 college football season began, I typically perused team schedules to check out what games I wanted to attend. I realized that I could possibly see nine teams that year that I hadn't seen in action before. That's when the idea hit me. Just how many D-I teams had I seen? I charted my personal history and found that I had already seen 58 of the 114 Division-IA teams play by then. Add the nine new teams in 2000 and less than 50 more such teams remained to be seen in person for me "*to see 'em all.*" Of course, more teams jumped into FBS fray as this adventure continued.

Revelations!

Could such an unimagined goal be possible? Could I actually get to see every IA team play in person at least once in my lifetime? Had anyone else ever done it? I didn't care. This was something that I'd *love* to do. I'd read about avid baseball fans making trips across the United States and Canada to see as many Major and Minor League teams play in as many venues as possible. Why couldn't I try something similar with my own great sports infatuation — college football? It wouldn't be easy based on time, extended travel, growing responsibilities, and of course, money. However, I felt real passion to make this happen. I didn't want to spend fall weekend after weekend sitting at home watching games on television. My desire drove me to see new places, experience the excitement at different venues, travel more of the country, meet with friends or family to spend an afternoon outdoors, visit friends, meet fans from different schools, and embrace the spirit ("electricity in the air") of competitive, college football games.

Granted, I would be focused on only one, maybe two games on a Saturday or over a weekend, causing me to miss many televised games. TV networks expanded more live coverage though, and new shows captured highlights broadcast around the country wrapping up college football Saturdays. It became easier to keep a finger on the pulse of college football nationally on weekends. During my early youth, we had to wait for the Monday newspaper sports sections to post the scores of games completed after their Sunday print deadlines out in that distant region known as *The Far West* - generally games played from the Rockies Mountains all the way to Hawaii.

What was stopping me from seeing every one of the 114 Division-IA college football teams play at least once? Of course, this couldn't all be completed in one season.

Maybe my wife's right when she says, "It's all about me (meaning me, not her)."

By no means did I have access to some private or corporate jet. Who would hire a business major whose experience was comprised of the following college football career:

- One season of "150-lb football," now known as Sprint football, at the Naval Academy where I never made the 158-lb weight limit to play in a game;
- A season of transfer ineligibility at Juniata College spent running scout-team offense for a D-3 program (my frosh cohorts and I called ourselves, "Scout-team All-Americans" to tolerate the three days a week running plays against the first-team defense);
- A year recovering from an ACL and menial meniscus injury from a spring, club lacrosse game self-inflicted over my own stick while

basically getting in shape for football;
- Coming back from that injury in the best shape of my life two football seasons later and eventually walking into the coaching staff meeting after a scrimmage against Millersville State my senior year to say, *"screw this"* (my parting words were, *"This ain't Notre Dame!"*).

Our original coaching staff under our late, great Head Coach Walt Nadzak had moved on to the University of Connecticut while I recovered from my injury. Had they not, things may have turned out differently. After graduation, I could not say I was a college football "player," but I was definitely a college football "practitioner."

Though my plan "to see 'em all" might take years, I knew doing this out of sheer desire would be an experience to savor. Also in 2000, with a wife and two kids, I'd have to figure out how I could get them to buy into my plan, cutting into quality, family time, and the household budget. Realize at that time, my endeavor wasn't to make it to every stadium. That would be divorce no matter how tolerant my saintly wife may be. I had to pick and choose games to attend with a time-constrained plan in place.

In accordance with that, I also still had to earn a living Monday-Friday. Now since 2021 settling into retirement, I'm glad I basically took in one game (and sometimes two) each weekend. As stated, no one paid me to do this. I wanted to do this. I possessed no desire to make a job out of this plan either. Employment doing this would remove the fun and add some pressure by eliminating the freedom of just wanting to enjoy this surreal adventure. I had enough pressure and responsibility along my professional career path. I'd enjoy college football as part of my work-life balancing act.

Finally: my plan and my vision

I developed plans looking at future schedules. How far could I drive to witness a team to add to my quest? Where would I possibly have to fly to? How could I afford it? Where would I stay? Who could I visit nearby to join me? Who could I get to go with me to a particular game? I desired to get this done, but I also wanted to have fun doing it. Of course, I couldn't have continued my "goal," hobby, infatuation, or maybe my "habit" over the years without the blessings of the aforementioned St. Laurie, patron saint of *college* football widows. Up to 676 games attended in all since 1972 to 2022. It's not over. The journey continues.

Keep this in mind as I share my life-long, unique journey

Some readers may find that I was unchallenged because the majority of teams played for the first time against the likes of Penn State, Navy, Army, or Rutgers, or at some neutral site like The Meadowlands. All were within four hours of driving distance as were many smaller school venues. However, I've attended another 250+ games since writing my first book published in 2011 - Tales from the Tailgate: From the Fan Who's Seen 'em all! During those earliest years reported, extensive travel was limited based on my starting salary. Earning $12,000 as a Junior Buyer for Alpha Wire Corporation starting in 1979, my entertainment budget determined where I could afford to go and how much I could spend. For years, I attended most games within a day's drive.

Of course, my initial football-focused budget paid for tickets, beer, gas, game-day parking, tailgate food, beer, and my just-developing, game program library. Of course, that salary also financed my non-football budget. It paid for necessities like rent, beer, utilities, a car, auto insurance, gym membership, softball travels, groceries, and beer (yes, I intentionally mentioned beer twice, for both budgets). Sometimes, I could actually afford to go out on a date.

As my career in Purchasing thrived professionally and financially and helped me rack up frequent flier miles over 42 years. Games played by these same schools later had more significance than the original games attended. I include these follow-ups after a "Fast Forward" notation. Example: In Alabama's chapter, my first-game report tells of me seeing Paul "Bear" Bryant coach twice against his bitter rival, Auburn. I finally attended at game at Bryant-Denny Stadium many years later. It's noted as a second byline in the same chapter starting like this: "Tuscaloosa, Alabama

- Fast Forward to Utah State at Alabama, 2022: I wouldn't attend my next Alabama game until 2013 during the Saban era..."

Each "Fast Forward" forges ahead to a specific, memorable event for that particular team following my original story. A few other experiences for that team leads up to the one I mention in the byline. Believe me, I'm amazed how many games I've attended that their loyal, living fans rate amongst their finest victories. In cases where I've seen a team maybe only once or twice, I share ideas for my Bucket List. A lot of my enjoyment from this adventure comes during my off-season planning. At times, it drives St. Laurie *nuts*!

Ready, break!

So, with my caveats and focus on the future, buckle up your chinstrap, or crack open a few cold brews. I hope you will enjoy reading about this adventure as much as I've enjoyed doing it.

Note: The numbers you will see listed with each school, for example, "(*1*) *Army,*" is based on the chronological order toward "The Goal to see 'em all." The numbers aren't rankings. They reflect the order in which I checked off each team during my escapade to see every team play. Each story starts basically about the first time I watched that particular FBS team play.

Also, please note along the way I continue to report my chronological order of seeing every team play at least once. I note scores of games attended toward the Goal without providing a story. I avoided writing full chapters in this chronicle for every team seen to date for two reasons. 1) Despite other good, fun and applicable stories, I preferred to balance the controversial matters (the Ugly) among what I think are among the best of my Good and Fun scenarios. 2) I didn't want to dilute the focus on the provocative issues I report in two essays after sharing so many memorable tales. I truly believe that these issues need to be addressed. I provide my input and analysis of these in two essays at the end entitled, "Vision of the Future" and "For the Love of the Game."

Acknowledgement

The lifelong adventure in this book is an acknowledgment in itself to so many since it could not have been done without the help and support of a lot of friends and family. They helped me enjoy these many years of traveling and attending over 600 college football games since I started doing this in 1979. Many of them have joined me at games to be quoted in my weekly Game Reviews on www.collegefootballfan.com as my Guest Game Analysts (GGA's). I got to stay at their homes and to tailgate with them when visiting out of town to attend games. Many helped with input, editing, and proofreading of my drafts to help finalize my manuscript for publication.

Special thanks go out to my long-time friends since the beginning: my Auburn connection, Charlie and Lynda Murren, and to my Penn State connection, John and Kelle Massimilla. I've attended games with them longer and more often with them than with anyone else. I also have to give kudos to friends like Jim "Bugaluga" Harton, Wake Forest alum, and the late Mr. San Diego State, Tom Ables, who presented me with other great stories to write about. And the list goes on to include many others who played key roles in helping me and joining me in this fun adventure. I couldn't have done this without them, and it's because of them, their friendships recorded in these tales tied this lifelong story together.

Of course, there are the stories about my wife, "St. Laurie," who lends different and conflicting perspectives to my adventure, and yet we still enjoy our life together tremendously. My daughter Alex and her fiancé Zach have added to this adventure, and we will hopefully continue to add more fun times in the future. It's wonderful to have many fond memories of Alex and our son Eric going to games with us as preschoolers and now into adulthood. Time flies! It was great to have the experiences taking Eric on bowl excursions before starting his career in the Navy. We get together for games now whenever time allows us.

As I said in my preface, I looked "to get some practical and professional guidance to help me seek input and strategies on how to present this unique story from a better perspective." I certainly did. Travis Jordan through Reedsy, who edited 40 sports books prior, and published sports articles himself, helped me greatly. He reviewed most of my more controversial topics and helped me restructure and reorganize the many pages of this book after I first wrote it. I knew I needed to reel some things in, but I didn't know how. His meticulous, ten-page, Editorial Assessment Summary was tremendous. I didn't agree with everything, but I liked his analogy of pulling back from a "shot-gun approach" and becoming more of "a sniper" when it came to effectively consolidating what I originally wrote compared to what I finished with. I can't thank him or recommend him enough to other potential writers seeking the same kind of support he gave me.

Regarding all photos (except for one acknowledged) and the book cover design, I took these over the years myself to use on my weekly game reviews on my website collegefootballfan.com to share the excitement of college football along with my reports. The cover design is a collage comprised from among hundreds of tickets over the years of games attended. That's as artistic as I get. Regretfully, new technology has led to the demise of my artistic opportunities. I thank Angie, contracted with Reedsy, for working with me patiently to finalize the finished book cover.

I

Tales - mostly the Good and the Fun!

Fun and interesting experiences and people met over the course of a lifetime. I hope you'll enjoy reading about them as much as I still enjoy living this adventure.

America's Teams - Forever

(1) Army vs. (2) Navy, December 2, 1972

Philadelphia, Pennsylvania - My introduction to this classic rivalry and to "big-time" college football started on a low, wooden, end zone bleacher seat on an unseasonably warm December afternoon at John F. Kennedy Stadium in Philadelphia. My father said he "wrangled" four tickets somehow to the sellout between 5-4 Army and 4-6 Navy. We drove three hours to Philly from north Jersey with extra warm clothes and bundles of blankets. We watched caped, gray-clad Cadets and Midshipmen in woolen, navy blue overcoats march along the cinder track and onto the plush, green field before us as we shed layers of jackets and sweatshirts on that unbearably hot, December Saturday. The Corps of Cadets formed their companies on the playing field to cheer for both teams, led in unison by semaphore from the upper deck of the host venue. From signals above, the Corps launched into traditional pre-game cheers, but half-heartedly for the opposition. Army cadets saluted their greatest foe with a muffled, nonchalant cheer of "N-A-V-Y. Go Navy! Fight!" Then on the next semaphore command, they performed a sharp, military about-face to their side of the stadium to the rousing applause and cheers of the Army faithful. The Corps took on new life. Out came their booming cadence brazen and bold for their own: "A-R-M-Y! Goo-OOO ARMY! BEAT NAVY!" Throngs for Army stood and cheered wildly. The Corps marched to the empty seats awaiting them, but the parade soon broke off into a run as cadets of all classes looked to meet up with fellow classmates in the stands. Plebes are responsible for the spirit on game day.

The Mids' march-on follows, and it's evident—"nobody does march on a ship"! And if you listened closely, after the Mids raise their hats to their alternative cheer of "BEAT ARMY!: Their hands drop hats back on to their heads before they align their thumbs along seams of their trousers with the muffled order from within the Brigade of, "Drop! Trou(sers)!" - inside humor from the Mids who speak in code laced with acronyms and abbreviations.

All the traditions of college football and more unfolded before us that day. Miniature tanks and ships fired bursts of blanks. Army Mules and the Navy Goats with handlers roamed the sidelines. Cheerleaders fired up spirit on both sides. The Army Band and Navy Drum Corps played their respective fight songs as Cadets and Mids sang along loudly.

Navy took a 12-0 lead in the first quarter. In the third, however, Army overcame the deficit as running back Bob Hines raced 43 yards for a touchdown. Later, a blocked field goal by Army's Tim Pfister resulted in an 84-yard touchdown return by Scott Beatty. A 21-yard scoring run by Bruce Simpson and a field goal by Jim Barclay put the finishing touches on Army's 23-15 win. The gun sounded to end the 73rd edition of college football's greatest rivalry.

In 1974, I became a member of the Brigade of Midshipmen. Thanks to my underwhelming skills in math and science, I stayed for only two years. I did make the Lightweight football team, now known as Sprint Football.

Now here this: calling all college football fans!

I continued to attend Navy football games over the years. Whether at the Meadowlands, in "Crabtown" (Annapolis), versus Army in Philly, or on the road somewhere, the Mids traditionally play hard. So do the Cadets. Every college football fan should experience an Army game at West Point and a Navy game in Annapolis at least once. Both uphold great traditions and display great team spirit.

I've seen Army play 58 games and Navy play 83 games against various teams since. Attended 17 of this epic classic, some more eye-opening and thrilling like the 28-24 Army win over Navy in 1996 that landed both teams in much-deserved bowl games since that first meeting in 1972. Navy leads when I attend, 10-7.

The teams turned out that the first two eventual "steps" on my long road to achieve my eventual goal started with the greatest of all traditional rivalries in college football! No other college rivalry can top Army-Navy in terms of true student-athleticism, bragging rights, tradition, and what it signifies to our nation. Case in point: The 2022 Army-Navy game with team records of 5-6 and 4-7 respectively drew 6.94 million television viewers. It ranked seventh highest among all 44 college post-season games.

If Army and Navy faced one another with 10 or more wins, who knows how many more would have watched? Ohio State and Michigan, both undefeated at 11-0, drew the highest regular season audience with 17.1 million viewers. How many fans nationwide would tune in if they had records of 5-6 and 4-7? Remember, these players from Army and Navy and all their classmates in the stands move on to play defense at the next level - not in the NFL, but for all Americans.

The Future is Now

Philadelphia, PA - Fast Forward to 2022 and beyond for both Army and Navy: What I really cherish about this game, having marched on the field with my Second Company classmates of the Class of 1978 and despite my departure from the academy only 20 months after starting, I can still call many of these guys my friends. From plebe summer, to "come-arounds" with Firsties (for civilians- senior Midshipman) in the confines of Bancroft Hall, to intramural sports, to third class cruise, and Saturday nights in downtown "Crabtown," we spent a lot of time together. I'm proud to have known them and still be associated with them. Many of them served in the Navy and Marine Corps during Desert Storm. Many became pilots, some went into submarines, surface line, and into the Marine Corps. I could list many great accomplishments and illustrious careers among all of them. I will make note though of one in particular who I roomed with for a while during my third and final semester.

FIFTY YEARS OF TAILGATE TALES:

John Semcken used to go away on weekend tours that semester with the Naval Academy Glee Club. He made the most of that experience during his navy career. Long story that John likes to tell is, as a lieutenant, somewhat by default, he became the Navy's official liaison for the hit movie, *"Top Gun."* A Top Gun pilot himself, he tells stories of some prime input he gave director Tony Scott over the course of the filming to assure adherence to Navy protocol. Also, leveraging his glee club experience, he told Scott that Tom Cruise and Anthony Edwards basically couldn't sing worth a lick to put it nicely. Challenged if he could do any better, John responded, "Yes, sir!" Next time you watch the movie and see the two stars crooning, *"You Never Close Your Eyes,"* to Kelly McGillis, the guy on the left who suddenly turns around and chimes is none other than one of my former roommates at the Naval Academy.

USNA 2nd Company Class of '78 at 2022 ArmyNavy game in Philadelphia: Mike, John, Will, Dennis, Alden "The Rock," Rick, Me (Juniata '79, Mark and Vinny.

Catching up with John and my other pals from Second company in the 123rd edition of this classic rivalry between Army and Navy was great! Tied to start the second OT, 17-17, Navy went on offense. With six running plays, the Mids got to the three for a second and goal. Anton Hall took the hand-off, went left, and lunged toward the goal line. Before he could reach the ball across, Army defensive lineman Austin Hill forced a fumble recovered by Darius Richards. Starting at the 25, Army focused to keep the ball between the hash-marks. From 39 yards out, Quinn Maretzki made good to finalize the victory for the Cadets. Unlike the two seasons my former classmates and I partied after beating Army in 1974 (19-0) and in 1975 (30-6), the Mids fell to the Cadets in the first ArmyNavy game played in overtime, 20-17. Regarding the future, God-willing, plans are already in place to attend ArmyNavy in Boston in December 2023, in Landover, Maryland 2024, in Baltimore 2025, in East Rutherford 2026, and back in Philly in 2027. I hope to catch up with all my great Navy friends again. Go Navy!

Academy football futures

The Naval Academy always takes pride in playing the best football schedule they can at a national level. The football program is the Navy's way of displaying the flag around the country against some of the best competition available. The changes in the American Athletic conference won't offer as much of that now.

On the other hand, with FBS programs open to NIL money and wide-open transfer portals, Army, Navy, and Air Force football will not be able to mix and match players constantly like these other teams. Academy athletes take on a four-year curriculum required of all graduates. They can leave on their own without penalty before their junior year. To play football or another sport, some have done that in the past. Will more players be tempted to do this in future? Probably. Not only are military academy academics on par with the Ivy League, but first-year Mids or Cadets have to start with the rigors of plebe summers to start college life all over again to indoctrinate into military life.

The primary mission of the academies is to train students to prepare to become military leaders. They have commitments to serve in the military after graduation. All of the academy students are full-time employees of the United States government. Name, Image, and Likeness (NIL) contracts are not available for them. For the academies to find good players willing to make the four-year commitment and to avoid offers from a very tempting market now will offer new challenges to retain their best players. I can say this: Navy football and her sister academies, win or lose, always thrive on great challenges. Go Navy! Go Army! Go Air Force!

Turncoat and Burnout / Close encounters

(3) Notre Dame vs. Navy, November 2, 1974

Philadelphia, Pennsylvania– I grew up a Notre Dame fan. On New Year's Eve 1973, I ran out of my family's house into freezing weather in just a t-shirt, shorts, and socks to celebrate the Irish's 24-23 win over Alabama in the Sugar Bowl for the 1973 National Championship!

November 2, 1974 became my personal day of infamy. I did something I never dreamed I would nor could ever do. For the first time, I was about to see the defending national champs for whom I'd rooted so hard on that previous New Year's Eve live and in-person. Only this time, for the first time ironically, I couldn't claim them as my team. Since I was now a Midshipman, the Irish appeared as the dreaded opposition. There would be no cheers "for old Notre Dame" from me for the first time ever. The 6-1 Irish came in as 30-point favorites. We were just 2-5. The Brigade was pumped up for this one, having fallen to the Irish during the eleven long years since Heisman winner Roger Staubach last played for Navy.

In Second Company, we approached the portal leading on to the Vet Stadium turf for the pre-game march-on. ND's male cheerleaders held their female counterparts over the entrance to show 4,000 Navy guys, especially about 1,200 female-deprived Plebes, what we were missing. Many jumped for a "touch" even though the targets were far beyond leaping capabilities. After march-on, we literally climbed the outfield wall at the

Vet into our designated seats. Many boosted fellow classmates to get up over the railing.

As one, four thousand raucous Midshipman — including one former, recent, die-hard Fighting Irish fan — were pumped up for today's game. Despite the daunting task ahead, we fed off a mutual appetite for the long-awaited win. We were caught up in it. Despite my years of dedication to Notre Dame, I was converted! There was no way I could root for my former favorite team on this particular day. Today, I was Navy all the way. I was a "turncoat" and proud of it—proud to be part of the Brigade. We stood and cheered our team throughout the first half to surprising success.

Every big play, especially on defense, sent us Mids into an uproar. We were fired up and going crazy! We went even more bonkers as our teammates on the field took a 6-0 lead over the big boys from South Bend. Classmate Dave Heinz, who went on to become a Major General in the United State Marine Corps, and I embraced and jumped up and down with enthusiasm. Salivating for Blue and Gold victory after eleven years of Irish domination, we began to anticipate the taste of victory—big victory! Mass hysteria, school spirit, and a proud tradition morphed into something bigger than just eleven guys out on the playing field.

Early in the fourth quarter, Notre Dame finally put the ball deep in the end zone with a low, five-yard pass from quarterback Tommy Clements to sliding tight end Pete Demmerle. After they converted the extra point for the 7-6 lead, the Irish "Subway Alumni" exhaled sighs of relief more than rousing cheers. With 2:12 remaining, Notre Dame defensive back Randy Harrison picked off Mark Roban's pass and returned it forty yards for a touchdown. It sealed the Irish victory, 14-6. Days after this game, Notre Dame's great, successful football coach, Ara Parseghian, who I greatly respected, decided to call it a career at South Bend. A close call against Navy revealed the enormity of pressure to win at probably the most famous of all college football programs. I was a turncoat. Ara felt burnt-out. It was the end of an era – for both of us.

In 2007, I left Beaver Stadium with my 12-year-old daughter Alex after Penn State defeated that traditional Irish nemesis, Purdue. I sat in the car to listen to the last two plays of triple overtime between Notre Dame and Navy on Westwood One Radio. An interference call went against the Mids on Notre Dame's two-point conversion. On the ensuing conversion attempt, Navy stuffed the Irish run. That day in South Bend, Navy had finally beaten the Irish, 46-44. After 43 straight losses, the streak finally ended. I finally got to cheer a Navy victory over the Irish. When Navy finally ended that losing streak against the Fighting Irish I heard on the radio, I remembered that November game in 1974. In October 2010, after personally witnessing seven Navy losses to Notre Dame, I finally saw a dominant Navy team sink the Irish myself, 35-17.

Surreal South Bend

South Bend, Indiana – Fast Forward to Notre Dame vs. LSU, 1981: Tony Lagratta transferred to Juniata College my senior year to become one of eight suite mates living together in 201 Flory in our dorm complex known as East Houses. With about 60 other Notre Dame fans that came to tailgate in Lot 17B on November 1, 1980, Tony brought along his contingent of Notre Dame die-hards from Maryland and Pennsylvania.

Missing from among Tony's entourage that day was Dane Taylor. Tony's old high school classmate from Cumberland, Maryland actually followed his dream to matriculate at Notre Dame. He also proudly served the program he loved by becoming lead student equipment manager for the Irish his senior year.

In 1981 at the invitation of Tony and Dane, about a dozen of us of us met at Tony's house in Lansdale, Pennsylvania where we climbed aboard a rented recreational vehicle (RV) to pay my first visit to the hallowed grounds of the Four Horsemen, Knute Rockne, and Touchdown Jesus We headed to South Bend to help usher in "the Bold Experiment." The Irish would play their first game ever under new football coach Gerry Faust. He came directly from Cincinnati's nationally-known, high school powerhouse oft times referred to as the "Moeller Steamroller." Notre Dame fans expected him to keep their loyal sons marching onward to victory starting with LSU at home for their season opener. In his 18 years at the helm of Moeller, Faust's Crusader teams won 174 games and lost 17.

Close encounters with a nice man and a legend

During one of our forays across the grassy, well-groomed campus, our group literally crossed paths with none other than the man "destined" to lead Irish football to new heights. Smiling, happy, affable Gerry Faust led his freshman players to some event across campus. Without hesitation he stopped, shook all our hands, and chatted for several minutes. In retrospect, as an experienced purchasing manager, I envision Gerry as an absolute salesman. As he talked, I noted this "roly-poly" freshman next to me, who looked like he had yet to pick up a razor blade. He didn't strike me as athletic, but he was a big kid, definitely a lineman. I thought, let me find out who this guy is and see if he ever makes anything of himself.

When I bought the Notre Dame vs. LSU Official Game Program the next day, I perused pictures of the Notre Dame roster to identify him for future reference. Found his picture— *"82 Mark Bavaro TE/DL—Freshman."* I made a mental note of it. Could I pick out future football talent or what? Not only did Mark Bavaro achieve All-American honors his junior and senior seasons at Notre Dame, he became an All-Pro tight end twice with the New York Giants during his nine-year NFL career. He epitomized the toughness of a football player his entire career. You never know.

As for Gerry

The game against Louisiana State reinforced Irish hopes. Despite a late score by LSU to make the final 27-9, the ND crowd turned up its chants of *"Gerry! Gerry! Gerry!"* They vaulted to No. 1 in all the polls the following Monday.

After witnessing the initial success of the "Bold Experiment," our excited but weary band of tailgaters headed home in our rented, mobile home from that memorable, "historic" weekend. Along Route 80 before we even left Indiana, a loud, deafening roar started from beneath the vehicle followed by a loud explosion! We pulled over to find that a rubber retread let loose from one of the tires. Luckily, we had double axles and four tires on each. Another exploded and let loose in Ohio. It happened again in Pennsylvania. We left remnants of rubber retreads in each state on our way back. Luckily, we made it through our ordeal in one piece.

The same could not be said for a formerly, successful, high school coach. The cheering didn't last long. Faust and the Fighting Irish lost the very next week to Michigan. It only got worse after that. The Irish finished the season at 5-6. *"Oust Faust!"* However, the administration lived up to its five-year commitment to the beleaguered head coach. After being fired, Akron surprisingly hired him as their head coach.

In retrospect against LSU, we witnessed to the "Bold Experimental Failure." Following a 30-26-1 record, two minor bowl games, and no national championships, these fell far short of the intentions Notre Dame bargained for when they signed Faust. After his team's initial win over LSU, the wheels on our recreational vehicle literally never came off after three blow-outs. We made it home safely. The same could not be said for Gerry Faust's career at Notre Dame.

Culture Shock! Dawg Days.

(4) Georgia at (5) Auburn, November 18, 1978

Auburn, Alabama - At the Lakeland Hills YMCA in Mt. Lakes, NJ during the summer of 1978, Charles Murren III pointed to the name of my current college on my bright, yellow t-shirt. How he got "Oneonta" out of J-U-N-I-A-T-A, I don't know, but it began the start of a long friendship. At least he didn't pronounce it *"Juanita"* as did many others. That day in the gym, Charlie was home on summer vacation from Auburn University. He studied for a degree in Civil Engineering. That summer, we talked about important stuff like my future trip to Auburn for a football weekend.

For Juniata's trimester break the weekend before Thanksgiving, I bought a cheap airline ticket for my first flight ever. Al Di Vite, one of our cohorts from back in Boonton, NJ would fly down as well. Charlie had the entire Auburn cultural experience planned for us. We bought beer at a local gas station. We got to ride on real construction equipment at night on a real highway under construction. For Civil Engineering at Auburn, I assumed this was a prerequisite.

The next day, we glimpsed football traditions up close and personal. Taking a tour of the training facilities, we watched the AU Tigers getting taped before Friday's practice. Friday night, we ventured out to Toomer's Crossing for the traditional pep rally. This was SEC football country! We had a great time.

War Eagle!

CULTURE SHOCK! DAWG DAYS.

Charlie had gotten us $2 student tickets for the game. Boy, did three guys from New Jersey stick out! We wore our flannel shirts, jeans, work boots, and ball caps among Auburn students dressed for a semi-formal affair. Auburn cheerleaders chanted:

"Track 'em Tigers, just like beagles, give 'em hell you War Damn Eagles!"

That was followed by:

"Weagle, Weagle, War Damn Eagle! Kick 'em in the butt big Blue! Hey!"

Charlie could have been Aubie if he only could have shouted, "Y'all!"

Southerners seem to like to throw a "damn" in there somewhere, like "damn Yankees!" Speaking of which, Charlie tried out for Auburn's amiable-looking mascot, Aubie the Tiger. In his enthusiasm to get crowd reaction, he hollered in typical Jersey dialect, "Come on, *you guys!*" He knew he blew it right away. His audience prepared more apt to get stirred up with,

"Come on, *y'all*!" Needless to say, he didn't get the job. "Jersey boys need not apply!" Charlie still loves his Tigers!

Joe Cribbs' second score of the day on a two-yard run gave Auburn the lead at the end of the third period, 22-15. The defenses held from that point on until Willie McClendon scored for Georgia from the one. 5:18 remained and the score stood, 22-21. A Georgia victory here would mean at least a share of the SEC championship and the Sugar Bowl. Future Hall of Fame Georgia Coach Vince Dooley took a lot of heat for his next decision. He elected to kick for a tie rather than by going for two to win. This crucial contest ended in a 22-22 stalemate, the only tie I'd ever see in 1-A play. No Sugar Bowl for the Dawgs. The Tide rolled the Tigers the following Saturday, 34-16, to head to New Orleans instead.

Thanks to overtime rules initiated in 1995 to determine an eventual winner, we'll never have to see a tie again. After sixty minutes of rock 'em, sock 'em, hard-hitting action with a championship on the line to boot, to finish with no winner and no loser is not only anti-climactic, it's downright depressing.

However, two visiting Jersey boys encountered our ultimate southern cultural shock the very next morning. Charlie took Al and me to James Brown's Diner in nearby Opelika for all-you-can-eat-southern breakfast. The event took place in the parking lot as Al and I digested leaning against Charlie's old, green Ford Pinto. Charlie talked to someone he knew inside, when *lo and behold*! From across the parking lot sauntered this beautiful, gorgeous, drop-dead, knock-out, strawberry blonde!

Al, where are we?

Wow! And she was walking unabashedly right towards us! She came right to us near that beat-up, green Ford Pinto with Garden State plates, smiled, and said, "Hey! How y'all doin'?" Al and I tried to recover quickly as our knees buckled like taking a hard, left jab from Joe Frazier. We looked at each other with smirks on our faces that said, "This doesn't happen back in Jersey!" Forget the *"y'all"* part!

Mystified, still in shock, we were able to make small talk for a few minutes when suddenly this guy, supposedly her boyfriend, shows up and says, "Hey! How y'all doin'?" Now this definitely NEVER happens nor would ever happen back in dear old NJ. There would be screaming, cursing, ranting, or crying, and things would eventually turn physical. Something would have escalated as we probably had no right to be talking to, no less approached by, a total "knock-out" like this one anywhere near her significant other! It was surreal! Where were we?

On the ride back to Auburn with Al and me still dazed, Charlie provided his insight with two words. "Holy Rollers," he deadpanned. Now, I go to Mass on Sundays, but if I ever had the notion to stay way down South in the Land of Cotton back then, I think it would have been very worthwhile to also attend a few prayer meetings in the Church of the Holy Rollers, too. Both very pretty people and very friendly people there.

Auburn, Alabama - Fast Forward to Penn State at Auburn, 2022: Forty-four years later, I retired and moved south to Tennessee. I was finally ready to settle into Southern Culture – music, weather, football, BBQ, and new friends. Laurie and I love it so far. A bonus for me is being closer to some campuses to add variety to this ongoing adventure. Charlie and his wife Lynda live outside Atlanta. They raised four nice kids and Charlie converted his degree at Auburn into a very successful construction business. Even this past season, he invited me to Auburn for the Penn State game. Over the years, I've met with him "on the Plains" for about half-a-dozen games. One season, his daughter Megan worked for Tommy Tuberville's staff as a student intern. She gave us a tour of the press box before the Arkansas game in 2004.

In 2022, Auburn hosted Penn State for the second part of the two-year home and home agreement. Charlie got me and Joe Rogers, a transplanted Pennsylvania friend now in Savannah, Georgia, two tickets. Joe had previously done some college football writing for The Bleacher Report. Better yet, Charlie met us at a great tailgate party organized weekly on "the Plains" with friends of his he went to school with. They also invited friends, family, and business associates affiliated with Penn State. A lot of good food and good-ribbing preceded the game. Penn State won, 41-12.

The Tigers disappointed with a 5-7 record, fired Head Coach Bryan Harsin and replaced him with Liberty's Hugh Freeze after the season.

Dawg Days

Lexington, Kentucky - Fast forward to No. 1 Georgia at Kentucky in 2022: As for Georgia, I didn't see the Bulldogs play again until their opener of the 2005 season with Charlie Murren and my 10-year-old son Eric in Athens against Boise State. Now living in Tennessee, when I put my 2022 slate together, I decided to make it a point to see the four preseason favorites since they all played games not too far from where I now live within driving distance:

- No. 1 Alabama plays about three hours away at Bryant-Denny Stadium.
- No. 2 Ohio State plays the Nittany Lions in State College every other year.
- No. 3 Georgia plays about three hours north when they play Kentucky.
- No. 4 Clemson I'd see at home for the first time with two Juniata friends.

My PSU buddy John Massimilla became a Kentucky Colonel and had an "in" now for tickets in Lexington. The Dawgs would struggle somewhat on that cold day against a good Kentucky defense. On the other side of the football, had a few errant passes been completed by quarterback Will Levis, U of K was close to pulling off a major upset. I wish I had invited Mel Kiper, Jr. to this game to see his favorite quarterback of 2022 in action. I'm not sure what he saw to evaluate Levis a top draft pick. Georgia defeated Kentucky, 16-6, to head on to win the 2022 Championship.

Georgia finished No. 1 at 15-0 for a long, successful season. However, a huge followed at the end that led to controversy and investigations involving a seamy side of college football.

Sad ending to a happy day

CULTURE SHOCK! DAWG DAYS.

After a huge victory party in Athens, Georgia on January 14 to celebrate the national championship, a high-speed street race after leaving a bar resulted in a fatal crash at 2:45 am the next morning taking two young lives involved in the Georgia football program. Offensive lineman Devin Willock, 20, was killed instantly. The driver, a young woman employed by the Georgia football program as a Recruiting Analyst, Chandlery Le Croy, 24, died at the hospital later. Two other passengers suffered severe injuries. Offensive lineman Warren McClendon, 21, and another Georgia Recruiting Analyst, Tori Bowles, 26, both suffered injuries.[1] Memorial services were held for the deceased.

Condolences to the families that will endure the losses of these young lives for rest of theirs.

UGA guard Broderick Jones (59) will don jersey No. 77 as a Pittsburgh Steeler in honor of his deceased teammate, Devin Willock (77), blocking at upper right against Kentucky.

FIFTY YEARS OF TAILGATE TALES:

[1] James Parks 01/30/2023, "New details emerge in car crash that killed Georgia football player, staff member", Fan Nation/College Football HQ. Retrieved July 23, 2023.

Stunners

(6) Syracuse vs. (7) West Virginia, September 15, 1979

East Rutherford, NJ– In its fourth year of existence in 1979, Giants Stadium at the Meadowlands announced a college football schedule made up primarily of Division I schools. With the current demolition of Syracuse's ancient Archbold Stadium, the Meadowlands obliged to aid the nomads. On this day, the West Virginia Mountaineers called on the Meadowlands to visit the Orangemen for a traditional battle between independent, eastern rivals. Without conference affiliations, 22 current FBS teams played as Independents back then for as many wins as possible to earn bowl bids.

The 76,000-seat venue easily engulfed the mere 10,366 that showed up that day. Charlie Murren, home from Auburn, and I listened to some old guy razzing a young, tall, geeky, SU, pain-in-the-ass fan named Myron. The old guy would croon, "My-ron! Hey! Myyy-rron!" We didn't know what instigated the old guy, but he kept at it throughout the game which turned out to be a snooze of a contest during the first half. The razzing became our primary entertainment. With so few fans in attendance, the old guy's crooning could be heard above everything else.

A 38-yard touchdown pass to Art Monk, followed by his fantastic, leaping catch on the two-point conversion gave the Orangemen a 21-0 lead at intermission. Mountaineer quarterback Oliver Luck finally put the visitors on the board in the fourth with a 19-yard pass. WVU's next drive went for 57 yards with Eldridge Dixon bulling over from the one.

Now trailing, 21-14, the Mountaineers recovered a Syracuse fumble at SU's 30, but officials called the play down by contact. Syracuse took advantage of the break with mighty Joe Morris, Syracuse's short but powerful, sophomore running back. He sped down to the one on a long run on this series. WVU held there, but Gary Anderson converted his third field goal of the day. Final score: 24-14, Orangemen win.

Oh yeah, on the way out to our car, we saw tall, geeky Myron about to get his ass whipped by some stout WVU-clad redneck who had a few beers too many. That Myron just seemed to irk everybody he crossed paths with that day.

Almost Heaven for West Virginia

Miami Lakes, Florida - Fast Forward to 2012 Orange Bowl, West Virginia vs. Clemson:

- The Mountaineers appeared at Penn State or against Rutgers in Big East contests.
- In 2008, I attended a game in Morgantown with Charlie whose business excavated nearby for shale gas extraction. His success relied on knowing where new opportunities existed – right place at right time. For my football endeavor, too! West Virginia dropped Auburn that evening, 34-17.
- Most memorable Mountaineer adventure came in the 2012 Orange Bowl.

Meeting with Charlie in Miami on January 4, we both anticipated balmy weather. Neither of us came prepared for the unexpected cold front that moved in. We actually had to go to K-Mart to buy additional layers of clothes before attending the anticipated heat of battle about to take place.

Atlantic Coast Conference (ACC) Champ Clemson ranked ahead and favored over Big East co-champ West Virginia. The turning point of the game occurred early in the second quarter. WVU led 21-17, but Clemson drove to their one looking to take the lead. On a dive play, Clemson fumbled and Mountaineer Safety Darwin Cook scooped it up and dashed 99 yards untouched for a sudden, extended 28-17 lead. Stunningly after that, except for a Clemson field goal in the first half, it was all Mountaineers. With Geno Smith at quarterback, WVU raced out to a 49-20 lead by halftime. West Virginia hammered Clemson unexpectedly, 70-33. Despite 103 points, that total stands as only the seventh highest scoring total among 676 games. The Mountaineers 70-point output stands at the top for total points scored by one team among 46 bowl games or any other game I've attended.

Back at the Dome

Syracuse, NY – Fast Forward to Clemson at Syracuse, 2017: The Orangemen appeared on my schedule many times playing eastern rivals mostly on the road. Their overall record in my presence stands at 12-12. Most often with friends whose kids attended Syracuse, I ventured up to the Carrier Dome for several interesting experiences. The most recent, significant, Syracuse memory, however, occurred on a Friday night there in 2017. Clemson at 6-0 came in ranked at No. 2 in the nation. They rode an 11-game winning streak that included beating Alabama in the CFP championship game of 2016, 35-31. The Orange played under their first-year Head Coach Dino Babers unranked with a record of 3-3.

Syracuse quarterback Eric Dungey threw three touchdowns among his 278 yards. Entering the fourth, with the score knotted, 24-24, Syracuse's Cole Murphy booted a 30-yard field goal with 9:41 remaining. The Orange defense stopped the Tigers to turn the ball back over on downs at their 41 with 6:10 left. From there, the 'Cuse offense effectively ran out the clock to win, 27-24. Upset! For me, no other upset comes close! It will be hard to top this one.

Ancient personal college football history

My first college football game ever attended before I started to keep track came during Fifth Grade in 1966 when Colgate visited Princeton. Two good teams. School buses packed with grade school boys along with a few adults, bagged lunches and without cell phones in the good, old days visited old Palmer Stadium on the Princeton campus. Teams still snapped the ball direct to halfbacks in this game where Colgate won, 7-0. The Red Raiders finished 8-1-1, and their fullback Marv Hubbard went on to an illustrious career playing for the Oakland Raiders of the up-and-coming American Football League (AFL). The Princeton Tigers went 7-2 with a 6-1 Ivy League record to tie Dartmouth and Harvard for the Ivy championship. Memories include the Princeton Tiger Marching band with straw hats, tiger-striped sport jackets, black pants and tiger tails tied to trombone slides. With money my parents gave for souvenirs, I bought two pennants from tables stacked with them - one for Princeton and one for Notre Dame.

New found college football friends

All during my fifty-year adventure, I attended games among Football Championship Subdivision (FCS) teams as well. This weekend's itinerary included a Saturday game in nearby Hamilton, NY to see a game at Colgate University for the first time. They hosted Fordham in a Patriot League match. I'd seen the Red Raiders play over the years at Princeton, Rutgers, Penn State and Stony Brook over the years.

On Saturday, I parked in the lot near Colgate's Andy Kerr Stadium and made several phone calls to a few friends to talk about Friday night's upset they watched on TV. A few parking spaces away, Colgate Red Raider fans Bruce, Sam, and Ray invited me over to their tailgate for some grilling, snacks, hospitality, and Ommegang Beer brewed in Cooperstown, NY. We shared "tales around the tailgate," - some good stories, football history, and laughs. Sam Cooper and Bruce, a Colgate grad, talked about the days when Colgate's primary rivals were the teams I mentioned. Ray grew up in Bergen County, NJ and commuted to Fordham in The Bronx to study there. He and I shared some history about Fordham basketball when "Digger" Phelps and Charlie Yelverton put the Rams on the basketball map in the late 60s before Digger left for Notre Dame. Sam mentioned that they had brought along their extra fourth ticket for today's game and invited me to sit with them at their 50-yard line seats with a great view. Colgate prevailed, 38-12. *"College football – what better way to spend an autumn afternoon?"*

Colgate fans - Sam, Ray, Bruce and yours truly. Fun time!

The End of the Beginning to Nowhere

(8) Rutgers at Princeton, September 29, 1979

Princeton, NJ - In 1979, I ventured out to see my home state's university, Rutgers, play for the first time. They had recently become college football's newest Division IA program. This game would be the next-to-last of the oldest of all college football rivalries. The Scarlet Knights and the Princeton Tigers were meeting at Princeton's Palmer Stadium for the very last time. The last game scheduled in 1980 at Rutgers Stadium in New Brunswick would be the final meeting ever between the two schools 16 miles apart. They started 110 years before at Neilson Field on College Avenue in New Brunswick, NJ, *"The Birthplace of College Football."* On November 6, 1869, Rutgers defeated Princeton, 6-4.

Cross-roads of the Revolution, 200 years later

In 1976, Rutgers picked up games against a few programs above "Ivy League" talent they were traditionally associated with. The Scarlet Knights finished 11-0. The Independence Bowl, one of only about a dozen post-season games at that time, offered RU to play 9-2 McNeese State. Instead of accepting the university's first ever bowl bid since their start in 1869, the Scarlet Knights felt they were more deserving of a better bowl bid than this. They turned it down. Big mistake! Any bowl for RU could've jump-started the recruiting for this program. They wanted Jersey kids to come to New Brunswick instead of heading to State College, Pennsylvania, Columbus, Ohio, or Lincoln, Nebraska among other national, football, powerhouse campuses. I believe this refusal blew a big opportunity for Rutgers football future while the iron was hot! I said that then as well as now.

On this overcast September day in 1979, the Tigers held on midway through the third period. The Scarlet Knights finally broke the game open with a touchdown pass from Ed McMichael to tight end Brian Crockett. The Knights went on to win, 38-14. After the final tick of the clock, the natural surface in Palmer stadium hosted the most bizarre, post-game "celebration" I have ever witnessed! No exuberance nor jubilation. No back-patting of players. No surrounding the coach to carry him off the field for one final triumph at Palmer vaulting their team forward into the much-desired big-time. Instead, RU fans separated into small groups to pound the hell out of one another - not Princeton fans, but fellow Rutgers fans! The post-game celebration entailed getting someone else on the turf and pummeling the crap out of him. Was this indicative of future celebrations for victories at the Division I level? Maybe this demonstrated a new tradition the Scarlet Knights would bring with them to "big-time" college football. I never saw anything like it before or since. However, I remember another game years later...

New Brunswick, NJ - Fast Forward to Louisville at Rutgers, 2006: Princeton maintained its staid, Ivy League status with pride. Rutgers continued its desire into D-IA with the wishful, underlying battle cry, *"If we can only keep the best players in New Jersey to play for Rutgers, we'll have a great football program!"* That mantra has lasted for many years. Even a 13-7 upset over traditional powerhouse Tennessee in Knoxville later in the *"What's a Rutger?"* game of 1979 gave them only a brief spark of legitimacy.

In 1991, Rutgers joined the newly formed Big East Conference. They struggled along capturing no bowls until the fifth season under Head Coach Greg Schiano. Athletic Director Robert Mulcahy retained faith in his hire after four losing seasons with a record of 12-34. In 2005, patience paid off with a 7-5 record to play in the Insight Bowl. Despite that loss, Rutgers football climbed to its apex in 2006.

Upstream Red Team! Rutgers, rah!

On a Thursday night on November 9, No. 15 RU (8-0) hosted No. 3 Louisville (8-0) in front of a sell-out crowd of 44,111. I attended with my cousin Frank Scarpa to see his Alma mater battle for first atop the Big East. The Scarlet Knights shut out the Cardinals in the second half to overcome an 18-point deficit. With 18 seconds left to play, Jeremy Ito's three-point attempt to win failed. However, a Louisville off-sides gave him a do-over five yards closer. From 33 yards, it sailed through for a Rutgers victory, 28-25. Rutgers Stadium exploded with jubilation marked by the astonishing Scarlet Knight comeback. That aforementioned Rutgers post-game celebration did not take place, however. Instead, one New Jersey State Trooper probably quelled any such reaction when he body-slammed one student who raced on to the field into the ground and escorted him out in cuffs earlier during this scoring drive. Fans celebrated on to the field and then dispersed to the bars and taverns in downtown New Brunswick.

Nine days later, as experienced in the past, the glory of Rutgers football evidently went to their heads. Often as in years past, Rutgers football dwelled on its own hype. The Knights fell to 5-5 Cincinnati, 30-11. Two weeks later, they went down swinging to West Virginia (11-2), 41-39. The program supported by local media seemed to feel that opponents should roll over _for_ them, not _over_ them. To me, Rutgers always appeared overconfident in their approaches to significant games. In 2014 after a season in the American Athletic, RU, enticed by TV money, joined the Big Ten who eyed the New York metropolitan television market.

Rutgers still struggles upstream

The ship to land the best players from New Jersey at Rutgers has already sailed. Early on, all New Jersey high school games were traditionally played on Saturday afternoons while many other states played under "Friday night lights." That took the focus off of RU football in-state going back to WWII. Despite gradual changes in this practice with more NJ high school contests played on Friday nights now, Rutgers fell short of the exposure to other programs nationally televised before they ascended to IA football.

Most likely, the Scarlet Knights will continue to achieve mediocrity in football at best. I'll be observing from a distance now in Tennessee. They stand 27-40 in games I've attended since 1979. I can't imagine they'll come out of the rut they're currently in. State demographics have lowered the volume of talent drastically, and the core of its best players continue to find better opportunities to play for better programs out of state.

Ups and Downs in Happy Valley

(9) Penn State vs. Syracuse, October 20, 1979

East Rutherford, NJ - The second game of the 1979 Meadowlands college football package featured perennial, eastern power Penn State "visiting" Syracuse during the Orangemen's nomadic season. My first Penn State game at the Meadowlands included nothing particularly memorable, but little did I have any inkling that day that this would be only the start of a long, steadfast journey following the Nittany Lions for many years to come.

PSU entered this contest at 3-2 with Head Coach Joe Paterno in his 14th season running the program. Fourteen years were considered to be a pretty significant tenure at the time for any head college football coach at one particular school.

Syracuse played in its second yawner of the season in front of a crowd at Giants Stadium, but this time they put 53,789 to sleep - five times as many as they had against West Virginia. The Nittany Lions fielded an awesome offensive line anchored by Mike Munchak and Irv Pankey. The half ended with the Nittany Lions in front, 28-0. With a 35-7 Penn State lead late, the fans who fell asleep before the fourth woke up after the game was over and saw the same score as the final.

After the 1979 football season, another new acquaintance made during a workout at the Lakeland Hills YMCA helped start my long association with Nittany Lion football. As with Charlie Murren, John Massimilla and I started our conversation in the small, cramped weight room.

"Altoona?" I asked. "Do you know...?" My stories about "Altoonians" attending Juniata were pretty extensive as a roommate, drinking buddies, and other assorted classmates resided in the same Podunk lying 30 miles west of Juniata located in Huntingdon, Pennsylvania. John bled Blue and White as a die-hard Nittany Lion fan and alumnus. He also possessed a proud association with the University of Iowa where at the time he was interning locally for Master's degree in Hospital Administration.

Happy Valley, here I come!

State College, Pennsylvania - Fast forward over ups and downs through 2022: In 1980, I attended my first game at State College, thanks to John. It was against an unlikely opponent, the Colgate Red Raiders. Bottom line: tickets were available. The most memorable highlight of the Nittany Lions game against the I-AA Raiders came on sophomore, running back Curt Warner's breakaway run.

Warner's shifty running capability broke him free past the Red Raider defense after a few nice moves for supposed, certain pay-dirt! Outracing Colgate defenders past the midfield stripe, Warner's legs suddenly went awry on the dry, plush green playing field for no apparent reason. He tumbled forward falling face first and rolled over several times until he finished lying flat on his back with legs and arms spread-eagle. He stared straight up at the clear blue, high sky over Happy Valley in front of 84,000 stunned Lion fans.

He must have set the record by a running back for the most time taken to get up off the ground in the history of college football. Too embarrassed to get up and face the partisan home crowd, all was eventually forgiven as indicated by the final score of 54-10 over the Red Raiders. Warner captured All-American honors in '81 and '82 before his eight-year career in the NFL where he played for his new boss in Seattle, a graduate of Juniata College, Head Coach Chuck Knox.

Through thirty-two years following Penn State football, I witnessed the following:

- Two national championships, some crushing defeats
- 24 bowl seasons
- Four of the five leanest years, between 2000-2004
- Promising recruits
- Graduating classes
- Beaver Stadium expansions
- Revolving all-Americans - especially linebackers
- Electronic scoreboard upgrades
- Escalating ticket prices
- Escalating parking prices
- Sprawling parking lots
- High-speed express lanes direct to Beaver Stadium
- Major traffic delays leaving late night games
- Independent status
- Big Ten membership
- Assistant coach turnovers
- New blocking schemes
- NCAA rule changes
- Following the Lions to the Rose, Outback and Alamo Bowls
- And the ever-evolving BCS system.

Of course, Penn State held one thing constant—Head Coach Joe Paterno.

Bride-to-be

One very memorable game occurred at Beaver Stadium on November 21, 1987 when the Nittany Lions hosted the Notre Dame Fighting Irish with Heisman Trophy winner Tim Brown on the team. The memorable game ended as Notre Dame's Anthony Johnson dove into the end zone to close the score 21-20 with 31 seconds left. However, the Lions stopped quarterback Tony Rice for a loss on their two-point conversion attempt. The unranked Lions (7-3) pulled off the upset over No. 7 Notre Dame (8-1).

More memorable though was bringing my girlfriend, Laurie, to this game where the temperatures were frigid. Winds of 25 miles per hour put the wind chill into negative numbers all game long. From where we sat high up in the east stands of Beaver Stadium, we could watch swirling snow storms heading toward us from the west. She impressed me. She stuck it out. Didn't complain. Like the main character in the movie *"Diner,"* I had a few tests along the way for the right woman. This was one of them. She stuck this game out in its entirety. When I mentioned to her after we got married that this was one of the factors that signified that she was the one for me, she had a quick response. "Are you kidding? I was so cold I couldn't move! My feet were freezing! They didn't warm up until we got out of the stadium, and I stuck them in a snow bank!" I still love her.

The "Joe-Pa factor"

As stated, when Joe showed up with his team at Giants Stadium in 1979, he coached in his 14th season. Who then could have imagined thirty-two years later, he'd still be coaching college kids for the same university he started with as an assistant back in 1951 under Head Coach Rip Engle? He coached Penn State football players for 60 years. On the flip side thirty-two years later, I couldn't have imagined the news about Paterno reported on my car radio returning from Philly after a night game between Temple and Miami (O.) at Lincoln Financial Field on November 9, 2011.

To this day, I can only reiterate that phrase attributed to the Chicago Black Sox scandal of 1920: *"Say it ain't so, Joe!"* Of course, in this case, my consternation applied to the Jerry Sandusky sexual assault scandal. Having closely followed the PSU program over the many years during Paterno's career, I have thoughts based on my personal observations and experience.

Going to Beaver Stadium to follow the Penn State football program that seemed to be run with integrity, interest in most games hinged on Joe Paterno. What was Joe thinking? What was his outlook on this aspect of college football or that? How was Joe approaching this game? What did Joe say to the media this week? Thoughts always persisted that Joe had the answer - the right answers.

Happy Valley generally loved Joe Paterno – mainly the students, and he loved it back. He brought honor and respect for the entire university as a community. He ran his program with integrity and put academics and the education of student-athletes among team priorities. Of course, he had his detractors, too. People wondered why he didn't play a certain guy. He ran this one player off the team.He should have punished this player, but he gave him a second chance. Why? Joe can't manage the clock effectively in late game situations. Joe can't develop good quarterbacks. Criticism came with the territory along with the accolades.

My PSU Connection for many years: John Massimilla, left, and his son Brian.

He resonated as the national voice of running college football programs for what the game was supposed to be about - running a clean program built for student-athletes to excel both on the field and in the classroom. In 1999, when my long-time Penn State connection and buddy John Massimilla told me the news that linebacker coach Jerry Sandusky of "Linebacker U." was leaving the program, it didn't make sense. He headed out to run his new foundation, the Second Mile, for troubled kids. Of course, we wondered what Joe thought. We understood he let him go undeterred, and Sandusky moved on.

In the past, we had heard Sandusky would be a major consideration to replace Joe when he retired. On the other hand, was his departure due to Paterno's desire to have his son, Jay, currently quarterback coach, eventually succeed him? Only rumors at that time, but that was a typical reaction to anything that occurred in Happy Valley. What was Joe thinking? Did he influence this departure, or did he regret it? We assumed he always tuned in to what was going on in the background at Penn State. Right or wrong, many like John and I following the Nittany Lion football program felt that the world of Penn State centered around him.

This is what I can't understand

What didn't make sense to me regarding the news of this entire scandal, fell on some of my personal experiences going on at this time. From 1998 through 2012, I spent much of my time outside of football season involved in youth sports, particularly Little League baseball and travel baseball. I did a few years as well with Rec League basketball locally. I managed teams during regular seasons as well as All-Stars. As a Little League board member most of those years, I attended meetings year-round to fund, to organize, to equip, to support, and to assure the safety of all players involved. My final season after my son moved on after he was too old for sanctioned youth league play, I remained for a year as Little League President.

A few years earlier, concerns were raised nationally and locally about the safety and security of the kids among adults who could put them at risk in any physical way. Enforcement involved all youth activities, not only sports. Now required, any adult involved with players on the field, in the dugout, traveling to games together, umpiring, running a snack stand, or even a parent participating on a field during practice not only had to file documents for background checks, but they had to be finger-printed as well.

It added a lot more administrative work and responsibility to all adults volunteering for kids' sports. Luckily, in my small town, Byram Township, while I was involved, we never came up with any feedback prohibiting any adult from participating. In New Jersey, even a Rutgers-sanctioned program had to be taken by every youth coach to reduce coaches' liability issues. It was necessary to allow adults to be exonerated from any accidents or injuries to young players. Without these programs, organized youth sports could no longer exist without adult support.

Head Coach Joe Paterno, affectionately known as "JoePa" to Penn State followers, students, and admirers nationwide, prided himself being a family man as well as a good man of Catholic faith. During these years, he had five adult kids of his own. All were Penn State grads remaining close to their father. They gave Joe and Sue Paterno 17 grandchildren among them. Being a sports-affiliated family, certainly the grandkids had to be involved in youth sports and activities around that time. For sure there had to be awareness, concern, and even discussion among the family including Joe at this time regarding these issues. It's difficult for me to imagine that some awareness of this possibility should have shown cause for concern when assistant coach Mike McQueery approached Joe with this matter between Sandusky and a boy at the football center.

I'll abide by what the report records indicate to date, but if he had such awareness of things like this from a national youth sports perspective, I would have thought Joe's response would have led him to take action to report this to law enforcement directly. His charisma around State College to take such action could have led to a quicker and more honorable solution to this scandal. It probably could have helped avoid health issues before he passed. Had he done so and followed up with a statement regarding the matter turned over to law enforcement, he could have exonerated his football program immediately stating something like: "We had a legal issue on site with a former coach. He was arrested and will be dealt with through legal channels. It was a horrible thing that happened, and we will support the system in bringing charges against this individual for what he did. The Penn State family will unite to assure that this can never happen again."

This makes it sound less complicated than what probably could have been done, but this direction could have been the right approach and would eliminate the embarrassment, shame, and maybe the consequences Penn State would eventually go through. One individual was responsible and deserved to be punished.

If Joe's concern was implicating the Penn State football program, his direction caused it much more harm than what this approach would provide. Again, I'll accept the resolutions absolving Paterno from the matter as a whole. Final investigations determined to reinstate his total of 409 wins, but it also has erased much of his venerable history with the Penn State football program. He built it on high standards he implemented until this incident occurred. His famed monument still lies somewhere in storage. Sorry it had to end for him and all of Penn State this way.

I only wish he had taken a more offensive approach based on what he had been told. In the end, maybe he wasn't aware of concerns exhibited through youth sport programs at the time. However, that's the part I still find hard to believe. For the victim and any others in Sandusky's wake, hopefully they recover wholly and live productive lives despite the incidents they suffered. Sandusky is evidently a very sick individual. Those who let him get away with this surely needed to be punished.

Right coach at a troubling time

Bill O'Brien did a fantastic job through the sanctioned years of 2012 and 2013 to keep this program from total collapse. In games I attended, O'Brien's teams went 5-0. The team of 2012 comprised of players who did not bail out on Penn State earned recognition on Beaver Stadium's Wall of Champions. The facade on the luxury suites on the west side of the stadium recognizes championship football teams of the Nittany

Lions. This team did not win a championship, but with a 6-2 Big Ten record despite the sanctions to de-emphasize Penn State football, the team received deserved recognition for their accomplishments in the face of adversity.

Since 2014, James Franklin appears to have things moving in the right direction, but the jury's still out on his game day decision-making processes. I've seen the Lions go 17-4 among the games I've seen him coach. Two losses came against Ohio State. He can recruit, but he still has to show he can get consistency every game with the team he puts out on the field. Though a much farther drive after my relocation to Tennessee, plans remain to attend at least one game a year in State College. And like 2022, I can now travel to some road games as well. I ventured to Purdue and to Auburn that season for some great tailgate parties. I'm still proud and excited to be part of the *"We are"* crowd!

College Football History 101 / From "Bear" to Saban

(10) Alabama vs. Auburn, December 1, 1979

Birmingham, Alabama—Records are made to be broken. Way before attending the JoePa "love-fest" in 2001 at his 409th victory, I actually had the opportunity to see the man whose record he had to break to exceed his 323 wins. In 1979, Paul "Bear" Bryant's Alabama Crimson Tide rode a 19-game winning streak. Charlie Murren invited me to see his beloved Auburn Tigers attempt to "Roll back the Tide!"

Now this is a bitter rivalry!
Bear Bryant leaned with his back against the goal post to watch his players dressed in civvies take a leisurely stroll on the field getting a feel for the playing surface. "Look at him! He's so drunk he can't stand up straight!" hollered a fired-up Tiger fan from somewhere in the already-packed Auburn student section. No love lost here—this was Auburn-Alabama! Only a few weeks before the Auburn game on his weekly television show, Bear Bryant openly remarked, "I'd rather beat Auburn than go to ten bowls." Quite a mouthful coming from a man who had already led his teams to 25 bowl games.

Auburn fans vented their feelings before this game with creativity. *"If you can't go to college, go to Alabama!"* Then in unison, they let loose their favorite chant, *"Around the bowl and down the hole, roll, Tide, roll!"* There wasn't just *electricity* in the stands like there had been at Jordan-Hare when I saw Auburn play Georgia. Pure hatred pervaded here. From across Legion Field came the chant of The Crimson Tide's faithful: *"Hey Auburn! Hey Auburn! We're gonna beat, the hell out of you!"* Sounded like they meant it, too.

Auburn took an 18-17 lead late, the only time all season that Bama trailed in the fourth quarter. The Tide offense started its next possession from its own 18. Quarterback Steadman Shealy scored on an 8-yard keeper for a touchdown with 8:17 left. His successful two-point run put Alabama in the lead, 25-18. Auburn running back James Brooks threatened to even the score on the ensuing kickoff. He raced 64 yards before a game-saving tackle by Tide Captain Don McNeal at the Alabama 31. With a little over four minutes left, a Charlie Trotman pass for the Tigers on fourth down fell incomplete at the Tide's 37. Shealy and Bama ran out the clock for a victorious final score, 25-18.

In 1980, I'd see the Bear coach two more times. The Tide came to the New Jersey Meadowlands where they just got by D-I upstart Rutgers, 17-13. Later that season, again I trekked back down to Birmingham where Bryant's team bested Auburn again, 34-18. To put a punctuation mark on the hatred portion of this rivalry, we didn't see it start and we didn't see it end, but driving out of the Legion Field parking lot, we saw two guys, literally "die-hard" supporters from each team, encircling around one another with large hunting knives drawn. Never witnessed that anywhere before or since.

Following the '82 season, Paul "Bear" Bryant suddenly passed away from cardiopulmonary arrest. I'm happy to say though, that I got to see him coach two games at his most rivalry-intense best versus Auburn.

During the 80's, Bama came north four times. I saw them play three epic battles at Penn State and once against Ohio State in the Kick-off Classic. Paterno won the first of the three against Bama coached by Ray Perkins in 1985. Later, Bill Curry's teams got the best of Paterno in '87 and '89.

Enter Nick Saban

Tuscaloosa, Alabama - Fast Forward to Utah State at Alabama, wouldn't attend my next Alabama game until 2013 during the Sab...

- The Tide won the national title game in Miami Lakes against Notre Dame, 42-14.
- They defeated Washington, 24-7, in Atlanta in the 2016 CFP semis.
- Bama beat Oklahoma, 45-34, in Miami Lakes again in the 2018 CFP semis.

After both CFP games, however, Saban's teams fell to Dabo Swinney and Clemson in the championship finals. Finally in 2022 with a three-hour drive from my new home, I made it to Bryant-Denny Stadium in Tuscaloosa to watch The Tide devour Utah State, 55-0. With the pre-game festivities, a 41.5 point spread and immediate domination, it made me think of what it must've been like in ancient Rome to watch the Christians get fed to the Lions. The Aggie defense held Bama to Will Reichard's field goal of 45 yards on their first possession. That turned out to be State's defensive highlight for the game. Every subsequent Bama score preceded a touch back on every kickoff through the second series of the third quarter. All but one of those forthcoming Bama possessions resulted in a touchdown. The other ended in a field goal. At halftime, Bama led 41-0.

Saban is a record-setting coach, no doubt. No coach knows better how to manipulate superior recruiting on the field against teams he invites to the slaughter. When it comes to a "level playing field" as demonstrated in his short stay in the pros with their equitable draft for talent and a game schedule determined by the league, it's not his game-day coaching that reigns supreme. Even playoff losses to Clemson and later to LSU and Tennessee in 2022, he lost to teams with comparable talent. College football depends mostly on recruiting, and that's where he has the upper hand.

FIFTY YEARS OF TAILGATE TALES:

Nick Saban enters with his Crimson Tide before the home crowd at Bryant-Denny Stadium.

Not just Basketball

(11) North Carolina State at Penn State, November 8, 1980

State College, Pennsylvania - The first time I saw the North Carolina State Wolfpack play, they visited Penn State's Beaver Stadium under Coach Monte Kiffin, father of Lane. The contest wasn't that memorable to report on. Penn State won, 21-13.

When I thought of NC State athletics, originally, I thought "hoops" - ACC basketball, the ACC Tournament, the Big Dance, Monte Towe to David Thompson on the "Alley-Oop!" Norm Sloan's team winning it all in '74. Later, Jim Valvano racing up court after winning The Final Four in 1983. In 1998, I ventured to see a game in Raleigh for the first-time. Football, I figured, was something just to keep NC State fans busy until the start of basketball season. Boy, was I wrong!

First-class, Red and White State Tailgate!

Raleigh, NC – Fast Forward to Syracuse at NC State, October 1998: On a business trip to North Carolina, a business acquaintance, Al Warwick, invited me and my Quality Control colleague from work, Tennessee fan Mary Jean Shannon, to come to his annual NC State tailgate party as two of about 100 guests. Al "howled" Wolfpack through and through. Syracuse showed up for a nationally televised game on a Thursday night. Aside from the anticipation of this early season game between two ranked teams, Al had organized a first-rate, pre-game tailgate party. Good old Southern BBQ was served up along with adult beverages in large, ice-packed coolers next to a sit-down buffet under a large, white tent.

The hot, tasty BBQ, ice-cold drinks, and fun company provided a fantastic pre-game atmosphere. Then, the festive tailgate party really started hopping when NC State's marching band, "The Power Sound of the South," marched into the tent with snare drums tapping and brass horns blaring! The Power performed their traditional fight songs getting us primed for the game. The Wolfpack cheerleaders and their dance team performed routines to music including their traditional fight song, "Red and White from State!" "Mr. and Mrs. Wuf," official Wolfpack mascots, honored Al's guests with their appearances. Al had planned the exhilarating tailgate party experience perfectly, but the NC State spirit didn't end under the tent in the parking lot.

The high-energy level filled the stadium during the entire game. The band played in the end zone throughout while the dance team constantly performed their rhythmic, gyrating, synchronized routines. The Wolf Pack's student body stood and cheered the entire game. Carter-Finley reveled with great football spirit, erasing my preconceived notion that NC State was nothing but a "basketball school" when it came to athletics.

The enthusiasm increased as the Wolfpack held Syracuse star quarterback Donovan McNabb in check. The Orangemens' Heisman candidate took a back seat that evening to his Wolfpack counterpart Jamie Barnette. He guided the home team to 525 yards of total offense - 282 through the air and 67 on the ground himself. State's defense turned up the intensity against McNabb. After opening with a 66-yard touchdown drive, the Orangemen offense netted only 17 yards by the end of the first half. NC State enjoyed an energetic, 38-17, win.

Raleigh, NC - Fast Forward to Texas Tech at NC State, September 2003: The atmosphere at Carter-Finley left me with quite a lasting impression. I returned again in 2003 to find that energy level still intact against Texas Tech. When interviewed by John McGrath of the Tacoma News Tribune for an article about my website in the Lindy's preseason publications for 2005, he asked me to name for my "bests." He shot out specific categories. "Stadium?" "Campus town?" "Tailgate party?" "Morning drive?" I had to think about each. "Best crowd?" Without hesitation I fired that one right back at him: "NC State!" The Wolfpack's Carter-Finley Stadium really rocks!

Why the among best stadiums?

What impressed me about the game atmosphere at NC State: I've been to 79 FBS stadiums and 31 neutral sites to see bowl games and other FBS contests. Even recently, I read about another rating of the college stadiums with the best atmospheres. Always, they include mostly the 90,000+ seat venues. In my long experience, atmospheres rise and fall depending on who the home team hosts. If it's a big rival, impact conference game, or a significant game against a hot non-conference team coming in, which is rare these days, the atmosphere ramps up. When I attended these Wolfpack games, Syracuse and Texas Tech were not slouches, but they also weren't key rivals. Both visited as non-conference teams. 'Cuse joined the ACC years later.

At both games, Wolfpack fans pumped up Carter-Finley. I watched Alabama host Utah State last season. All the pre-game, on field fanfare was there, but Bama fans anticipated what was going to happen. An Auburn visit would create a totally different atmosphere no matter what the records were. In the past, Nick Saban's complained about Bama students leaving games by half time. No wonder, I attended the 55-0 Utah State slaughter, but the fans can't be blamed facing an opponent with a 41-point spread.

From my experience, the NC State Red and White crowd still rocks, no matter who they play. That's why I rate Carter-Finley among the best in any stadium or atmospheric poll. Regrettably, the last time I visited Carter-Finley back in 2009, I attended an early season game against South Carolina. The Wolfpack crowd remained ecstatic despite my second ever lowest-scoring contest in a 7-3 loss. I was headed from there to my first game ever in Knoxville, Tennessee. Didn't have any big tailgate plans at Carter-Finley this time.

I'm due to go to another exciting Wolfpack game in Raleigh. I'm itching to get back there, and I'd like to do it soon. It's on my ever-growing Bucket List.

Prelude to a Championship / "The Fridge"

(12) Clemson at (13) Maryland, November 15, 1980

College Park, Maryland - This game for me—I must honestly confess—was more of a party. John Massimilla and I met up with some of his old Altoona buddies attending grad school at the University of Maryland. I read the paper the next day to find out how the Terps and Tigers got to the final result. Guaranteed, I was definitely there. I could easily prove it until we moved to Tennessee, but I still have a picture.

Before the game played on a cold, overcast day, we enjoyed simple concoctions cut with soda that came in fine-looking plastic cups from concessions outside of Byrd. I bought several of the white, 16-ounce *"Snappin' Terp Territory"* cups that displayed a Terrapin standing upright with claws on hips standing in front of a big, bold, red "M." More were negotiated away from other nearby fans in Byrd as I explained that I needed to collect as many as I could as wedding gifts for my future, yet unknown, bride-to-be. I left Byrd with twenty-seven cups! They stacked so neatly that by the end of the game I could still drink from the top one while grasping number twenty-seven at the bottom.

My future wife, who wouldn't have the pleasure of meeting me for five more years, just never did appreciate my effort and the benevolence of others to build this cherished collection for her. She eventually disposed of this unique gift idea along with other various works of art gathered during bachelorhood - treasures for a single guy, but unappreciated valuables viewed as "junk" in holy matrimony. A few collectible "Snappin' Terp" cups resided on my garage workbench for years where they invaluably held nuts, bolts, pencils, and other assorted, unidentifiable pieces of hardware - sometimes they even contained worms for fishing. However, most of my college football soda cup collection had to be disposed of to make room in kitchen cabinets for stuff like bowls, plates, coffee mugs, wine glasses, and eventually - "sippy" cups. However, there is no way I will ever part with my cherished ticket stub and game program collections!

It was an impressive Terrapin victory. They handled the Tigers winning easily, 34-7. Head Coach Jerry Claibourne led his team to an 8-3 finish and its seventh bowl game in eighth years at College Park. This game turned out to be a significant low-point for Clemson. One week after attending Maryland's 34-7 win over the Tigers, I headed south on I-95 on my way to "vacation" in Alabama to attend my second consecutive Iron Bowl in Birmingham with Charlie Murren. On Sunday while driving through South Carolina, several cars passed with newly printed bumper stickers that proclaimed, "Clemson 27 South Carolina 6."

Unbeknownst then, of course, was the significance of the recorded score on the bumper stickers. They trumpeted the first of thirteen straight victories for Danny Ford's Clemson Tigers. The thirteenth, a 22-15 win over Nebraska in the 1982 Orange Bowl, earned Clemson the 1981 National Championship. Only one year after I attended their fifth and final loss of the 1980 season by twenty-seven points, the Clemson Tigers reeled off 13 straight victories to win the NCAA National Championship!

Terps open up under "The Fridge"

Orlando, Florida - Fast Forward to Champs Sports Bowl, Maryland vs. Purdue, 2006: Maryland football appeared on my schedule 16 times over the years. The best of Maryland football came under the tutelage of Head Coach Ralph "the Fridge" Friedgen from 2001 to 2010. In his first season, he helped me add Troy State (now Troy University) to my list of new programs joining the FBS. His Terps soundly defeated the Trojans,

PRELUDE TO A CHAMPIONSHIP / "THE FRIDGE"

47-14, on their way to the ACC championship, a 10-2 record, and a No. 10 ranking after their loss to Florida in the Orange Bowl. The following season, they opened for me in The Meadowlands losing to Notre Dame, 22-0, in the final Kickoff Classic played.

The Terps defeated Florida International in my presence in 2006, 14-10. After finishing the regular season at 8-4 for second place in the ACC Atlantic, my son Eric and I followed them to Orlando at the Champs Sports Bowl. The Fridge's team defeated Purdue, 24-7. For me, that's as good as it got for Maryland football. Ralph Friedgen was the icing on Maryland's football program. His 10-year record of 75-50 by far outshines the Terps' record of 56-84 over 12 years since Maryland released him.

Aside from visiting Penn State in early years, I saw them host the Nittany Lions later after joining the Big Ten. They've faced severe domination now after dissing Penn State under their former assistant coach James Franklin by avoiding pregame handshakes in 2014. The Terps caused their own fallibility in this Big Ten East rivalry. The Lions will probably never forget! For my benefit, the Terps loaded up scheduling some wayward teams that I would not have traveled farther to see otherwise. They hosted Eastern Michigan and Florida International on Saturday evenings after I attended Navy games just east 30 miles due east in Annapolis. Conveniently, Navy played mid-day games to turn Saturdays in Maryland into much-needed double-headers to see 'em all!

My Clemson Climax

Miami Lakes, Florida - Fast Forward to Capital One Orange Bowl featuring Clemson vs Oklahoma, 2015: I've already reported on two infamous losses for Clemson in my West Virginia-Syracuse chapter. Besides losses at Maryland and to WVU in the Orange Bowl, the Tigers fell twice in games I attended against their intrastate rival Gamecocks of South Carolina. With the Tigers winless in my long history, I headed to Florida for three bowl games in 2015 – I sandwiched the Russell Athletic in Orlando and the Outback in Tampa sandwiching around the No. 1 Clemson Tigers (13-0) playing the No. 4 Oklahoma Sooners in the CapitalOne Orange Bowl in Miami Lakes for the CFP semi-final on December 31, 2015, the premiere game of my bowl season

After a hard-fought first half, Clemson trailed the Sooners, 17-16. In the second half, however, Clemson just dominated. Dabo Swinney's team drove 75 yards with Wayne Gallman scoring on a one-yard run. Defensive Coordinator Max Venable's defense rose up to crush the Sooner offense. On the very next drive, they a halted a fourth and one at their 30 to take over on downs. They held Oklahoma to 121 yards the rest of the game.

The Tiger offense responded with DeShaun Watson's pass to Hunter Renfro who shook a tackler and raced for a 35-yard touchdown. The Tiger defense stopped the next Sooner possession intercepting a Baker Mayfield pass. Next, the Tigers forced a punt to take over at midfield. Gallman punctuated the next Clemson drive with another one-yard score to go up, 37-17. With 7:32 left to play and Oklahoma threatening to score at the five, linebacker Ben Boulware leapt high to pick the ball off to thwart any chance of a Sooner comeback. Clemson celebrated briefly before heading to the Fiesta Bowl to face Alabama.

Bama triumphed over Clemson, 45-40, in Glendale, Arizona for the College Football Playoff Championship of 2015. However, I at least finally got to witness one glorious, shining moment in Clemson football history.

PRELUDE TO A CHAMPIONSHIP / "THE FRIDGE"

Roger Arnold, center, and Dave Bender, right, both Juniata alum, and I display my battle flags at Clemson tailgate vs. Louisville in 2022.

In 2022, I finally made it to a game at Memorial Stadium in Clemson to see the Tigers defeat Louisville, 31-16. This game featured ESPN's top play of the week when running back Will Shipley hurdled a would-be tackler into the end zone for a 25-yard touchdown. Great time at Clemson that day with fellow Juniata friends and alumni Dave Bender and Roger Arnold. Now that we're all retired, we can finally enjoy some games together. Dave's brother, Dick, has been an assistant basketball coach with the Clemson Tigers for many years. He was a two-year letterman and team MVP at Western Maryland, where he ranked third in the nation in free throw accuracy for NCAA Division III players with a 91 percent clip in 1985-86.

Bowling Cougars / Charlie's Corner

(14) Houston vs. Navy, Garden State Bowl III, December 14, 1980

East Rutherford, NJ - On a cold, blustery Sunday December afternoon, the Houston Cougars ventured to the northeast for the first time since 1962 to compete in the third edition of the Garden State Bowl at Giants Stadium. Key injuries suffered by three veer option quarterbacks spoiled the Cougars' anticipated success to a 6-5 record. Their opponent this day would be the 8-3 Midshipmen of Navy. The Cougar's deceptive veer option offense, crafted by West Point grad and Head Coach Bill Yeoman, depended on the leadership of his quarterback Terry Elston.

The Cougars came ready to play. The Mids, atypically, didn't. The Midshipman defense couldn't stop the Cougars' veer. Houston also held Navy to 200 yards of offense. Houston tailback Terrell Clark earned MVP honors with 163 yards on 26 carries for 3 scores. The game ended figuratively in the third period, 35-0, as the sky turned dark gray, the swamp winds swirled, and heavy snow began to fall. Clark went to the bench. My friends and I sat in a snow storm until the game was over. Then and in the future, I never (OK, rarely) considered a game attended unless I remained to the absolute, bitter end.

After the game, we traveled locally in search of beer, food, and warmth. On snow-covered Paterson Plank Road in Secaucus, we pulled up next to a place called "Charlie's Corner" in the middle of downtown. It was quiet outside. We didn't know what to expect inside.

Eventual home-away from apartment

A middle-aged couple, though she seemed younger, sang country music and Christmas carols on the small stage behind the four-sided bar. The big, busty, blond woman wore a short, red skirt and Santa cap while playing guitar and vocalizing. Her *ex-husband* played the keyboards - perfect for country music. They epitomized a country song!

We stayed late into the evening before a go-go dancer performed between sets of a rock band that came on stage. This was a first anywhere - a bar that displayed a poster of Pope John Paul II on the wall while a go-go dancer performed. John Paul had a big grin on his face!

Brothers Charlie and John Krajewski had inherited their family-owned, local bar. We got to know both owners pretty well. Krajewski's became a meeting place before and after many games thereafter at The Meadowlands. It was classic Jersey! Springsteen considered using the bar to film his video *"Glory Days"* a few years later, but the ceiling was too low. He chose another bar in Central Jersey and had it decorated just like Charlie's Corner to film the video. Pictures of him with John and Charlie still adorned the walls last time I stopped by.

My first bowl game was not very entertaining on the field as Houston totally dominated Navy. However, our serendipitous, post-game discovery that day hosted my friends and me after games attended at the Meadowlands for many years to come. By the way, this was another test my girlfriend Laurie passed. Matter of fact, one night I brought her into Krajewski's when my car radiator started leaking. I asked Charlie if he could help me out, and he had a confused look on his face. He drove me over to his place to get a can of sealant to temporarily plug the leaks. We went back, and Laurie and I hung out for a while. John told me later that he wasn't sure if I really wanted my radiator fixed, or if I had some alternate plan in mind? Great guys! On another occasion, one of my Purchasing assistants at Myron Manufacturing, Flo Stein, and I stopped there for lunch on the way back from a trade show at the Jacob Javitz Center in Manhattan where we couldn't find a convenient place to eat. We walked into Charlie's Corner several minutes after they just closed the kitchen.

They asked us if we wanted anything, and they gladly fired the grill back up and made us lunch. Flo whispered to me, "Are you related to these people?" They really did make me feel like family there.

Texas Bowl highlight

Houston, Texas - Fast Forward to Houston vs. TCU, Texas Bowl, 2007: With my 12-year-old son, Eric, we flew to Texas to see four bowl games in five days. Our first stop was the Texas Bowl in Houston at Reliant Stadium. The match-up turned out to be all Texas - Houston from ConferenceUSA vs. TCU of the Mountain West in front of 62,097 fans. Both had squared off regularly in the now-defunct Southwestern Conference. This game featured two pretty potent offenses under quarterbacks Case Keenum and Andy Dalton respectively. Both would move on to respectable careers in the NFL. In this game though, an anticipated shootout turned out to be a defensive battle. Each quarterback accounted for a touchdown. Keenum tossed a 67-yard scoring pass and Dalton ran for a three-yard score. Keenum threw for 335 yards and Dalton for 249. Dalton earned the MVP award as TCU won, 20-13.

The real highlight for me occurred earlier before the game in the stadium parking lot. The Texas Bowl announced opportunities for autographs before the game, one participant being former Houston Head Coach Bill Yeoman. Another was Bruce Matthews, 19-year All-Pro offensive lineman with the Houston Oilers and Tennessee Titans. Not only was Yeoman the Cougar Head Coach at the Garden State Bowl in 1980, he was also a West Point graduate. Not a big collector of autographs, I brought my 1980 Garden State Bowl game program from my collection. I looked forward more to asking him a question. Eric and I got on line, and we waited to meet the venerable College Hall of Fame coach.

I asked him, "Coach, with Navy starting to turn the corner winning with the triple option now, how well do you think a similar offense like your veer option would work to help Army's program to become more successful?" He sat up straight, folded his arms, looked me in the eye, and said, "Well COACH…" and went into the intricacies of the effectiveness of his veer working today.

I didn't get past much after he called me "*coach.*" I turned my head to look at Eric to see his reaction. My son of few words just gave me a sideways glance. He heard it. "*Coach?*" Me? I coached Eric's baseball teams since he was four, but my question about the veer made this College Football Hall of Famer respond to me almost as an equal, not that we were, of course. I got the autograph and some valuable insight, but getting some unwarranted respect as a "coach" (Little League baseball, at least) from this man who I respected for the great career he had just made my day. Fun memory!

Of Feathers, Flame and Philadelphia History

William & Mary at (15) Temple, September 5, 1981

Philadelphia, Pennsylvania - John relocated from New Jersey to Abington, Pennsylvania, north of Philly to start his hospital administration career near the City of Brotherly Love. This provided a new launching pad to venture out in search of new game opportunities. Timing is everything. John's cousin, Mike Kneidinger, originally from Voorhees, NJ, headed up from Williamsburg, Virginia, with his fellow Indians from The College of William and Mary. They opened the '81 season at ancient Franklin Field in Philadelphia against the Temple Owls.

 I'd met Mike, the W&M starting defensive tackle, just the summer before. His father, Otto, played for Penn State under Rip Engle before he went into the football coaching profession. That included stops at Delaware, Penn, and Rutgers. When Otto was head coach at West Chester State University, John and I stayed with the family one summer weekend to attend the Philadelphia Eagles preseason camp held on the WCSU campus. We had the pleasure of partying with Mike one night and hoisted flaming shots together. Eventually, Mike got around to demonstrating how he could even ingest flaming potato chips! I preferred shots.

 Mike and his Indians didn't put up much of a struggle against Temple that evening. It resulted in a total romp and stomp by the Owls over the Tribe (the name politically-corrected later). Temple's junior halfback Jim

Brown, tallied four rushing touchdowns and also caught a two-yard pass for a score from quarterback Tink Murphy. In the end, the Owls ran rough-shod for 472 yards in their 42-0 victory over the FCS program.

John caught up with Mike down in Orlando in 2006. Our night out that summer in South Jersey must have been an omen. Mike became Chief Operating Officer of Operations for the Hard Rock Cafe International Chain. Since then, he's been President of Bahama Breeze, and now he is the President of Yard House Restaurants. His calling evidently gravitated more toward food than football as displayed by his penchant for inhaling flaming potato chips! One of many fun memories of fantastic people I've met during this great college football adventure.

Fly Owls (not Eagles), fly!

Fast forward to September 2015, Penn State vs. Temple at Lincoln Financial: After John's career start in Philly, he relocated once again to Central Pennsylvania and invested in season tickets to support his beloved Nittany Lions. I joined him often and still do all these years later. John worked it out with me to get a handful of games each season. We balanced my PSU schedule to see good opponents along with lesser competitive teams. So, when I saw PSU host the likes of Alabama or Notre Dame, I would offset with another ticket to see Temple as that lesser foe. Heading into 2015, I watched the Temple Owls play 26 games overall, seven against Penn State - six away and one in Philly. Lost all.

The closest score came surprisingly in the first of those in 1985 with PSU winning, 27-25. Among all others, PSU scored at least 41, and the most the Owls could ever muster totaled only 15. When St. Laurie (*surprise!*) and I saw these two teams finally meet again in Week One of 2015, things had changed for both programs. Penn State was still digging out of the Sandusky sex scandal with second-year Head Coach James Franklin. The O-line talent struggled to say the least, and so did the accuracy of quarterback Christian Hackenberg. Happily, for PSU, they finished with a win over Boston College in the New Era Pinstripe Bowl the previous season.

Franklin's reputation as a superior recruiter preceded him. Improved talent was expected. On the other hand, Temple came into this season under their third-year head coach and former Penn State walk-on, linebacker Matt Rhule. If anything, the previous season demonstrated vast improvements for the 6-6 Owls on the defensive side of the football. Could Rhule improve the offensive output coming into his third season with this program?

At halftime in front of 69,176 fans at Lincoln Financial Field in Philly, State led 10-7 at halftime. The Lion defense held the Owls until a late 93-yard drive closed the margin. The contest seemed to be going as anticipated. In the second half, however, fans noticed that the Temple's coaching staff focused more on adjustments than did Penn State's.

Temple turned up the pressure defensively while their offense picked up steam. Christian Hackenberg misfired and struggled with accuracy. Owl signal-caller P.J. Walker took it in from the one for a 17-10 lead with a minute to go in the third.

In the fourth period, at the PSU 24, Owl running back Ahad Thomas stiff-armed a would-be Lion tackler on his way into the end zone for a 24-10 lead. It appeared the "great recruiter," James Franklin, was being out-coached by former Lion linebacker Matt Rhule. Many Penn State fans had seen enough and started toward the exits. The Lions didn't seem to play with any sense of urgency. Very unusual for Penn State, they seemed to be throwing in the towel. Temple went on to win, 27-10. The Owls came away with ten sacks. Linebacker Tyler Matakevich recorded three among his seven stops on the day.

OF FEATHERS, FLAME AND PHILADELPHIA HISTORY

In 2015, the Temple Owl defense swarmed over Penn State to defeat the Lions for the first time in 74 years.

Another historic day in Philadelphia

For the first time in 74 years with a record of 0-38-1 against perennial powerhouse Penn State, Temple finally halted that streak. They went on to finish this season 10-4. Later that season, I ventured back to Franklin Financial where I saw the Owls fall 24-20 to a very good, 10-3 Notre Dame team. It was a banner performance for the Temple Owls in the regular season. However, they fell in the AAC Championship to 13-1 Houston and then to 10-2 Toledo in the Boca Raton Bowl.

Tigers from Guinea Pigs to Top Dogs

(16) Louisiana State at Notre Dame, September 12, 1981

South Bend, Indiana - There wasn't much to dwell on regarding LSU in the initial Notre Dame game I attended from the Tigers' perspective, aside from being the Guinea Pigs in the "bold experiment" for the Fighting Irish. I mentioned them briefly in that tailgate tale.

- In 2008, I ventured to Baton Rouge for their 34-24 win over Mississippi State.
- At The Grove at Ole Miss in 2013, the Rebels upset the Tigers, 27-24.
- The following season in the Music City Bowl, Notre Dame topped the Tigers again, 31-28.

Regarding my first game in Baton Rouge, special thanks to Mike and Carol Barish for inviting me to their tailgate hosted at their early model mobile home they called the G&G Express, affectionately known as "Stinky." Tremendous experience. I have to visit Baton Rouge again for a significant game in the future. Bucket List!

Finally, Geaux Tigers!

Atlanta, Georgia - Fast Forward to LSU vs Oklahoma, Peach Bowl, December 2019: I watched an LSU team in an unforgettably, dominant performance when Heisman-winner Joe Burrow and company riddled Oklahoma and quarterback Jalen Hurts in the CFP Peach Bowl, 63-28.

It wasn't even that close. Burrow led No. 1 LSU over N(
throwing for 493 yards and seven touchdowns in the first I
led at intermission, 49-14. Burrow tied the all-time bowl record for ɪᴅ
passes in a game. Wide receiver Justin Jefferson tied the all-time bowl record with his four touchdown receptions, again all in the first half. Burrow ran for another score in the second half.

Among 22 performances by Heisman Trophy winners personally attended over the years, Burrow's performance ranked as the best and most memorable among all winners in games I've seen. In addition to his extraordinary stats achieved this evening, one play stood out more than any other.

On a third and two from his 22, avoiding heavy pressure, he rolled right. Nearing the sideline, in one motion, falling out of bounds, he demonstrated his accuracy submarining a pass down field 24 yards to Terrace Marshall for a first down. The drive resulted in another touchdown pass, but on that play alone, the great quarterback for LSU showed me and millions of others he was something special. I was gratified I saw this talent displayed in person. Of course, after sitting on the bench at Ohio State for three years, Burrow became the "poster boy" for the transfer portal.

In the CFP finale two weeks later, LSU celebrated the national championship in New Orleans of all places. They soundly beat undefeated defending national champ Clemson, 42-25, to finish 15-0 under Louisiana native Ed Orgeron. It doesn't get any better than that for any national champion – a win near home under a home-state coaching icon and led by the Heisman Trophy winner to finish undefeated and No. 1! All there is left to say is, *"Geaux Tigers!"*

FIFTY YEARS OF TAILGATE TALES:

Heisman Trophy winner Joe Burrow (9) led LSU to a 15-0 record in 2019.

From Low-scoring Affairs to Travels with St. Laurie

(17) Virginia at Rutgers, September 18, 1981

East Rutherford, NJ - I took a date to The Meadowlands to see 2-0 Rutgers host 0-1 Virginia. In the final period, Virginia had the ball fourth and short at Rutgers' sixteen. UVA Head Coach Dick Bestwick decided since his Cavalier defense put the stops to RU all evening, he would put the easy three up on the scoreboard and hope for his defense to maintain its stinginess. Wayne Morrison trotted out on to the field to give his team the lead with a fairly routine 33-yard kick. Wide right!

Like the previous season, Rutgers' Alex Falcinelli got his chance to give the Scarlet Knights a late lead after a Morrison miss. With 3:02 left in the game, his kick sailed through the uprights from thirty-seven yards away. During the final three minutes, Bestwick's defense held, but so did Rutgers'. Both offenses remained as ineffective as they had during the first fifty-seven minutes of the game. In the end, the final score laid claim to the lowest scoring affair ever witnessed in over my fifty years of watching intercollegiate play. Final score: Rutgers 3, Virginia 0. Results of the date - like the Cavaliers, I did not score.

Fast Forward to Kickoff Classic, Virginia vs. Notre Dame, 1989: The next time I saw the Virginia Cavaliers play, I did not bring a date. Instead, I brought my new wife, Laurie. We had only returned from our Hawaiian honeymoon about twelve days prior when the Cavaliers clashed with

Notre Dame in the Seventh Annual Kickoff Classic at The Meadowlands. The Fighting Irish, defending national champs under Head Coach Lou Holtz defeated UVA under former Navy Head Coach George Welsh, 36-12. Since arriving in 1982, Welsh had brought some respectability to the usually anemic program. More competitive were conversations with Laurie of how long I was going to continue to attend all these games. These conversations could not be shied away from. We met at work both employed by Myron Manufacturing, and we commuted together daily each way for over an hour. Talk about a tough schedule! This Classic kicked off my 11th season. I responded that I started this before I knew her, I did it while we dated, and why would I stop now?

Travels with St. Laurie

She's tolerated my adventures since. Eventually along the way before each season starts, she'll say, "I'm only going to two or three games, you let me know which and when." She got to go to The Rose Bowl (parade only as desired), New Orleans, Vegas, Colorado, and other "exotic" locations to break down her resistance. Then there have been a few Penn State games, Princeton games, Army-Navy (she usually just hangs in the parking lot), a Harvard-Yale bus trip, and weekends to Annapolis.

When I could get four tickets, she and I and the kids would all go. We would even tie trips to visit family or go to an amusement park, visit the USS Nautilus Museum, a cavern, an aquarium, or some other form of entertainment or interest on the drive to or from. Fewer opportunities came along as the kids got older and more involved in their sports and with friends. Of course, when Alex attended South Carolina, Laurie would definitely go, even drive by herself as our son Eric and I would fly down the next morning after his Friday night high school football games. The three of us all drove back together.

We also negotiated a major trade-off. She tolerates my fall football weekends, and I tolerate her inability to go anywhere beginning in January through around April 15 - tax season! She works for a CPA on other peoples' taxes. Nothing else in life matters in her daily agenda during that time-frame. Our tolerances for each other's "priorities" have kept us married into our 35th year.

Pitt Pride Pays Me Well

Syracuse at (18) Pittsburgh, October 24, 1981

Pittsburgh, Pennsylvania – My Juniata College friends Toni-Anne Svetkovich and Cheryl Ondrejek graduated a year after me and roomed together while they attended the University of Pittsburgh for post-grad studies. Our relationships were strictly platonic. Like many of my Juniata friends, they grew up in the Pittsburgh area. Of course, all the "Burghers," as we non-Pittsburgh Juniatians referred to them, loved their Pittsburgh Steelers, Pittsburgh Pirates, Pittsburgh Penguins, and Pitt Panthers.

In the fall of my senior year in 1978 after I decided to stop practicing football, I ventured down to Annapolis to attend Navy's game against William and Mary. The Mids won, 9-0, to remain undefeated at 6-0. The following week, the No. 15 Pitt Panthers (5-1) were coming to Annapolis. I brazenly told my Burghers friends that Navy would defeat Pitt. They all told me I was crazy, and then asked how many points I wanted. I said, "No points! Navy is going to flat-out win." I really felt that confident, and I rarely bet. I made bets for money, cases of beer, bottles of vodka, and food. Toni-Anne and Cheryl wagered "hoagies," or "subs," as we called them in Jersey. My confidence rang true! Navy pulled off the shocking upset, 21-11. I was congratulated and collected all my winnings in short time. Never been as certain about an upset as I was then, and I won!

The girls invited me out to the 'Burgh when I told them I'd be interested in seeing the Panthers play a game at Pitt Stadium. Under Head Coach Jackie Sherrill, Pitt ranked second in the nation. When I rolled into town, I would see them play a familiar team, Syracuse. The Orangemen struggled with a record of 1-4-1.

This staunch Panther defense allowed only 18 rushing yards per game. Joe Morris ran it in from seven yards out to take a surprising 10-0 lead at the end of the first following a 65-yard drive. After "Snuffy" Anderson's 32-yard field goal for Pitt in the second, it was all Dan Marino and the Panther defense for the balance of the game. Dan Short's interception resulted in Marino's 13-yard touchdown pass to John Brown followed by a 13-yarder to Julius Dawkins. They gave Pitt a lead it never relinquished.

Neither team scored in the third. In the fourth, Marino sealed the game with a 5-yard spot pass to Dwight Collins. Marino threw for 282 yards and three TD passes, but Syracuse kept the high-scoring Panthers in check with four interceptions. Pitt's record remained unblemished at 6-0, and they remained in the national championship race winning, 23-10.

Fast Forward two weeks to Pitt at Rutgers in The Meadowlands and four weeks later at Temple in Veteran's Stadium: The Dan Marino years marked the apex of seasons among Pittsburgh's fifteen games I attended. Two weeks after Pitt handled Syracuse and landed at No. 1, they visited the Meadowlands. They blasted Rutgers (5-3) in front of 34,600. RU actually led 3-0, but Pitt responded with 47 unanswered points to remain No. 1. Marino threw three touchdown passes and ran for one.

On November 21, I caught the Panthers again at Philadelphia's Veteran's Stadium among 32,600 against Temple (5-4). This time, Pitt's offense started quickly for a 21-0 lead in the first 15 minutes. Marino's first two of four scoring passes went to wide receiver Barry Compton. The defense, led by All-American linebacker Sal Sunseri, shut down the Owl offense for the final score of 35-0.

The Panthers hosted rival Penn State a week later looking to enhance their No. 1 ranking into bowl season. Not that I went, Marino threw two TD passes in the first quarter for a 14-0 lead. PSU came back with a vengeance though and defeated the Panthers, 48-14, to knock them out of No. 1. On New Year's Day, Marino threw a late, game-winning pass in the Sugar Bowl to defeat No. 2 Georgia, 24-20.

Sentimental Souvenirs /"And Almost Oh"

(19) Wake Forest at Richmond, November 14, 1981

Richmond, Virginia – I hadn't seen Charlie Murren since the previous season. He relocated to Atlanta after graduating from Auburn and came back to Jersey to visit in the fall. Along with his friend T.J. Nelligan from Charlie's hometown of Montville, NJ, we took the opportunity to travel down to Virginia to see T.J.'s Alma mater, Richmond, host the Demon Deacons of Wake Forest at Richmond City Stadium.

The Richmond Spiders, considered a mid-level D-I program, held on to a 15-7 lead late into the third period until the Deacons offense came alive. Within eleven minutes, Wake rallied with 27 unanswered points. Kenny Duckett hauled in a 28-yard pass from sub quarterback David Webber for their final touchdown. Richmond scored again on Steve Krainock's 31-yard pass to Clayton White for the 34-22 final.

For me, souvenirs we collected provided lasting memories of this game. "Go Spiders" painter hats with spider webs printed on that we collected became novel gifts appreciated by many after we went home. John Massimilla's housemate, Jack, wore his to a concert at the Spectrum in Philly. In the men's room, he was greeted by enthusiastic, Spider fans. In traditional UR fashion, they wiggled their fingers and waved their hands up and down shouting, "Go Spiders!" Jack admitted, he was not in a convenient position to return their "salutes."

Also, Charlie and I decided we needed to have one of the homecoming banners hanging from the stadium fence after the game as a memento. We got our souvenir! On the white sheet had been hand-painted a large, blue spider web with large, red lettering, "Mary Washington College says Go Spiders!" Dozens of girls had signed the banner, but none left phone numbers from the all-girl school located about 50 miles north in Fredericksburg. Too bad!

That banner hung as tapestry in my bachelor apartment back in Elizabeth, NJ until 1989 when my new wife and married life moved in. It's a shame how all the neat things you collect along the way during bachelorhood suddenly get categorized as "garbage" when marriage sets in.

As for Charlie's friend, T.J. Nelligan, I found out years later that he headed up a successful sports media company of his own, Nelligan Associates. I wonder if our weekend adventure to the Wake Forest-Richmond game helped him develop an appreciation for sports marketing? *Go Spiders* (arms up and down, fingers wiggling)!

Winston-Salem, NC - Fast Forward to the Demon Deacons vs. Louisville and vs. Texas A&M in the Belk Bowl, 2017: Up through 2008, I attended four games played by the Demon Deacons, the perennial doormat of ACC football. They won all four – two at West Point against Army and two against Navy. The wins over Navy in 2007 and 2008 could not be taken lightly as Head Coach Jim Grobe took over the Deacs and had them on the upswing since he took over in 2001. The second win over Navy (8-4) came at the Eagle Bank Bowl, later named the Military Bowl, 29-19.

"Bugaluga"

In 2015, my purchasing career turned down the homestretch to work for Solvay USA in Princeton, NJ. With almost a two-hour, daily commute to work, I left early in the morning and beat traffic to work out at the company gym before business hours. Among a few other early risers, I worked out regularly with Jim Harton, a president of one of Solvay's other Global Business Units. Jim and I sometimes talked about business, but more often about other topics, mostly sports. Jim happened to be a die-hard Wake Forest alum.

In 2016, Jim's Demon Deacons finished 6-6 and earned a bid to the Military Bowl ("consolation game") in Annapolis. I referred to this as a consolation game for Wake because as the number of "bowl" games continues to expand due to primarily filling airtime for television programming. Bowl games in my book should only go to teams that established themselves as rightfully deserving a bowl trophy. I consider teams that win nine games or more as bowl teams. Any team in postseason play with eight wins or less should be considered as playing in a consolation game. However, Temple (10-3), American Athletic champs having defeated Navy in Annapolis only 23 days before for the title, returned as their formidable foe. Jim's son-in-law was a Temple grad, and Jim wanted to win badly. He and his wife Courtenay were in! They came and tailgated with me and my Navy friends to see his Alma mater in action. Once again in my presence, Wake triumphed, 34-26. His Deacs held a record of 6-0 in my personal history.

About that time, Jim had announced his retirement. The following year, he planned to retire back to "North Cackilacky," as he often referred to his Alma mater's home state. Of course, he would live back near Winston-Salem to cheer on his Demon Deacons. Realizing under my personal watch that his "Deacs" owned a record of 6-0, I'd be invited to future Wake Forest home games. Amazed, Jim, a Wake graduate of 1974 who included former NY Jets punter Chuck Ramsey among his Wake Forest buddies, said, "Nobody has ever seen Wake play that many times without losing!"

A year later, another Solvay gym-rat, George Lazarides, and I traveled down to Winston-Salem together to meet up with Jim at his new home. Interestingly, he had moved it to property his wife Courtenay's family had been awarded by the United States government after the American Revolution. They supplied the American Army with produce during the war - talk about History! We tailgated with Jim who introduced us to his fellow alumni, all by nicknames earned in college.

Jim had been designated two. "Bug," depicting him as in hidden-in-the-woodwork, was what he was called when he went off to study with his "smart friends." When he accompanied his "fun friends," fraternity brothers in non-formal educational, weekend activities, he earned the moniker, *"Bugaluga."* Today, we only met his fun friends – One Iron, Goober, Wheels (the only female), and Earl who somehow retained his first name, but according to Jim, now possessed 47 nicknames. Jim's roommate who became an Army General couldn't join us this time. He always refers to him by his nickname, "Large Wally." Even George had earned a moniker assigned by Bugaluga in the company gym at some point. He dubbed him "Iron Man" - definitely not for George's work-out efforts, but more aptly for his dedication to running.

A nickname for which Wake can never lose again!

After a great pre-game tailgate, Wake Forest enjoyed a 35-17 lead over Louisville heading into the final period of my 547th game, thanks to four touchdown passes from quarterback John Wolford to his favorite target, Greg Dortch. The final score still remained in doubt until the waning minutes. Louisville was led by 2016 Heisman Trophy Winner Lamar Jackson. Despite Wake's early domination, Jackson became more elusive later in the game rushing for total of 161 yards and three touchdowns. He completed 22 of 44 passes for 330 yards and one score. Wake finally triumphed in this ACC Atlantic clash, 42-32.

Known before the game among the happy tailgaters of their Deacs being 6-0 in my presence, with the win today they bestowed upon me my Wake Forest nickname. I accepted it proudly: "7 and oh (as in zero) Koreivo." Such an honor! After this win, I caught up with Bugaluga and friends at the Belk Bowl in Charlotte that season against 7-5 Texas A&M. The contest was an exciting, high-scoring shoot-out down to the wire. A&M took a 42-41 lead into the final period. The Aggies and Deacons exchanged the lead three more times until Wake Forest's Matt Colburn powered over from the one with 2:28 remaining. A&M drove to their 44, but the Demon Deacon defense halted them thereafter. Wake enjoyed their second bowl victory in two years for the first time in school history, 55-52. My name was updated: "8-oh" Koreivo.

Since then, I've attended four more Wake Forest games. A close, last-minute loss to Louisville did not entirely corrupt my nameplate before they defeated NC State, Boston College, and Vanderbilt in my presence. Bugaluga and company still exalt in my Wake Forest successes. For the time being, I am known as "Eleven-and-almost-oh" Koreivo among the Deacon faithful. Still has a nice ring to it! It may be a challenge to maintain that moniker though. I'm considering the Demon Deacons versus some ranked foes in the future to leverage my successes for the Deacs. Whom I gonna call? *Buga-luga!*

Demon Deacon contingency at tailgate before 2017 Louisville game: Iron man, Bugaluga, One-Iron, Goober and Eleven-and-almost-Oh!

Orange Streak to Six Bowls /"Wild Horses" to the Fifth Quarter!

(20) Tennessee vs. (21) Wisconsin, Garden State Bowl IV, December 14, 1981

East Rutherford, NJ - Garden State Bowl IV was billed as Big Ten Strength versus SEC Speed. John Massimilla and I perched in great seats for the game since I bought the season ticket package that year. They put us ten rows up from the 40-yard line behind the Wisconsin bench. Kenny Gallagher, Bob "Polecat" Marcello, and I retained six great seats for every college game we saw at Giants Stadium through 2002.

The Badgers took a 7-3 lead on a 68-yard drive in the first period, but on the ensuing kickoff, we all witnessed a blazing streak of orange! Orange-clad, Tennessee, US Olympian track team member Willie Gault zoomed 87-yards down the sideline right in front of us for a Tennessee touchdown that still remains the best and fastest return in my memory. With 8:23 left in the game, Vol quarterback Steve Alatorre finished a drive with a six-yard touchdown run. When the Vols got the ball back with over five minutes in the game, they ate up the clock. Jimmy Colquitt punted down to the UW one with less than a minute to play. Time ran out for the Badgers, and Tennessee triumphed, 28-21 in the fourth Garden State Bowl.

As memorable as Willie Gault's kickoff return that day was, the halftime performance by the University of Wisconsin Marching Band also remained a vivid memory. In the bowl game program, their band director Mike

Leckrone referred to his musicians as "a team of wild horses."[1] They nearly blew John and me out of our tenth-row seats. Their brass section performed loud and strong! It might have been because of where we sat, but to this day, I remember that team of wild horses more than any other D-IA marching unit I've seen perform at a college football game.

This would turn out to be the last Garden State Bowl played. Within the next year, the N.J. Sports and Exposition Authority announced it finalized negotiations with the NCAA to initiate the first edition of a pre-season "bowl" that officially became known as The Kickoff Classic. Now, I'd have opportunities each fall to possibly add one or two more teams from far away for my football-viewing pleasure. It also provided me with more opportunities to visit Krajewski's at Charlie's Corner in Secaucus before or after each game.

Call these "Orange Bowls"

Florida cities and Nashville, TN - Fast Forward to Tennessee bowls in 2007, 2014, 2015, 2016 and 2021: Talk about Bowls and Tennessee! Six years later, the Vols came back to The Meadowlands to play in the Kick-off Classic. Considered a "pre-season bowl," they defeated Iowa in a close battle, 23-22. As of 2022, I attended 46 true, post-season bowl games in all. In most cases, I planned to attend bowls based on seeing as many as I could in close proximity to one another within the shortest time possible.

This basically meant flying to one airport within driving distance to multiple bowl sites. Early on, I booked many of these excursions with my young son Eric after his seasons playing youth and high school football. Over these years, I planned our bowl travels to Florida, Texas, Tennessee, and an Arizona-California combo. Before bowl committees selected teams, I bought the tickets. With that strategy, I ended up at Tennessee Volunteer bowl games five times.

My earliest trip with Eric featured Penn State's 24-10 win over UT at the 2007 Outback in Tampa. Joe Paterno analyzed from the coaching booth after sustaining a leg injury after he got rolled on the sideline against Wisconsin. Three of the other four resulted in dominant Tennessee wins over Big Ten West teams:

- 45-28 over Iowa at the 2014 Taxslayer in Jacksonville.
- 45-6 over Northwestern in 2015 Outback in Tampa.
- 38-24 over Nebraska at 2016 Music City in Nashville.

Now living in Tennessee, for me the Music City will most likely become a perennial local bowl game tradition. In 2021, the Vols played Purdue in an exciting game, but came up short at the very end, literally, and lost 48-45.

Time to harness those Wild Horses

Madison, Wisconsin –Fast forward to an eventual date at Camp Randall: As for Wisconsin, I've never seen them in another bowl. However, they returned to that pre-season "bowl" in The Meadowlands in 1997. Syracuse shut down the Badgers, 34-0. The Orangemen held eventual 1999 Heisman Trophy winner and New Jersey native Ron Dayne to only 46 rushing yards. Seen the Badgers win just one of six games all on the road:

- In their only win, they defeated Penn State on the final play in 2003, 30-23.
- After Detroit area business meetings in '08 with MSU alum Adam Kalmbach, Sparty edged Bucky, 25-24.
- In 2012, Penn State took a win in OT, 24-21.
- In Wisconsin-like cold of November 2018, the Lions bested the Badgers, 22-10.

The "Jump-around" and the Fifth Quarter are Camp Randall traditions I need to take part in, but I want to participate because I like to party, not because I'll be freezing my butt off! It would be great to take part in that tradition with those "wild horses" of Wisconsin. Hopefully, they still play with that same bold sound that practically knocked John and me out of our seats over 40 years ago!

FIFTY YEARS OF TAILGATE TALES:

[1] Anonymous, <u>Garden State Bowl IV Game Program</u>. "Wisconsin Band's 'Fifth Quarter' is a vast Polka Party," December 13, 1981, p. 57.

You Call This a Classic? / Husker – Power!

(22) Nebraska vs. Penn State, Kickoff Classic I, August 29, 1983

East Rutherford, NJ - Joe Paterno's Nittany Lions beat previously undefeated Georgia and Heisman Trophy winner Herschel Walker, 27-23, to win the 1982 National Championship. The first-time, Kickoff Classic committee invited the "defending champs" to the play in the inaugural, pre-season game. They made an excellent choice in Nebraska for the New Jersey venue. Several key players from their highly-ranked program would get a chance to play in front of their home state fans. Under my budget constraints, it worked to my advantage. I couldn't afford the time nor money during my early college football endeavors to travel to Nebraska. I planned to make up for limited travels later on.

Good idea with major flaws

After every college football season, a phenomenon known as "graduation" tends to deplete experienced rosters. Many players graduate, and others just run out of eligibility of some sort after playing four years. This particular year, Penn State's roster was seriously impacted. The financial bonanza at the ticket office before 71,123 fans unfolded into a boring, one-sided blow-out. The NCAA's leading rusher from 1982, Penn State's Curt Warner, graduated. Their quarterback Todd Blackledge also moved on with a degree. The Lions' second, third, and fourth leading receivers all moved on. Most '82 key starters finished their PSU football careers the previous season.

Meanwhile, the Huskers brought back a strong, experienced core. Their last loss prior to their current 10-game winning streak came at the hands of the '82 Lions. Penn State beat them with only four seconds remaining in a 27-24 win. The returning Huskers carried that as an added incentive into this game. Penn State showed up with a revamped roster to kick-off a new season. You call this a classic? Brand names impress, but key returnees bring necessary game experience to compete. The Huskers enjoyed a 44-6 laugher over the "defending champs" on their way to an 11-0 regular season.

Nebraska running back Mike Rozier of Camden, NJ started his monster 1983 season with a mere 71 yards against Penn State before sitting down in the third. He'd rush for over 100 yards in each of his following eleven games to win the 1983 Heisman Award.

In 2006, he was inducted into the College Football Hall of Fame along with the opposing coach from this first Kickoff Classic, Joe Paterno. In the 1983 national championship match-up at the Orange Bowl, Tom Osborne called for a gutsy, two-point conversion for the win in the waning moments. The attempt failed. The undefeated Huskers fell to Miami who won the national title, 31-30.

Masters of The Meadowlands, and then...

East Rutherford, NJ - Fast Forward to Kickoff Classics VI and XII: Powered by Head Coach Tom Osborne, the Huskers became a Kickoff Classic committee favorite. They returned twice in later seasons. In 1988, they defeated Texas A&M in the season opener, 23-14. In 1994, they returned to Giants Stadium again, and they dominated West Virginia, 31-0.

In 1996, the Big Eight dissolved and the original eight teams consolidated with four teams from the Southwest conference to form the Big XII. The Huskers won the first two Big XII titles under Osborne in his last two seasons. In 1997, they won the national championship defeating Tennessee in the Orange Bowl, 42-17. Hall of Fame Coach Tom Osborne retired after the 1997 season with a career record of 255-49-3.

The Husker program started to decline when I saw them play in 2002 after Osborne's retirement. Nebraska entered Beaver Stadium 3-0 against Penn State under Osborne's hand-picked successor, Frank Solich. His record at Nebraska prior to this game stood very commendable at 45-9. In State College that evening, however, the Nittany Lions roared, 40-7. The northeast corner of Beaver Stadium flowed crimson like it bled to death. Scarlet-clad Husker fans exited down the aisles from the upper deck during the third period through steadfast blue and white Penn State fans and outside the stadium and into the parking lots.

Without any national championships since Tom Osborne's career and wallowing in mediocrity since the release of Frank Solich, Nebraska desperately seeks direction back to national prominence. A Bucket List game in Lincoln will be in the works soon to witness a highly anticipated transition under new Head Coach Matt Rhule.

FIFTY YEARS OF TAILGATE TALES:

Cornhusker cheerleaders at Music City Bowl, 2016.

"How's the Corn ...?" / Hawkeye Happenings

(23) Iowa at Penn State, September 17, 1983

State College, Pennsylvania - John Massimilla, my buddy Greg Hardman, an Army vet who worked with me at Alpha Wire Corporation as Shipping Manager, and I sat in the thick of the visitors' section at Beaver Stadium again. More Hawkeye fans showed up than Colgate Red Raider followers had during my first visit to State College in 1980. Unlike that earlier visit, we dressed in "Iowa camouflage." John had just presented me with a black and gold Hawkeye t-shirt from his second Alma mater, his graduate school. In line at a port-o-john prior to the game in the parking lot, undoubtedly a farmer, acknowledged my attire: "How's the corn growing out in Iowa this year?"

"Well, I don't know about Iowa, but it looked pretty healthy in Jersey when I drove out yesterday." I replied too honestly. "Hmmph!" He grumbled and looked away. "I thought you were from Iowa. "Sorry!" But not as sorry as the two of us cheering on Penn State would feel after the game.

The Hawkeyes racked up 587 yards under fifth-year head coach Hayden Fry. Iowa overcame a 21-14 halftime deficit scoring three of four touchdowns following Penn State fumbles in the second half. Their impressive offense outscored the Lions, 42-34, for the win.

After the game, we partied around State College. That evening Greg and I crashed on couches at John's brother Joe's apartment on Beaver Ave. Joe, being hospitable, slept on a pile of blankets on the floor between us in separate twin beds in his one-bedroom loft. When we woke up the next morning, Joe sat up on his pile of blankets – dazed!

"You - S.O.B.'s!" he said being not as hospitable as the night before. "I couldn't sleep last night! One of you would snore, and when one would stop, the other would start – only louder! You did it all night long! You, sonsofbitches!" Greg nor I heard anything. The secret to a good night's sleep during a road trip like this was to party hard after the game and to fall asleep before anyone else. Greg and I were tailgate party veterans. Joe was still in college. We drove back to Jersey the next day well rested. Joe had to stay awake to study for an exam on Monday while I tried to forget those days. By the way, I did notice that corn stalks on our drive back home looked a vibrant, healthy, green.

Iowa City, Iowa - Fast Forward to Penn State at Iowa, September 1984: The Hawkeyes played some pretty memorable games I attended over the years, not only for on-field performances, but regarding experiences off the field as well. A year later, due to a new job undertaken in 1984 at Myron Manufacturing only two weeks prior, I had to consolidate a previously planned weekend to see the Hawkeyes play at home in Iowa City. With no new days available to take off yet to take a long weekend, I had to do it all starting Friday night through Sunday night. John had gotten us tickets for Penn State at Iowa. Originally, the plan was for me to head out to Pennsylvania on Friday and to join him with friends whose family owned a big, new recreational vehicle. I would ride out with them to Iowa City on my day off. I looked forward to my second RV trip to tailgate!

No-frills airfare, a Japanese rental car, and a mobile home

Instead, on Friday night after work, I took a "no-frills," People's Express flight (later merged and acquired with United Airlines) to Chicago from Newark, NJ. Passengers got herded onboard like cattle and paid cash to stewardesses with carts walking up the aisles to sell tickets. I picked up a rental car in the outreaches of O'Hare Airport in the dark, some new

Japanese car model called a Toyota Camry. The high beams weren't on the floorboard that I was used to, always having driven American cars. The headlights flashed from darkness to high beams with controls on the column halfway out of the city until I pulled over to figure out how to get the low-beams to work.

While pulling off to the side to check this out, the driver ahead of me pulled over, too. As I'm under the dashboard looking to figure this out, he approached my window. He asked if I was signaling him. *"No dammit! I can't figure these (darn) lights out!"* He went back to his car and drove away, luckily for me, I guess. Was he waiting for someone to signal him? He didn't offer any help. I trekked on westward for three and a half hours toward Iowa City.

I arrived at the designated mobile home in a parking lot somewhere outside of Iowa City. It was pitch-black, around 3 am. "Is that you, Steve?" came a voice without a face from the side door. Still in the dark, I jumped in on a bare mattress with no blanket. I froze my butt off in the blackness. Didn't sleep for long, and when the sun came up, I realized a blanket was neatly folded about two feet beyond my reach. Darn, it was cold! Call this adventure, *"No-frill planes, Japanese cars, and recreational vehicles."* John Candy just beat me out with *"Planes, trains, and automobiles."*

Penn State extracted revenge from the previous year by beating Iowa and quarterback Chuck Long, 20-17. In 2006, I attended Long's head coaching debut at San Diego State.

Hawkeye happenings

Nashville, Tennessee – Fast Forward vs. Tennessee in Music City Bowl, 2022: In other Iowa games along my history, they played Tennessee in the 1987 Kick-off Classic. UT freshman quarterback Reggie Cobb drove his team downfield, and Phil Reich kicked a field goal with eight seconds left to down the Hawkeyes, 23-22. NC State defeated them in the 1992 Meadowlands Classic, 24-14. A memorable Iowa win came in 2004 certainly not for style, but for historic trivia. They defeated the Nittany Lions in State College. Of note, though the scoring rules changed since

1869 when Rutgers defeated Princeton in the inaugural college football game that year - the original Kickoff Classic, it resulted in the same score, 6-4.

My most treasured Iowa memory though remains frozen in my mind at Yankee Stadium on the evening of December 27, 2017, when the temperature dipped well below freezing! Frank Scarpa and I avoided our cold, aluminum right field bleacher seats after touring the stadium baseball monuments in center field. We decided to stand instead by the outdoor bar in the upper deck over the outfield goal post. We had a good end zone view of the game action, but even better I can still visualize my beer in my jumbo, plastic cup. It turned into an alcohol "slushie." The water was separating from the barley, corn, and hops and turning into ice. Never thought that could happen to beer, and so quickly! I needed a spoon to finish it during the Iowa 27-20 win over Boston College in the New Era Pinstripe Bowl. And I thought it was cold in that RV out in Iowa City.

In 2022 to my chagrin, and that of others who purchased tickets before the teams were announced, Iowa, averaging 17.4 points per game on offense, came to the Music City Bowl to play Kentucky. In November, I watched the Wildcat defense hold No. 1 Georgia in check at home losing, 16-6. For the Wildcats, Iowa presented no problem offensively. Also, Kentucky's over-rated, "star" quarterback, Will Levis, opted out.

For the Hawkeyes, the Cats presented no problem offensively. Saw U of K struggle without Levis against South Carolina in an earlier "upset" by the Gamecocks. As expected, this year's "Clash in Nash" came nowhere near the drama of the previous Music City Bowl when Purdue edged Tennessee in overtime. Iowa's first two touchdowns came on pick-sixes. Could have canceled the second half. Iowa won a sleeper for fans like me hoping for a competitive game, 21-0.

"HOW'S THE CORN ...?" / HAWKEYE HAPPENINGS

Iowa entry into TaxSlayer Bowl at Jacksonville, Florida in 2015.

How about those Hurricanes? / Collective Caveat.

(24) Miami (FL) vs. Auburn, Kickoff Classic II, August 27, 1984

East Rutherford, NJ - Over the years, I became pretty adept planning tailgate parties for 20 to 100 or more people. Kickoff Classic II would start for TV at 9 p.m. EDT. We started our tailgate party around 4 p.m. A few friends and family vacationed with me down the Jersey Shore that week, so we got into the Giants Stadium parking lot to tailgate early. I booked an entire row of about thirty seats for most of the revelers, many of them joining us after they got out of work. As usual, my fellow season ticket holders and I sat at our seats ten rows up from the forty. The pre-game Hurricanes concocted with three rums, fruit punch, and other juices were a big hit in the parking lot, especially among the women. The Miami Hurricane football program had also been flowing quite smoothly prior to the upcoming season as well.

For the second time in two years, The Kickoff Classic had invited the reigning national champions. However, the 'Canes constituted a more formidable returning champion than the Penn State edition. Miami concluded the 1983 season knocking off 12-0 Nebraska in the Orange Bowl, 31-30. They leapfrogged several teams including Auburn to No. 1. Sophomore quarterback Bernie Kosar, the Orange Bowl MVP, along with his entire offensive line known as the "Blitzbusters," returned intact for this Classic.

HOW ABOUT THOSE HURRICANES? / COLLECTIVE CAVEAT.

Former Miami Head Coach Howard Schnellenberger, who had turned the floundering program around, left for supposedly greener pastures in a new, pro league called the USFL. After scouring the nation, Miami replaced him with former Oklahoma State Head Coach Jimmy Johnson. We were attending his Hurricane debut. On the flip side, Auburn entered this game ranked at pre-season No. 1 in several polls. Its formidable rushing tandem of tailback Bo Jackson and fullback Tommie Agee provided one of the best one-two punches in college football.

The vengeful Tigers enjoyed a 15-14 lead going into the fourth. However, Miami's defense held Bo Jackson to 96 yards on 20 carries, and more importantly, out of the end zone. They knocked him out of the game with a leg injury in the final period. Miami's Greg Cox booted a 45-yarder to start the final period. Auburn's Robert McGinty matched his distance to retake a lead for AU. With 6:08 in the final period, Cox converted a 25-yarder for the Hurricane lead.

Miami defensive end Julio Cortez recovered an Auburn fumble on a pitch with less than three minutes to play. From there, Kosar, who finished the game with 329 passing yards on 22 of 38 attempts, led Miami down to the Auburn two. There, time expired to preserve the Hurricane's 20-18 Classic victory.

How 'bout those other Hurricanes?

We had polished off all the rums mixed with Hurricane "juices." Our start five hours before kickoff, everyone had a good time during our tailgate - apparently too good a time. At halftime, one of our partiers up from the shore, Laura Dixon, ventured over to visit our fellow revelers sitting in the full row of tickets purchased for the game. She happened upon an unexpected sight. The entire row had passed out! They truly enjoyed the tailgate experience, but most of them had no inkling as to what happened during the game. Hey! How 'bout *those Hurricanes?* One of my specialties.

Under Jimmy Johnson, the Miami program would improve and become infamous for building an arrogant swagger. Along with Johnson's successful 52-9 record and 1987 national championship before he moved on, the attitude disenchanted fans of other programs. In the annals of my personal college football history, the Hurricanes played on the road seven times against solid teams like Ohio State, Penn State, and Pitt. Among teams I'd seen play a minimum of six times by 2011, the 'Canes remained the only undefeated team.

After Johnson's inaugural 8-5 season, his Hurricane's challenged for the national title each of his next four years before he left to coach the Dallas Cowboys. As a Penn State fan, I didn't attend the Fiesta Bowl in 1986, but I celebrated mightily when linebacker Pete Giftopolous intercepted a Vinnie Testaverde pass. With 18 seconds left to play, he sealed the 14-10 victory to defeat the Canes for the national championship. A year later, Miami won it all at 12-0. Johnson injected swagger into the Miami program before heading to coach the Dallas Cowboys for his Oklahoma State teammate, Jerry Jones.

Coaches change, but swagger stays

State College, Pennsylvania - Fast Forward to witness Hurricane swagger: In games I attended later, Miami remained successful under other head coaches. Dennis Erickson guided them to national championships in 1989 and 1991. I saw his Canes best PSU in 1992, 17-14, led by Heisman Trophy winner, quarterback Gino Torretta. In 1994, led by Bronko Nagurski Defensive Award winner Warren Sapp, they beat Rutgers, 24-3. Under Butch Davis in 1996, Miami dominated hapless Rutgers (2-9) again, 33-0.

The Canes returned to New Jersey for the Kickoff Classic in 1999 to take on No. 2 Ohio State from the previous season. Ohio State swimming champ and colleague from Allied Signal, Greg Masica, joined me to voice his vocal support for his Buckeyes. A 44-yard touchdown run by James Jackson and a 67-yard scoring reception by Santana Moss from Kevin Kelly gave the Canes a 23-12 victory. Greg went home hoarse with remorse. Davis left Miami after the 2000 season to coach the Cleveland Browns. In his wake, he left a lot of talent behind for his offensive coordinator, Larry Coker, who took over as head coach.

HOW ABOUT THOSE HURRICANES? / COLLECTIVE CAVEAT.

In 2001 under Coker, John and I watched the Hurricanes decimate Penn State in the opening game for both teams in Happy Valley, 33-7. The outcome was decided in the first half – a rarity and a shocker for the Lions in State College. The Miami roster featured some of the greatest football talent ever assembled on a collegiate roster. Many went on to perform at the highest levels of pro football.

- Running backs Clinton Portis, Frank Gore, and Wills McGahee
- Tight end Jerome Shockey
- Wide receiver Andre Johnson
- Offensive linemen Jerome McDougal and Bryant McKinney
- Defensive linemen William Joseph and Vince Wilfork
- All-American linebacker Johnathan Vilma
- Safety Ed Reed and defensive back Mike Rumph

These Hurricanes dominated college football in 2001 outscoring opponents, 512-117. They finished 12-0. They stamped their championship with a 37-14 win over 11-1 Nebraska in the Rose Bowl. The swagger instilled by Jimmy Johnson still remained at Miami, but eventually, to a fault.

Hurricane Warning for the Future

After Coker's departure in 2006, a scandal came to light at Miami. Convicted felon, Ponzi-schemer, and Hurricane football booster Nevin Shapiro was accused of providing Miami athletes with improper, excessive benefits from 2002-2010. He allegedly provided team members with cash, goods, prostitutes, and excessive favors. Under University President Donn Shalala, Miami imposed significant penalties on itself. It suspended eight football players and declined any post-season bowl contention for one year.[1]

Before the NCAA declared more costly sanctions for these violations, it was found the NCAA's enforcement team called upon University of Miami personnel during a separate legal deposition for Shapiro's bankruptcy.

They attended with a specific list of questions to investigate the scandal at the school. A legal review determined the NCAA had no subpoena power in this matter. The exposure of these over-extended activities by the NCAA combined with the university's self-imposed sanctions avoided further and even harsher punishment on Hurricane football.[2]

Miami avoided a potential Death Penalty, but still paid a heavy price

The penalties administered in the case of Miami set the program back, and it continues to recover from the scandal. "The U" has not challenged for the national title since they left the Big East after 2003. In 2017, the closest they came was when they played for the ACC championship and lost to North Carolina. My personal 7-0 Hurricane winning record derailed when they fell to Maryland in 2011. Al Golden debuted as head coach to bring some integrity to the much-maligned program. In 2018 under Mark Richt, they fell again at Boston College. The swagger had dissipated.

Former offensive lineman Mario Cristobal who played for Dennis Erickson's Hurricane teams that went 44-4 from 1989 to 1992, took over in 2022 after successfully coaching PAC-12 power Oregon. In his first season, the Canes finished 5-7 indicating the new Hurricane honcho has some work ahead to turn things around in Coral Gables. If he returns the swagger, Miami Hurricane followers will be elated. On the other hand, those not big fans of "The U" hope they will continue to struggle according to perspectives heard from fans of other programs. Not just Miami, but all schools need to closely monitor who's representing their collectives to avoid the pitfalls Miami faced.

[1] Andrea Adelson, ESPN.com October 22, 2013, <u>Nevin Shapiro</u>, "University of Miami Scandal." Last page edited 21 April 2023

[2]Ibid.

From Royal plan to "Dodge-ball" to Super-Conferences

(25) Texas vs. Penn State, September 29, 1984

East Rutherford, NJ - One week after its loss to Miami, preseason No. 1 Auburn hosted No. 2 Texas, falling to the supposed, rebuilding Southwestern Conference's Longhorns, 35-27. Two weeks after that big win over the Tigers, Texas ventured to the New Jersey Meadowlands to "host" 3-0 Penn State. Host? In New Jersey?

Texas Longhorn Athletic Director and former Head Coach Darrel Royal sought a game in the northeast, but he insisted on a site other than State College, Pennsylvania. The Meadowlands obliged. Three weeks before the game at a meeting of the Metropolitan Football Writers Association, a coin flip determined the "host" team. Texas won rights to wear their home, burnt orange jerseys and to take the bench on the sideline opposite the press box.[1] Neither of these home team "advantages" affected the outcome of this game, of course.

The Texas Longhorn running tandem of Terry Orr and Jerome Johnson excelled against the Lions that day. The Longhorn backs ran for 108 and 72 yards respectively. The days of the dreaded, efficient Texas Wishbone under Darrel Royal officially became the offensive Longhorn strategy of the past. UT confirmed the successful transition in the second period when quarterback Todd Dodge linked up with William Harris for an 84-yard score, third longest in Texas history. The Longhorns introduced their own version of "Dodge-ball" as their quarterback's namesake that day. Texas held Penn State to 273 total yards of offense, most of them came late in the second half. It took a late field goal to keep Paterno's non-shutout streak on offense intact in the 28-3 loss.

Todd Dodge went on to become a great high school coach in the state of Texas. Like Gerry Faust at Notre Dame, Dodge's previous success marked by high school championships, national coach of the year recognition by several publications while at Southlake Carroll High School, and sending scholar-athletes to play in college and beyond, especially quarterbacks like Chase Daniel of Missouri and Greg McElroy of Alabama, did not equate to comparable success in wins and losses at the collegiate level. Like Faust, though not at a private school, Dodge coached several top Texas high school programs running his spread offense where he compiled a career record of 248-71. Moving on to become head coach of North Texas State from 2007-2010, his wide-open offensive philosophy with the Mean Green resulted in a record of 6-37 before he was released to seek other opportunities.

Austin, Texas - Fast Forward to Kansas State at Texas in Austin, November 2019: The Longhorns rarely came anywhere within driving distance of my home in New Jersey. I did not see Texas play again until 1990 when they visited State College and defeated the Nittany Lions in Week One, 17-13. When I could fit a Lone Star State trip into my budget, I'd add other Texas teams to help build toward my goal to see 'em all! I visited Rice who hosted Hawaii. I combined a two-fer excursion at SMU and at North Texas State for a day-night double header. As mentioned previously, my son Eric and I attended four bowl games in five days for a Texas two-step around the Lone Star State in 2007. We missed the Longhorns who ventured out to San Diego to face Arizona State in the Holiday Bowl that season.

My new Texas connection

My true Texas connection finally started in 2019 when my USC Gamecock daughter, Alex, landed her first job in Austin. Two weeks after her arrival, I went down to visit her, and we watched the Longhorns defeat Kansas State, 27-24, in Darrel K. Royal Stadium-Texas Memorial Stadium. Her true football affiliation in Texas, however, goes through her fiancé Zach, a Penn State grad she met at a dog park in Philadelphia during their respective internships. After interning at Temple, Zach became a Business Developer Manager for the Texas State University Athletic Department in San Marcos.

Though my obligation is to TXST games when St. Laurie and I visit, I look for opportunities seeking out other games played by other Texas teams nearby. I did not see the Longhorns play again until 1990 when they visited State College and defeated the Nittany Lions in Week One, 17-13. Last Thanksgiving, I attended UT's game in Austin against Baylor on Friday. The Longhorns overcame a 27-24 deficit in the final period on the running of Bijan Robinson and Roschon Johnson to best Baylor, 38-27.

"Where's the Beef?" asked the little, old lady. Here he is - Bevo in Austin, Texas!

FIFTY YEARS OF TAILGATE TALES:

[1] "Six years and a flip! ", Texas vs. Penn State Official Game Program (29 September 1985), p. 25.

Classic Lesson: Bring us your Quarterback! Strategic Coaching Lesson: Don't!

(26) Brigham Young vs. (27) Boston College, Kickoff Classic III, August 29, 1985

East Rutherford, NJ - The Meadowlands administration should have learned at least one lesson from Kickoff Classics I and II. To have a successful, meaningful, competitive game on the field, be sure the teams invited return with some star power intact, especially at quarterback. Nebraska and Miami did and won. Auburn competed with a returning starter. Penn State imploded with inexperience at that position and others. Of course, for this edition, The Meadowlands committee could bank on another nearby fan base from the eastern corridor from Boston to New Jersey, a fertile recruiting area for both football and the general student population.

Fresh off their first National Championship with a record of 13-0, Brigham Young University (BYU) was loaded to the hilt with key returning lettermen including four receivers with 168 receptions among them. Tossing passes to the likes of wide receivers Glen Kozlowski and Mark Bellini came Associated Press 1984 Third Team All-American quarterback Robbie Bosco. Boston College traveled down Interstate 95 following a great 10-2 season finishing at No. 5, including a 45-28 Cotton Bowl victory over Houston in 1984. Missing from Kickoff Classic III, however, was the field general who led the Eagles to new, soaring heights - last year's Heisman Trophy Winner, Doug Flutie.

Bosco back; Flutie flew to a higher level

Long passes from Bosco to Kozlowski set up BYU's first two scores. The duo completed a bomb to get to the six to score first on a six-yard pass from Bosco to Bellini. The second came on a short run after another long completion to Kozlowski. BC knotted the score 14-14 in the third on Tryon Stratton's five-yard run. A second scoring pass to Bellini followed for a 21-14 BYU lead. Bosco connected with Kozlowski for a 22-yard touchdown and finished off BC with a final score of 28-14.

Bosco finished with a career game-high of 508 passing yards. Flutie's replacement, Shawn Halloran, started off slow in his first start. His three interceptions were topped by Bosco's four. Despite the turnovers, the returning passing attack made the difference in this game. For the season, too - BYU went on to a record of 11-3. BC finished the season with a record of 4-8. The Classic turned out to be a microcosm of both teams' seasons. The main difference – Bosco returned to BYU. Graduated, Flutie moved on to the Canadian Football League. Early season success in college football generally means having an experienced quarterback. In recent years, however, top programs like Alabama and Ohio State attract some of the best freshman talent to their rosters to reload.

Chestnut Hill, Massachusetts - Fast Forward to Miami at Boston College, 2018: Regretfully, I didn't get to see Doug Flutie play during his collegiate career. In 1982, I attended the Princeton-Brown game where Doug's brother, Bill, played wide receiver for the Bruins. Princeton defeated Brown , 28-23, in a very competitive game.

However, I saw Bill's son, Billy, play for Boston College his freshman year against Maryland in the final home game of 2008. Doug's nephew made up for what I never got to see during Doug's career. As holder on the field goal unit, Billy faked a pitch over his head. He then rolled right to throw a 34-yard scoring strike in the Eagles' 28-21 win. At that point, I could actually say I saw Flutie throw a touchdown pass in college despite being 26 years after the original BC Flutie won the Heisman!

In my attendance, the Boston College Eagles hold a record of 11-8 overall. They have not fared well in bowl appearances having gone 0-3 against Penn State, Iowa, and of all teams, Vanderbilt. I've seen them at home and at seven other northeasterly venues.

In more recent years, through friends at Navy games, I got to meet up with Boston College Eagle stalwart Bob "Pops" LeBlanc, class of 1971, and his BC die-hard tailgate co-hosts, Dave and John. Bob holds great tailgate parties from parking space No. 1 right outside the main gate of Alumni Stadium. Dave and John do most of the grilling and have even served some lobster dishes during some tailgates. They heat up the tailgate grills whether Pops shows up or not. A very successful graduate with a BS degree in Chemistry, Pops enjoyed a very successful career in the chemical manufacturing industry. He retired as Chief Executive Officer of Handy and Harman, and relocated from his native Connecticut to retire in North Carolina. He flies back often to support the Eagles when they play home. Living in Carolina, he's an avid golfer but he also attends BC games when the Eagles visit some of their ACC foes nearby. He made major contributions to Boston College's beautiful, new indoor football practice facility adjacent to the stadium, and he also endowed a football scholarship to the memory of his father at BC.

FIFTY YEARS OF TAILGATE TALES:

I never got to see Doug Flutie play football at BC, but I did get to see him play drums next to Pops LeBlanc's tailgate on Red Bandana Night against Miami in 2018.

The Red Bandana Tradition

In 2018, I attended BC's celebration of its traditional Red Bandana Game held since 2002. Each fan receives a red bandana on the way into Alumni Stadium. Eagle players wear them, don red bandana stickers on their helmets or have them sewn into other parts of their uniforms. The celebration pays tribute to the late Welles Crowther, Boston College '99 alumnus and lacrosse player. On this Thursday evening, Boston College hosted the Miami Hurricanes.

On 9/11, working as an equity trader on the 104th floor of the South Tower of the World Trade Center, he reportedly saved at least a dozen lives while giving up his own. A volunteer fire fighter since the age of 16, wearing his red bandana to protect himself from smoke and dust, he appeared through smoke to rescue injured and frightened employees trapped inside. At Boston College, friends knew him to always carry his red bandana while playing lacrosse. His parents, Jefferson and Alison, waved from the field on this night as the stadium crowd of 41,892 honored his memory with a standing ovation. It does so traditionally every year since he passed heroically. I was glad I was able to witness BC's tribute to him as a true American hero during the 27-14 win over Miami.

Catching up with BYU

Provo, Utah - Fast forward to BYU vs. Alabama-Birmingham in Independence Bowl, 2021: On the other hand, BYU played only once more before I caught up with them many years later. In 1989, the Cougars ventured to Annapolis with Heisman winning quarterback Ty Detmer. He completed 26 of 35 passes for 353 yards and two touchdowns on a rainy day. BYU defeated Navy, 31-10.

In 2021, I ventured to Utah from Nashville to attend games at two venues in Utah, both for the first time. Utah State hosted Hawaii at midday, and BYU hosted Virginia in the evening. In BYU's aptly-named Lavelle Edwards Stadium for the Cougar head coach whose teams thrived over his career with a wide-open passing attack. A lot of yardage and scoring came through the air this evening. In the end, BYU triumphed, 66-49. The 115 points ranks third now among my games with most points.

In December of the same year, BYU, without injured quarterback Jaren Hall, traveled to Shreveport, Louisiana for my first Independence Bowl. For the second time, running back Tyler Allgeier impressed as he did against Virginia gaining 193 yards and scoring three touchdowns. On a cold, rainy wind-swept day, the Cougars fell to the UAB Blazers, 31-28.

I look forward to seeing the Cougars play again at Lavelle Edwards Stadium again, hopefully for a day game to take in the surrounding view I missed during the night game against Virginia. Cougar fans insist they hope the move to the Big XII will mean more day games for their team. Like my experiences at Saturday evening games at Penn State, it makes for a long day with an early morning at home.

FIFTY YEARS OF TAILGATE TALES:

(28) North Carolina 21 Navy 19
Navy-Marine Corps Memorial, Annapolis, Maryland, September 7, 1985

Game MVP quarterback Sam Howell looks downfield against Temple in Carolina's 55-13 2019 Military Bowl victory in at Navy-Marine Corps Memorial Stadium. Holding? No flags.

Against Gators,"No-Show Bo!"/ Later, Best of Gators.

(29) Florida at Auburn, November 2, 1985

Auburn, Alabama – Life was certainly a-changing, especially for some of my friends. Charlie Murren and I continued to stay in touch. We talked about me heading down south again some weekend for an Auburn game. Of course, Charlie no longer had any youthful contacts back at his Alma mater. Instead, after he picked me up in Atlanta, he took me to Snellville, Georgia, where he and Lynda not only settled in with Charlie IV, but now also baby daughters Megan and Laura. Afterward, Charlie and I crossed the Alabama state line to rehash some fun memories of game weekends when I visited him back at Auburn. This trip provided my first gander at the visiting Florida Gators. On paper, this promised to be a typically brutal SEC affair.

Auburn (6-1) with a 14-game unbeaten streak at home, hosted the Gators (6-0-1). AU Heisman candidate Bo Jackson already amassed 1,402 yards and 13 TDs on 198 carries. This game had SEC championship implications written all over it. However, with all the pre-game hype focused on offense, defenses dominated right from the start.

Unexpectedly, entering the final period, Florida led, 7-3. In the first half of the second game I went to see Bo Jackson play in, the Heisman hopeful "No-Show" rushed for only 48 yards on 15 carries. Regretfully, he left the game for good after a no-gain in the third quarter. Just like the Kickoff Classic in 1983, Jackson could neither score nor answer the bell physically near the end of a tight game. Auburn grabbed a 10-7 lead early in the final period, but quarterback Kerwin Bell led the Gators on a 61-yard scoring drive to take the lead with his second scoring pass of the game to Ray McDonald from 8 yards out. The Gators won this big one, 14-10. On the post-game, radio call-in show, we listened to Auburn fans lambaste Jackson for his ineffective performance. Bo Jackson was a great athlete in college and in the pros in both football and baseball, but regretfully, my timing was off both times to see him play at his best during his Auburn football career.

Best of the Gators, later.

New Orleans, Louisiana – Fast Forward to Florida vs. Florida State in The Sugar Bowl, January 2, 1996: Although my saintly wife didn't know she was helping rack up points, we earned two bowl game tickets through a credit card rewards program. One day, she noticed that we had accumulated enough points for a toaster oven. What? I wasn't running up credit card expenses and paying interest to burn bread! "No way! We're going to a bowl game!" I had to come clean. I had a plan in place already for St. Laurie and I to travel to New Orleans to see No.1-ranked Florida State play No. 3-ranked Florida in the Sugar Bowl for the National Championship of 1995. She was stunned, but before she could counter, I was ready.

With a growing balance of frequent flier miles, I told her I had saved enough points for at least one round-trip ticket to New Orleans. Having booked her parents to watch our kids and three days for us at an inexpensive hotel in the Big Easy, this proved easier than expected. To my advantage regarding the hotel cost, Nebraska originally expected to be in New Orleans, but flamed out at the last minute by losing the Big 12 title game to Texas. I knew St. Laurie would be tempted any way. She had always wanted to go to Brennan's in The New Orleans French Quarter for breakfast, her favorite meal of the day! She definitely wanted "in" despite having to tolerate a football game.

It's hard to find a bad place to eat in New Orleans. When we arrived, we hit a restaurant specializing in crepes and drank authentic Hurricanes at Pat O'Brien's. We spent New Year's Eve celebrating at Jimmy Buffet's Margaritaville. Despite having no kids along, we visited the New Orleans Zoo. Brennan's breakfast was expensive, but it was a once-in-a-lifetime experience just for its turtle soup and Bananas Foster. Thanks to my ... well... our spending and a championship bowl game, we enjoyed a great mini-vacation in New Orleans away from kids. In retrospect, with my wife, it was a totally different experience than my Mardi Gras trip there my senior year in college. Ah, the good old days!

Sweet Sugar for Gators

On Saturday night, we watched the Gators, led by Heisman winner Danny Wuerffel, torch the Seminoles with three touchdowns and 306 yards. Only 33 days earlier, the Seminoles dished out some hard shots to the resilient quarterback in Tallahassee for their 24-21 win. Florida State emerged as the only undefeated team left standing at the end of regular season. They jumped to No. 1 with their victory. In the rematch, former Heisman Trophy winner Steve Spurrier, coaching his Heisman-winning quarterback (a college football first), set him up in the shot gun to offset the over-powering Seminole rush. The Old Ball Coach's strategy paid off. Florida won its first national championship, 52-20.

Down to the wire...and beyond! / OSU vs PSU Rivalry.

Alabama vs. (30) Ohio State, Kickoff Classic IV, August 27, 1986

East Rutherford, NJ – Long before overtime was even a figment of the NCAA's imagination in 1995, the fourth Kickoff Classic provided action after regulation time had already expired. Two great college football programs clashed at The Meadowlands for their first-ever regular season meeting despite long, storied football traditions. The Alabama Crimson Tide and the Ohio State Buckeyes combined for more than 1,200 wins, with only one of these played between them. The Tide had defeated OSU at the end of the 1977 season in the Sugar Bowl, 35-6.

Three strikes, Buckeyes down and out!

Trailing 16-10 with only 55 seconds remaining and starting from his own 21, quarterback Jim Karsatos led his Buckeyes into Crimson Tide territory. As time expired, Alabama's Derrick Thomas was flagged for defensive pass interference giving Ohio State one more chance to score. Strike one! On the next play, Thomas was called for pass interference a second time on the drive. Strike two! Ohio State remained alive for a possible tying touchdown and the winning extra point to boot, pardon the pun. At Alabama's 18, Karsatos caught a glimpse of Cris Carter open in the end zone. As he fired the ball, fast-closing defensive back Chris Goode, who replaced Thomas, and Britton Cooper, knocked the ball down. Strike three! Bama's win in the season opener gave them the edge over Ohio State in the early season polls.

This Classic actually came down to - and even went beyond - the wire. Three plays ran with no time left on the clock. The selection committee came up with the right formula in Alabama's 16-10 thriller for their second win in their second meeting with Ohio State

Linebacker Chris Spielman of Ohio State became the first defender to capture the honor. In this defensive struggle, it seemed appropriate that a stalwart defender be picked as the game's MVP. He not only became the first defensive player of two ever in the Classic to win the award with his sixteen tackles and one interception, but he also became the only member of the losing team to ever win the award.

At the end of the season, despite identical 10-3 records and a head-to-head loss, Ohio State finished at No. 6 and No. 7 in the AP and UPI polls respectively. The Crimson Tide finished No. 9 in both.

Ohio State – Penn State rivalry

State College, Pennsylvania - Fast Forward to my personal favorite, non-traditionally recognized rivalry, Ohio State at Penn State. The Buckeyes hold an 8-7 overall mark with me among all their games I attended. That includes a home win at Ohio Stadium against the Fighting Illini in a driving rain storm in 2009, 30-0. My brother-in-law Frank Lorito joined me on the trip to Columbus. Great tailgating in a dorm garage nearby that was hosted by a classmate of a former business colleague, Greg Masica. Greg still held swimming records posted at the OSU Aquatic Center on campus. He and I worked closely on successful projects together at Allied Signal, now renamed Honeywell. He joined me at Kickoff Classic XV in 1999 when his Buckeyes fell to Miami, 23-15. I also got to see the Buckeyes romp over arch-rival Michigan at The Big House in 2015, 42-13.

However, when it comes to an intense Ohio State rivalry, I've seen them clash with Penn State nine times, all in Happy Valley. The Lions hold the edge 5-4 . Aside from the first one, a blow-out, the head-knockers generally resulted in hard-fought finishes. In 1994, the Nittany Lions (5-0)

thrashed the Buckeyes (5-0) and future Heisman winner Eddie George, 63-14. On their way to an undefeated record and a Rose Bowl win, the Lions finished 12-0 for No. 2 that season. In 1997, PSU (4-0) went on top 31-27 early in the fourth on a Curtis Enis touchdown run to defeat Ohio State (4-0). The Buckeyes led, 27-9, in 2001. However, substitute freshman quarterback Zach Mills made a dazzling scoring run in the third for the Lions (1-4) and upset OSU (4-2), 29-27. The victory marked Joe Paterno's historic 324th win to surpass Paul "Bear" Bryant's record at the time.

In my presence, the Buckeyes (7-1) finally got the best of the Nittany Lions (2-6) in 2003. OSU's Michael Jenkins caught a five-yard pass with 1:35 remaining to take a lead. As time expired, Lion kicker David Kimball's 60-yard attempt fell just short and slightly wide right. Final: 21-20, Buckeyes. In 2005, PSU (5-0) led 17-10 over Ohio State (3-1) with 2006 Heisman quarterback Troy Smith early in the third period. A hard-hitting defensive battle endured until the Lions forced Smith to fumble late in the game to preserve that lead. The Nittany Lions and Buckeyes finished ranked third and fourth respectively at the end of the season.

In a battle between two top defenses in 2009, both quarterbacks each totaled only 125 passing yards. The difference resulted with Buckeye Terrelle Pryor passing for two touchdowns and running for another. Ray Small's two long punt returns set up two Buckeye scores. Lion quarterback Darryl Clark threw an interception and ran for only one score. Ohio State (7-2) came out on top of the Lions (8-1), 24-7. Both teams finished 11-2 that season.

In 2016, OSU (6-0) led PSU (4-2), 21-7 in the third period. Spurred on by the Beaver Stadium "White-out," a blocked Buckeye punt resulted in a Lion field goal, and a blocked OSU field goal attempt resulted in a 60-yard touchdown return by defensive back Grant Haley to pull off a 24-21 upset by Penn State. Another close one in 2018 pitted two 4-0 teams. Penn State took leads by twelve and thirteen points, but Ohio State overcame both. The last on a 24-yard pass from the late Dwayne Haskins to K.J. Hill for the 27-26 lead. After three consecutive time-outs on a fourth and five, Buckeye defensive end Chase Young stuffed quarterback Trace McSorely and running back Miles Sanders together in their tracks for a loss of yardage and the game.

In 2022, the Lions led with 9:46 left, 21-16, over the No. 2 Buckeyes. In the final period, Buckeye defensive end J.T. Tuimoloau strip-sacked QB Sean Clifford to set up T.J. Henderson's second score. Next, Tuimoloau gathered in Sean Clifford's pass thrown directly to him for a 14-yard pick-six return for the last Buckeye score. They outscored the Lions 28-10 to seal their eighth win, 44-31.

Overall, the Buckeyes lead the series, 23-14. Since Big Ten play, they lead the Lions 21-8 with one win vacated by OSU in 2010 due to improper inducements to Pryor. I have not attended any OSU-PSU games in Columbus. Though the Buckeyes lead there since 1993, 11 wins to two, often times games were determined late. In my experience, it's been a great rivalry. I make this match-up a priority for me whenever Ohio State ventures to State College.

From Low-budget to New Heights

(31) Cincinnati at Penn State, September 19, 1987

State College, Pennsylvania - For over one full year, not one new, unseen team had been added to my schedule. However, I couldn't complain about my 1986 travels after the Alabama-Ohio State game. I watched Penn State and Joe Paterno win three of their 12 victories on the way to their second National Championship in four years. I pieced together my usual Penn State plans before the '87 season with John Massimilla. As usual, I selected "good" games balanced with the "bad" and the "ugly." This year, the good games were against Alabama and Notre Dame. The bad, well not so bad, was against West Virginia, but the ugly was definitely against Cincinnati.

It turned out to be an unremarkable 41-0 rain-soaked PSU victory by the defending national champs against a team with an offense expected to threaten under the controls of "Heisman Candidate" Danny McCoin – not even close! The most memorable detail about this trip was seeing a Bearcat defensive back talking on a pay phone in the hallway at our hotel in Lamar, Pennsylvania the morning before the game. I always booked economy–class hotels and less. During my many pregame overnight stays, I had never even seen a visiting team at a hotel I stayed in. You need no better proof to confirm that the University of Cincinnati was definitely a low budget football program! Friends who've traveled with me to games over the years will attest to this.

Cincinnati, Ohio - Fast Forward to Cincinnati vs. Houston for AAC title, 2021: UC football from the deepest depths to new heights! The most significant aspect of the Cincinnati Bearcats in the annals of my personal history reflects on how they lost and lost big! Besides the 41-0 loss in State College, Syracuse smoked them during my first Carrier Dome trip in October 1997, 63-21. However, the Bearcats' third loss provided the charm. They visited the winless Black Knights of the Hudson on October 9, 2004 in a Conference-USA game.

At the expense of Cincy, Army lore

Army, on a 19-game losing streak, led 41-29 going into the final period. The Bearcats drove to the Army nine, but on a fourth and eight on to the right side, the Cadets halted them to take over on downs. Next, Tielor Robinson got great blocking downfield to ramble 93 yards for Army's final score of the day. The Black Knights of the Hudson won, 48-29. The Corps erupted! Cannons exploded! The goal post nearest the Corps of Cadets went down quickly in a sea of gray. Disassembled, an upright was paraded around the stadium by giddy Cadets. It met the same fate as the other. Both ended up at the bottom of Lusk Reservoir. Half the Corps had never, ever seen their team win a football game. For them, it was a long-awaited first. For Cincinnati, it was another loss - not to an overpowering favorite, but to an underwhelming underdog. No matter who I watched the Bearcats compete against, the result was always the same—a lop-sided loss.

What a difference good, no less great, head coaches can make. Despite the loss to Army, Mark Dantonio took them to 18-17 before he left for Michigan State. Brian Kelly used Cincy as a stepping stone with a 34-6 mark before landing at Notre Dame. Butch Jones led them to a 23-4 mark before struggling elsewhere later. Tommy Tuberville brought them moderate success after Auburn at 29-22 before turning to a career in politics. However, I just never got to see any of those teams play.

Bearcat budget attains new heights

Luke Fickell took over the Cincinnati Bearcats program in 2017. He served as defensive coordinator at Ohio State when they won the CFP in

2014. In this game, with friends on what was becoming an annual tailgate tradition in Annapolis, we watched Fickell's first edition of Bearcats lose to Navy on a blistering, heat-exhaustion-inducing hot, sunny day, 42-32. The Bearcats finished the season at 4-8. Same old, low-budget Bearcats? Not quite. Under Fickell, they finished 11-2 the following season. Our rain-soaked, tailgate party watched them defeat Virginia Tech, 35-31, in Annapolis once again in the Military Bowl. They won the American Athletic Eastern Division the following year. They finished 11-3 by blowing out Boston College in the Birmingham Bowl, 38-6.

Combined Navy and Bearcat fans celebrate Cincinnati's Military Bowl win over Virginia Tech in 2015.

Covid-19 hit college football hard in 2020. Restrictions for travel, required face masks, limited attendance capacities, and even cancellations due to players health squelched opportunities for fans to attend games. I made it to only three this season. Luckily, the state of Florida was not impacted as much. I was able to get a one-day round-trip ticket to go to Orlando. There, the 7-0 Bearcats faced the 5-2 Golden Knights of UCF.

Trailing 25-22 at the end of the third quarter, Safety Darrick Forrest picked off a Dillon Gabriel pass tipped in the air. Gabriel came into the game ranked third in the nation with 188 consecutive passes without a pick. Forrest returned it 20 yards to the UCF 16 to start the short touchdown drive. Bearcat quarterback Desmond Ridder dove over extending the ball from the one for his second touchdown on the ground. Next, he followed up with a seven-yard touchdown pass to lead No. 7 Cincinnati past Central Florida with its high-powered passing attack, 36-33. CU finished 9-0 before falling to 8-2 Georgia in the Peach Bowl, 24-21.

A year later for the first time, I drove up to Nippert Stadium only about three hours away now living in Nashville. The No. 4 Cincinnati Bearcats (13-0) defeated the Houston Cougars (11-2), 35-20, to win the American Athletic title. Cincy back Gerard Ford's spectacular MVP performance of 18 rushes for 187 yards and two explosive touchdowns runs keyed the victory. Houston exchanged scores with Cincy early. The tenacious Bearcat defense adapted and shut the Cougars down from the second period on. With that, they secured their selection into the College Football Playoff. No. 1 Alabama loomed as their next opponent at the Cotton Bowl on December 31. The Bearcats achieved the "honor" of being the first Group of Five team to ever earn a bid among the final four in the CFP.

Rutgers 19 - (32) Kentucky 18
The Meadowlands, East Rutherford, NJ, September 26, 1987

Welcome, "New Ball Coaches"

(33) Duke at Rutgers, October 3, 1987

East Rutherford, NJ - Another college football "two-fer," this one consisted of two D-I games. I squeezed in the Wake Forest-Army game at West Point before heading down the Palisades Parkway in dreary rain immediately afterwards to catch the Duke Blue Devils play Rutgers at Giants Stadium. The Demon Deacons beat the Cadets, 17-13, in a noon start. St. Laurie and I headed up to that game with my Boonton High classmate, Jim Lewis, who now dwelled in Manhattan. Jim came with us on last-minute notice. Now enduring bachelorhood in his 30's now, he realized a hint of hitting a strange new attitude that actually gave him some comfort. A woman had canceled their date that evening. He wasn't upset as he would have been in earlier years. Instead, he relished the positives in that he could join us for the game, and in the evening get his laundry done as well. Between games, I dropped Laurie off at her house as she had attended one game, but wouldn't withstand a second whether or not with or without the impending downpour. I dropped Jimmy off to catch a bus back to New York to get his clothes cleaned.

On my own, I forged on to the nightcap of my Saturday D-I doubleheader in The Meadowlands. Despite being a decent match-up between fledging programs, the fans stayed away from Giants Stadium in droves. New head coach and former Heisman Trophy winner Steve Spurrier coached his Blue Devils (3-1) in his first season against the Scarlet Knights (2-1).

That evening, I avoided my prime, rain-soaked seats ten rows up from the 40 on the press box side for drier climes under the mezzanine. Everyone else in attendance had the same idea. Looking down from my dry, covered perch, not one red seat visible above or below the mezzanine in the 76,000-seat stadium supported a single human being. It had to look totally empty on a television screen. With so few attendees, Rutgers and Duke players seemed to be playing in front of their families, a few close friends, and one die-hard college football fan. Maybe five or six thousand showed up in the rain that night all fine, but the no-shows didn't miss much – offensively any way.

Following a pass interference call by Duke in the fourth quarter, Rutgers tailback Harry Henderson scored on a two-yard run with 5:41 left for the only score of the game. RU recorded win 500 in school history, 7-0.

Two Steve Spurrier rarities witnessed in one evening

The no-shows missed two unique, historical, football footnotes. I claim them among my most unique of game experiences. Very few fans witnessed either, and they can never be experienced again! Spurrier's 5-6 Duke team of 1987 would be his only squad with a losing record at any school; and the 7-0 loss represented only one of two times the "Old Ball Coach" would ever get shut out. His South Carolina squad lost to Georgia, 18-0, in 2006. Besides the 500th historic win for Rutgers that rainy night at The Meadowlands, how many fans can claim to have ever seen Steve Spurrier coach during a losing season or get shut out? Along with about 5,000 other attendees under cover at Giants Stadium that evening, I witnessed both.

West Point, NY - Fast Forward to Duke vs. Army, 2009 and 2015: Regarding Duke, the more common, desirable trip to Durham is to attend a basketball game with the "Cameron Crazies" rather than to watch their football follies at Wallace Wade Stadium. Since my initial intervention experiencing Blue Devil football, I've attended only three other Duke games. They've rarely deserved the attention. In 1993, they returned to the Meadowlands again to play an equally challenged Rutgers team and lost in a very competitive game, 39-38. The next time they made my slate, I hosted a bus-trip/tailgate with my company's Employees' Club at the time to see them face Army at West Point.

In 2009, they traveled to play Army again under second-year Head Coach David Cutcliffe. He seemed to have things looking up for the Blue Devils at the time. Duke won, 35-19, on their way to five wins which totaled the most wins for Duke on the gridiron since they won eight in 1994! One personal memory for me that game entails Saint Laurie bringing a book to read on the bus trip to West Point! Figured she didn't know many people from my work, but who does that? It's supposed to be a tailgate party! Food, drinks, fun, laughs! Initially, not the case for my saintly Laurie.

Duke football, not basketball, rebounds

In 2015, Duke and I returned to West Point again. They drilled a struggling Army program, 44-3. They scored every time they had the ball. The victory there was their fifth of eight they would win on the year including wins over Virginia Tech and a Pinstripe Bowl victory over Indiana. Cutcliffe's teams brought moderate success the next few years with quarterback Daniel Jones under his tutelage. However, after three straight losing seasons following Jones's graduation, Duke released him.

In 2022 under "new ball coach" Mike Elko, who came from Notre Dame where he was defensive coordinator, the Devils finished 9-4. The Blue Devil football program seems ready to rebound. My hope will be that Duke starts playing some more meaningful football games. That way, I hope to catch up with some Cameron Crazies at their Wallace Wade Stadium for the first time. That would be a plus for the Bucket List.

"♪Yogi Bear is smarter than the average bear....♪"

Nebraska vs. (34) Texas A&M, Kickoff Classic VI, August 27, 1988

East Rutherford, NJ - The Aggies of Texas A&M, winners of three consecutive Southwestern Conference titles, marched into The Meadowlands to kick off the 1988 season against the first team to ever return to play a second Kickoff Classic, the Nebraska Cornhuskers. The selection committee did an excellent job choosing competitive teams for its sixth season opener. Within NCAA constraints, they had to invite each major conference within the first seven years of the Classic.

Like Ohio State's traditional dotting of the "i" in *Script Ohio* by "the best dam band in the land" (OSU's description), the Kickoff Classic introduced the NY-NJ metropolitan area's college football followers to the Fightin' Texas A&M Aggie Marching Band. The precision, military-like unit in campaign hats, brown tunics, khaki trousers, and whose seniors wore polished, knee-high, tan riding boots, performed impressively to the "Aggie War Hymn". They march impressively in tight precision formation.

Sorry if this bugs Aggie fans, but...
What always struck me funny is how their proud War Hymn reminded me of the *"Yogi Bear Cartoon"* theme song. Only difference - a slower, more methodical beat. Yogi's theme is more upbeat! Next time you hear it, sing along. *"Yogi bear is smarter than the average bear. Yogi Bear is always in the*

Ranger's hair. Have a picnic basket you will find him there, ♪..." I'm sure it's just a coincidence, but those words enter my mind whenever I hear the Aggies play their war hymn. I haven't taken the time to learn the real words because I always liked the lyrics to *"Yogi Bear"*.

This Classic turned out to be a little bit Yogi Bearish. Though I'd say it reminded somewhat of Yogi and his little pal, Boo-Boo Bear. Nebraska failed to score after recovering two A&M fumbles in the first half to trail, 7-6. Nebraska's score came on Steve Taylor one-yard pass to Nate Turner early in the third. Early in the fourth, Taylor connected with tight end Todd Millikan who carried two defenders bear-hugging him into the end zone on a 20-yard pass play.

A 20-7 Husker lead woke up the Aggie offense after the punt team recovered a Husker fumble on a return at the 44. A&M back Randy Simmons narrowed the margin, 20-14, on a 2-yard run. Nebraska's Greg Barrios booted his third field goal of the contest, a 48-yarder for a Classic field goal distance record. He finalized the scoring at 23-14 with just over seven minutes left. Both defenses prevented any further serious scoring threats.

Steve Taylor garnered the Flynn Award as MVP in one of the Classic's more lackluster offensive MVP performances. The voters for MVP evidently could not see their way to select another defensive player as they had in 1986. Surprising though because of all the pre-game hype regarding the reputations of the linebackers featured in this Kickoff Classic. Despite linebacker John Roper's impressive reputation and stats at A&M, and despite two All-American seasons at linebacker for Nebraska's Broderick Thomas, neither captured the award that evening.

Aggie Bowl Blues

After experiencing two losing Kickoff Classic losses by the Aggies, they didn't fare any better in bowl games I attended. I crossed post-season paths with them twice. Eric and I watched them fall to Penn State in the sold-out Valero Alamo Bowl during our Texas Two-step to See Four Bowls Trip in 2007, 24-17. The Nittany Lions overcame an early 14-point deficit to defeat the Aggies. PSU's Evan Royster broke a 17-17 tie with a 38-yard touchdown run in the third period to win their 23rd bowl game under Joe Paterno. Wake Forest did them in late at the aforementioned Belk Bowl, 55-52.

Johnny who?

Columbia, SC - Fast Forward to Aggies at South Carolina, 2014: In between bowl losses, I watched Texas A&M win their opening game of the season at South Carolina, 52-28. This was my daughter Alex's senior year in Columbia, SC. Aggie quarterback Kenny Hill surpassed Johnny Manziel's game-high record throwing for 511 yards. On my Bucket List, I plan to see a game at Kyle Field, home of the Aggies, for the first time in the near future.

With Alex now living in Texas, I'm probably going to rely on her to go see an Aggie game with me there in the future. Maybe Alex will go see her Gamecocks play at Kyle Field this year. However, like me, she's saving up for her big wedding plans in the Lone Star State next spring. I told her I'd be very happy with Zach's help to plan her wedding reception at TXST's Bobcat Stadium. Tailgate wedding party! End zone reception area, marching band music to play South Carolina and Penn State's fight songs live, football videographers to film, replays on video board, big BBQ buffet, beer trucks, and The Strutters Dance Team! I would plan a fantastically, fun wedding reception. She and her mother just ignore me though. I don't know why.

"Wunderbride" and "Wunderkind"

(35) Southern Cal vs. Syracuse, Kickoff Classic VIII, August 31, 1990

East Rutherford, NJ – Before I reflect on my memory of watching USC play for the first time, let me mention that 1989 turned out to be another season void of new teams. Primarily, two big commitments also took over life that year. As mentioned previously, I was adjusting to married life. Also, I was attending non-football Seton Hall University at night to work on my MBA. Many weekends focused on papers, studies, and projects depriving me of football attendance. Three years of grad school remained ahead to rein me in. I couldn't travel as much now, so I limited my adventures to within short, driving-distances if I could attend any game at all.

    A year after grad school in 1993, we had our first baby, Alexandra. Two years after her, Eric arrived. Times became more challenging for me on the football front, but I continued to enjoy fall weekends as much as I could. Not always with the blessing of Laurie at first. She constantly reminded me that she should be exalted for the sacrifices she was making. My "Wunderbride" claimed no other woman would put up with it. I wasn't backing off either though. I did this before I knew her and while we dated. So, what made her think I was going to stop altogether now? I assured her that I would make this work for both of us. Entering our 34th year together, I can say that we worked it out very well. She remains my Wunderbride!

"WUNDERBRIDE" AND "WUNDERKIND"

Hollywood plays off-Broadway

The USC Trojans ventured east for their first trip in 39 years. They became the first PAC-10 team (later PAC-12) to participate in the annual Kickoff Classic. Their appearance would fulfill the obligation of the Classic contract with The Meadowlands to invite all seven major conferences as participants within seven years. Southern Cal, known as Tailback U. for its tradition of outstanding running backs, this year's offensive spotlight instead fell upon Trojan quarterback Todd Marinovich.

USC appeared with their starting sophomore quarterback known in certain circles as "Robo QB," or as "America's first test-tube athlete." From his mother's womb, his father, Marv, a former USC and AFL lineman, raised Todd to be the "purest" natural athlete possible. He committed his wife to give up cigarette smoking and insisted she consume a high protein diet. As a youngster, Todd's dad planned strict work-out regimens and ensured no fast-food products ever entered his son's body. Marv's admitted goal for his son was to make him the first high school athlete ever to be pictured on the Wheaties cereal box – seriously![1] The family nurtured Todd to be a "Wunderkind."

The opposition for the Trojans that evening would be the former, short-term denizens of The Meadowlands, the Syracuse Orangemen. With USC leading 14-10 in the third period, the teams traded field goals. Next, Marinovich threw a 46-yard scoring strike to flanker Gary Wellman for the 24-13 lead. In the final period, linebacker Scott Ross and company held the Orangemen to a field goal. The Southern Cal Trojans scored the last ten points to seal the victory in Kickoff Classic VIII, 34-16. Neither team lived up to promising, pre-season expectations. Instead, the most intriguing epilogue to this game was the plight of the game's MVP, "Robo QB" or "Wunderkind" Marinovich. He eventually earned another nickname - Todd "Marijuanovich."[2]

The strain of Marinovich's relationship with Head Coach Larry Smith gradually intensified, and after encounters with the law for drug abuse and rape charges, the prodigy raised from the womb to become a football player first and foremost, opted early for the NFL draft in 1991. Al Davis, owner of the Raiders, the same organization for whom his father had played in 1965, drafted him in the first round. He signed for $2.27 million. His debut in the final game of his first season would be the highlight of his NFL career. He threw three TD passes before his release in 1992. He flirted with the Canadian and Arena Football Leagues for a few years, but he did more than flirt off the field as he was served with three paternity suits and arrested for more drug abuse convictions. In 2004, ESPN rated him seventh among "The 25 Biggest Sports Flops." Exactly seventeen years after his Kickoff Classic MVP Award, the 38-year-old Marinovich was arrested for felony possession and resisting arrest on the Newport Beach, California pier after being stopped for skateboarding in a "No Skateboarding Zone!"[3] Despite or perhaps because of his parents' selective and controlled cultivation, the 38-year-old Marinovich still hadn't grown up.

Lessons from Big Brother's mistakes?

In 2008, Todd's younger brother, Mikhail Marinovich, a highly recruited tight end, entertained scholarship offers from USC and Texas Tech among others. Eighteen years after his brother's MVP Kickoff Classic performance, Mikhail ended up, ironically, on the roster of Syracuse, USC's opponent that evening off Broadway. He saw little action as a defensive end entering his senior season in 2011. Good news though is that Mikhail graduated with a B.S. degree from Syracuse to go on to a career in business. He made great use of his college football scholarship in the long run.

USC's Traveler gets ready to Fight On against UCLA!

Los Angeles, California - Fast forward to USC vs. UCLA at Los Angeles Coliseum, November 2017: I attended other Trojan contests of note later in my annals. They lost to PSU at State College, 38-14, during the Lions' first Big Ten title to play in the Rose Bowl. In 2000, the Trojans with Heisman Winner Carson Palmer defeated the Lions, 29-5, in the Kickoff Classic. In 2015, at the invitation of Dave Plati, Sports Information Director at Colorado, I got to see the Trojans defeat the Golden Buffaloes, 27-24, in my first game at Folsom Field in Boulder. I made it a priority, however, to finally venture out to the Los Angeles Coliseum to see USC host cross-town rival UCLA, for me a must-see rivalry.

Traditionally, this rivalry on national television in the 60s and 70s right before Thanksgiving indicated bowl season implications. Usually, this battle laid claim on what PAC-10 team would go on to the Rose Bowl to play the Big Ten champs. More than that though, it brought sunshine and plush green grass into the cold, dark, dank, late Saturday afternoons of eastern living rooms. The "Far West" rivalry always played a few weeks after turning clocks back to Eastern Standard Time bringing darkness around 4:30 pm. Their timely kickoffs, even on black and white TV (in color eventually), would just brighten up a living room with a game played in bright, warm sunshine. In 2017, I finally made the journey to Los Angeles to witness the colorful clash live and in-person.

Fight on!

The No. 12 Trojans came in a heavy favorite at 9-2 against the Bruins at 5-5. In 2000, the rivalry stood deadlocked with each team owning 34 victories. Since then, the Bruins only enjoyed the pleasure of taking home the traditional, prized Victory Bell in four of the past seventeen meetings. Both came to play with supposed top pro prospects at quarterback. On this day, neither impressed. I gave Trojan quarterback Sam Darnold the edge over the Bruins' Josh Rosen.

In reality, the spectacle featuring Traveler, the Trojan Horse; the stirring tune *"Fight on!"*; scarlet and powder blue home jerseys worn by the respective teams; the Olympic flame; the USC Song Girls; and more so based on where I sat, the UCLA Bruin cheerleaders, made the long flights across the country worthwhile. Witnessing unique traditions like these leave lasting memories of attending great rivalries throughout the country.

Cheerleaders uphold one of the great traditions in the USC vs. UCLA rivalry.

The Bruins started the fourth quarter trailing, 21-14. Their next drive starting from their 14 fizzled at the Trojan nine resulting in a 26-yard field goal. Unlike Rosen of UCLA, USC's Darnold showed how to spark a sense of urgency. The Trojans needed to score. He led Troy on a 90-yard drive for a touchdown. USC tailback Ronald Jones II broke over from the two for a 28-17 lead with 5:19 left. UCLA fans now hoped to see Rosen show leadership to upset the Trojans. USC focused ahead on the PAC-12 championship.

Rosen led his team back to within five points with a 27-yard pass to John Lasley, his third score through the air. His two-point pass attempt failed. Recovering an onsides kick, Southern Cal started from their 49 with 2:36 remaining. After two Bruin time-outs, USC converted a first down to seal the Trojan victory. This being a classic, cross-town rivalry, the score ended closer than most expected, 28-23.

[1] Anonymous, www.biographicon.com/history/lpdc4/Todd_Marinovich (Jan. 2008).

[2] Mike Sager, "Todd Marinovich: The Man who Never was." *Esquire*, April 14, 2009.

[3] Ibid.

Battles for Bowls

(36) Michigan State at Rutgers, September 29, 1990

East Rutherford, NJ– In my first Michigan State encounter, the Spartans whipped the Scarlet Knights into reality with a 34-10 victory and captured their 500th overall win. With six straight victories, they finished the season strong including a Sun Bowl victory over USC and its "Wunderkind." RU finished the season at 3-8. To paraphrase the late, great broadcaster Lindsey Nelson of Notre Dame highlight fame, "...we move on to further Spartan action..."

East Lansing, MI - Fast Forward to Wisconsin at Sparty along Red Cedar River in 2008: Until a Big Ten game at Penn State in 2002, MSU did not appear on my slate again. With no geographic or historical ties, the Big Ten tried to promote this annual series as some kind of instant rivalry. After the Nittany Lions joined, they tried to pitch the "Battle for the Land Grant Trophy." It never really sparked any excitement - kind of lame. *"This land is granted to you; this land is granted to me?"* As for Rutgers, I would see them play many more times over the years. They still trumpeted their battle cry, "If only we can keep the best players in New Jersey ..."

In 2002, 2014, and 2016, Michigan State and Penn State battled on my slate - all played in State College with the Lions taking two of three. The winner of each game rolled the other. In 2002, the Lions won big behind the running of Larry Johnson, 61-7, to head on to the CapitalOne Bowl. Sparty rolled, 34-10, finishing 10-2 before eclipsing Baylor in the 2014 Cotton Bowl, and PSU won 45-12 to finish 10-2 to move on to beat

Wisconsin for the Big Ten title before falling to USC in the 2016 Rose Bowl, 52-49. The winning teams always brought a superior record; the other lagged behind in the Big Ten. However, the Spartans won exciting finishes in road trips critical toward bowl battles toward successes at two other venues.

In 2008, I made it to Spartan Stadium in East Lansing with my Supply Chain colleague at BASF, Adam Kalmbach, his wife, and their two little kids. A grad of "Sparty," Adam seized the opportunity to host me and his young son and daughter to our first game on campus. Without tickets, I helped him approach the right fan to get them a good deal for four tickets. He was amazed! I understood the parking lot markets pretty well by then. Today's electronic tickets on cell phones obliterated those opportunities.

In front of 75,000 fans, MSU came in at 7-2, 4-1 a week after a win over in-state arch-rival Michigan. With a previous loss to Ohio State, they had to beat Wisconsin (4-4, 1-4) this week. Games later against Purdue and Penn State had to be victories to vie for the Big Ten title.

Clock management decides in B1G Battles for Rose and CFP

The Badgers scored in the final period with just over nine minutes to play to lead, 24-13. Head Coach Mark Dantonio's team responded with a 64-yard scoring drive aided by an unsportsmanlike call against UW Coach Bret Bielema. State's try for two points failed. The Spartans held the Badgers to a three and out. Sparty's Brett Swenson responded with a 50-yard field goal to trail, 24-22. Two penalties by Wisconsin forced them to move back and punt from their 40. With 1:19 to play and no time-outs left, the Spartans took over from their 17.

Brian Hoyer completed three passes to put MSU at the UW 29 with only 12 ticks left. However, to unwittingly save the day for the Spartans, the Badgers' Bielema called for a time-out instead of letting time expire! Embarrassingly, he used his second to try to "ice" Swenson. It didn't work. The kicker with three conversions including a 50-yarder on a pretty calm day, nailed it from 44-yards to win it for MSU, 25-24. The Spartans defeated Purdue one week later, but Penn State supplied their knockout punch with a 49-18 win to represent the Big Ten in The Rose Bowl. The Spartans (9-3) settled in to play Georgia in the CapitalOne Bowl.

Frank Scarpa with his award-winning pizza and portable oven at RU vs. MSU tailgate.

New Brunswick, NJ – Fast Forward to Michigan State vs. Rutgers along the banks of the Old Raritan, 2015: On an October Saturday evening, at our pre-game tailgate with Rutgers fans and Michigan State fans from Philadelphia, cousin Frank Scarpa served a contingent of about 15 fans with his hand made, oven-baked style pizzas on his grill with a new pizza oven hood. His award-winning BBQ pizza recipe of the New Paltz, New York BBQ Fest at the Ulster County Fairgrounds the previous August tasted great! It was a winner for all in attendance.

As for the game, the Scarlet Knights tied the score, 24-24, with 4:21 to play on a 22-yard field goal by Kyle Federico at the end of a 91-yard drive.

Late heroics and another opponent faux pas were in order again for the No. 4 Spartans (5-0, 1-0) to get past Rutgers (2-2, 0-1). The Spartans retaliated with a 76-yard drive capped by a three-yard run by L.J. Scott with 43 second left. RU, playing freshmen defensive backs due to suspensions of key starters and playing under interim Head Coach Norries Wilson taking over from fired Kyle Flood, tried to mount a last-minute comeback.

At the 50, after two incompletes and a 10-yard sack by Malik McDowell, RU lost track of downs and spiked the football on fourth down. Game over with three seconds left for the Spartan win, 31-24. It was intense, exciting, and an unexpectedly fun football game to attend. On Monday, because Rutgers stepped up, the still undefeated Spartans drifted down to No. 7.

Michigan State pressed on to defeat undefeated Iowa, champions of the Big Ten West, 16-13, at Indianapolis to finish at No. 4 for the College Football Playoff. However, they came up nothing but empty in their CFP semi-final loss to Alabama, 38-0. Bama defeated Clemson for the National Championship, 45-40.

Fumble-fest to a Miracle on Techwood Drive

Penn State vs. (37) Georgia Tech, Kick-off Classic IX, August 27, 1991

East Rutherford, NJ - The Kickoff Classic invited its fifth defending national champion to its ninth edition. Georgia Tech came in under Head Coach Bobby Ross, recipient of the 1990 Bobby Dodd Coach of the Year Award, following a storybook, 11-0-1 season in 1990. (Why are southern football coaches named Robert or Bob called "Bobby"? - i.e., Bowden, Ross, Johnson, and Dodd. I found in business if you don't call a true Southerner by his formal given name, you get a dirty look, or hear about it).

The Yellow Jackets crushed Nebraska in the Florida Citrus Bowl, 45-21. They earned the No. 1 ranking in the final UPI Coaches poll. The polls split the national championship that season. The AP writers' poll selected 11-1-1 Colorado. The Buffs played a schedule arguably better than Georgia Tech's. They also beat Nebraska in Lincoln, 27-12, during the regular season.To me, a coaches' poll exudes nothing but politics. Glad it's not used any more among championship considerations.How can a coach rank 25 of 131 teams when every week they can only focus on two? Their own and their next opponent.

This evening, Penn State led 13-3 into the second half. In the third quarter, PSU quarterback Tony Sacca continued to fire away. He tallied three touchdown passes following three straight Georgia Tech turnovers. The first touchdown followed one of quarterback Shawn Jones's three fumbles. Sacca flipped a five-yard scoring pass to O.J. McDuffie. Following Matt Baggett's interception, Sacca lofted a tight spiral down the right sideline to a leaping, twisting, turning, diving McDuffie for an exciting, 39-yard touchdown catch. On the subsequent drive, outside linebacker Rich McKinzie forced Jones's next fumble. One play later, Sacca's screen pass to Richie Anderson resulted in a 52-yard catch and run to give the Nittany Lions a commanding 34-3 lead. In the fourth quarter, Tech made the score respectable. They scored three touchdowns to make the final 34-22 in favor of Penn State.

Immediately after that season, Ross left Tech to become head coach of the San Diego Chargers. In 1995, he coached the Chargers to Super Bowl XXIX. After years of coaching professional attitudes, he returned to the college ranks. In 2004, I saw him coach Army late in his career as the highest paid employee of the federal government.

Slow to Fast times at Georgia Tech

- Syracuse with All-American DE Dwight Freeney outplayed Tech to win, 13-7.
- Under Paul Johnson, the Jackets fell to VA Tech in Blacksburg in OT, 20-17.
- At the 2013 Music City's rain-slicked field, the Jackets lost to Ole Miss, 25-17.

Despite the Georgia Tech losses I attended, the next season, I watched Johnson coach the Yellow Jackets in their seventh straight bowl game and their second New Year's Day Six Orange Bowl under him. On that New Year's Eve in Miami, Tech quarterback Justin Thomas led the triple option offense to an Orange Bowl record of 452 rushing yards. No. 12 upset No. 7 Mississippi State, 49-34. Thomas garnered MVP honors while his defense did enough despite the Bulldog's Dak Prescott passing for 453 yards. GT (11-3) finished ranked No. 8 in the AP poll. However, with Thomas as one of few key members returning the following year,

Johnson's Georgia Tech team would suffer his worst season there.

Atlanta, Georgia - Fast Forward to Georgia Tech vs. Florida State, 2015: Florida State (6-0, 4-0) came to Atlanta ranked No. 9 in the nation under Head Coach Jimbo Fisher. Struggling Georgia Tech (2-5, 0-4) surprisingly hosted the Seminoles for their homecoming! Generally, the homecoming opponent normally hails as a struggling, long-time patsy invited for the alumni "feast." I decided to attend this game before the season started figuring it would have some bearing with both squads vying for the 2015 College Football Playoff. Regretfully on paper this particular evening, this contest did not live up to that expectation.

As the first half expired, Roberto Aguayo split the uprights again to give Florida State a 16-10 lead. In the third, Harrison Butker cut the lead for the Yellow Jackets with a 40-yard field goal. Neither team scored again until he converted again with 54 seconds remaining to play from 35 to knot the score, 16-16. As usual, the 'Noles started from the 25 thanks to another Butker kickoff resulting in a touch back. FSU worked the sidelines and the clock to get to Tech's 38. An incompletion near the sideline brought Aguayo out to attempt a 55-yarder. What a finish!

Amazingly on the winning field goal attempt, defensive back Corey Griffin knocked the ball out of mid-air. His secondary-mate, Lance Austin, hesitated to pick it up on the right hash mark at his 22. When he finally did, he sprinted left, picked up great blocks, and brought sudden bedlam to Bobby Dodd Stadium! I got to witness one of the school's greatest regular season, comeback victories ever.

My business colleague Chris Harken (Ohio State fan), his buddy Ron (LSU grad), and I were overwhelmed by a crush of "white-out" wearing Georgia Tech fans while Austin returned the blocked kick. He returned it 78 yards on the last play in regulation for the game-winning touchdown to upset Florida State, 22-16. The three of us lost track of each other though standing next to one another ten rows off the end zone where Austin crossed the goal line in a shocker of a play. We unraveled. Chris's new cell phone got lost briefly in all that Georgia Tech exuberance and broke.

Georgia Tech fans rushed the field at Bobby Dodd Stadium after Lance Austin's 78-yard TD run to defeat No. 9 Florida State, 22-16, as time expired.

Rambling Wrecks

After the game, Ron commented, "You know, we were probably a broken arm away from spending the rest of the evening together in some emergency ward!" Aside from Chris's broken cell phone, we survived the deserved, unexpected, explosive mayhem around us. After the frenzy, we were astonished and amazed to have witnessed an unexpected comeback victory by the Rambling Wrecks.

We found the stadium reaction reminiscent of the Auburn field goal return seen on TV in their big win over Alabama in the Iron Bowl two seasons before. Tech knocked FSU off its unbeaten pedestal and out of the Top Ten to No. 17. Amazingly, now 3-5, Tech lost all four remaining games after that. The victory was dubbed as the infamous *"Miracle on Techwood Drive."* It ranks as one of the best games ever in Georgia Tech

Football history.

Some pundits dubbed this particular date as "Upset Saturday." My friends and I witnessed it first-hand from 10th row seats along the end zone while getting knocked around to see that reality set in right in front of us as Austin amazingly crossed the line for the final score. What sport is more exciting during its regular season than the short, hard-fought season of college football?

King of the Commander-in-Chief's Trophy / Into the Wild Blue Yonder

(38) Air Force at Navy, October 12, 1991

Annapolis, Maryland - In 1975, as a Third Classman in the Brigade of Midshipmen, I had helped cheer Navy on to victory over Air Force at RFK Stadium in D.C. Our team shut down the Falcons for a 17-0 win. Navy won the second of the fourth Commander-in-Chief's Trophy. Since 1972, the Trophy went to the winner of the round-robin rivalry among the three military academies for football supremacy. A three-way tie would remain with the previous year's winner.

By 1991, Navy had taken home the Trophy five times, but the last time was back in 1981. Air Force dominated academy football now. They'd taken the hardware back to Colorado Springs six times since, including three of the previous four seasons. Air Force had become a much-improved team since 1984 when offensive coordinator Fisher DeBerry took over the head coaching job. He turned Falcon football fortunes around by implementing his vaunted wishbone attack that best suited the quick, smart, smaller athletes the academies recruited. Since 1984, DeBerry had guided the Falcons to a 55-30-1 record and five bowl games.

To this game came St. Laurie, her brother Tom, his wife Linda, and their son, five-year old Brian Bramhall. They attended to see the "rivalry" between the 5-1 Falcons against 0-4 Navy at Navy-Marine Corps Memorial Stadium. On top of the rivalry, today marked the 1,000th game in Navy football history. Fans of all factions came to see this one. Tailgating next to us were some die-hard Michigan fans who, for some reason, got caught up in singing *"Hail to the Victors!"* Then, to remind them of their 51-31 loss two weeks earlier to Florida State, I performed the "Tomahawk chop" and Seminole War Chant at them. They ceased singing with some embarrassed laughter.

The pre-game festivities included a flyover by a squadron of F-14 Tomcats commanded by former Navy punter, Lt. Commander John Stufflebeem, USNA class of '75. He punted against Notre Dame in the 14-6 loss chronicled earlier. In 1973, he punted in Navy's 800th game played against these same Air Force Falcons in a 42-6 romp. Eighteen years later on this day, he flew over Annapolis where the final score would be similar, albeit with different victor. During Operation Desert Storm, Admiral Stufflebeem regularly reported the status of military events on national television as military advisor to the White House.

A tale of two halves

Navy Coach George Chaump threw a curve at Air Force. He started Plebe Jim Kubiak at quarterback for the first time. In front of the second largest crowd in Navy-Marine Corps Stadium, Navy trailed their second biggest rival, 7-6, at half time. Kubiak fumbled on the second play of the second half, and the Falcons capitalized with Jason Jones' seven-yard run for a score. Navy turned the ball over four more times in the half giving the USAFA good field position each time. Falcon quarterback Rob Perez completed only two of six passes on the day. One went for 40 yards to take a 25-6 lead by the end of the third. The visitors didn't need to pass. Their vaunted wishbone finished the day with 407 yards rushing. Air Force sank Navy, 46-6, the most points ever scored by either team in this traditional rivalry.

It was the tenth straight time the Falcons bested the Mids. In 1991, Air Force won its fourth consecutive C-I-C Trophy. Under the tutelage of Fisher DeBerry, the Air Force domination over its sister academies didn't stop then. During the next eleven football seasons, USAFA swept Army and Navy nine times to keep the Trophy in Colorado Springs.

Air Force influence?

West Point, NY - Fast Forward to Air Force at Army, 1998: Air Force dominated Army at West Point, 35-7, with the same adults, and now 12-year-old Brian in attendance once again. Tom, St. Laurie's brother, thought he had some influence over parking matters. He placed a banner across his windshield proclaiming his status as a former Army Sergeant figuring the non-commissioned officers directing traffic would find him a prime spot. That got us a space in "general parking," just like everyone else! This season, DeBerry coached the Falcons to a 12-1 record and a number 13 ranking in the Final Top 25.

It's hard to know if the two dominant Air Force victories attended by young Brian over Navy and Army had any influence on his career path. Eight years later, he served his country in his first tour of duty with the 177th Fighter Wing of the US Air Force in Iraq. As a fire fighter, he extinguished flames from after-burners and dodged mortar fire. Two years after, he served as a Staff Sergeant on a second tour in Kuwait.

Fisher DeBerry coached the Falcons until the end of the 2006 season. During his 23 seasons leading the Falcons, his team won the C-I-C Trophy outright 14 times and shared it once. He finished with a combined record of 34-8 against Army and Navy. He retired as the winning-est coach in any service academy history with a record of 169-109-1.

Win or lose; Falcons always fight to the finish

After DeBerry's retirement, Air Force hired former alum Troy Calhoun. In 2007, I saw him coach his first team at the Armed Services Bowl in Fort Worth with Eric for our third bowl of four attended in Texas. The fight lasted to the end before quarterback Sean Carney suffered a severe leg injury in the third. The Falcons went down to defeat against California, 42-36. In 2011, Eric and I attended in the Military Bowl at RFK Stadium in Washington, D.C. On fourth and three at the Toledo 33, Air Force scored on a pass with 56 seconds left play to close the score, 42-41. Rather than kick to tie, Calhoun called for a two-point conversion. On a pitch-out, the ball went low and rolled out of bounds. Toledo recovered the ensuing onsides kick to seal the victory. The Falcons lost a close, exciting, well-played bowl game.

Only at the Air Force Academy.

Colorado Springs, Colorado – Air Force vs. Utah State in "The Wild Blue Yonder," 2015: Over the years, I've seen Air Force go 2-4 against Navy and 3-0 against Army. In the only regular season action against neither Army nor Navy, I finally made it to Falcon Stadium in 2015 after attending Southern Cal at Colorado the evening before. The Falcons (6-3, 4-1) hosted the Aggies of Utah State (5-4, 4-2) in an important Mountain West confrontation.

The Air Force Academy displayed air superiority with some traditional pre-game festivities:

- Aerial acrobatics performed in a glider by a cadet high above Falcon Stadium.
- USAFA jump team, Wings of Blue, parachuted delivering the game ball.
- Immediately before kickoff, a B-52 Bomber roared overhead with awesome power.
- The Falcon mascot swooped from the press box to catch bait swung at midfield.

Leading 21-14 entering the third period, the Falcon football team demonstrated unusual air superiority forgoing their dominant ground game. Quarterback Karson Roberts lofted a high pass to 6'4" Jalen Robinette who leaped high into the air with a defender on his back, shook him loose, and flew downfield for a 74-yard catch and run to go up 28-14. The Aggies closed the score late and trailed, 35-28. USAFA's win was not assured until Safety Weston Steelhammer broke up Kent Myer's 18-yard pass attempt into the end zone on fourth down with 36 seconds left. Great game! In the end, Air Force tallied 580 yards, but not in typical Air Force fashion as they balanced a passing attack for 271 yards with a typical run output of 309.

Last season, Air Force defeated Army, 13-7, and Navy, 13-10, to win the C-I-C Trophy once again. Army defeated Navy in their first overtime meeting ever, 20-17. The three compete as hard as ever for the Commander-in-Chief Trophy.

Air Force Falcon Dance Team performs prior to 2015 home game versus Utah State

This Side of the Rainbow and Back / First Class Coaches

(39) Florida State vs. (40) Kansas, Kickoff Classic XI, August 26, 1993

East Rutherford, NJ - When the Kansas Jayhawks came to The Meadowlands in 1993, Dorothy's words from the Wizard of Oz never rang truer: *"Something tells me we're not in Kansas anymore, Toto."* No kidding, Jayhawks! You're in the swamps of Jersey playing preseason No. 1 Florida State coming off an 11-1 season with Heisman Trophy candidate Charlie Ward at quarterback, *my Pretties*! And while Scarecrow didn't have to worry about balls of fire today, it was 118 degrees on the Giants Stadium playing surface.

This year's Kickoff Classic added two more schools to my ever-growing, life-long list. While I enjoyed adding the Jayhawks, Kansas didn't. They got rolled flatter than their home-state prairie. FSU rolled to an easy 42-0 win. Unbelievably, the highlight of the game for KU was an early goal-line stand. This Kickoff Classic romp was definitely not my most memorable FSU game. For me, one lasts longer, albeit not for Seminole fans. For Bobby Bowden's squad, they rolled on to "somewhere over the rainbow" defeating undefeated Nebraska in the Orange Bowl for the National Championship at the end of the '93 season.

Aside from two wins in the Kickoff Classic over Kansas and Texas A&M (23-14), the meting with Florida for the National Championship in the Sugar Bowl and another game to be reported on later, the only other

Seminole game I attended was their 38-20 victory over Syracuse in 2014. With Jameis Winston winning the Heisman, the Noles finished 12-0 before falling big to Oregon in the Rose Bowl, 59-20. My Bucket List has Doak Campbell Stadium inked in as a priority to attend a game after all these years.

Best in Class

What I savor more than anything regarding Florida State football, is that I had the honor of seeing Bobby Bowden coach twice. Following his years as head coach and what I saw as a man from afar, I always had the utmost respect for him. In years when other programs started ducking competitive foes to load up on automatic wins, Bowden always sought to play the best.

Samford University's honored Alumnus!

After FSU joined the ACC, he never complained or backed out of commitments to play tough, in-state rivals Florida and Miami year after year. When schedules expanded from 11 to 12 games, he'd schedule teams like Notre Dame, USC, BYU, and Oklahoma for the open dates. Since he retired in 2009, Seminole slates, aside from the recent, neutral site clashes with LSU, are usually void of tough non-conference foes except for the traditional season-ending rivalry against Florida.

Bowden exemplified a class guy, good family man from stories others told in memorial services and other tributes when he passed on. Seemed like a very nice guy from my perspective. Loved the Lord and always carried a great sense of humor. I gained more respect from the scene in *"We are Marshall"* showing the tribute to the team in Huntington, West Virginia that went down in the crash. Impressed many by helping new Thundering Herd Head Coach Jack Lengyl to implement the wishbone offense he coached at WVU. This past season, I was privileged to remember him while attending a game at Samford University. His Alma mater honors him where he started his coaching career. In broad letters, you're greeted at Bobby Bowden Field. Adding a game in Tallahassee is a given on the Bucket List!

Coach-building for Jayhawks

Memphis, Tennessee – Fast Forward to Arkansas vs. Kansas in the Liberty Bowl, 2022: It took 39 years since that Kickoff Classic beatdown to Florida State to find a Jayhawk game worth attending! To be honest, once KU hired Lance Leipold as its new head coach, I knew the atmosphere in Lawrence would change for the better. Being a D-3 grad, I still have a penchant to monitor what goes on at that level. I followed Leipold's progress at Wisconsin-Whitewater winning six championship, Amos Alonzo Stagg Bowls.

In 2006, I ventured to Salem, Virginia with Eric to attend the D-3 national championship game for our first time. Since 1996, the Mount Union Purple Raiders under Head Coach Larry Kehres dominated the division. On my website www.collegefootballfan.com, I often referred to the D-3 national champion playoff as "the Mount Union Invitational Football Tournament." At this particular game, Mount Union defeated the University of Wisconsin-Whitewater Warhawks under Head Coach Bob Berezowitz for the second year in a row, 35-16.

A year later, UW-Whitewater and Mount Union squared off in the championship once again. In his first season as head coach in 2010, Lance Leipold led the Warhawks to a Wisconsin Intercollegiate championship. My fellow "scout-team All-American" from Juniata, Steve Ciesla, and I ventured to Dover, Delaware. We watched Leipold coach his Warhawks in a D-3 semi-final against Wesley College to triumph, 27-7. They finished 14-1, and went on to defeat the Purple Raiders in the championship game, 31-21. For the next four years, these two programs would compete in the championship finale against one another. Leipold's teams took the last three to finish No. 1 at 15-0 each season. The playoffs were no longer dominated by the Purple Raiders, but the Warhawks! With an eight-year record of 109-6, the University of Buffalo, an FBS team in the Mid-American, enticed Leipold to come turn their struggling program around.

Team builder extraordinaire

In his first two seasons, his Bulls won seven games and lost 17. In the first, I caught up with one of my working buddies Bill Knab and his fiancé Liz who had retired to Buffalo where his mother still lived. Why else would anyone retire to Buffalo? We got to see one of UB's only two wins that season. They defeated Army, who eventually finished 8-5, 23-20, in overtime. I also saw them defeated by 11-2 Penn State, 45-13, early in the 2019 season. However, Leipold had them on fire later that season winning six of their last seven to finish 8-5.

Kansas knew a good up-and-coming coach when they noted his improvements. Leipold is a proven program builder and KU regarded him as the best available up-and-coming coach. He only won two games with the Jayhawks in 2021. Not much could be expected of a new coach hired by a program with only 18 wins over the past ten years. In addition, how can any coach build a competitive team when hired after spring practice? Generally, all the recruiting that could be done was completed for the upcoming season. His roster was intact. One win of the two came with a big 57-56 upset over Texas in 2021. Noting the final scores over the course of the entire season, the Jayhawks demonstrated some improvement with closer final scores.

Before the season started in 2022, on a podcast with Stephen Hiegel of JustCollegefootball, he asked me for some predictions. "Coach of the Year?" he asked. I replied that if Lance Leipold won six or more games, he would be my choice. Well, he won six, and darn, I just saw him coach and miss number seven. Lawrence, Kansas is now a go-to football destination. There should be some worthwhile games to be seen in the near future in the expanding Big XII. I added a game in Lawrence to my Bucket List!

Ten + one = Big Ten? / Game 600!

(41) Minnesota at Penn State, September 4, 1993

State College, Pennsylvania - The Minnesota Golden Gophers visited Beaver Stadium not only for the first time in their first game ever versus Penn State, but they visited as the Nittany Lions' first opponent from their new conference, the Big Ten. PSU decided to give up 106 years of college football status as an Independent to join up with the ten major, traditional, Midwestern football programs that had been playing each other for conference championships since 1953. Personally, I had mixed emotions about the move into conference play.

First, if the Lions were to join a conference, my preference leaned to continue to see them play Syracuse, WVU, Pitt, and Boston College who could only get stronger playing each other while building on solid and thriving traditions. Likewise, I always enjoyed seeing games against the aforementioned, but I also enjoyed the flexibility Penn State had of scheduling diverse opponents each year like Notre Dame, Alabama, Texas, Nebraska, Miami, and a few others. The scheduling flexibility Penn State surrendered to join conference play took away possibilities to see big-time games with national implications. Of course, with the upcoming play-off format announced starting in 2024, my perspective is changing.

One great opportunity

One advantage I realized right off saw the entry of Penn State into the Big Ten provided a major possibility of going to the Rose Bowl. I called my good friend since grade school, Jim Lewis, who was relocating with Henson Productions from New York City to Burbank, California. I told Jim that when the Lions beat Ohio State and Michigan in the same season, get ready because we're going to the Rose Bowl! Those words would prove more prophetic than I initially imagined.

Wide receiver Bobby Engram had a big day in front of 95,387 fans for Penn State against Minnesota returning after a one-year suspension by Coach Paterno. He nabbed four catches from John Sacca for touchdowns to set a new school record. Those started Penn State 1-0 in Big Ten play with a 38-20 win.

Time to can the "Big" Numbers

Of course, Penn State joining a conference that already had a great name and 10 teams presented a numerical challenge. The Lions became the 11th Big Ten team. John Massimilla pointed out the Big Ten logo on the scoreboard to show me that the powers-that-be compensated by overlaying the digit "1" along each side of the "T" in Big Ten to indicate 11 schools.

This didn't make sense in 1993, and it makes even less now. Can't these institutions of academia be more creative? Leave numbers out for flexibility. How about "Big Monsters of the Midwest?" Now there are geographic overlaps with conference alignments as well. All right: "The Big U.S." "Trans-American Athletic Conference." "United Football Conference of America." How about, "The Conference formerly known as the PAC-12." Use some imagination since no one seems willing to stay put for the benefit of conference television revenues. The Big Ten Conference will range now from New Jersey to California with 18 teams, and then possibly all four corners of the "Continental 48."

Minnesota Memories

Minneapolis, MN - Fast Forward to Middle Tennessee at Minnesota, *2017:* First though, in October 2009, Minnesota brought plenty of snow, but no offense to State College, PA. The Lions won, 20-0, but we dedicated fans who showed up had few places to park. The snow-covered grass lots closed to prevent a huge mess afterward. I never experienced as much snow in mid-October for tailgating in State College before or since. For my friends from town, Ed and Kristin Bonnefond, they joined me in this one for their first ever there. We still tailgated behind their work van in a plowed-out, local hotel parking lot. Bringing our growing sons and a few of their friends with us, their van provided us with necessary space we needed for this excursion. Despite this unexpected wintry experience, Ed and Kristin have gone back with me since. *"College football—what better way to spend an autumn afternoon?"*

Next, I attended the Buffalo Wild Wings Citrus Bowl in 2015 when the Golden Gophers played the Missouri Tigers in one of only a handful of games I observed from the press box. There are a few advantages of the pundits I got to enjoy, like a free buffet, unobstructed view, and a nice, light souvenir BWW jacket I still wear on colder days working at home. I also got to attend the post-game celebration on the field as Missouri bested Minnesota, 33-17. With press credentials, I attended the post-game press conference to listen to head coaches Gary Pinkel of Missouri and Jerry Kill of Minnesota. Tiger defensive end Markus Golden with ten tackles spoke as game MVP.

Despite some enjoyable benefits, I learned that I preferred watching games out among the crowds. No cheering or emotions allowed in the press box. Stuffy as a non-press outsider. As for my personal experiences with Minnesota football, one of the most cherished came about as a result after attending a Golden Gopher home game.

In September 2017, I got to experience Minnesota football at TCF Stadium (now Huntington Bank Stadium) on campus to witness a re-energized football program under first-year Head Coach P.J. Fleck. My connection to get to this game against Middle Tennessee State came through another cousin, Anthony Cavalli.

Recently out of the Air Force as a Flight Surgeon, he now studied at U of M Medical School and served as a resident physician. Since both a student and a staff member, Anthony got us tickets right in the student section in the upper deck. College kids wondered how these two "old guys" got to sit among them. It was truly an energizing experience. The Gophers went 3-0 defeating my future local team, Middle Tennessee, 34-3. After the game, Anthony and I ventured into "Topcats," a local bar with over 100 beers on tap across the street from where he resided in downtown Minneapolis.

We got to meet some Gopher fans much closer to our age in Dave Herbeck and Kevin Linstrand along with their wives. They were very fired up about the team under new Head Coach P.J. Fleck who had taken over after a recording a 13-1 record at Western Michigan. They also told us about their group of friends who attend home and away games referred to themselves as "Gopher Tails." They mentioned that they often traveled to support the team on the road. They'd been to all except two Big Ten Stadiums at that point – Michigan State and Rutgers. We agreed that when they planned to come to Jersey to see Rutgers, we'd plan to meet. Our timing couldn't have been better!

Planning my schedule for 2019, I would attend my 600th game since keeping track in 1979. Rutgers would host the Golden Gophers on October 19. I called Dave Herbeck and he verified the Gopher Tales planned to be there. I arranged a busload with my Knights of Columbus Council to set up a fundraising, tailgate party for local charities and for the parking facility's owner Chris's Great Strides Cystic Fibrosis Foundation. His lot offers tailgaters a perfect parking spot within walking distance to the game. We had tables to set up, games to be played, and planned extra food and beer for our visitors coming from Minnesota. Great, sunny, autumn weather showed up also. What a great tailgate celebration set-up for Game 600!

Happy Hours

New Brunswick, NJ - Fast Forward to Game 600, Minnesota at Rutgers, The Birthplace of College Football, 2019: The Minnesota fans drove or *"Ubered"* over to our tailgate from local hotels. Amongst the food, beer, and games, people who had just met for the first time enjoyed a great day together. The Gopher Tails introduced us to some of their pre-game traditions (*Ski-U-Mah; Row the Boat!*), and of course alcohol bonded everybody in spirit!

As for the game, Minnesota scored first on its second possession with Rodney Smith's three-yard run to finish an 87-yard drive. Smith led the Gopher running game with 111 yards on 19 carries and two scores. Gopher corner Phil Howard picked off a pass. Seventy-seven yards later, Rashod Bateman caught a 13-yard TD pass from Tanner Morgan. Six RU drives in the first half accumulated only 28 yards. You surmise that the Gopher D was tough. However, Rutgers with a third string quarterback, a head coach with only high school experience until three weeks before, and without a key running back who decided to red-shirt after the exit of uninspiring Head Coach Chris Ash, struggled against all comers to say the least. Most of our college football tailgaters in section 116 decided they'd seen enough, and preferred the enjoyment of tailgating back in the parking lot. The Minnesota fans understandably watched their team continue to play for an undefeated season. Their current Head Coach P.J. Fleck assisted former Rutgers Head Coach Greg Schiano, and now seemed to have the Minnesota program going in the right direction. The undefeated Gophers romped over Rutgers (1-5) as expected, 42-7.

Minnesota finished 11-2 for No. 10 in the final 2019 Associated Press Poll. P.J. Fleck keeps the Gopher fans generally happy. I'm sure they'd love to see a West Division and Big Ten championship as well as a CFP bid. Since his first season when I saw his team finish 5-7, the Gopher record stands at 44-23. They've won all four bowl games he's coached them to.

Joe Benvenuto, a good friend from my former neighborhood in Byram, approached me few days after Game 600. He said, "Steve! What great time. Those Minnesota people were a lot of fun. No wonder why you like going to these games. You not only get to travel to see great games, but you get to meet up with such great people!" Joe's right about that. After St. Laurie and I get to celebrate our daughter's wedding next spring, I have to sort through my plans and get back in touch with Dave and Kevin to see when I can meet up with the Gopher Tails once again! I definitely want to do

FIFTY YEARS OF TAILGATE TALES:

make that a Bucket List repeat!

The Minnesota Gopher Tails joined us for a great tailgate party at Rutgers in 2019 to celebrate my 600th college football game attended since 1979!

Rush hour in Un-Happy Valley / Cheerleader – Not!

(42) Michigan at Penn State, October 16, 1993

State College, Pennsylvania - The Nittany Lions remained undefeated and ranked No. 7 in their inaugural Big Ten season leading up to their first showdown with Michigan. The Wolverines led the Big Ten with most championships (37) since the start of conference before the turn of the 20th century. It was time to find out if the Nittany Lions could challenge the Wolverines for some of their traditional territory. This would also be the first PSU game for three other people who made the trip up with St. Laurie and me.

With only two tickets for the first really significant Big Ten showdown at Beaver Stadium, we planned to bring our six-month-old daughter, Alex, to meet our Penn State tailgating partners, John and Kelle. Since Laurie planned to spend her day hanging out in the parking lot with Alex, we brought along our two neighbors, John and Jan Hosler, for the overnight trip.

Affectionately, they became known as Grandma Jan and Pop-pop John to our kids over the years. I still refer to John as "the Superintendent." With adjacent properties, I was never lacking for tools, and even more, for advice for any job around the house or yard. The plan for this game was for John to join me at the game while Jan would hang out with Laurie and Alex to tailgate.

Improvise and overcome

This plan benefited us more than anticipated. With a noon time start and a record-setting crowd of 96,719 converging into State College all at about the same time, all roads leading into Beaver Stadium parking lots were backed up by 10 a.m. Traffic crawled. Full parking lots caused most tailgaters to diverge from their normal parking arrangements. State College was not prepared to absorb this sudden vehicular surge for expanded capacity with an early kickoff.

Kickoff approached as we crept along Route 322 to our usual parking lot. I eventually realized we weren't going to make it on time. Our arrangements paid off though. St. Laurie (daughter of a Marine veteran) took over the driver's seat. John (a Marine veteran) and I took our tickets and hopped out of the mini-van to start our unanticipated hike to Beaver Stadium. In the age before cell phones, we planned to meet Laurie, Jan, and the baby by the traffic light next to the intramural gym after the game. John and I parked our fannies in our aluminum bleacher seats just minutes before kickoff. We didn't miss a play in PSU's 1,000th football game. We arrived so late though that all programs for this game were already sold out. It's one of a few missing from my cherished collection.

In the third, Michigan's Mercury Hayes made a diving catch in the end zone. With the 16-yard pass from Todd Collins, U of M took a 14-10 lead. After that, the Lions challenged Michigan's staunch defense, pounding up front with plunges close to the goal line. The Wolverines stuffed Kerry Collins on quarterback sneaks twice. Twice more, they stopped Ki-Jana Carter at the one to halt a potential comeback series with a goal line stand.

Penn State struggled to contain Michigan's powerful rushing attack. Tyrone Wheatley gained 192 yards, one of the highest totals ever given up by a PSU defense. The Lions closed the score at 14-13 with a field goal. Todd Collins retaliated with a touchdown pass to Che Foster to end the scoring with 5:12 left. Penn State had just suffered its first Big Ten loss, 21-13.

Wolverine tales

It would not be the last time the 18th-ranked Wolverines would leave Happy Valley denizens unhappy. Whether I watched these two teams play, or tried to. In 1997, Michigan throttled Penn State, 34-8 on their way to winning a national championship. I witnessed junior Charles Woodson that year become the only one-way defensive player to ever win the Heisman Trophy.

In 1999, I drove up to State College the night before another noon kickoff. I missed the game next day played by a Wolverine quarterback named Tom Brady. My four-year-old son, Eric, woke up sick to his stomach several times during the course of the night. I sold our tickets in the hotel lobby the next morning for face value and drove him home. Brady led Michigan to a late come from behind victory, 31-27. Wished I'd been there to record that, one though the Lions lost. As Eric grew older, I reminded him of this once in a while when watching the New England Patriots play.

The 2001 game was the worst for PSU. The Wolverine defense showed no fear of the Lions' offense, shutting them out, 20-0. The loss launched the first 0-4 start for a Paterno-coached team in 36 years. In 2006, Michigan defeated Penn State at one of its celebrated Beaver Stadium "white-outs," a 17-10 win where the Lions got down to their third-string quarterback. By far, no Big Ten team has brought more unhappiness to Happy Valley than the Michigan Wolverines.

Ann Arbor, Michigan - Fast Forward to Penn State at Michigan, 2009, and beyond: Since those earliest of Penn State-Michigan Big Ten meetings, the Nittany Lions still struggle with the Wolverines. In my case, however, like Wake Forest, I must bring the Lions some luck. They won the last four times I watched these two teams play. Three were blow-outs including my first stop at the Big House in 2009. This game came compliments from a good friend from work who I had to pressure to expose a secret he never revealed to me.

Another good friend and business colleague at our BASF Southfield, Michigan plant, Mike Meyers, threw this question at me during a lunch break. He asked, "Did Dave Imrick ever tell you he was cheerleader at

Michigan?" Imrick – a cheerleader? I was all over this! Dave and I coordinated a lot of projects together. He was the assistant to our President of Automotive Coatings. He had no choice but to explain this to me! When he went to Michigan, he planned to walk-on for a couple of other varsity teams. However, a female friend from high school approached him about joining her on the cheerleading squad as she explained they needed some guys to come out. Dave declined figuring he couldn't picture himself a cheerleader. He always played sports. The walk-on plan at the Big Ten power wasn't working out for him though. His friend pushed him enough until he gave in and finally attended a meeting. When he got there, he met a bunch of other guys who like him played sports in high school. He figured; they were regular guys like him so this might not be a bad gig after all. He could go to a few away games each year, stand along the sideline for all the home games, hang around with a bunch of nice-looking girls he could throw into the air or could sit on his knee, and he could have some fun. So, he joined and enjoyed the experience.

Dave Imrick and me. Who's the cheerleader?

We finally planned to go to this 2009 Penn State-Michigan Homecoming game as his wife and kids had other plans, and he was getting together to tailgate with a bunch of friends who were ex-cheerleaders like himself. On a cold blustery day, we grilled and drank and had a good time. At one point, a couple of younger women stopped by who also claimed had been Michigan cheerleaders. These cheerleader guys had the "in." I was a few years older than most of them, but I gave it a shot to get in on the conversation. So, I said, "Hey, I was a cheerleader, too!" The girls stopped, looked at me for about five seconds, and said, "Nah!" I didn't push. I didn't offer to lift one over my head holding her feet to prove anything because I knew I would lose my balance. I don't know what it takes to look like a guy cheerleader, but I gave it a shot for a brief moment. All I could say at that point was "Beat Michigan!" And Penn State triumphed, 35-10.

Last game was in 2014. Bill O'Brien coached PSU in his second and final season in State College to keep the program afloat. Give him a lot of credit here. The Nittany Lions started with struggling quarterback Christian Hackenberg and a suspect offensive line. The 2-3 Lions beat 5-0 Michigan in four OTs, 43-40. I plan to get up to State College to see them play again with Jim Harbaugh leading the Wolverines. They dominated Penn State in 2022, 41-17. Beaver Stadium will be buzzing when they return!

Ann Arbor, Michigan – Fast Forward to Ohio State at Michigan, 2015: One other Michigan game of note, the big one! I attended the Ohio State - Michigan rivalry at the Big House. No doubt it was must-see rivalry, but turned out to be another adventurous travel experience. I flew planes to Detroit and back from Chicago, a bus to the stadium canceled, and I experienced my first Uber. The latter, came with thanks to some friendly Wolverine fans who let me share a ride from the bus depot to their tailgate party at the stadium parking lot. I never Ubered before, and had no idea how to with my flip phone.

Longer story short, but another unique story of "cheap travels with Steve." The game experience was more memorable for me than for these Michigan fans. Their 9-2 Wolverines under first-year Head Coach Jim Harbaugh took a 42-13 shellacking from arch-rival Ohio State. The outcome might have been motivated by the 12-1 Buckeye upset loss the week before. They crashed hard on a late, crazy play to Michigan State, 17-14. A fan Wolverine sitting behind me told me that a fan sitting behind him suffered a fatal heart attack right after the game! No doubt the emotions run high for this one.

Penn State 38 - (43) Indiana 31
Beaver Stadium, State College, PA, November 6, 1993

Upset! Upset! Upset! And Avoiding Deacon Blues

(44) Louisville at Army, October 15, 1994

West Point, NY– Army allowed Louisville to score two rushing touchdowns and two two-point conversions within 34 seconds. LU Cardinal quarterback Marty Lowe heated things up with 19 completions for 245 yards. For the Cadets, kicker Kurt Heiss was also on target with a 37-yarder and two more from 30 yards. On this sunny, cool, brilliant fall Saturday along the Hudson River, Army, on a four-game losing streak, trailed the Cardinals, 29-23.

With 3:17 remaining, Army's Ronnie McAda fired a 10-yard pass to fullback Joe Ross to tie the score. Heiss booted the extra point for a 30-29 Black Knight lead. The Cardinals drove to retaliate, but Louisville's Anthony Shelman fumbled a pitch for a nine-yard loss at Army's 28. A second U of L possession ended with David Aker's 46-yard field goal attempt wide right with 1:35 left. The Black Knights ran out the clock for an exciting, Army upset. I got to enjoy it this particular Saturday with good friends Tracy and Dave Headden. St. Laurie was back at home taking care of 18 month-old Alex who had already attended her first three games the previous season. With our second kid expected in about six months, St. Laurie just wasn't up for a short trip to West Point with a toddler.

This didn't turn out to be the most memorable game I saw between Army and Louisville, however. That came five years later and ended with the second of "Upset! Upset! Upset!" On a dark, chilly, overcast Thursday evening on October 7, 1999, the Army-Louisville game, to accommodate television scheduling, would be the first weekday night game ever played at West Point. With my friends and supplier of recycled PET (primarily plastic drink bottles) Paul Zordan and Jim Baker joining me from upstate New York, we sat on the visitors' side to watch this Conference-USA clash. With Heisman hopeful Chris Redman quarterbacking for Louisville and Army coming in at 1-3, the game looked like a mismatch in favor of the Cardinals.

Army guys? Secret weapons? Big guns?

Shockingly, Army's offense looked unstoppable in the first half as Michael Wallace ran around, over, and through the poor-tackling Cardinal defense. In their second year of Conference-USA play, the Cadets looked like world beaters. They built a 45-17 lead. In the second half, however, the Cardinals did not pack it in. This would make for what would for one of the wildest, most exciting games ever played at Michie Stadium. Paul and Jim noted the key to Louisville's offense in the second half, tight end Ibn Green. Wherever he lined up, the Cards followed.

Following that strategy, Louisville rallied in the second half with 28 unanswered points. They tied the game late in regulation, 45-45. On a night of firsts at Michie Stadium, both teams played in their first overtime periods ever. On their first possession, Louisville took a seven-point lead on a ten-yard run. Army quarterback Joe Gerena capped the extra Army possession with a nine-yard pass to Brandon Rooney to tie it up.

To start the second overtime period, Gerena, who played a heady game for Army, didn't let up. He posted a seven-yard touchdown run to take a 59-52 lead for the Cadets. Louisville's next possession got to the Army eight to set up a fourth and seven. Redman stepped up into a pocket and fired to a seemingly wide-open LaVell Boyd at the back of the end zone. Army's Derrick Goodwin closed quickly. Boyd went high, had the ball in his hands. Bang! Bang! He and the ball hit the turf at the same instant. The Corps roared! Howitzer volleys fired from across Lusk Reservoir. Army won a thriller on its first weekday night game and in its first overtime game ever.

A record-breaking score

In the annals of my personal game history, the one-hundred and eleven points totaled the most ever scored in one game. It was a fantastic, exciting football game – long scoring plays, big lead, big comeback, and not one, but two overtime periods. Fans moved from one end zone to the other to be closer to the action when the teams went from the south end zone to the north in the extra periods. College football couldn't get much more exciting than this!

As for the third of the memorable triumvirate of Louisville upsets, there was the previously documented Thursday night game in 2006 played along a different river, the banks of the Old Raritan. The Knights that evening wore scarlet, not black. In the end, a 25-7 Cardinal lead turned into a 28-25 victory for Rutgers . Make that the third "Upset!" for the Cardinals on the short-ends of "Upset! Upset! Upset!"

Turning around the Upset Table

Winston-Salem, NC - Fast Forward to Louisville at Wake Forest, 2019: Louisville split another pair of games with Rutgers I attended in New Brunswick during Big East confrontations. Before my move south though, two visits to see games with my retired Wake Forest friend Jim "Bugaluga" Harton in Winston-Salem became the highlights of further Louisville memories. In 2017, the Deacons and Cardinals led by quarterbacks John Wolford and 2016 Heisman winner Lamar Jackson, respectively, led their teams in a hard-fought game right to the finish.

Jackson ran for three scores to trail Wake, 35-25, in the fourth. Wolford, who had his best game ever according to die-hard Demon Deacon followers, faked a hand-off to the dive back and rolled right on an attempted option, stopped, stood, and fired the ball 44 yards for a score. The Demon Deacons extended their lead, 42-25. Jackson threw a touchdown pass of 20 yards to close the gap, 42-32. Wolford finally took a knee in the victory formation just once as time expired. Great game! Exciting plays. Impressive players. Though Louisville fell in my presence again, this marked the prelude to another classic Louisville last-minute scorcher.

And records also get broken...eventually

Two years and two days later, Louisville and Wake Forest appeared for a rematch at BB&T Stadium in Winston-Salem for a night game. New quarterbacks appeared for both squads. The third period ended with the Cards in the lead, 45-31. Despite many Wake fans already leaving, I felt this game was still within reach for the Demon Deacons. After an exchange of punts, Louisville thrived with their overall team speed. Their reserve quarterback Evan Conley, who replaced Micale Cunningham injured earlier, tossed the ball to Dez Fitzpatrick who turned on his afterburners for a 50-yard touchdown. The Deacs responded with 59 yards culminating in a three-yard run by Ken Walker III. Five minutes and 35 second remained when Blanton Creque put up another field goal for a 17-point Cardinal lead, 55-38.

Most of the Wake "faithful" already filtered out. Jim promised to give his frat buddy, "One-Iron," a ride out near Greensboro Airport. It was already well past 11 pm. I had a long ride to Charlotte to catch a morning flight home. I hate evening kick-offs! Jim and I sauntered out, made a "pit stop," and continued out to our now disassembled pregame tailgate close to the stadium. A few of Jim's Deacon contingent lingered to share their disappointments. Deacon Blues? I never experienced that. Suddenly, a couple of roars let out from the remaining crowd inside BB&T. The Wake band belted out, "Oh here's to Wake Forest!" And a couple more times!

What's going on? Louisville speed killed, Wake Forest special teams struggled, and time's running out! Out came all the cell phones. Updates varied. WTH? 55-52? We missed two Deacon scores? Turned out Wake quarterback Sam Hartman, the starter from a year ago, hit Scotty Washington for a 22-yard scoring play. A successful onsides kick recovery put Wake at LU's 47. Three plays later, Hartman completed a 21-yard scoring pass to tight end Jack Freudenthal. I'm heading back into BB&T Stadium.

I go inside and easily find a seat. I see a first down challenge under review for several minutes. The replay video on the scoreboard froze up. It showed Conley's knee definitely down a yard short of the marker to the embarrassment of the refs, who were horrible all night. Louisville finally breaks from the sideline with their offense, not their punt team. Fourth and one at the Wake 41 means the game here. First down or a turnover on downs.

Conley fakes a handoff to a back through the middle, takes it along the right side of his protection, turns up field past one defender, and then bolts 41 yards untouched for a score – unbelievable! It looked too easy. Untouched. Did Head Coach Dave Clawson think his Deacs could score twice trailing 62-52 with 2:15 left. *Nah!*

I start walking out, but stop! Two more Deacon scores? No way! Stragglers cheer again? *"Oh, here's to Wake Forest!"* In only 65 seconds with seven plays, Hartman gets the Deacs back on the board with a one-yard run following his 27-yard pass to Sage Surrat. With 1:10 left, the onside kick gets recovered by Louisville. The Cardinals run out the clock. Had the Deacs recovered, no doubt they would have won. Unbelievable. Louisville wins in regulation time, 62-59.

Their win here bests my original highest score of 111 points by ten which Louisville contributed to in their 1999 overtime loss at Army, 59-52. It happened three days short of the 20th anniversary since that record was established over this long history. The Deacs dropped out of the Top 25. Louisville overwhelmed them with speed. Wake's special teams stunk. Their defense couldn't tackle, but *"Oh, here's to Wake Forest!"* Speaking of Oh! As reported in my Wake Forest chapter more than anything, my "Eight and Oh," Wake Forest moniker was revised to "Eight and almost Oh Koreivo." I will feel more challenged now any time I see Wake play again, thanks to Louisville. Regretfully, whenever I go to see Bugaluga's Demon Deacons play, I hope I don't have to sing, *"Deacon Blue."* My aura may be tested soon. However, I'm not looking to see the Deacs host Elon or any other patsy on their slate. I called "Bug" to avoid hiding like he did with his chemistry constituency in school. I want to put it all on the line with Bugaluga and the fun friends when the Deacs play someone highly-ranked, like Florida State!

Historic Doormat No More / Wildcat Leader

(45) Northwestern at Penn State, November 19, 1994

State College, Pennsylvania - When Penn State joined the Big Ten, one team that could be counted on for a "W" annually was Northwestern. The one private institution playing football for years against bigger state institutions with bigger stadiums, larger student bodies, larger state budgets, and slightly lower academic standards had been struggling for years. During my college years, Sports Illustrated featured an article about the beleaguered Wildcat football and basketball programs. It included a photo where a bit of humor was added to a sign somewhere along Interstate 70. Below "Interstate 70," someone spray-painted, "Northwestern 0!" Things hadn't changed much for NU since.

Despite the losing seasons every year since 1971 including an NCAA record-setting 34-game losing streak from 1979 to 1982, the Wildcats stuck it out in the Big Ten. I watched Columbia erase their record in 1986 when they lost to Princeton for their 35th straight loss on the way to 44! For me, NU became the school traditionally "traded-off" in my annual ticket plan to balance out the Penn State schedule to get Michigan or Ohio State tickets. The 1994 season was no exception to the rule.

However, the Wildcat game against Penn State presented historical significance to the Lions. Ranked No. 2 in the nation with a 9-0 record, 6-0 in the Big Ten, a win here would make the Nittany Lions outright conference champs. It would mark their first championship to send them on their way to The Rose Bowl, despite the possibility of losing to Michigan State in their final game.

The Wildcats would not disappoint the Lions in their first visit to Happy Valley. Four first half turnovers by NU resulted in 28 points for PSU. Surprisingly, however, the Wildcats had outgained the Lions by 65 yards! State's tackling was horrible, but interceptions and fumbles halted NU drives. The Lions extended the nation's longest winning streak to 15 games with a 45-17 victory. Despite the score, Penn State did not jump to No. 1.

Its defense, suffering the losses of four starters to injury and losing a fifth starter in this game, allowed 475 yards of total offense to Northwestern. The Cats finished the season in typical Wildcat fashion at 3-7-1. With their Big Ten record of 2-6, the Wildcats finished just ahead of 1-7 Minnesota. The Golden Gophers ousted them from their typical, last-place finish as Big Ten doormat. PSU headed to meet "Gran-daddy" Rose Bowl.

Wildcat-bred leader

From 1993 to 1996, Pat Fitzgerald starred at linebacker for Northwestern. At Penn State games he started in when I attended, he had begun to fire-up a Northwestern turnaround. In 1994, the Wildcats (3-7-1) fell to the undefeated No. 2 Nittany Lions, 33-19. When they returned to State College in 1996, the No. 7 Lions (11-2) defeated the No. 15 Wildcats (9-3), 34-9. In his junior and senior seasons, Fitzgerald earned consensus All-American, he won Big Ten Defensive Player of the Year, the Bronko Nagurski Award, and the Chuck Bednarik Award. He took home the Jack Lambert Linebacker Award in 1996 as well. Someday, there should probably be a Pat Fitzgerald Linebacker Award. Well, probably not now as Fitzgerald was released by NU before the 2023 season for alleged knowledge of his players hazing teammates. He looks to legally challenge these allegations that got him fired. With that, I still report on his history here with the Wildcats. Without him, they may have remained nothing but a perennial door mat.

In 1995, Northwestern finished 10-2, 8-0 in the Big Ten. It included a victory at home against Penn State for its first winning season since 1971. As Big Ten champs in their first Rose Bowl since 1949, they fell to Southern Cal. With their rise, Temple became my trade-off with John to get my seat for Northwestern in 1996! As mentioned, a Northwestern ticket to a Penn State game became my traditional trade-off with John. Their record stood at 0-6 in games I attended when the Wildcats visited State College, and in one when I traveled out to see these teams meet at Ryan Field in Evanston, Illinois.

Fitzgerald returned to Northwestern in 2001 as linebacker coach and recruiting coordinator. I saw the Cats win a game in exciting fashion a year later when they defeated Navy in Annapolis, 49-40. Tragically though after the sudden death of Head Coach Randy Walker in 2006, luckily his replacement turned out to be the right man at the right place at the right time for the future Northwestern football. Fitzgerald took over as head coach for the Wildcats at the age of 31. In his inaugural 4-8 season, I watched him on the sideline at Beaver Stadium. As youngest FBS coach at the age of 31, his Wildcats fell to the oldest coach, 80-year-old Joe Paterno, 33-7.

New York, NY - Fast Forward to Northwestern vs. Pitt in the New Era Pinstripe Bowl, 2016: My Northwestern highlight game finally came about in 2016 in the New Era Pinstripe Bowl at Yankee Stadium. With good defense and with the running skills of Justin Jackson, who impressed with 224 yards and three scores, it was a seesaw battle. Fitzgerald's Wildcats held Pitt's James Connors in check before he left the game with a head injury. They held him to only 32 yards. They surprised a good, No. 21 Pitt team, 31-24. Jackson took MVP honors.

A short stop to baseball history along the way
In going to the exciting, competitive game on a cold afternoon with my great friend of many years, Bob "Polecat" Marcello, a die-hard Yankee fan, our trip into the city introduced me that day to *Red Foley's Bar* on 33rd Street in Manhattan. The eating and drinking establishment doubled

as a museum packed with sports memorabilia. It displayed everything from original stadium seats, to hundreds of autographed baseballs, and the tallest porcelain urinals utilized anywhere. From there, we took the D Line subway to Yankee Stadium. The late Red Foley served as official scorer in the major leagues for almost four decades, and worked in more World Series, 10, than any other scorer in modern history. He covered Sports for the New York Daily News for 34 years. Regrettably, his namesake, nostalgic landmark has closed since.

Where does Fitzgerald go from here?

Despite the recent release of Pat Fitzgerald from his coaching duties due to his alleged knowledge of hazing practices among his players, his impact until now had been the most positive, sustainable era in the history of the Northwestern Wildcat football program. Without him, there was not much else that could be reported about this program from a positive perspective. Legal matters pending will determine the final legacy of his overall impact as a Northwestern head coach.

Rose-colored Frog / Oregon Trails

Penn State vs. (46) Oregon, The Rose Bowl, January 2, 1995

Pasadena, California –In 1993, my friend Jim Lewis, who I'd known since second grade, moved from New York City to beautiful, downtown Burbank, California. I was sorry he was moving so far away, but I also realized that we now had real Rose Bowl possibilities. I told him to be ready. If Penn State beat both Michigan and Ohio State in any given year, we had to find our way to the Rose Bowl! My prophetic words to Jimmy became reality quickly when they beat both to win the Big Ten and head to the Rose Bowl on the second day of 1995. The Rose Bowl is never played on a Sunday.

When my wish came true, I called him. He said, "If you're still serious, let me know. I may have a connection." Could I be any more serious? The next long-distance conversation went like this:

"I'll make a call, but how many tickets do we need?" Jim asked.

"Well, there are you and I, and I know John Massimilla will definitely go. Laurie says she's not interested in the game, of course, but says that she's always wanted to go to the Rose Bowl Parade."

"I'll ask if we can get tickets for that, too. How many?"

"Well, you and Judy, me and Laurie, Alex, John, maybe Kelle..." Jim decided to ask for eight.

"I can't promise you anything. I'll probably call you back next week." Amazingly, we had our second conversation the very next day.

"I called this guy and I told him that some Penn State friends of mine were interested to come out for the game, and I'd like to see if we can possibly get any tickets?"

"Sure! How many would you like?" responded Jimmy's contact.

"Three."

"How's the fifty-yard line, halfway up?"

"Great! How much do you want for them?"

"Don't worry about that. You and your friends will come as my guests. Would you like seats for the parade as well?"

Wow! This was bigger than the time a few of us as 14-year-olds went to Madison Square Garden and were told by an usher to give him a buck and go to gate 105 and ask for "Ike." Jimmy couldn't have come up with a better contact. W.H. "Bud" Griest happened to be the Vice Chairman of the Tournament of Roses Committee that year. The following year, Bud would be Chairman. The Chairman gets to select the Grand Marshal for his parade. The only consideration that we needed to make for the tickets was not to divulge who Bud's Grand Marshal would be in 1996 Tournament of Roses. The secret was safe with me and I never let the cat, or I can now say frog, out of the bag. Kermit the Frog was Bud's choice as Grand Marshal. My old Boonton pal Jimmy was artistically responsible for "Kermie" at that time. So, thanks to the green frog, I saw the green and gold Ducks play for the first time - and in the Rose Bowl!

Once-in-a-lifetime must-see

The fabulous Tournament of Roses Parade came first. We enjoyed reserved parking spaces and reserved bleacher seats below the television camera booth. We walked past "Jeopardy" host Alex Trebek on our way to bleachers. It figured. St. Laurie never liked him. She said he thought he was so smart because he had all the answers in front of him. Unlike him, I only asked her questions like, "Did you see where I put my...?" Probably how we've lasted so long. The PSU and Oregon bands came along to cheers from their respective fans. Horse units, US Marines, Morris Brown University Marching Band, and other marching units were great, but I have to admit that I found myself very amazed seeing the floats in person for the first time. I know it struck a chord with my little daughter. For a very long time, Alex would remember the event as "bears and flowers."

After the parade and a short drive to the stadium, we enjoyed a great, buffet lunch under a huge bubble in the parking lot as guests of Big Ten and PAC 10 officials and Grand Marshal Chi-Chi Rodriguez, the golfing legend. Saint Laurie, Jim's wife Judy, and Alex left after lunch, not that they had any interest in watching a football game to begin with. Laurie and Judy were both awaiting arrivals of baby boys in the spring. Jimmy, John, and I headed to the Rose Bowl to meet Bud at our seats. There we presented him with a Penn State sweatshirt as a token of our appreciation. He graciously accepted, but for obvious reasons did not put it on to maintain his neutrality. We couldn't put him on the spot, but we hoped that he'd wear it eventually.

A win with long-term impact

PSU's Ki-Jana Carter tied a Rose Bowl record with three rushing touchdowns for the Lions among his 156 yards on 21 carries. Oregon quarterback Danny O'Neill riddled Penn State's defense as well completing 41 of 61 passes for 456 yards and two scores. Penn State went on to defeat the "Quack Attack," 38-20, to finish the season 12-0, the fifth undefeated season ever during Coach Paterno's long career.

Penn State's win set off a much-needed controversy, however. Undefeated PSU let loose on the media charging that they were as deserving of the national championship as was Nebraska. Their arguments exposed the weakness of a national championship determined along television network alignments and bowl coalition ties. The Rose Bowl was not affiliated with the coalition sticking to its Big Ten vs. PAC-10 roots. Despite the arguments, Nebraska was crowned as national champs. Two undefeated teams remained standing at the end of the 1994 season. Even Cornhusker Head Coach Tom Osborne suggested succinctly, "If there's two undefeated teams, you ought to get them together. Joe Paterno would rather be here."[1] The powers-that-be eventually formed Bowl Championship Series (BCS) which wasn't exactly perfect, but it started the wheels turning to make some changes that definitely beat deciding on a national champion with secret ballots.

From a personal perspective, this Rose Bowl experience was the opportunity of a lifetime—first-class all the way! We couldn't thank Bud enough for his great hospitality, and before we parted at the end of the post-game celebration, he told us, "The next time Penn State plays in the Rose Bowl, you guys are invited back any time." I left Bud with this thought, "Bud, no matter who's playing, I'll be glad to come back any time!"

A year later, Kermit the Frog presided over Northwestern's first trip to Pasadena since 1949 to face the nearby Trojans of USC. Regretfully, the Lions did not return until 2008, and even more so, we couldn't track down Bud. If I ever did get back to the "Granddaddy of 'em all," I'm sure it will never top the experience enjoyed on January 2, 1995 unless Penn State's there playing for a CFP championship. I got to see Team No. 46, the Ducks from the University of Oregon, thanks to my acquaintance with Kermit the Frog.

On a historical note, it turned out I had watched that game with a celebrity. My pal James Lewis won an Emmy award in 1998 for Outstanding Children's Programming for his work on *Muppets Tonight*. He was also nominated again in 2003 for a movie he wrote, *Kermit's Swamp Years*.

Eugene, Oregon - Fast Forward to an Oregon Duck game along the Oregon Trail in the future: I haven't caught up with these Ducks since. Distance has basically precluded me from catching up. Of course, now it looks like I'll be following them against some Big Ten or whatever the conference to be named later team might be. With Dan Lanning now head coach at Oregon, the Ducks seem primed to continue to play well.

[1] George Vescey, "Sports of the Times: Osborne is Finally the Champ," *New York Times*, January 3, 1995, Section B, page 7.

🎵 Goin' to Carolina... 🎵 / Easy Pickings and Black Sheep of two Families

(47) Vanderbilt at (48) South Carolina, October 21, 1995

Columbia, South Carolina - The year 1995 offered me a new career opportunity. This caused me to pull up roots from my native New Jersey to start work with Tupperware® Manufacturing in the middle of nowhere—Hemingway, SC. I first moved down by myself as St. Laurie stayed in NJ waiting for baby number two, Eric, to arrive in May. By September, we settled into a condo complex Georgetown, SC. I determined the incentive to relocate was for a better salary in an area and lower cost of living. Ha! It was really to get closer in proximity to attend more SEC and ACC games.

With a two-year-old and a five-month-old, and with no known babysitters yet, trips to Clemson didn't make sense at the time. The South Carolina Gamecocks played two hours closer in Columbia. When Mike Morgan, a corrugated supplier of mine, and his wife Pam invited us to go to a game, we jumped at the chance.

Commodores: Just what Carolina ordered for easy pickings

A big crowd showed up at Williams-Brice Stadium despite the ineptitude, or maybe because of the ineptitude, of the competition. South Carolina Head Coach Brad Scott entered this weekend 3-3-1 by beating the likes of Louisiana Tech, Kent, and Mississippi State. With 0-5 Vanderbilt showing up, what else could be expected? Talk about convenient scheduling.

FIFTY YEARS OF TAILGATE TALES:

USC's pony-tailed QB Steve Taneyhill threw for two touchdowns and 187 yards in the first period alone. His first toss for six tied a school record of 21 scoring passes for the season. He blew away the record before the day was out with five. We watched SC tear up the hapless Commodores, 52-14. As the onslaught took place with Eric and Alex trading places on their mother's lap and mine, I struck up a conversation with the USC season ticket holder sitting to my left. My voice gave it away that I wasn't from South Carolina. After I explained how we were in the process of settling in from New Jersey, our conversation turned to South Carolina basketball. He spoke of how much he and the Gamecocks both missed their New York City connection over the years since Frank McGuire's days. The coach from NYC recruited players from the metropolitan area when he coached the Gamecock basketball program up until 1980. Basically, we discussed some good college hoops during a bad college football game.

Funny thing though, despite all this supposed offense, the Gamecocks 4-3-1 record never improved in the win column for the balance of the season. Carolina took advantage of weak competition like Vanderbilt, but couldn't beat any teams of equal or better talent. The Gamecocks got their tail feathers kicked in by the likes of Florida, Tennessee, and Clemson. They lost to all by a combined score of 157-45 to end their season 4-6-1. The offense averaged 65.5 points per game (ppg) in games won, but only 21.5 ppg in those lost. Brad Scott stayed for five seasons. He left with a 23-32 record. Evidently, the win column was very suspect.

My move to South Carolina ended about a month later. It wasn't the career opportunity that was right for me. Another company back in Jersey offered me a better position. It was a welcome relief after a tumultuous time—new job, no job for the wife, new baby, buying a house, selling a house, new surroundings, and looking for a new job again! Having a young family, I was pretty fortunate that things turned out the way they did.

As far as "big-time" college football within four hours of moving back to where we lived, nine different 1-A campuses hosted games within driving range. Multiple I-AA football schools and some competitive Division II and Division III programs competed nearby, too. Also, one of the best

♫♫ GOIN' TO CAROLINA... ♫♫ / EASY PICKINGS ...

sports complexes for major college football games and two pro football teams existed in The Meadowlands. I learned South Carolina is great for nice, relaxing vacations, but as for college football, I now appreciate New Jersey more as it's the Birthplace of College Football, and its greatest fan!

It doesn't get more historic than this for Vanderbilt football

Nashville, Tennessee -Fast forward to Vanderbilt vs. Boston College in the Music City Bowl, 2008: Having not seen the struggling Commodores play since 1995, a game of epic proportions as far as VU football lore stands presented itself to me. Vanderbilt met Boston College at Nissan Stadium in Nashville for their first bowl game in 26 years. At 6-6, in the grand scheme I've mentioned before, this game fell into the "consolation" category. However, this was Vanderbilt, and for historical purposes, call this a bowl. Thirteen-year-old Eric and I visited Tennessee on our annual bowl tour.

On a cold, overcast New Year's Eve Day, Boston College (9-4) led Vandy (6-6) at the half, 7-6. The Dore's punted at the BC 41 after the Eagles stopped them on their opening drive of the second half. The punt bounced off BC's returner and went into the end zone. Sean Richardson recovered for Vanderbilt. The refs signaled a touchdown. Commodores up, 13–7.

A defensive battle ensued. Neither scored until late in the fourth. The Eagles Dominique Davis connected with Colin Larmond, Jr. for a 45-yard touchdown to lead, 14–13. Vanderbilt retaliated. Bryant Hahnfeldt kicked a 45-yarder to give VU a 16–14 lead with 3:26 left to play.

The Commodore defense forced the Eagles to a three-and-out on their next possession. They took possession with 2:24 left. BC used all three of their timeouts, and forced a Brett Upson punt from the 20. To put the game away, defensive back Myron Lewis intercepted a Davis pass with 1:36 left. The Commodores ran out the clock for its first bowl victory in 53 years, a year before I was even born. Long time in the making.

The Commodores converted only one of their 15 third-down attempts. The Eagles' three turnovers included the fumble into the end zone for the Commodores' only touchdown. Thirty yards of penalties picked up by the Dore's on the final scoring drive lifted them to the final score. A very unique outcome of this game: Vanderbilt punter Brett Upson won MVP honors. He averaged 42.6 yards on his nine punts to keep the Eagles deep in their territory all game.

Black Sheep of two families

Columbia, SC - Fast Forward to Clemson at South Carolina, 2013: I have family members on both my mother's side and my father's side who are proud Clemson graduates. However, when it comes to Clemson, my immediate family and I are proud to be the Black Sheep of both families. My daughter, Alex, selected the University of South Carolina as her choice to further her college education. She's proud to be a Gamecock fan and alumnus now. While at USC, the Gamecocks defeated the Tigers their first three seasons before succumbing to the Tigers her senior year (2014). She actually admitted to me eventually that I had been a big influence on her college choice. She wanted to go to a school with a "big" football program. My daughter and my money left home to support the Gamecocks and Steve Spurrier.

Among three of her four seasons in traditional South Carolina garb of a black dress and cowgirl boots, she and her classmates cheered the Gamecocks on to 17 straight victories at Williams-Brice Stadium. I rolled along similarly myself with her Carolina team. Ever since we brought her to that first game as a toddler back in 1995, her Gamecocks enjoyed a record of 8-0 when I attended. When Alex attended school, the Cocks defeated Vanderbilt, Navy (just got by 24-21), Clemson, Missouri, and Kentucky. For Thanksgiving weekend 2013, we got together for the second time in three years to see the No. 10 Gamecocks (9-2) host No. 6 Clemson (10-1) in their annual, in-state, arch-rivalry to punctuate the regular season.

With Clemson tying the game, 17-17, the Gamecocks went to work from their 26. Into the final period, they retook the lead capping the drive on Mike Davis's two-yard run. The Gamecock's forced quarterback Tahj Boyd to fumble on the Tiger's next series and recovered it. Clemson forced

♪♪ GOIN' TO CAROLINA... ♪♪ / EASY PICKINGS ...

a Carolina punt. However, the Gamecocks jarred the ball loose again, and took over at the Tiger 34. On a halfback option pass, Pharoah Cooper connected with Brandon Wilds for a 26-yard scoring play to lead, 31-17.

Boyd went to the air, but this time linebacker Skai Moore picked it off. SC punted. Once again, a linebacker, T.J. Hollomon, intercepted. Carolina ran out the clock. The Gamecock fans among 84,174 at Williams-Brice Stadium exploded to celebrate a record-setting game. For the first time in the history of this bitter rivalry, Carolina set the mark for its fifth consecutive win. USC would defeat Wisconsin in the Capital One Bowl, and Clemson defeated Ohio State in the Orange Bowl. The Gamecocks finished ranked No. 4 in the AP Top 25. Dabo Swinney's Tigers landed No. 8.

After quarterback Connor Shaw's graduation, regrettably for my daughter and her classmates, their senior year didn't go well. Among games I attended, they fell to Texas A&M in the opener, to Missouri on Parents' Weekend, 21-20, and at Auburn, 42-33. Now living in Tennessee, St. Laurie and I saw them upset Kentucky in Lexington, 24-18, and they finished 2022 ranked No. 23. The Gamecocks own a respectable 12-4 record among the games I've attended now. They supposedly enter 2023 with the toughest schedule among FBS teams, but based on how this is determined, I whole-heartedly beg to differ. I address this in one of my two essays later, "For the Love of the Game."

Seeing Red! Now Orange, thanks to "Jersey Mike"

(49) Purdue at Penn State, October 12, 1996

State College, Pennsylvania - The Purdue Boilermakers showed up in State College to play the Nittany Lions for the first time since 1952. The Lions won their sixth of seven games that day, 31-14.

Four years later on September 30, 2000, the Penn State-Purdue game became etched in my memory for an unusual encounter that day. Purdue QB Drew Brees had one final chance to bump off the Lions his senior season playing at State College. St. Laurie and I also looked forward to tailgating with some other good friends.

Business associate Barbara Glazar, a Purdue alum with a degree in chemical engineering, and her husband, Denny, were joining us in the Happy Valley parking lot to tailgate before the 3:30 pm kickoff. Barbara liked to reminisce about her fantastic experience as a student at the Rose Bowl in 1966. Her Boilermakers defeated the Trojans of USC, 14-13.

Bob Jones, another business associate, lifetime PSU season-ticket holder, and not only a Slippery Rock grad, but designer of and original wearer of the school's "Rocky the Rock" mascot, planned to meet us to tailgate along with his mom, a die-hard Penn State fan for many years. It would be the first time that we would get to unfold our new, red canopy for our first football tailgate party that season. However, a strange thing happened in the parking lot that remains a mystery to us to this day. Only one conclusion makes any sense.

Bob Jones at Slippery Rock Archives with his creation of "Rocky the Rock." Without such an icon his freshman year, he designed a mascot that was "unique, like Slippery Rock." (photo credit courtesy of Judy Loney Silva, Slippery Rock Archives)

Prepared to party despite desperate times in Happy Valley

By mid-morning we were unfolding the frame of our tent in a lot north of the stadium just west of the Agricultural school buildings. Traffic was lighter than usual coming into the Beaver Stadium parking lots that day. On the positive side, a 3:30 kickoff meant everyone didn't converge into State College at the same time. On the negative side, traffic was light because Penn State was off to its worst start ever, 1-4.

A week earlier, Ohio State hammered the Lions, 45-6, in Ohio Stadium. On top of that, PSU freshman cornerback Adam Taliaferro suffered a severe spinal injury with 1:39 left in that game. He was removed from the stadium on a stretcher and transported to Ohio State Medical Center. There, he underwent surgery for a cervical spinal injury. By the following Saturday, it was still too early to tell if the 18-year-old athlete would ever be able to walk again.

Maybe the outcome of the previous week's defeat and misfortune had something to do with what happened to us next. Some guy walked up to us and congenially started a conversation while we rigged the red canopy up over our out-stretched frame. Next, the guy says, "I have to warn you that these canopies cause traffic problems and are not allowed here. I have to ask that you put it away. If you don't take it down right away, I'll have to get security people and confiscate it." What?

Now I'd been attending Penn State games in Happy Valley for twenty years. One of the reasons it's so "Happy" is because a lot of people come up and gather on football weekends in RVs, vans, trucks, and cars. They love to set up tents, grills, kegs, and more to enjoy themselves before and after Nittany Lion football games. However, this was my first time in this particular lot. There weren't a lot of tailgaters around yet.

I looked around trying to prove that this guy was not telling the truth. I couldn't, to my surprise! There wasn't an awning of any kind in sight yet. Was it too early still? Never seemed to be. Did this parking lot have different rules than others? Did the school suddenly change the rules just because I finally brought a canopy to tailgate under?

I had a hard time believing the school initiated such a new policy. This guy said they were now banned because they created traffic problems? No kidding! All of a sudden, I have this nice, new, "red" canopy that we bought primarily for tailgating. Suddenly, it's forbidden? I looked around for security people, but noticed none. I was really getting pissed off, but since I couldn't disprove this mystery man, yet, and not wanting to get into a physical confrontation over a tent, I acquiesced.

What the...?

We pulled out a cooler full of beers and snacks. Thank the Lord, food and alcohol weren't banned. We drank somewhat dumbfounded as the guy headed toward the road where traffic was finally starting to build. He just kept walking never to be seen again. Calming down a little, I left St. Laurie to wait for our guests. I walked eagerly to the crest of a hill for a vantage point to witness a tent-less Happy Valley Saturday. Who was this guy kidding, and where did he come from? Overlooking the lots to the east, blue and white canopies filled the landscape galore! What the...? Blue and white? Was that this guy's issue? Did this idiot see a scarlet canopy as an association with last weekend's dreadful loss to the Ohio State Buckeyes? Was that the reason for his threat?

By the time I got back to our car, a couple new rows of tailgaters had begun to form behind us. Tables, chairs, coolers, grills, AND canopies started to fill traffic lanes. Among all the blue, white, gray, and probably black and gold ones, we pulled our frame back out. We rigged the red canopy on top. The guy never came back. No security approached us. It had to be the strangest damned experience I'd ever had in any parking lot. It still ticks me off thinking about it today! Where were all these other tailgaters when this guy came by?

A passing Brees in State College

Quarterback Rashard Casey took it in from the two and PSU closed out the third period ahead of Purdue, 22-13. Drew Brees brought his team back on the next drive. It culminated in a 39-yard touchdown to Vinny Sutherland with 11:30 left to close the gap, 22-20. His completion tied the

Big Ten record for touchdown passes in a season with 74. Purdue missed a 46-yard field goal attempt. The game wasn't over.

Brees tossed one last *"Hail Mary"* into the end zone. Defender James Boyd batted the ball to the ground for State. Brees finished his collegiate career against Penn State at 0-3 despite career Big Ten passing records including most completions, yards, and touchdowns. The emotional week after Taliaferro's severe injury probably played a hand also in helping the struggling Lions defeat a team ranked higher than them for the first time since 1996.

We partied late under our red canopy after Penn State's second win and Purdue's second loss of the season. Cars crept out of the parking lot slowly. Most stayed to watch the final outcome decided on the final play. I still wonder if the color of our canopy caused that mysterious jerk to make threats to have it confiscated. That guy was there one minute and gone the next. His timing was perfect with no other canopies or security around. I still see red over the whole incident. It was weird.

John Massimilla and I attended the opening game at Beaver Stadium the following season. We watched a poorly played 33-7 loss by the Lions to eventual National Champ, Miami. The Canes dominated the Lions to the point where ABC-TV switched coverage at halftime to the Oregon-Wisconsin game. The bad news for Penn State football was that they continued on into their second consecutive, losing season with a record of 5-6. The great news for Penn State football that opening night – over 100,000 people stood and cheered for Adam Taliaferro when he walked out of the Beaver Stadium tunnel prior to the kickoff.

Purdue Pitfall and Pride in The Music City

Nashville, Tennessee – Fast Forward to Purdue vs. Tennessee, Music City Bowl, 2021: Now residing in the Nashville area, I looked forward to my short trip to conveniently attend this bowl game for the sixth time. However, I had trepidations when Purdue was matched up with local favorite Tennessee. Only three seasons before, I watched Purdue put up one of the worst performances ever in any bowl game imaginable. At halftime, Auburn led, 56-7! My great Auburn friends Charlie and Lynda Murren and I walked over to the bridge back to downtown Nashville for drinks and to discuss my idea about my future move to Nashville.

Losing that game, 63-14, I could only hope that the Boilermakers would not embarrass themselves against Tennessee playing in front of their big home crowd. The Music City set a record with 69,489 in attendance. A field goal by Tennessee's Chase McGrath gave the Vols a 31-30 lead in the third period. The Boilermaker defense avoided more damage by stopping the Vols next drive at their 24 before taking over on downs. Two possessions later from their 38, Aidan O'Connell connected with tight end Payne Durham on a crossing pattern. Hit and pushed toward near the sideline, Durham broke free and raced downfield for a 62-yard catch-and-run to score. O'Connell connected with Payne for a two-point conversion to give the Boilermakers a 38-31 lead.

To start Tennessee's next drive from the 35, Hendon Hooker connected with Cedric Tillman on a slant across the middle for a tying touchdown with 3:37 left. Purdue responded on its next series when O'Connell connected with Broc Thompson on the right sideline. He beat his defender who fell, and raced 70 yards for a 45-38 Purdue lead with 2:57 remaining. O'Connell's fifth touchdown pass tied him with two others for the Music City Bowl touchdown pass record. With 1:35 remaining and not to be outdone, Hooker tied the same record connecting on a two-yard fade pass to Jaylin Hyatt who made a diving catch just keeping his feet in as he landed out of the end zone. Purdue punted after gaining only six yards. The Vols drove to the Boilermakers' 42. With two seconds left, McGrath's 56-yard attempt fell short. Overtime!

It took the Vols six plays to get to the Boilermaker two. Defensive end Jack Sullivan's sack put UT back at the eight. On fourth and goal at the one, Jaylen Wright got tackled short of the goal. Lying on top of two defenders before a whistle blew, Wright reached the ball out over the goal for an apparent six. However, after review, the official call upheld the ruling that forward progress had stopped before the ball broke the plane. Purdue took over on downs. A seven-yard pass to Durham put the Boilermakers on the eighteen. Two running plays centered the ball, and Mitchell Finneran's chip-shot gave Purdue an exciting, 48-45, victory. Fantastic game to be at! Purdue definitely made up for that debacle against Auburn last time they played at the Music City.

Belated Boilermaker Connections

West Lafayette, Indiana - Fast Forward to Penn State at Purdue, 2022: With our recent move to Tennessee, destinations out of reach from New Jersey now fell within driving range. Purdue was one of those destinations. Of all teams, the Penn State Nittany Lions visited West Lafayette, Indiana to open the Big Ten season against Purdue. PSU fans saw this as another kick in the teeth though. Most recent conference openers for them started on the road. For my sake, this worked out very well. Not only had I not yet attended a game at Ross-Ade Stadium, but because Laurie and I have a great Boilermaker affiliation with friends from NJ. They came out for the opener as well.

I also developed a more favorable aspect regarding Purdue. Recently through Ancestry.com, I found out that my great-grandfather who immigrated from Poland, worked as a boilermaker for the Pennsylvania Railroad in Newark, NJ. So now when I see Purdue Pete along the sideline, it makes me feel proud how our family started here and where we've gotten to today. Go Boilermakers!

Our own personal "Jersey Mike"

Our good friends from NJ, Mike and Amy Pirrello, have a daughter Julia who started her senior year at Purdue. Along with Rick and Kristie Blount of the same town whose son Matt also attended Purdue, they came to West Lafayette to celebrate the opening game of their kids' senior season. On a beautiful day, they treated us to a party in the back yard of Matt's house shared with other friends located only a few blocks from Ross-Ade. Mike and Rick worked over hot grills making some of our favorite NJ specialties - Taylor ham, egg, and cheese sandwiches along with sausage, peppers, and onions on sub rolls.

FIFTY YEARS OF TAILGATE TALES:

We all brought various samples of favorite brews to go along with burgers and dogs while sharing many Tales around the Tailgate. My Penn State cohorts from over the many years, John Massimilla and Dr. Wayne Hoover (Juniata,'83) came up from Chambersburg to root for Penn State. We all had a great time tailgating with the Purdue students and parents who welcomed us there. Everyone enjoyed a tremendous tailgating experience!

With two seconds left in the first half, PSU tight end Brenton Strange shed two tacklers and rambled down the right sideline 67 yards to give Penn State a 21-10 advantage at halftime. Purdue fought back to take the lead into the final period, 24-21. On a slant pattern over the middle, Penn State Lion KeAndre Lambert-Smith hauled in a 29-yard pass from Sean Clifford and spun off a tackler to bounce down the middle of the field to put PSU ahead, 28-24.

On the Lions' next possession, Boilermaker S Chris Jefferson dimmed Penn State's spirits. He intercepted Clifford's overthrown pass and wove his way 72 yards back for a Purdue touchdown with 8:29 left in the game. "Boilers Up!" as Purdue fans say, 31-28. Purdue seemed to have the game well in hand. However, with 57 seconds remaining, Clifford connected with Keyvone Lee on a nine-yard swing pass to seal the Nittany Lion win capping an 80-yard drive. Last minute touchdowns in both halves by Penn State keyed the outcome. Penn State fans came away happy with a victory, 35-31, capping a fun day at Purdue.

The Pirrello's also have son at Ohio State, but I burned that bridge for Penn State playing there in 2023 since I'm deeply committed to Air Force at Navy that same day. However, Mike's youngest daughter, Taylor, graduated from high school, and started looking at colleges to attend in 2023. I gave Mike a list of priorities for Taylor's education and our future tailgate considerations. Update: of all schools, she chose the University of Tennessee. Now, I'll have to go to a game or two in Knoxville and have to wear dark glasses to block out all that bright, Tennessee orange!

SEEING RED! NOW ORANGE, THANKS TO "JERSEY MIKE"

Penn State at Purdue Tailgate, 2022!

Army 34 - (50) Tulane 10
Michie Stadium, West Point, NY, October 19, 1996

From the Ashes to the Rising Sun Belt

(51) Marshall at Army, September 6, 1997

West Point, NY - My late father grew up in Lyndhurst, New Jersey about nine miles from the entrance to the Lincoln Tunnel. Both sets of grandparents lived in that same town through the 1970s. My father always spoke with great pride about the athletes and teams that came from his hometown. During the height of my youth baseball career in the late '60s growing up in Boonton Township, NJ, he took me to see a few games one weekend when the Lyndhurst American Legion baseball team played for the state championship in nearby Dover.

The Lyndhurst lineup consisted of players playing college baseball as freshmen at Notre Dame, Seton Hall, Princeton, and Lafayette, among others. The team's catcher was a broad-shouldered kid with a gun for an arm. According to my dad, a former sports editor for the local paper near Lyndhurst, The South Bergen News, he went to "some small school down south."

Ted Shoebridge played catcher for the Lyndhurst Legion. Between Legion baseball and a semi-pro baseball circuit known as the Metropolitan League that played at Bergen County Park in Lyndhurst, we saw many of these same players compete over the next few years. As an All-Star catcher in youth baseball, still learning the position myself, I focused on Shoebridge playing catcher when I watched those teams play.

He was a solid hitter, a hustler, and a take-charge leader on the field. In one, quick motion from the crouch, he'd spring straight up, take one short stride, and bring his arm straight up over his head. Within a split second, he'd nail runners trying to steal second. Surely, pro scouts drooled. As a 12-year-old, I didn't emulate the Reds' Johnny Bench nor the Mets' Jerry Grote, two of my favorites. When I was behind the plate, I tried to play like Ted Shoebridge!

Little did we know

In the fall of my first season playing football as a high school freshman, our head coach informed us about the news regarding the horrific plane crash in West Virginia before our Sunday afternoon film sessions. Most of the Marshall team perished on their return trip from East Carolina on November 14, 1970. But for me, it became more poignant the following Monday. For some reason, our varsity team hosted a game on Monday instead of Saturday. We freshman attended in the stands. After the game, my dad came by to pick me up. He looked me square in the eye and asked, "Do you know who died in that Marshall plane crash?" I never really had heard much about Marshall. Until the news of the tragedy, I rarely heard about Marshall no less knew of anyone who went there. Before I gave it much thought, he blurted, "Ted Shoebridge."

Shocking! Until then, we never knew that the "small school down south" Shoebridge attended was Marshall. Nor did I even know that the baseball prospect I admired with a rifle of an arm also played quarterback anywhere. Marshall Head Coach Rick Tolley started to revitalize The Thundering Herd football program. He expanded the program's recruiting efforts to states rarely considered before – New Jersey, Texas, Alabama, and Florida.

On that terrible day in college football history, Shoebridge led a comeback against East Carolina that fell short in a 17-14 loss. In the second half, he came off the bench. In his efforts, he completed 14 of 32 attempts for 188 yards and a 16-yard touchdown. His Lyndhurst High School teammate, Marcelo Lajterman, who doubled as kicker and punter for The Herd, also perished that day. At the crash site, rescue teams never recovered Ted's body. I remember a photograph in *The Sporting News* after the tragedy. It showed Ted's somber parents presenting a huge floral arrangement in a memorial at the Marshall campus. Years later, I dealt with a chemical sales rep, Steve Smith, who as an ECU student, attended the game. He said an eerie depression overcame the campus when students heard about the tragedy the following day.

Rise of Marshall football witnessed first-hand

Marshall traveled to West Point to play Army on September 6, 1997, twenty years and a day since my father passed away at the age of 47. It was almost 27 years since the horrible plane crash that took the lives of Ted Shoebridge, Marcelo Lajterman, and seventy-three other people returning from a college football game played in Greenville, NC. I looked forward to seeing The Thundering Herd football program that had risen from those ashes play Army that day. The football program started taking on the new challenge stepping up to play IA football. As depicted in the 2007 movie release, *"We are Marshall,"* the efforts to continue the football program under new Head Coach Jack Lengyl began the season after the loss of 34 players, five coaches, and seven staff members.

From 1971 to 1981, the Marshall program never achieved more than four wins in a season. In 1982, the school administration decided to take a step back to play at the IAA level. That move eventually revived the football program to new heights in the long term. The program thrived, even winning the IAA national title in 1992. Under first-year Head Coach Bob Pruett, they won it again going 15-0 in 1996.

In 1997, Marshall returned to Division IA as a member of the Mid-American Conference. They played in the MAC years before from 1954 to 1969. Today's game against Army marked their second in their return to IA football since 1980. They fell at West Virginia in their opener the previous Saturday, 42-31.

Marshall sophomore wide receiver Randy Moss showed his speed early by catching a short pass from quarterback Chad Pennington. He streaked past Army defenders for a 90-yard touchdown. Army countered another Pennington touchdown pass with running scores by Joe Hewitt and Ty Amey. However, missed extra points kept The Herd in the lead, 14-12. In the third, Moss did it again. He caught a short pass and hurdled an Army defender for an exciting, 79-yard score. Later, Marshall nose tackle Larry McCloud pulverized Hewitt who fumbled, and suffered a concussion. Herd linebacker Ricky Hall picked up the loose ball to sprint 43 yards for a score giving Marshall a 28-12 lead. Army actually outgained Marshall that day, 527-337 yards, but the visitors came up with the big, scoring plays.

Marshall earned its first D-1 victory since 1980, 35-25. Moss and Pennington would have a lot to do with that early Marshall success back into big-time football. During the 1999 NFL Draft Show, ESPN continuously highlighted the two big plays Dave Headden and I witnessed that day. Moss took two short Pennington passes and turned them into two long touchdowns against Army. The Minnesota Vikings drafted Moss. The New York Jets drafted Pennington.

I consider witnessing the beginning of Marshall's rebirth in IA football a highlight amongst my personal annals of college football history. Under Head Coach Bob Pruett, re-entry into Division IA football for the next eight years resulted in a 79-23 record. Five MAC Championships, five bowl wins, and a couple of Top 25 finishes proved that the Thundering Herd arose from the ashes that horrific day in 1970. Surely, Rick Tolley, Ted Shoebridge, and their deceased Herd teammates would be proud of that the Marshall team of 1997. They revitalized what the Marshall football program had set out to do back in 1970.

On November 14, 2009, 39 years to the day of the tragedy, my friend Steve Ciesla and I arrived at the campus in Huntington, West Virginia. We attended the annual Memorial and the Marshall-Southern Mississippi game, won by USM, 27-20. The ceremony is held near the Memorial fountain that gets turned off every year on the anniversary of the tragedy. We met Ted's brother, Tom, who was presented with a memorial quilt. A player who was injured and missed traveling to the game, Joe Gillette, class of '73, reminisced as keynote speaker to honor his deceased teammates.

The team and the date will never be forgotten in Huntington. Steve and I were glad that we had the chance to be there to share the occasion with those this hit so hard. It's a solemn and beautiful service to remember the many young lives and those with them that perished on November 14, 1970.

From Mid-American to rising Sun Belt

Annapolis, Maryland - Fast Forward to Marshall vs. Maryland in the Military Bowl, 2013: This was the last season Eric and I would be able to attend bowl games together. This came during the holidays of his senior year in high school before he would join the Navy after graduation. Marshall, still of the MAC, met Maryland of the ACC at The Military Bowl in Annapolis.

The two teams battled throughout this contest. Marshall took a 17-13 lead into halftime. That score held through the third. Maryland scored on a touchdown pass from C.J. Brown to Dave Stinebaugh to give the Terrapins a 20-17 lead early in the fourth. However, The Herd bounced right back with a 63-yard drive as Essray Taliaferro ran it in from the seven. On their subsequent possession, Marshall quarterback Rakeem Cato threw a scoring strike to Gator Hoskins into the end zone from the eight with 3:42 left. Plenty of time remained for the Power Fiver Terrapins to overcome their deficit. However, Marshall Safety A.J. Leggett picked off a poorly thrown pass, and The Herd held on to celebrate their bowl victory, 31-20.

A personal highlight of this game for me was seeing linebacker Cole Farrand play for the Terrapins. His father George and I were high school friends and teammates. Cole, easily recognized playing with a long ponytail draped from his helmet, achieved a unique distinction of honors during his playing career. In 2013, he earned the ACC Defensive Player of the Week Award in the Terps' game against Clemson. A year later when Maryland joined the Big Ten, he won Defensive Player of the Week Award versus Indiana in that conference. Not sure if any player has done this since with all the recent conference realignments, but he had to be probably the first to accomplish this feat.

Marshall now belongs to the Sun Belt East. Other Sun Belt teams have demonstrated competitiveness against non-conference teams and within the conference itself. I'll look to future opportunities when The Thundering Herd will face off against other Sun Belt East foes. Appalachian State, Coastal Carolina, and James Madison among others will clash in entertaining games against one another other. The Sun Belt now offers good, tough, competitive football that's worth watching!

Penn State 34 - (52) Southern Mississippi 6
Beaver Stadium, State College, PA, September 5, 1998

(53) Miami (O.) 14 Army 13
Michie Stadium, West point, NY, September 12, 1998

Historic West Point after fall foliage on a football Saturday.

Greatest Game Ever! / Killing the Moment

(54) Virginia Tech at Syracuse, November 14, 1998

Syracuse, NY - Over the years, I attended thirteen Syracuse games. The Orangemen always played before me as road warriors. Even when they "hosted" games at the Meadowlands while the Carrier Dome was under construction or played there in Kickoff Classics. I traveled to see them play at venues in Annapolis, State College, Pittsburgh, and Raleigh. Finally in 1998, 23 years after seeing them play in Annapolis, I finally got to see them play not one, but two games in the Carrier Dome. Bernie Olszyk, a friend through work, purchased a season-ticket package at Syracuse while his daughter, Heather, attended school there. Initially with "Bernardo," we witnessed a typical 63-21 blow-out of Cincinnati in the Dome, but five weeks later, my friend since kindergarten, Les Di Vite, and I attended the most thrilling football game I ever witnessed in over 30 years attending college football games. It set my high standard for excitement.

    Les and I trekked up I-81, and we shunned the satellite parking lots this time for a chance to park closer to the stadium. As luck would have it, we turned on a street near the SUNY Upstate Medical Center. A nurse who must have just come off her shift approached her parked car along Adams Street. I slowed to stop, she waved, got in her car and left. We had a free parking space literally in the "shadows" of the Carrier Dome. The spot was not more than a stone's throw from The Dome. I always looked for ways to minimize expenses so I could continue to afford to do this.

One other pre-game note of interest, this was the first time in twenty years attending an on-campus athletic facility that sold beer! We took seats chosen personally by Bernardo in Section 328, Row H, high above the end zone sitting right between the uprights in the south end of the Dome. They turned out to be perfect for the game about to unfold before us.

Big Game in Big East

This important Big East match-up took place between the 6-3 Orangemen led by quarterback Donovan McNabb against the vaunted defense of the 7-1 Virginia Tech Hokies. As expected, Frank Beamer's special teams were forces to be reckoned with. His punt-return team already had nine blocked punts to their credit. McNabb started the game with the thumb on his throwing hand wrapped. However, the bandage came off early in the contest.

Trailing 3-0 early in the first period, Virginia Tech fullback Jarret Ferguson broke through a hole over left tackle. He sprinted away from us untouched for a 76-yard touchdown—wearing only one shoe for 60 of those yards no less! By game's end, his run would account for more than fifty percent of Tech's rushing yards. What's more, this one jaunt also totaled more than twice the passing yardage that Hokies' quarterback Al Clark would throw for that night.

You wouldn't expect this to be such an exciting game with such an anemic offense, but this night's game would epitomize classic "Beamer Ball" – big, special-team plays. Right below us, on Syracuse's ensuing possession to start the second quarter, VT's Anthony Midget blocked the SU punt into the end zone. There, Ricky Hall recovered it for the Tech lead, 14-3. Before the first half ended, Beamer's defense would get the chance to strike again.

Syracuse moved into field-goal range. On an attempted reverse, wide receiver Maurice Jackson had the ball knocked from his grasp into the air by free safety Keion Carpenter. Cornerback Loren Johnson picked it off in mid-air. He sprinted 78 yards for the defensive score to take a 21-3 Virginia Tech lead. Syracuse responded with a field goal, a 36-yarder by Nate Trout to dent the Hokie lead, 21-6. The majority of the 49,336 in attendance this evening expressed extreme discontent for the Orange and Blue as the teams left for intermission. Coach Paul Pasquoloni's troops knew their first half offensive performance was dismal.

Aside from Jarret's run, the SU defense held Tech in check. Donovan McNabb and the offense would have to step things up. Were they up for the task? In the third, the Orangemen defense continued to stifle the Hokies. McNabb finally got the Orange into the end zone with a one-yard scoring pass to tight end Stephen Brominski to complete a 10-play drive. A second 10-play drive resulted in three more points. Trout converted again from 30. By the end of the third period, Syracuse only trailed by five, 21-16. With twelve minutes left to play, the Orange finally took the lead on a one-yard plunge on fourth down by fullback Rob Konrad.

The 22-21 lead lasted briefly. Beamer's special team defense team found another way to take it back! Loren Johnson played the culprit once again. He picked off McNabb's pass attempt on a two-point conversion and raced away from us for Tech's 99-yard two-pointer. On another unusual, long play, Tech re-took the lead just like that, 23-22. Following the two-point turnaround, the Hokies' offense finally came through with its second score, a 49-yard field goal by Shayne Graham at the end of a short 29-yard drive.

A finish to remember

With 4:33 left in the game, the Orange started from their 17-yard line trailing, 26-22. They'd have to play for six to have a shot to win the Big East Conference still within reach. A second conference loss would eliminate them from contention. On a fourth and six from his 46, McNabb came up big. His 39-yard run gave SU a fresh set of downs at Tech's fifteen. On his hands and knees along the sideline, McNabb puked. His 14-yard pass to Maurice Jackson brought the Orange to the one-yard line right below our vantage point. McNabb heaved some more – not the ball, his guts.

With less than a minute remaining, the Hokies stopped a Konrad run for no gain. After an incompletion to Brominski, Syracuse moved half a yard closer courtesy of a VT penalty. McNabb bootlegged left only to be sacked by defensive end Corey Moore, the Big East's Defensive Player of the Year, for a 12-yard loss. No time-outs remained. The Orange hustled back to the line of scrimmage. McNabb spiked the ball. The clock stopped with time remaining for only one more play on fourth down. This was it.

McNabb rolled to his right, stopped, suddenly looked all the way back to his left, turned, jumped, and floated a pass high to Brominski. He positioned himself in front of linebacker Michael Hawkes. Brominski went high to make the grab. He pulled it in while falling to the ground, and clutched it to his chest for the most exciting finish imaginable! No time left. No extra point needed! The SU squad piled on top of Brominski. Syracuse students raced on to the field in celebration. Hokie players collapsed to the turf in disbelief. It was a wild, unforgettable finish—a true classic determined on the game's final play, 28-26!

My primary purpose to attend this game was to see Virginia Tech play for the first time. I was starting to try to specifically schedule teams I hadn't seen play. Yet, this game became a classic featuring a number of unusual, exciting scoring plays leading to a classic finish for the ages. In his FoxSports.com article, "100 Greatest Finishes," Pete Fiutak rated this game No. 58 among the elite in this category. Each game required three primary requirements: 1.) won on a final play or drive; 2.) played for some significance; and 3.) remembered in college football history.[1] Syracuse won the Big East championship. In over three hundred college football games, none topped Syracuse versus Virginia Tech in excitement from beginning to end in the quest to "see 'em all!" I was there. I remember! How can I forget?

Blow-outs and good action seen with the Fighting Gobblers

Hilton Head, South Carolina - Fast Forward to vacation in Hilton Head, South Carolina, 2018: Since my "greatest game ever," I attended eight more games played by the Hokies. Among them, I attended six while Frank Beamer coached until his retirement in 2016. In '99, I watched

Michael Vick and company maul Rutgers at the Birthplace of College Football, 58-20. In VA Tech's farewell tour to the Big East in 2003, Eric and I traveled out to Pitt with a stop to the historic Gettysburg Battlefield Park. We witnessed Tech's final decision in a last-minute loss, 31-28, to a Big east foe. For my first trip to Blacksburg, the Hokies rudely introduced me to the Western Michigan Broncos in 2004, 63-0. I watched the Hokies (Gobblers) start on their road to the ACC Championship in 2010 in a 33-30 loss in the opener to Boise State at FEDEX Field. I saw the Hokies' win their 2012 home opener over Georgia Tech in overtime, 20-17.

After Beamer retired, I watched his successor, Justin Fuente, keep games close three straight years from 2017-2019. First, at FEDEX Field to open once again, they defeated West Virginia, 31-24. The following season, a 6-6 record landed them in a downpour at the Military Bowl. Improving Cincinnati capped an 11-2 season with their 35-31 victory. In the opener the following season at Boston College, they fell to the Eagles, 35-28. I attended a lot of mostly good, competitive Virginia Tech games settled in the final minutes of play during the course of my history.

Killing what could have been a great moment

Despite so many great, down-to-the wire games I'd seen Virginia Tech play, my most vivid memory of Hokie football turned out to be somewhat disappointing. And this wasn't at any game. It was on a vacation in the summer of 2018 in Hilton Head, SC. Saint Laurie and I enjoyed the beach, a local microbrewery, visiting friends who retired there, and a Ghost Tour in nearby Savannah hosted by five different bars! From there, we packed up to spend a few more days in another favorite city, Charleston, SC.

We pulled into a gas station in town to fill up on the way there. I parked behind a white sedan similar to our rental car where the wife filled up their tank ahead of us. Her husband walked off to the convenience store on the other side of the pumps to our right. After I finished filling our car, I got in and we all waited for the husband who'd gone into the store. On the left, we were blocked in by a few lawn maintenance vehicles working there.

As we sat, I noted to my right that the guy we were waiting for was walking directly to our car, not his. He started to reach for the door to get in. Suddenly, I realized and said, "Hey! It's Frank Beamer!" Now my saintly wife did not calmly look up and reply to ask something to the effect of, "Oh, how do you know him?" Instead, she lifted her head from what she was reading, scrunched her face, and with a high-pitched shrill, exclaimed, "*Who?*" Frank suddenly realized wrong car, smiled, waved apologetically, and headed toward his car ahead of us.

What a moment killer! Immediately I knew this would go nowhere with her even if I explained. There was no time to. With cars coming in behind, I had no way to start a conversation and turn this into a "Kodak memory." Not that I ever did anything like that before, but being away on a relaxing vacation and running into someone like Frank whom I always admired, I "coulda, shoulda, woulda" if I had the time and cooperation I needed. He always ran a great program with much success as a Hall of Fame coach. It would have been nice to talk briefly about some of those great games I attended.

When South Carolina hired Shane Beamer, his son, as head coach a few years later, I reminded St. Laurie about this chance meeting. Telling her it was even more regrettable now since that Gamecock connection could have made this a cherished "family" photo. She could have cared less. Not that I would have been on a vacation with any of these other guys, but it would have been probably been a totally different story if John or Charlie or Les or Frank or Eric or Cat could've been there! As I often like to say, timing is everything.

Penn State 41 - (55) Arizona 7

Pigskin "Classic,"Beaver Stadium, State College, PA, August 28, 1999

Syracuse 47 - (56) Central Michigan 7

The Carrier Dome, Syracuse, NY, September 11, 1999

(57) East Carolina 33 - Army 7

FIFTY YEARS OF TAILGATE TALES:

Michie Stadium, West Point, NY, October 2, 1999

[1] Pete Fiutak, "100 Greatest College Football Finishes," http://cfn.scout.com/2/657471.html (9 July 2007)

Location! Location! Location!

Central Michigan (56) at Syracuse, September 11, 1999

Syracuse, NY - Bernardo, Steve Ciesla, and I ventured up to Syracuse to watch the Chippewas of Central Michigan wander into upstate New York. The highlights of our final trip to Syracuse together came before the 8 pm kickoff. We picked up beer and food in town before meeting Heather, now a senior, at what she proclaimed as the best "tailgate" spot on the entire Syracuse campus – 708 Comstock Avenue. It was the shortest walk to the Dome of any student housing on campus. Three 40-plus year-old guys barged into the downstairs apartment with sub sandwiches, buckets of fried chicken, and cases of beer, ready to pig-out and party before the game. Hearing the commotion, Heather came downstairs to get us. Wrong apartment! Guys lived here, but they weren't in. So instead, we started to set up our "tailgate" on Heather's screened-in deck overlooking Comstock. Evidently though, no one had been there since spring semester. Dust, pollen, and dirt coated the floor and furnishings. Three guys way over college-age ready to feast had to do a little house-cleaning first. The girls didn't have paper towels! Steve and I swept off the deck, and Bernie barged back into the boys' apartment downstairs to get a roll of paper towels to wipe down the table and chairs. We cleaned so we could finally feast on the deck of 708 Comstock.

Eventually, we strolled over to the Carrier Dome nearby to watch the Orangemen's home opener. The Chippewas punted on their first four possessions and the Orangemen capitalized. Troy Nunes threw his third of four TD passes to Quinton Spotwood on a 34-yard pass, and defensive back Will Allen recovered a blocked punt in the end zone for a 31-7 SU lead at the half. Syracuse swamped the Chippewas in the end, 47-7.

Honor thy Father

A few years later, Bernie found out he contributed a little more to Heather's education than he knew of. According to Heather, our tailgate party at 708 Comstock was nothing compared to what she described as "one of the best and biggest parties in SU history" thrown there by her and her roommates right before graduation. She gave credit where credit was due though. Bernie's monetary contribution helped pay for a few kegs, and in his honor, Syracuse University students toasted Bernie Olszyk at the best tailgate spot on the Syracuse campus, 708 Comstock. What an honor!

By the way, Paul, one of the guys who lived downstairs became Bernardo's future son-in-law. And all Bernie took from his apartment was a roll of paper towels!

(57) East Carolina 33 Army 7
Michie Stadium, West Point, NY, October 2, 1999

Try this at your local super market! / Aggies look to Jerry Kill

(58) New Mexico State at Army, October 23, 1999

West Point, New York – Sixteen days after Army's 59-52 overtime win over Louisville, on a brilliant, fall Saturday morning with good friends and football fans Charlie Roberts and Dave Headden, I returned to West Point. Charlie grew up attending many Yale games with his grandfather who lived within walking distance of the Yale Bowl and became an avid Eli fan. As a boy, Dave would reminisce about attending many games at West Point driving up with his dad from his home in Jersey. We headed up the NY State Thruway this morning to meet up with "Slippery Rock" Bob Jones to make up our football foursome. New Mexico State came all the way out from Las Cruces to play the Cadets, so I benefited greatly adding the Aggies to my growing list of teams seen.

With two cars loaded with food, grills, and coolers of beer, we exited before the first toll on the Thruway to take Route 6 East to West Point's Stony Lonesome Gate, the back entrance to the huge, historic college campus/military base. At West Point, you never know where you'll end up parking for an Army football game. Once you enter the military reservation patrolled and directed by Military Police, they direct us civilians to general parking wherever the flow of traffic takes you. For Generals, especially West Point grads, they park where they want to. For us, today's parking space turned out to be one of the most unique and memorable of all locations parked in at any football game.

As we entered the Stony Lonesome Gate, traffic just crawled along. I feared it would take us forever to get to a parking space to start tailgating. I was sure that they were going to direct us all the way out to the farthest reaches of tailgating lots down along the river by the water treatment plant. I'd parked there several times before. We'd have to unpack, eat fast, re-pack, and walk to a bus to get to the game on time. The bus might even get caught in traffic—been there, done that!

To my surprise, an MP in front of me suddenly directed me to turn my car with his very military-like signal to take an immediate left. I made sure he directed Bob to follow me into the same lot that looked like a busy, local super market. Sure enough, we ended up in the middle of the West Point Post Exchange (PX) parking lot. The PX is the military equivalent to your friendly neighborhood supermarket.

We unloaded chairs, coolers, grills, a table, and food into an adjacent parking space. Army wives unloaded and loaded kids and groceries into cars bound to and from home. We had the radio blasting as we tailgated. Try drinking beer and grilling burgers at 10 a.m. some Saturday morning at your local supermarket among women pushing shopping carts and carrying grocery bags with kids in tow. See how quickly you're appreciated.

"Come on down! Tailgate in our super market parking lot!"

I can imagine a few irate homemakers in over-sized SUVs challenging for a convenient parking space filled with coolers, a table, and chairs on a crowded Saturday morning. Other guys might join you for a few early morning cocktails. That is until their wives or more likely the local cops show up. The beauty of this, however, was that the military cops directed us here! The experience was surreal. We cooked out and drank beers and Bloody Mary's as families passed us to do their grocery shopping. I can hear St. Laurie complaining already if she ever witnessed this at our local super market! On the other hand, she'd probably laugh, shake her head, and realize the people tailgating were friends of ours. The entire town would be hanging out eventually. To get ready for the game, we put our stuff away. We caught our school bus alongside the PX for the climb up the steep hill to Michie Stadium.

Army keeps rolling along

Army's record-setting Michael Wallace scored from six yards out to open the second period. The Cadets again appeared unstoppable. The offense performed a repeat of the first half of their win against Louisville. Omari Thompson's 72-yard run gave Army a 28-6 lead by halftime. State put up two field goals and a touchdown after intermission, but Army scored last on Calvin Smith's 25-yard burst in the fourth. The Cadets nailed the Aggies with their fourth loss of the season, 35-18.

After the game, we went back for a few more beers back in the PX parking lot. The store was now closed. Only a few other cars remained for post-game cook-outs. I think back to that day when we had the grill going and drank alcohol in the super market parking lot. Only at West Point could we ever savor such a tailgate experience. Where else would local law enforcement direct you to have a tailgate party with adult beverages in a super market parking lot? Try this at your local supermarket—I dare you! By the way, the PX no longer exists in that location at West Point.

Aggies pin future to hard-charging Jerry Kill

Las Cruces, New Mexico - Fast Forward to some New Mexico State game in the future: New Mexico State football has two things going well for it in the future. The hire of revived Head Coach Jerry Kill, and entry into ConferenceUSA. Jerry Kill has had past, but interrupted, success as a head coach due to epileptic seizures. He suffered from kidney cancer, now in remission. Over his career, seizures continued to impact the gutsy coach's presence.

Since 1994, despite missing five and a half seasons to battle health issues, he sports an overall record of 165-110. Coaching stints at the FBS level include Northern Illinois and Minnesota. As reported previously in 2015, I saw his Golden Gophers fall to Missouri in the Buffalo Wild Wings Citrus

Bowl, 33-17. He had returned from health-related issues that relegated him to the press box in the second half of the previous season. His team went 8-5, 6-3 to earn him Big Ten Coach of the Year honors. After a 4-3 start in 2016, he retired to address his health issues once again.

In 2022, Kill took over the New Mexico State program that totaled seven wins over the previous three seasons. He led them to a 7-6 record albeit two wins came over FCS programs. The NCAA granted the Aggies a waiver to play in the Quick Lane Bowl. One of the two FCS games played replaced a cancellation by San Jose State. They went on to defeat Bowling Green, 24-19.

Note here: The Quick Lane could not come up with another qualified FBS team with an acceptable record. I don't blame Jerry Kill for requesting a waiver to play. On the other hand, with only four FBS wins, why couldn't the NCAA reach out to invite James Madison to go to this bowl? They finished 8-3, won the Sun Belt East, and the only reason they didn't participate was because the NCAA said they're not eligible in their first year of FBS competition. To start with, why is this even a rule? Is there any brain power actually at the top of the NCAA to consider a more deserving team here? Secondly, what precluded James Madison University from requesting a waiver? Maybe they did, but why not award that to them?

The other good thing happening to Aggie football, NMSU moves on from independent college football status to compete in Conference USA. It gives the Aggies some stability in scheduling and an opportunity to win a conference championship. Over the next few years, I will get to see them play one of several teams within my local range among some other C-USA members. No longer will the Aggies have to look to fill a complement of home dates while overflowing with options to play top competition for pay-outs on the road.

I look forward to seeing this team play and develop under the grit and determination of Jerry Kill. I'll also continue to watch for opportunities to see games at Aggie Memorial Stadium in Las Cruces. My hope is to schedule that with a UTEP game about 50 miles away on the same weekend when convenient. New Mexico in Albuquerque offers potential 225 miles away.

I've seen games in 37 states and Washington, DC. I'd like to add New Mexico. Note to St. Laurie add this trip to her Bucket List!

Watch a Blow-out, Fix a Flat / At West Point, Who'll Stop the Rain?

(59) Louisiana Tech at Penn State, September 9, 2000

State College, Pennsylvania - Before the 2000 season, a review of my personal history showed that I had seen 58 of the 114 teams in 1-A football play. This season finally started my first concerted effort to kick off my goal to "see 'em all!" I identified eight teams as possibilities to see play at campuses within driving distance in 2000. In previous years as mentioned, I reviewed the Penn State home schedule with John to determine which games I'd prefer to see in State College. My priorities had been to see good games and balance them with lesser games. Now "The Goal" became my new focus. The Nittany Lions' home schedule wasn't particularly enticing before the 2000 season began. However, I decided that the Louisiana Tech Bulldogs and the Fighting Illini would be added as new teams for my revised priorities.

Tech appeared first between the two. They scored first following a Penn State fumble on Brian Stallworth's 10-yard pass to Sean Cangelosi for a quick 7-0 lead against 0-2 PSU. That was it for the Bulldogs. Rashard Casey followed Larry Johnson's 65-yard return with a five-yard scoring pass to Eric McCoo. James Boyd returned a Tech fumble for a six-yard score. McCoo scored again on a 41-yard jaunt. Omar Easy blocked a Bulldog punt, and Casey threw a 10-yard score to Tony Stewart. The game got uglier for Tech. Casey tied Tony Sacca's five-touchdown pass record against Georgia Tech I attended in 1991. At halftime, State led 43-7. Penn State sent the Bulldogs to the doghouse, pounding them, 67-6.

The heat was on!

I broke tradition with this one: with a 43-7 halftime score, a despondent wife, a seven-year-old girl, and a five-year-old boy on a hot, stifling, sun-blazed afternoon, we bailed early and headed back to the hotel swimming pool. Based on what they put me through watching such a lop-sided contest, my obligation to add LA Tech was fulfilled!

The "fun" didn't end before we left though. Upon return to our mini-van in the hilly, grass parking lot, the right rear tire was flat. How appropriate to fix a flat after witnessing such a blow-out! Saint Laurie and the kids sat drinking juices and eating snacks while they watched me change the tire. Watching me change a flat outside the stadium was definitely much more entertaining to them than watching the blow-out they had just witnessed inside Beaver Stadium! To achieve my new Goal, sometimes I had to watch the bad play bad.

Pouring it on again at West Point

West Point, New York - Fast Forward to Louisiana Tech at Army, 2008: In the only other LA Tech game attended, Charlie Roberts and I sat in a cold, downpour in Michie Stadium from kickoff to final whistle. We sat with our backs to the wall in the last row of the visitors' side that provided some blockage of the elements. Both teams came in struggling – Army at 2-5 and Tech at 3-3. The weather added to the struggle that day, more for the Bulldogs than for the Cadets. The Cadet defense thrived on the slippery, wet turf. They sacked LT five times and tallied six rushing losses holding the ground game to 68 yards. Meantime, Army lost three fumbles and threw an interception. Running back Ian Smith scored first for Army on a one-yard run to start. Following an Army fumble in the third, Louisiana Tech's RP Stuart finished a 34-yard drive with a two-yard run. In the final period, Cadet Smith caught a two-yard pass from Chip Bowden for the 14-7 lead with ten minutes remaining to finalize that final score.

Charlie and I remained through the cold, wet end reverting to my original, hardline tradition. I couldn't leave a Bulldog contest early again because of weather. To the Bulldogs' credit, they kept it close this time. For Army, this turned out to be the final win of their 2008 season finishing 3-9. LA Tech on the other hand, returned to conference play in the Western Athletic and reeled off four straight wins to finish at 7-5. They even went on to the Independence Bowl in Shreveport close to their campus to defeat Northern Illinois, 17-10.

Temple 31 - (60) Bowling Green 14
Franklin Field, Philadelphia, PA, September 16, 2000

Snatched from the Jaws of Defeat! / Memphis vs. Mids

(61) Memphis at Army, September 23, 2000

West Point, New York - Driving to overcome the six-point deficit with 4:50 left, Army's Curtis Zervic lofted a pass toward Bryan Bowdish in the end zone that could have given Army the lead. However, Memphis safety Idrees Bashir swooped in front to snatch the pass from Army's jaws of victory. With 100 yards of unobstructed green turf ahead of him, Bashir raced unscathed for a touchdown - a Michie Stadium record. A late safety for Army made the final score 26-16, in favor of Memphis. Bashir, the future Indianapolis Colt, took the game from pending Memphis defeat to assured victory, making it a memorable play for nephews Matt and Ben, Eric, and me watching it all unfold from Army's Family Fun Zone.

Annapolis, Maryland - Fast Forward to Memphis vs. Navy games in the American Athletic, 2018 and 2021: When Navy joined the American Athletic Conference in 2015, Memphis and the Mids met every season since. Most times, they battled early each season for key conference battles. In the first three seasons, these two each won the AAC West title. In 2018, Memphis led 21-9 based on 78 and 58-yard runs by Darrell Henderson among his 214 rushing yards. The Mids came back though following a fumble recovery and a three and out to add two scores. Quarterback Malcolm Perry zigzagged 19 yards for the first, and his back-up Zach Abey muscled it in from the two. Defensive end Anthony Villalobos sacked Brady White on a fourth down to seal Navy's victory, 22-21. Navy mustered only three wins that season, but Memphis finished 5-3 in the AAC, 8-5 overall, to become champions of the AAC West once again.

Memphis Tiger secondary breaks up a pass vs. Navy in 2018.

Mids and Memphis continue Match-ups to Mix it up

Memphis, Tennessee – Fast forward to Navy at Memphis, 2021: With our new digs in Tennessee, St. Laurie and I traveled to Memphis for a Thursday night game when the Mids visited the Tigers. We met Rick Selak my old Auburn friend for lunch, and then Laurie and I visited Graceland. There, we followed GPS and got called back out by Security for driving into Elvis's actual driveway where he used to ride his go-carts seen in pictures at his museum later. Memphis speed on both sides of the football destroyed Navy that evening. Long passes by quarterback Seth Henigan set up scores. Memphis kayoed Navy, 35-17.

With some new members joining the AAC, there will be options annually to see Navy play at Memphis, Charlotte, or UA-Birmingham. The latter two will easily be new FBS venues to add.

Not your Father's Homecoming / Breakdown in long-distance communications?

(62) Illinois at Penn State, October 21, 2000

State College, Pennsylvania - Despite the announced sell-out of 96,475, the alumni and students stayed away in droves. College football, unlike the pros, does not deduct "no-shows" from their announced attendance.[1] Who could blame the alum or students for not showing up at this one? People wandered parking lots with stacks of tickets available for sale. Never saw this ever before a game at Beaver Stadium. Empty seats abounded in the expanding stadium. Homecoming co-founder W. Elmer Ekblaw of Illinois envisioned the homecoming football game as a festivity where students and alumni "could come into closer touch with one another."[2] Penn Staters must have found some other places away from the game to gather this season.

This wasn't a typically good Penn State football team. This was not big brothers' typical Penn State Homecoming, never mind fathers' or grandfathers! Averaging 265.1 yards per game on total offense, the Nittany Lions ranked 105th out of 114 IA teams. However, those that did refrain from using their Beaver Stadium Homecoming ticket that day could not have imagined what they would miss—on one particular play any way.

The Lions led 14-10 at halftime. PSU (2-5) played its best football of the year and led 32-25 with just under six minutes left. What happened next was a play for the ages. After completing a 36-yard pass for a first down to the Illinois 39, Penn State quarterback Rashard Casey started to roll to his right looking to option the ball back. When the defensive end positioned himself to thwart a pitch-out, Casey completely reversed field. He faded back deeper while running all the way back to the near sideline. It looked like he would step out of bounds.

Avoiding what looked assuredly like a big loss, Casey escaped two would-be tacklers near the sideline and reversed back across to the far side of the field once again. However, he found a seam and turned up field around right end at the original line of scrimmage. He raced up field for a dazzling 39-yard touchdown run.

He ran three times that distance on that play for the final score of the game. For him it was a long home-coming via the scenic route! The 39-25 win gave Joe Paterno win No. 320 for his long career, putting him in sole possession of second place in all-time collegiate wins. Now one ahead of the legendary Glenn Scobey "Pop" Warner, he trailed now only three behind Alabama's Paul "Bear" Bryant.

History of Homecoming

Further fun Homecoming facts: Illinois students Clarence Foss Williams, class of 1910, and W. Elmer Ekblaw, class of 1912, are credited as the originators of Homecoming. Other schools previously featured alumni games. Bringing back alum to play against the current varsity squads, Homecoming inspired a new goal to gather alumni to attend a game rather than to play against them. The students' money-making proposal included the idea of holding a series of events on campus during the fall. Underclassmen, seniors, and alumni could all gather without all the distractions present during the typical, commencement week activities.

The first Homecoming took place on October 15, 1910 when Illinois' rival, the Maroons of the University of Chicago under Amos Alonzo Stagg, came to town. Ekblaw, also chief reporter for the campus newspaper, *The Daily Illini*, predicted "a particularly and distinctively Illinois institution which if successful will without doubt be followed by other universities."[3]

Mr. Ekblaw was a man with great foresight at such a young age.

Whatever happened to smoke signals and fax machines?

State College, PA - Fast forward to Illinois at Penn State, 2013: As chronicled previously, next time I saw the Illini play they fell to Ohio State during a downpour in 2009 at Columbus, 30-0. After that, the Illini made another call on Happy Valley for homecoming in 2010. Illini fumbles kept the Lions in this game. Dominance by the visitors became more evident in the second half. After intermission, Penn State punted the first four times it had the ball. The Fighting Illini took advantage of decent field position in its first three possessions. The score was closer than it should have been. Illinois wrapped it up defensively over the last 8:55. They headed home with a 33-13 victory.

In the last game I attended between the two, significant, off-the-field turmoil added to the intensity on the field. In 2012 when sanctions due to the Sandusky Scandal were brought against Penn State, the NCAA allowed PSU players to transfer without any penalties requiring them to sit out. Illinois Head Coach Tim Beckman blatantly took advantage of the opportunity. He sent six coaches to the Lasch Football Building parking lot to recruit available PSU players in July.[4] As can be imagined, the appearances of Illini coaches on the State College campus with transfer forms and briefcases did not sit well with the Penn State student body nor Lion Coach Bill O'Brien, in particular.

In this year's gridiron battle, the ramshackle Nittany Lions came up with 201 rushing yards from running back Bill Belton. The Illini had overtaken the Lions' early 14-0 lead by three points with 5:30 remaining on a pass from Nathan Scheelhaase to Josh Ferguson. With 41 seconds to play, State's Sam Ficken booted a 35-yard field goal to send the game into OT. Christian Hackenberg connected with Kyle Carter for a 15-yard scoring strike in the end zone. On the Illini's subsequent play, Safety Ryan Keiser picked off a tipped Scheelhaase pass to seal the Penn State win, 24-17.

Among Big Ten venues, I only have four left to visit. Champaign, Illinois, home of the Illini, now withing a day's striking distance, is an easy addition to my Bucket List.

[1] Nels Popp, Jason Simmons, Stephen L. Shapiro, and Nick Wantanabe, "Predicting Ticket Holder No-Shows: Examining Differences Between Reported and Actual Attendance at College Football Games," fitpublishing.com. March 23, 2023.

[2] University Archives' Student Life and Culture Archival Program, "Origin of the University of Illinois Homecoming," http://www.library.csi.cuny.edu/dept/history/lavender/footnote.hmtl, (2005)

[3] Ibid

[4] Anonymous, CBS News Chicago. "Illinois Coaches Head to Penn State Campus to Recruit Players". July 25, 2012.

Rockets Sink Navy

(63) Toledo at Navy, October 28, 2000

Annapolis, Maryland - The Toledo Rockets came in battle-tested sporting a 6-1 record under Head Coach Gary Pinkel. I didn't anticipate a thrilling last-minute victory by either team at Navy-Marine Corps Stadium. Surprisingly, Navy (0-7) led 14-0 before the Rockets even had the ball! They held on to a 14-13 halftime lead.

Navy coach Charlie Weatherbie outsmarted himself as his team attempted an onside kick into the wind to start the second half. Starting at Navy's 45, Tavares Bolden scored on a five-yard run and on the two-point conversion. The Rocket defense and strong winds played havoc with the Mids in the third period. Navy's next punt got held up by the wind. Bolden took advantage with the wind at his back to pass 19 yards to Dontl Greene for Toledo's next score. The wind held Navy's next punt up for only 24 yards. Three plays later, Chester Taylor broke off an 18-yard run finalizing the score, 35-14, for the Toledo win.

Win or lose, Annapolis is a great town for a family weekend. We savored a great seafood dinner downtown that evening, and spent Sunday morning touring the Yard after services at the Naval Academy Chapel. Chesapeake Bay is picturesque. Preble Hall is my favorite museum anywhere. It depicts the history of the U.S. Navy starting with John Paul Jones right up until today. Much of the history evolves around Navy grads who walked the same grounds where visitors stroll.

ROCKETS SINK NAVY

Kids with Mids - future Chief Petty Officer Eric, Bill XXVIII and Alex pose with Midshipman Goat Handlers before Toledo-Navy game in 2000.

Advance to the Big-time! / UConn's Man Dan / Portal traps

(64) Middle Tennessee at (65) Connecticut, November 4, 2000

Storrs, Connecticut - In 2000, Division I-A football welcomed several new programs into the fold. I'd seen the UConn Huskies play games since 1974 against the likes of Navy, Yale, Lehigh, Rhode Island, and Hampton when they played at the I-AA level. Now I ventured to see them play as newcomers to I-A football against another team new to my eyes and to I-A football - the Middle Tennessee State Blue Raiders. MTSU had also jumped into the realm of "big-time" football this season albeit not with the momentum and fanfare of the Connecticut program.

Connecticut had a national reputation as a basketball power house, and the Big East invited its football program to join in a few years as well. The Blue Raiders would eventually join the fledging Sun Belt Conference. I took 10-year-old nephew Matt Wylie with me to add these two debutantes to The Goal. We drove three hours for what I promised him should be a fairly competitive football game. Wrong!

By halftime, the Huskies had lost their bark and bite to trail by a stunning score of 52-7! Blue Raider Dwone Hicks gained 184 rushing yards and scored four touchdowns on only 17 carries. I predicted stardom for him on Sundays. MTSU's Mel Counts completed 17 of 21 passes for 221 yards and a score. Cornerback Kareem Bland returned an interception 70 yards for a first-half score. In short, the Raiders came to Storrs and made the

ADVANCE TO THE BIG-TIME! / UCONN'S MAN DAN / PORTAL TRAPS

UConn Huskies look like dog dirt.

You know my rule now no matter what the score, but how do you keep a 10-year-old interested in a game while hordes of "die-hards" leave the home team behind getting slaughtered, 52-7, at the half? This didn't faze my 10-year-old guinea pig at all. I brought him to experiment before I'd take Eric to games when he got older. Turned out Matt was much more immune to bad games than his cousin Eric would ever be. He enjoyed the surroundings and fired off question after question after question. He became very preoccupied with French Fries served in a large, dog bowl-type dish – something a real Husky could eat from. Despite Middle Tennessee mercifully posting the final at 66-17, Matt never begged me to leave. On the flip side, I started to wonder why I ever came up with this rule. Believe me, it would be totally different with Eric.

Was this the right move for UConn? Rutgers, in a state more respected for its home-grown football talent, had not even come close to cracking the top of Big East football after ten years of conference play and twenty years at the I-A level. "If only we can keep the best players in New Jersey …" What made UConn think that it could fare any better?

The Huskies' answer was right in front of us

"There he is!" said one fan to another sitting near us as the remaining stragglers began to saunter away from the large, concrete bleacher known as Memorial Stadium. He pointed to some tall, lanky kid in a navy blue and white, Shelton (Connecticut) High School varsity jacket.

"I hear he's probably going to Purdue," remarked the guy next to him. Matt and I didn't know we were witnessing the prescription UConn football ordered to advance into big-time football. The kid was a highly-sought recruit named Dan Orlovsky. Now, you see him on television as an NFL analyst on ESPN with Steve Levy and Louis Riddick, and as a college game analyst more than anyone could have imagined back in 2000. Regarding Dwone Hicks, he never made it to the next level. Wrong again on my part!

Season highlight played well before the Fiesta Bowl

Glendale, Arizona - Fast forward to UConn vs. Oklahoma in the Fiesta Bowl, 2010: Once Dan Orlovsky set up under center for the Huskies, they became an annual fixture on my schedule. They not only got better, but their I-A status as an Independent provided more opportunities to see new teams to add to my schedule like Utah State, Kent State and Akron. At least, UCONN started to improve. The first three years Orlovsky started from 2001-2003, as an Independent football program, the Huskies won two, six, and nine games each year. In his senior season when UConn joined the Big East, they won eight including their first bowl bid defeating Toledo in the Motor City Bowl.

After Orlovsky graduated in 2005 and got drafted by the Detroit Lions, Head Coach Randy Edsall continued to coach Connecticut through 2010. The Huskies won only five games in each of the first two seasons following Orlovsky's graduation. They rebounded though after those two with four straight bowl seasons. In 2010, they won the Big East. Their key win came against West Virginia.

I attended this Friday night contest on October 29 after returning from a business trip the night before from Germany. A sales rep I dealt with at that time who graduated from West Virginia happened to be in town for it. I agreed to join up before my trip. Great timing! For me, not so much for him.

The Mountaineers fumbled the ball away four times to the Huskies. The player of the game for UConn (3-4, 0-2) was linebacker Sio Moore. Among his 17 tackles, he caused two fumbles and recovered two. Regulation ended with the score tied, 13-13. West Virginia (5-2, 1-1) went on offense in overtime first. At the one, the Mountaineers fumbled and Husky linebacker Lawrence Wilson recovered. With a 27-yard field goal, Dave Teggart converted his third of the night to give the Huskies a 16-13 win. This victory turned out to be the tie-breaker that got them to the Fiesta Bowl as the Big East representative since these two tied for first with two losses each. No one that evening envisioned that this win sealed the Fiesta Bowl bid for the UCONN Huskies.

The result for the Huskies surprised me especially, and somewhat, regretfully. In planning a west coast bowl trip this year with Eric, I came up with the Holiday Bowl in San Diego and the Fiesta in Phoenix. I figured the Fiesta would offer a big game with two powers among the Top Ten at least. I bought two tickets in advance figuring these would be "hot." However, the bowls this season were relegated to conference champs. UCONN finished 8-5 winning their last five Big East games. They won the conference title. This head-to-head win I attended put them up against No. 7 Oklahoma (11-2), Big XII champs. I didn't look forward to seeing unranked 8-5 UConn who I had seen over the years play the No. 7 Sooners. Instant mismatch.

The sparse crowd at Phoenix University Stadium void of Husky fans and only a few Sooner fans indicated total apathy for this match-up. Husky fans probably stayed back in Connecticut focused on their championship men's and women's basketball programs. With 2008 Heisman-winning quarterback Sam Bradford pitching for Oklahoma, the Sooners won easily, 48-20. The Fiesta Bowl did not become the memorable game I had hoped for. More could be said for UConn's highlight win over West Virginia University.

Blue Raiders Beckon

Murfreesboro, Tennessee - Fast forward to Middle Tennessee with season tickets: After my introduction to both new programs back in 2000 following the Blue Raider win, they fell all four times during our common history together. I mentioned their loss at Minnesota in 2017. Since my move to Tennessee, I hoped they'd turn the corner. In 2021, I watched them beaten by Western Kentucky in Bowling Green, 48-21. Despite that, I announced in front of a Blue Raider preseason gathering including Head Coach Rick Stockstill that MTSU would be my adopted Tennessee team.

I admitted to all that Tennessee Orange hurt my eyes experienced when sitting among mass quantities at all their bowl games I attended. As far as Vanderbilt, I could not see following a team that continually lost by a lot of points, more often than not. Happy to hear of my commitment to

Blue Raider football, Master of Ceremonies and MTSU broadcaster Chip Walter proclaimed me as a "Sidewalk Alum." MTSU wants more of them!

My commitment didn't lead to a turn-around in my presence - yet. In 2022, I watched them lose to UTSA, 45-30, and to WKU again, 35-17. On the other hand, they finished 8-5, upset Miami (F.) early, won their last three C-USA games, and flew to Hawaii to play in the Aloha Bowl on Christmas Eve. There, they defeated San Diego State, 25-23.

At the 2022 preseason Blue Raider Blitz get-together, Head Coach Rick Stockstill was good enough to answer my questions about the changes regarding NIL and control of the transfer portals. Regarding the NIL, he said, "Recruits are no longer asking about playing time, positions, and classes. Instead, they ask how much money they can make, and they question facilities." As for the transfer portals, he said, "There needs to be a time limit as to when players can transfer." New guidelines came up in the news after the 2022 season.[1]

With my upcoming self-imposed travel limit due to Alex's upcoming wedding, the Blue Raider schedule in nearby Murfreesboro works well in my favor. Going forward, their weekday ConferenceUSA schedule allows me to build up the number of games I can attend. This may enable me to eventually meet or exceed my current record of 27 games attended in 2017. I also look forward to games from where I can get home shortly after, especially after played under the lights on weekday nights.

[1] James Parks, January 12, 2023. "NCAA makes changes to college football transfer portal", CFB-HQ on Fox Nation. Retrieved January 12, 2023.

One Burnt Cookie / Greatest FBS Comeback

(66) Alabama-Birmingham at Army, November 18, 2000

West Point, New York - My friend Les Di Vite's dad had passed away in recent years and my own mother was widowed for the second time eight years earlier. With the Family Fun Zone package at Army, Les and I brought our respective mothers, Barbara and Kathleen—known by her eleven grandchildren as "Grandma Cookie"—to enjoy a little tailgating at an Army game on a cold, sunny, November afternoon. My mother had told me that her first date with my dad was to an Army-Columbia game back in the 50s. Army hosted the University of Alabama-Birmingham Blazers in the first game ever between the two this day. Both were now members of Conference-USA. For the Cadets who had struggled all season long, this was their season's home finale. Alabama-Birmingham (UAB) visited Michie Stadium with a record of 6-4, primping for a bowl bid.

After tailgating in the lot right inside the front gate close to the Thayer Hotel where we enjoyed hot-buttered rum, the four of us bussed up the hill to Michie. Tickets in hands, Les and I passed through our gate well ahead of the two grandmothers who each carried a couple of blankets to place over cold, aluminum bleacher seats. Deep in football conversation with Les, I suddenly heard the blood-curdling cry of *"Stephen!"* I turned quickly to see my mother clutching the blankets against her chest standing next to the security guard. "He's getting fresh with me!"

FIFTY YEARS OF TAILGATE TALES:

The gate attendants, a man and a woman, stood looking at me with hands at their sides. Mrs. Di Vite said nothing. Unlike my mother, I don't have proverbial eyes in back of my head. I didn't know if the guy was really getting fresh with my mother, or if she just took offense that he was searching for bottles in her blankets. As far as I knew, we left our libations back in the car. Would Grandma Cookie??? She always liked her Scotch. I wouldn't put it past her on this cold day, but I don't think so. Security always checked blankets and bags going into Michie. I finally stepped forward and said, "Let's go!" Off we went without any further inspection. She never offered me any small bottles either.

Army (1-8, 1-5 in C-USA) trailed at halftime, 10-7. In the third, one play after the referee warned the Army band to stop playing when UAB had the ball, quarterback Jeff Aaron heaved a 63-yard scoring pass to a wide-open Leron Little to increase the Blazers' lead. UAB took a 24-7 lead in the fourth quarter following a 72-yard interception return by Wes Foss. Seasonal statistics showed that it was the sixth pass intercepted and returned for a pick-six against Army that season – fourth one in the fourth quarter a la Idrees Bashir of Memphis.

After that, I ventured out to the concession stand to get four grilled chicken sandwiches and drinks. There, I learned how environmentally conscientious the Army is. They did not provide lids for the cups, straws for drinks, nor any small trays to carry cups in. What a hassle for one person to carry food back to our seats. I had to go get Les to help me out. When we all hungrily unwrapped aluminum foil from our grilled chicken sandwiches, it turned out two of the chicken sandwiches were burnt!

Grandma Cookie got pretty agitated to say the least. One was hers, of course. She made threatening remarks about the food service at Michie Stadium. She was right. I think she could have used some more hot-buttered rum back at our tailgate. UAB won, 27-7, for its seventh win of the season. Army's record fell to 1-9 with struggling Navy waiting to play in two weeks for their annual rivalry. UAB stayed home during bowl season despite their final record of 7-4.

Fleeting fame

With my well-intentioned Goal now seriously underway thanks to a nice shot in the arm with the addition of eight new teams in the year 2000, I reached out to several media outlets and asked them to check out my new website www.collegefootballfan.com to see how they liked it and to introduce them to my unique Goal. *ESPN The Magazine* caught on and provided their analysis on their page entitled *"The Pulse: The Wired World of Sports"* in their October 2001 edition. Though they submarined my attempt at providing a tailgate party checklist, they admired the fact that I was already more than halfway to my lofty Goal.[1] As heard in the past, any publicity is good publicity.

However, it wasn't until after a few days of gloating over the small article that I noticed the photo of a hamburger bun below. I then noticed what looked like burnt chicken in between. What the...? I laughed my ass off! Of all the events I reported on during the 2000 season, they selected one snippet from one game review. Taken from the Army-UAB game, from which no editor pointed out my poor, late-night grammar, the line probably endeared itself to the publication's adolescent readership. Under a caption entitled "25 words (or less)," it read:

"Two of the four chicken sandwiches were badly burnt, which prompted Grandma Cookie to want to throw [them] back in the concessionaire's face! —A review of the chow at Army's Michie Stadium on collegefootballfan.com." [2]

How many guys have had their mother written about in a national sports publication? Well, I have! The point being made was that despite the beautiful and festive setting West Point offers along with all its traditions on football Saturdays, disorganized parking, congested entry ways, lacking concessionary supplies, and poor food quality took away from the enjoyment of attending an Army football game. I found Grandma Cookie's quotation may have had some influence.

Since then, improvements have been noticed around the stadium, especially regarding the food service. At a game a few years later, I found their hot dogs to be pretty tasty and actually hot. The parking situation still stinks, and tight security slows entry into games. That's a necessity now since 9/11. However, I think someone at West Point might have read Grandma Cookie's comment and did something about it. Ten years and two days since the day of this game, Cookie passed away. With a few friends and family members, she's enjoying better food, her Scotch, and tailgating in a better place now, probably on some beach like she enjoyed on the Gulf Coast of Florida.

Greatest FBS comeback ever

Shreveport, Louisiana - Fast Forward to UAB vs. BYU in the Independence Bowl, 2021: Amazingly as of 2022, the Blazers have been to six straight bowl games. They've won the last three. What makes this most amazing comes from the fact that the school shut down the program in 2014 and 2015 due mainly to perceived financial difficulties and lack of fan support. The move to dissolve UAB football caused an uproar with the avid, abandoned fan base. Factions started donating millions more for support, and releasing documents to contradict administration statements about the lack of financial funding. They also started pushing for changes regarding the University of Alabama System's (UAB) board of trustees. While this continued, the Blazer football program received more financing and media exposure than ever before.[3]

At the behest of rallying supporters, the administration hired a new consulting firm, College Sports Solutions (CSS). It was argued that previous decisions made considered no financial models with Conference USA revenue. UAB weighed staying in C-USA without football, but the conference refused membership without Blazer football. CSS found that keeping or cutting football and other sports offered both advantages and disadvantages.[4]

It seemed though that maintaining them would allow UAB to capitalize off renewed interest in school athletics. A major boost appeared as Birmingham businessmen met with UAB president Ray Watts to offer more financial support for Blazer football. In the past, some of these businessmen had traditionally not been associated with UAB.[5] With a growing economy in the Birmingham area, this seemed like a win-win opportunity for the university and local business alike. Basically, six months after termination, the decision to revive Blazer football came to fruition. Play would begin again in 2017. As they say, it takes a village – great example here.

Adding a new Bowl Venue

Now living in Tennessee, I decided to take a road trip to Shreveport, Louisiana for my first Independence Bowl. UAB came to clash with No. 13 Brigham Young who I'd seen defeat Virginia, 66-49, at home earlier in the season. On a gusty, rainy day in Shreveport, the two battled back and forth. Momentum swings for both teams set the tone. Dewayne McBride rushed for 183 yards and one score for UAB. BYU running back Tyler Allgeier had a second banner day in my presence this season. He tallied 193 yards and three touchdowns.

Blazer quarterback Dylan Tompkins passed for 189 yards, one touchdown, but threw one interception. Subbing for injured starter Jaren Hall who suffered a foot injury in the final game against Southern Cal, the Cougars' Baylor Romney matched Tompkins adequately. In the end, however, the difference came down to a completed pass fumbled by the Cougars' Sam Nacua on a late drive. After that, the Blazers controlled the clock with McBride and Jermaine Brown picking up first downs. BYU utilized its three time-outs. The Blazers ran out the last 3:36 of the game and pulled the upset over the Cougars, 31-28.

For the Blazers, it turned out to be their final victory under UAB Head Coach Bill Clark. He had taken over since 2015 to quickly rebuild this dismantled program into an immediate winner. Back problems halted his career. Assistant Bryan Vincent stepped in to cover to continue his success in 2022.

Enter former NFL quarterback Trent Dilfer to take over as head coach of the UAB program in 2023. His only head coaching experience comes at Lipscomb Academy, a private high school team in Nashville. For UAB, he's hopefully not Gerry Faust nor Todd Dodge who made jumps from coaching high school to FBS programs unsuccessfully. Maybe Dilfer's

NFL pedigree will make a difference for him in recruiting at this level, but we'll wait and see.

[1] "25 Words (or less)," *ESPN The Magazine* (29 October 2001): p 32.

[2] *Ibid*

[3] Jon Solomon. "UAB football is back, reinstatement announcement set for Monday," http://www.cbssports.com/college-football. 1 June 2015.

[4] Ibid

[5] Ibid

Eli's Comin'! So are reviewable plays / The Grove!

(67) Mississippi at Auburn, September 8, 2001

Auburn, Alabama - It had been 16 years since I visited Charlie and Lynda for an Auburn football game down on "the Plains." With his excavating business, C.A. Murren & Sons, booming in the thriving Atlanta market, Charlie had access to some great Auburn seats through his suppliers of heavy construction equipment. C.A. Murren built several venues for the 1996 Olympic Games in Atlanta. In 2001, Charlie IV and Megan now followed the footsteps of their parents along the "Tiger Walk."

Analyzing the Auburn schedule before the season, I checked for SEC teams to add to The Goal. The Tigers hosted Ole Miss and Mississippi State. The Rebels provided the better opportunity to allow me to maximize the number of new teams to see and the best combination of games possible for each weekend. So, I picked the Rebels' invasion of Jordan-Hare Stadium this season not just to add them, but to see quarterback Eli Manning, son of Archie and the younger brother of Peyton, perform. Watching Eli play against Auburn, in case he ever amounted to anything, I figured I could say that I at least attended his SEC debut.

Replayed, but not reviewed

For three quarters in front of a record crowd of 86,063 at Jordan-Hare Stadium, Auburn presented more obstacles than the supposed sophomore sensation could handle. Ole Miss never crossed the 50 on its first ten possessions. Rebel punter Cady Ridgeway didn't help matters much averaging only 32 yards on five punts. Auburn led 13-0 at halftime. In the third, the Tigers scored following an interception of a Manning pass. After that, Eli finally seemed to get the Rebels on the move. They thought they had six when Omar Rayford hauled in a long heave in the end zone, but officials signaled he didn't come down with a foot in the end zone. Instant replays later revealed Rayford caught it inbounds—but replay reviews didn't exist in 2001!

The very next play, Auburn picked off Manning again. Casinious Moore ran it in from 36 yards for his third score of the day. AU held a 27-0 lead. Eli didn't bail out though. He showed signs of leadership guiding Ole Miss back in the fourth to trail, 27-21. Eli could have possibly worked some more magic for a late score, but the Rebels roughed the Tiger punter late in the game and never got the ball back. Auburn preserved a 27-21 victory. Rayford's near-touchdown turned out to be a big play after all. Though Mississippi reeled off five straight victories at the end of the season, a final record of 7-4, 4-4 (SEC) was not enough to earn a bowl bid. Another sign of how times have changed in college football. As anticipated, much more about Eli would be heard during seasons to come.

I had problems getting home from Atlanta to Newark the next day. On September 9, 2001, my Air Tran flight delayed. Then engine problems turned my plane back to Atlanta to arrive home much later than expected. That turned out to be a mere inconvenience compared to what happened to four jetliners leaving Boston and Newark less than 36 hours later. Our world was about to change.

Before and after 9/11

September 15, 2001 was the Saturday of the week that "sports stood still." All college football games were canceled or postponed. My plan to watch California as my 68th team against Rutgers was postponed until the end of the season. After the cowardly events of 9/11, security at all sporting events took on new measures as we all became more wary when gathering in large crowds.

Eerily, I recalled the Virginia Tech-Rutgers game I attended with a group of friends in 1999. We saw Michael Vick and the Hokies defeat Rutgers that night 58-20 on their way to the national championship game. At one point though, a small, white, propeller plane with ID numbers blacked out underneath the wings and along the fuselage buzzed the stadium from behind us. Several minutes later, it returned from the opposite direction. From where I sat with ten guys who got together for this one, the plane looked like it was heading right down toward us. Thankfully, it pulled up suddenly and flew straight overhead never to return again! Not until after the game did any of the other guys admit that they felt the same way I did - we were all ready to bail!

The proximity to New York City, the covered-up numbers, the threat to buzz a venue with a good-sized crowd made me think about it again after 9/11. I never read anything about it in the papers the following day, but I still remembered it. I'll never forget how my heart raced as the plane approached us head-on! In retrospect, I still think it was one of those *bastards* from the Twin Towers attacks on some kind of a practice run. Later, it was reported the murderers practiced in similar planes at the municipal airport in Venice, Florida where Grandma Cookie had retired.

Games resumed the weekend of September 22-23. Everything carried into a stadium was inspected thoroughly. At the UMass-Delaware game I attended, our country demonstrated a renewed spirit of cohesiveness and patriotism. The Fighting Blue Hen football team raced on to the field at Delaware Stadium with three American flags in the lead. Crowds paid tribute to those who perished in the World Trade Center attack. Everyone prayed. Travel and large gatherings remained under close scrutiny probably will be forever due to the attacks of 9/11. Proudly, we still haven't given in to the evil that terrorism brought to our country that day.

The Grove

Oxford, MS - Fast forward to LSU at Ole Miss in The Grove, 2013: I move on to lighter times in the future regarding the Ole Miss Rebels. At the 2012 ArmyNavy game, a group of us tailgating together discussed opportunities the following season to meet up somewhere that none of us had ever attended a game before. We stayed in touch the next few months and all agreed that a game at Ole Miss in Oxford, Mississippi was a must-see. The Grove outside Vaught-Hemingway Stadium on the Ole Miss campus ranked high on the priority list for all. *"Hotty Toddy, Gosh Almighty!"* We came up with a plan.

No doubt, back on the Bucket List!

About ten of us from all over the country came away looking for a great time. One drawback in Oxford though, it lacks hotel space. We rented a town home for the weekend that basically cost each of us a monthly mortgage payment, and that's pretty steep in New Jersey. One of the guys, however, came up with a contact through another friend who had season tickets for the Rebels. Better yet, he had a reserved spot in The Grove.

The night before the game, we wandered the square in Oxford and came up with some great BBQ, of course. At a local bar with a band, we ended up partying most of the night with some nice-looking Ole Miss women. Despite some of us with kids in college, the pretty ladies and us just had a great time dancing to the music. Next morning, after partaking of Bloody Mary's for breakfast, we carried cases of beer and shopping bags of snacks to find our pre-game tailgate arrangement. Joe Rogers, a Pennsylvania guy but an LSU fan who proudly wore his Bayou Bengal ball cap amongst us, was the only one who got stopped and searched when we entered The Grove.

Upon meeting our host and all his friends and family at their tailgate site, we couldn't have had a nicer bunch of people to party with. They, like many others with season tickets had reserved tailgate spaces. The night before, Ole Miss students they hire come in and set up their canopies, tables, chairs, grills, televisions, music systems, kitchen sinks, and whatever else they stored locally. All the electronics were hooked up and ready to go. All the revelers brought in food and snacks including decorated baked goods specially made for the day's contest. As we learned later wandering around the Grove, Mississippi fans were very hospitable to display their set ups, their Ole Miss decorations, and share some good talk along with food and even drink, possibly. Of course, all are invited to chant along with them in their traditional Ole Miss cheer:

Are You Ready?
Hell Yeah! Damn Right!
Hotty Toddy, Gosh Almighty,
Who The Hell Are We? Hey!
Flim Flam, Bim Bam
Ole Miss by Damn!

We hoisted a lot of toasts. We met other people like us from all over, even a few Penn State fans, who wandered around The Grove taking in the full atmosphere. I have photos toasting with the other guys, pictures with Ole Miss Cheerleaders ("Hide the beer, please!"), and even the LSU Tiger mascot. I wondered how difficult it was for him to get in compared to Joe with just the LSU hat on. And I have to say, like Juniata roommate Pat Daly and I noted on our Southern swing years ago returning from Mardi Gras through Mississippi, there were a lot of very pretty women at The Grove - of all ages.

Couldn't ask for more, but we got it!

Oh, and by the way, a football game started. Not all of us who came together today sat together. Once inside, I was on my own. No problem. Today, Ole Miss (3-3,1-3) hosted No. 6 LSU (6-1, 3-1). Surprisingly, the Rebels charged out to a 17-0 lead they held into the third period. The defense picked off three Zach Mettenberger passes in the first half. The Tigers finally put together a scoring drive of 61 yards taking it in from the one. A Rebel fumble on their next drive gave LSU possession on their 49. The Tigers drove again for a three-yard touchdown to close the score, 17-14. Ole Miss responded late in the quarter with a 26-yard run to extend their lead.

In the final period, LSU punted but the Ole Miss returner fumbled it away. The Tigers now had the ball at the Rebel 13-yard line. Stops and penalties pushed the Tigers back. They settled for a Colby Delahoussaye 41-yard field goal. The Rebels looked to retaliate going down to the Tiger eight-yard line for an Andrew Ritter field goal attempt. However, the Tigers blocked it. They took over at their 20. With 3:19 left to play, Mettenberger connected with Jarvis Landry for a four-yard pass to tie the score, 24-24. Quarterback Bo Wallace started his Mississippians from their 15. They drove all the way to the LSU 24. With two second left, Ritter put it up as the ball just made it inside the right upright for the Rebels upset victory, 27-24. Great game!

Hey! Where'd everybody go?

One revelation to pass on after a game here: The Grove we partied in was entirely dismantled by the time the game was over. Night had already fallen. Crews of students worked their way through piles of equipment to be stored away. Nothing was recognizable. No landmarks of anything familiar that existed before the game remained. The Ole Miss students probably had parties to attend elsewhere and wanted to high-tail it out of there. I had no way of knowing how to get back to the place we stayed at. I discovered I wasn't alone in this boat.

In my meandering, I found a distraught Joe Rogers sitting on a door step of some academic building nearby. Head in his hands from both drinking and his Tigers losing, we were both relieved to find one another. With combined guesswork, we eventually pieced together where we were and how to get back. A lesson to pass on after a game at The Grove.

I saw Head Coach Hugh Freeze's Ole Miss team play again later that season. I met up with Joe and his Pennsylvania buddy Steve Dawson at the Music City in late December. Ole Miss (7-5) came to town to meet Georgia Tech (7-5) under Paul Johnson. It was a miserable, rainy day, but this was one of a few games I'd gotten a press pass for. In addition to the dryness of the press box, I also had a complimentary lunch on the showboat, General Jackson, down the Cumberland River. So, I ate and drank and at least stayed dry on board.

Like the LSU game, Ole Miss took a 23-7 lead into the four quarter. Then a Tech run of 72 yards and a field goal put them back in striking range, 23-17. Ole Miss added a safety on a 14-yard loss by Tech to win it, 25-17. OK, already been to an Ole Miss game and The Grove, but his is definitely a do-over to include on my Bucket List!

Making new acquaintances with Ole Miss cheerleaders at The Grove in 2013! Hotty Toddy, Gosh Almighty! A Bucket List Do-Over!

A Whole, New World

(68) Washington at (69) UCLA, October 13, 2001

Pasadena, California - I booked a trip to Los Angeles in the spring of 2001 in anticipation of a great game between two teams out west. Despite trepidations now due to 9/11, I still carried out my plan to fly from Newark to LAX one month later to add two missing PAC-10 teams to my Goal—undefeated Washington visiting undefeated UCLA. My brother Chris and friends Jim Lewis and Jim Buckley comprised a foursome for my *Left Coast Tour*.

This would be my first flying experience since the attacks of 9/11. The flight from Newark to Los Angeles turned out to be an awakening to a whole, new world. The experience indicated the world undergoing some significant and scary changes.

Screening procedures to get to the plane became understandably more intense and comprehensive than ever before. I left for the airport early to compensate for two additional hours of processing. Security personnel checked IDs and scanned everyone with electronic wands from head to foot. They opened each citizens' luggage and searched, sometimes exposing travelers' under-garments for all to see. Guards selected some customers to go through more intense scrutiny than others. The airport atmosphere was tense. Pre-screening took longer than prior to 9/11. Travelers felt on edge. Reports indicated armed U.S. Air Marshals would be aboard certain planes. You eyed other people wondering if they were bad guys. Once through security, I waited in a chair near the gate—a little more relaxed now that I'd gotten through all the new, necessary, but nerve-wracking rigmarole.

"Whose bag is this?" yelled a security agent to no one in particular right in front of me. I and four others looked up from what we were reading, looked at one another, shrugged shoulders, and admitted it belonged to none of us. One guy said he saw some woman drop it off and then walk down to the other end of the terminal.

Since no one claimed it, the guard made a quick call out on a hand-held radio. Another guard with a cart showed up in a New York minute. Security took no chances. They carefully loaded the bag on the cart and whisked it away. How could anyone be so stupid in light of what the country was trying to recover from? Or were terrorists still among us? You could feel the tension. Boarding passes and picture IDs had to be shown again to board and slowed the process.

Could this trip get any worse?

I took my window seat somewhat drained from the new boarding process. I thought I could relax a little now aboard, but then an airline rep came through the cabin looking for a particular passenger. No one responded. This individual checked luggage and had a ticket, but never came aboard. The person's luggage made it on board though! We sat at the gate an extra twenty minutes while airline personnel rummaged through the cargo hold to find and remove the unaccompanied bags. I wondered if things like this always happened before and just weren't as scrutinized, or were people who hated us still trying to get us. I would be glad when the luggage was unloaded. On the right side of the L-1011, happily I had three seats all to myself.

I thought that I could actually take a nap on this flight, something I can rarely do on a plane, but I was ready to nod. However, the intensity of my flight ratcheted up suddenly and more than a notch or two. A late passenger arrived, and they let him on board. He headed right toward my row. Not only was he of Middle Eastern descent, he wore a turban! Sure enough, he took the aisle seat in my row. I couldn't sleep now! I'd have to keep my eye on this guy the entire five-hour plus flight. *No rest for the weary*. Seriously, how could I relax? He could be the nicest, most innocent guy in the world, but who knew? For me, the flight turned out to be even more intense after getting through airport security. This put me on edge to say the least!

What really miffed me was that this guy fell asleep shortly after take-off, and I couldn't. The stewardesses brought out meals. At least I could eat. When I got served though, I was shocked! They provided me with a stainless-steel fork—not plastic! Knives, metals, or potential weapons of any kind were prohibited from being brought on board, but here they were providing anyone with a potential weapon right from the plane's galley. When he finally awoke from his long, pleasant slumber, the stewardess asked him if he would like some dinner. My adrenaline perked up. I was on my guard if this guy got hold of some real tableware. Thankfully, I evidently wasn't the only one watching. When they served him, he got plastic! What a relief. I felt a little better.

A few hours later on this cross-country flight, I had to get up, cross in front of the man sitting in my aisle, and make my way to the men's room. When I came back though, he wasn't in his seat! He sat in mine – looking out over the Rockies. This was getting to be too much. What a crappy flight. I sat in his aisle seat keeping my eye on him. He finally noticed that I had returned. He tried to make nice conversation, but instead, he reinforced my suspicions even more.

Everything he said seemed friendly and tolerable until he gazed out over the Rockies again and said, "I'd like to drive over those someday, *if* I ever come back." - "If" with emphasis! What the *hell* was that supposed to mean? *If?* Was this guy busting my chops, or was he actually part of some terrorist plot? Was I just on edge, or did he really mean he'd enjoy exploring the country to enjoy the sights? I sometimes think about doing that, too. It was the way this guy said it though. I didn't know what to think. We finally exchanged seats. I watched him out of the corner of my eye. I continued to keep my guard up making sure everyone aboard arrived safely. What a relief to finally get off that plane!

I could've kissed the ground

Because of airport security, my brother could not pick me up at LAX. Only commercial shuttles and taxis were allowed to pick up passengers. So, we planned for or me to take a *Super Shuttle* van to a hotel near his home. I relaxed a little more in the shuttle after my ordeal during the flight. I noted a high school game being played on the way through Long Beach. The crowd danced in celebration at the top of a small stadium. It got my mind off of that flight. It was good to be on the ground again. The ordeal made me appreciate even more the things we take for granted in this country - things like travel, visiting friends, family, different places, and enjoying sports! Sometimes we just don't realize how good we have it.

I stayed at my brother's that night and had dinner with him, his wife Jill, a UCLA grad, and their kids Emily and Nick. With Chris, I planned to attend the big showdown the next day along with the Emmy-award winning Jim Lewis and his fellow pundit Jim Buckley. Buckley, like Lewis, was a writer, but for *Sports Illustrated* among other publications. We had the pleasure of meeting when he came to several of my big tailgate parties in the Meadowlands when both Jim's lived and worked in New York City. A Cal grad, Jim Buckley now lived and worked back in his native California. He drove from Santa Barbara for the day.

Unlike previous games we attended together at Giants Stadium, this one would not be preceded by a big tailgate party. Chris coached his daughter Emily's soccer game that morning. Though we finally arrived for the game shortly before kickoff, our timing could not have been better for parking. We were directed through and around Rose Bowl parking lots to a space in the first parking row adjacent to the famous stadium's north end. We literally parked in its shadows.

Too bad we didn't have a tailgate plan. But if we did, we probably would have arrived earlier and not landed in such prime California real estate. We had to go through two security check points on long lines before entering the stadium. We took seats in the southwest corner of the end zone a few seats to the left of an ABC-TV camera platform. This game was so big that

Keith Jackson sat in the broadcast booth. Two PAC-10 powers met with 4-0 records - No. 7 UCLA and No. 10 Washington.

Foster, Fantastic!

The Bruins offense blemished the Huskies' defensive reputation very quickly when running back DeShaun Foster put Washington's Wondame Davis flat on his back on the way to a quick 7-0 lead. Another Foster touchdown and a fumble-return gave UCLA a 21-0 lead with just over two minutes remaining in the first period. The game did not turn out competitive as hoped for. Washington finally got a late first-half score. Taylor Barton subbed for Washington's injured starting quarterback, Cody Pickett.

To start the second half, Foster put his team back on track on the first play from scrimmage. He raced 64 yards before getting tackled at the Washington one. He scored from there. His most exciting jaunt of the game was yet to come. In the fourth, right below us from his 8-yard line late, he burst through the line down the left sideline, and then veered steadily to his right, outracing Husky defenders all the way to the far-right corner of the end zone for a 92-yard touchdown. Exhausted, he latched on to a sideline security guard until his teammates finally caught up with him.

For Foster, it was a long, exhilarating, exhausting run on that hot sunny, Southern California day – the kind of weather I'm not used to watching at a game in mid-October. I witnessed the longest and probably most exciting touchdown run from scrimmage by any back taking a hand-off. In the 35-14 UCLA victory, Foster finished with four touchdowns and the school-record of 301 rushing yards.

Selected by the Carolina Panthers as the 34th pick in 2002, an injury during preseason put him on injured reserve for the year. He played five seasons for Carolina. His career featured some fantastic playoff performances, but injuries hampered his career throughout. Shows you how much tougher they play at the next level. He returned to UCLA as running back coach in 2017. In 2022, he was inducted into the UCLA Athletics Hall of Fame.

The Jim's, my brother, and I settled in after the game at a bar called *Pinocchio's* in Burbank. Foster's record-setting performance was memorable. The flight home is a blur - luckily uneventful. However, like Foster's record-breaking performance, I'll never forget the flight on the way out to see UCLA host Washington. It introduced me to a whole new world that we live in today. Too bad for all of us.

Far West missions to be accomplished

Fast Forward to the future: Aside from not yet attending a game at Husky Stadium in Washington, I can say that I've fulfilled most of my desires to see these two programs perform on the gridiron. If and when the opportunity presents itself, I will consider a weekend trip to Husky Stadium to tie two games together among the four FBS teams playing in Washington and Oregon. Bucket List additions, but can't say they're high priorities at this time.

Regarding the Bruins of UCLA, I've seen them play home games at the Rose Bowl twice and also against nemesis USC in the LA Coliseum. The other trip to the Rose featured Utah in a 31-10 Bruins' win. Eric and I also watched the Bruins compete when they ventured east in 2009 for the Eagle Bank Bowl (now Military) in Washington, D.C. There, they defeated Temple, 30-21. I consider their powder blue uniforms and Temple's Cherry-white home jerseys with squares along the seams of their pants as my favorites. My best bet to see the UCLANs play again will probably be when they face off against some new Big Ten opponent whose campus I haven't been to yet, or possibly even at Penn State. I'm game to see them play if they're competitive and help me add a new FBS stadium to my incredible journey.

From Toys of Troy / To Transfer Portals

Troy (70) at Maryland
November 3, 2001

College Park, Maryland - I returned to Maryland's Byrd Stadium for the first time in 22 years. High atop Byrd, I sat looking in the distance at our nation's capitol still not believing what actually happened there on 9-11. Below, Coach Ralph Friedgen's surprising Terrapins (7-1) took on a D-IA newcomer, Troy. Maryland, smarting from its first loss of the season a week earlier to Florida State, toyed with the Trojans right from the start. On one of two touchdown passes from quarterback Shaun Hill, Marc Riley scored a 69-yard touchdown to get things going early. Nick Novak booted his first of four field goals that day.

Hill threw for 228 yards, and stalwart linebacker E.J. Henderson blocked a punt to dominate the first half. The Terps dominated their toys of Troy racking up 509 offensive yards in the first half alone and took a commanding 34-0 lead. The Maryland defense sacked Brock Nutter eight times for 72 yards. The Terps toyed with the Trojans down on the turf below on their way to a 47-14 victory. This game was ugly, but I recorded Troy State toward the Goal as intended.

Maryland finished 10-2, ranked 10th in the nation for quite an impressive one-year turn-around under "The Fridge." Troy State (now Troy University), coached by Auburn grad Larry Blakeney, finished its first D-IA season at 7-4. Its biggest win came at Mississippi State. Besides Troy's loss to Maryland, it earned the distinction of being the only team to lose to both teams in the 2002 BCS championship game, Miami (F.) and Nebraska. Two Troy defenders had brighter futures ahead of them despite performing as non-entities in this one-sided contest. Defensive ends Osi Umenyiora (junior) and DeMarcus Ware (freshman) enjoyed great careers on Sundays following their days at Troy. Pro teams have a knack for finding such hidden gems at lesser-known schools.

Bowling Green, Kentucky - Fast Forward to Troy at Western Kentucky, 2022: Before the 2022 season started, quarterback Jarret Doege left West Virginia through the transfer portal to become a graduate transfer at Western Kentucky. The previous two seasons, he started at quarterback for the Mountaineers. Prior to WVU, he had transferred there from Bowling Green State. Now a graduate student with the Hilltoppers, he landed a supposedly great opportunity. WKU demonstrated a dedicated, developmental quarterback pipeline thriving under Head Coach Tyson Helton. I watched the Hilltoppers in action three times in 2021.

Helton loses offensive coordinators annually. They move on elsewhere with what they learn. However, Helton's program develops and promotes assistants from within his system prepared to step in. Under offensive coordinator Zach Kittley the previous season, Hilltopper quarterback Bailey Zappe set NCAA single-season records passing for 5,967 yards and 62 touchdowns. The New England Patriots selected Zappe in the fourth round of the 2022 draft. After the 2021 season, Kittley moved on to take over similar duties at Texas Tech. In his place, Helton promoted three offensive coaches all to take over offensive coordinator responsibilities in 2022. What more could a gifted, young quarterback ask for as a great learning experience to prepare for the next level?

Graduate School "calling"?

Only ten days before the Hilltoppers' season opened, Doege took advantage of the very loose transfer portal process. Taking a back-seat to incumbent back-up Austin Reed as starter, he transferred once again and joined the Trojans of Troy. As a team, no matter how one looked at it, Doege turned his back on his post-grad, chosen teammates. What if Reed went down or faltered during the season? Doege exited WKU through the uncontrolled portal system in the final days of summer practices right before the first game. It evidently and rightfully left a bad taste among the Toppers in Bowling Green.

Now with a few weeks of practice remaining, WKU needed to reassess their quarterback depth. Remaining quarterbacks would get more reps, but at what point should any player arbitrarily determine if he stays or when he leaves at the expense of his team? Even more, why? On short notice, was there definitely a better opportunity for him at Troy? From another perspective, how can another school even accept a transfer, graduate student so quickly? Troy's fall classes had started in mid-August. In my personal experience, it took longer than a few days to get accepted into a graduate program for my Master's degree.

Planning my season schedule, I had already penned in the Troy-Western Kentucky clash on October 1. Looked to be a good, competitive game played a short trip away for me. With the departure of Doege before the season, this meeting clearly added a potential incentive for REVENGE! This game between the Trojans and Hilltoppers started out "smash-mouth" more than any game attended in quite a while. It was ready-made for a tense, hard-hitting, abusive, exciting football game.

Troy secondary mixes it up with Western Kentucky.

Vengeance doesn't always extract revenge

To my disappointment and surely to that of the Hilltopper team, Doege did not show up as the starter for Troy. His move through the portal didn't benefit any supposed intended goal to become the starting quarterback for the Trojans. Late in the third, however, starting quarterback Gunnar Watson took a hard shove along the WKU sideline. He laid face down in a twisted heap before being escorted gingerly off the field. The one-handed shove looked intentional, but didn't look that hard. Enter jersey No. 9, "Doege," much to the "delight" of the Hilltopper team. He stepped in to take Watson's place. More than anticipated, the Toppers pinned their ears back. With the score tied, 20-20, they intended to take it out physically on their prodigal "brother" more than expected. The already intense atmosphere on the field spiked up immediately. Doege's first pass landed incomplete on a third down.

Trojan Head Coach Jon Sumrall decided to go for the first. Doege obliged with an 18-yard completion. Two plays later under pressure, Doege lofted a long pass far beyond his receiver in the end zone. The refs flagged him for intentional grounding! However, they also flagged WKU for roughing the passer. Replaying the down, his next pass went for a three-yard loss. Doege's third completion then provided the charm for Troy. He connected with Jabre Barber for a 16-yard touchdown pass. While doing so, to the chagrin of Topper fans, he absorbed another roughing the passer penalty. From their perspective and my objective one - questionable call.

As the Trojans lined up to kick off from the 50, Doege was jostled, back-slapped, and supported by many teammates along the sideline. They anticipated the greeting received from his former, angry, revenge-driven teammates. On the ensuing Hilltopper drive, with a fourth-and-two at the Trojan 39, the Trojans stopped them and took over on downs. Doege and his offense went back to work. With 7:14 left, his 10-yard scoring pass to Tez Johnson not only widened the lead, 34-20, but Doege incurred another roughing the passer call to kick off again at the 50. The Hilltoppers' revenge factor cost them.

No quit in the Hilltoppers

At the six, on third-and-goal, Reed fired a pass to Daewood Davis at the back of the end zone for six points. The PAT was good. With 4:20 left to play, the Toppers trailed the hated Trojans and their prodigal brother, 34-27. The Trojans again punted on fourth down. The home team started from their ten with 1:56 left on the clock. A 26-yard pass put the Hilltoppers on the 50. A 12-yard run by Reed got the Toppers to the 32 for second-and-8. Next play, back under pressure, he scanned down field, and drew his arm back. From behind, linebacker Richard Jibunor reached out to knock the ball loose. Troy recovered. They ran out the clock in an exasperating win, 34-27. Great, physical intensely played game, heightened later than anticipated by Doege's late insertion.

Lesson here

As for Doege, like others, the grass may seem greener on the other side, but that's not always the case. He couldn't beat out Austin Reed at QB for Western Kentucky. In 2022, Reed led the FBS with 4,744 passing yards in 2022. Despite starting at West Virginia for two years, maybe Doege wasn't as good as other quarterbacks outside of that program. An indicator is that he also sat the bench behind Gunnar Watson until the latter's injury against the Hilltoppers. Doege played against Southern Miss the following week. Beyond that, his stats indicate he only saw spot duty thereafter. He completed 44 of 64 passes on the season for 575 yards, five touchdowns, and threw three interceptions. On short notice, the grass wasn't greener than at Western Kentucky. At that point in his career, he may not have made the best choice in either of the two programs he selected. On April 23, 2023 Doege signed with the Edmonton Elks of the Canadian Football league. Maybe he gets a chance to prove himself at the next level to reach his ultimate NFL goal.

The great news for Troy resulted in a 12-2 record, the Sun Belt Championship, and taking an 18-13 victory over ConferenceUSA champ UTSA (11-3) in the Duluth Trading Cure Bowl. The Trojans finished ranked No. 19 in the nation.

In the future, I'll continue to keep an eye on the Trojans to see them play a significant game at their Veterans Memorial Stadium. Bucket List!

From Storrs to Logan to Tuscaloosa.

(71) Utah State at Connecticut, November 10, 2001

Storrs, Connecticut – This weekend, my family and I ventured up to Rhode Island for family birthday festivities. Of course, I conveniently planned to add another new team on my list since we were on the go. Utah State visited nearby UConn which made it very convenient to add the Aggies into the fold. I gained pardon from St. Laurie and other women in the family because this trip would be rather convenient compared to traveling out to Logan, Utah just to catch an Aggie game. With Eric and me came my brother-in-law Gunther. Such a dedicated, fantasy football fan of pro football, final scores of any games meant nothing to him.

Way ahead of his time for sports betting

Back in the last millennium: "Hey Gunther, the Packers just scored again - up, 14-0!" I informed him about scores shown at the bottom of the TV screen as he would return back into the room from doing something else as we'd watch games on Sundays together. "Who scored?" That's all that mattered to this fantasy fanatic who used to kept reams of statistics on green bar paper under his couch cushions to scout and select his players back then. "How da heck do I know?" With the growing popularity of fantasy football, individual stats are reported up to the minute as a priority now.

With him to the UConn-Utah State game came his 4-year-old son, Blake. Anticipating the cold weather, his mom bundled him up to enjoy his first

FROM STORRS TO LOGAN TO TUSCALOOSA.

I-A college game with the rest of the boys in the family. Blake had already been in Uncle Steve's training program having tailgated at some University of Rhode Island and Princeton games. Also with us were cousins and college football veterans, Matt and Ben Wylie.

Orlovsky takes the field

The Aggies and Huskies seemed to be an even match on paper with 2-5 and 2-6 records respectively. Dan Orlovsky stayed locally to help develop the program in Storrs. His decision earned him the starting nod at UConn his freshman year. Utah State struggled with mediocrity most years. Two exciting skill players led their offensive attack. Emmit White led the nation in all-purpose yards with 201 yards per game. Kevin Curtis led the nation in yards per grab with 9.6 every time he caught the ball at wide receiver.

We took seats high in Connecticut's Memorial Stadium on a cold day with a little snow flurry action in the mix. Utah State moved the ball easily on its opening drive against the underlings. The Aggies took advantage of Orlovsky's inexperience. USU led by halftime, 28-10. It looked like the benefit of adding another team to the Goal in Storrs was going to be another painful, first-game experience. Troy State, Washington, UConn, Bowling Green, and Louisiana Tech recently came on board in disappointing one-sided scores the past year.

Utah State stretched its lead, 38-10. The weather got colder and our four, young boys grew bored while the remaining home team fans had nothing to cheer about. Tough! They had no choice but to stay until the bitter end or their parents would have to take up a collection to pay my airfare to Logan, Utah for an Aggies' home game! I thought about it anyway.

Other kids came by horsing around ran into our section. One wore only a T-shirt over his scrawny torso. Our boys stared wondering if they could get away with that. Gunther noticed the kid in the t-shirt and hollered, "*Hey, Kid! You cold?*" The skinny urchin turned to look directly at my brother-in-law probably waiting to get yelled at. "No!" came back his terse reply.

Gunther wrapped his arms around himself and in a high-pitched voice feigned to shiver and chattered through his teeth, "Then give *me* your t-shirt! Because *I* am!" The kid paused, stared briefly, and then ran off. We laughed as we all knew this was typical Gunther. He didn't.

Huskies have something going on here

The Connecticut Huskies finally sparked some excitement when Dan Orlovsky connected with Wes Timko for a 34-yard touchdown in the third. Running back Emmett White of the Aggies stood on the sideline with his knee packed in ice. The Husky defense held. The offense responded when Orlovsky threw another touchdown to Cliff Hill to cut the lead, 38-24. With five minutes left, the Huskies rolled to another score when Orlovsky plunged over from the one. Suddenly, the score was 38-31 with time left for either team to score. The home crowd finally got fired up. Our boys had something to cheer about now. Two struggling teams with dismal records each battled for their third win.

When State got the ball back, the ice pack came off White's knee. He got back into the game. The Aggies couldn't score, but they ate up the clock before turning over to the Huskies on downs. UConn moved the chains, but inexperience raised its ugly head. Orlovsky's low pass got picked by defensive tackle Jorge Tapia. He rumbled to the Husky seven-yard line. Game over, but no blow-out!

UConn came up short with the help of costly Aggie penalties in its hard-fought comeback bid, 38-31. By the time the final gun sounded, the two teams had combined for 222 yards in penalties, but at least both teams showed fight right to the end after the Aggies got out to a 38-10 lead.

Aggie Land

Logan, Utah - Fast Forward to Hawaii at Utah State, 2021: I finally began to venture west more often late in my adventure. First to see the Aggies, I traveled two new stadiums one weekend - Colorado's Folsom Field for Southern Cal at Colorado Friday night; and the following afternoon I visited Colorado Springs where Utah State visited Air Force. My plan worked out well for excitement. The USC Trojans prevailed 27-24 and the Falcons of Air Force defeated the Aggies, 35-28. I couldn't ask for better timing to see not just one, but two good, competitive games.

My third and fourth Aggie experiences exemplify what a difference a year makes and what a difference an opponent makes. Again, I was able to take advantage of my move to Tennessee to fly to Utah to attend two new venues in the state of Utah. Shorter flights and fewer frequent flier miles than from the northeast. In this case, I actually scheduled two games on one Saturday. In the morning, I drove up I-15 from Salt Lake City to beautiful Logan. I caught the Aggies hosting Hawaii at high noon.

Great game atmosphere in beautiful setting

On a picturesque, Saturday afternoon on Merlin Olsen Field at Maverik Stadium surrounded by scenic mountains in front of an enthusiastic, Utah State, Halloween-clad, student body, the Aggies got off to a fast start. They scored on their first three possessions. Aggie receiver Brandon Bowling scored the last two touchdowns for State – one on a pass reception and one on an unusual kickoff return. He picked up a one-hop onsides kick and returned it 45 yards for the Aggies final tally.

Defensively, Utah State held the Rainbow Warriors to 12 yards rushing and recorded five sacks. An early Warrior drive was halted by an interception in the end zone. State raced past Hawaii and fended off several late comebacks to win their sixth game of the season, 51-31. The Rainbow Warriors left Logan with a 4-5, 1-3 record. USU quarterback Logan Bonner racked up 361 passing yards and four touchdowns. Deven Thompkins snagged seven catches for 176 yards, and Elelyon Noa carried 23 times for 111 yards and a score. The Aggie offense looked formidable against Hawaii.

Under Head Coach Blake Anderson, the Aggies finished the season 11-3, 6-3. They manhandled San Diego State in the MWC championship at San Diego, 46-13. They triumphed in the Los Angeles Bowl over Oregon State, 24-13. With Bonner returning the following year, I looked forward to seeing how they would do. Immediately after this game, I jumped back down I-15 south to Provo to get there by 7:15 pm where BYU hosted Virginia.

You can almost hear the emperor command: "Let the games begin!"

Tuscaloosa, Alabama - Utah State at Alabama, 2023: What a difference a year and an opponent among the handful of "blue bloods" can make as depicted in my previous tale, "College Football History 101." Within three Aggie offensive plays, The Tide always got the ball back. All but one of those forthcoming Bama possessions resulted in a touchdown. The other ended with a field goal. At halftime, Bama led 41-0. Final score, 55-0.

Of course, Bama had an "off season" finishing 11-2 and not going to the CFP. State, on the other hand, lost to FCS Weber State the following week at home, 35-7! They battled back late in the season winning five of their last seven. Finished 6-6. They lost to 6-6 Memphis in the First Responder "Bowl" in Dallas, 38-10. If it wasn't for available television air time, neither team would be playing in the post-season to get over .500 in the win column. This match-up definitely epitomized a "consolation game" as I depicted previously in my tale, "Sentimental Souvenirs; 'And Almost Oh.'" I believe 134 teams are just too immense for the Football Bowl Subdivision. Due diligence later.

FROM STORRS TO LOGAN TO TUSCALOOSA.

Blake and Eric suited up to join in if needed at UCONN-Utah State game!

(72) California 20 Rutgers 10
Rutgers Stadium, New Brunswick, NJ, November 23, 2001

(73) Oregon State 35 Temple 3
Franklin Field, Philadelphia, PA, September 5, 2002

Now that's what I call service! / Blind-side Block

(74) Stanford at Boston College; September 7, 2002

Chestnut Hill, Massachusetts – Two nights prior to my first Stanford adventure, I added Oregon State in the first of two games this week. Schedules luckily fell into place to my advantage to start the 2002 season. Two teams from the PAC-10 that I hadn't seen yet would be within driving distance for a Thursday-Saturday doubleheader. For Oregon State on Thursday night, I hooked up with a Juniata bud, Ned Ehrlich, now a true, Philadelphia lawyer. At Juniata, he was our trainer and head student equipment manager for football. Ned's training career lasted for a brief time after college. I saw him at the Meadowlands in August 1980 working with the training staff of the Philadelphia Eagles before an exhibition against the Jets. He later decided to forgo sports medicine in favor of a law career. His sports experience put him in position to eventually negotiate individual NFL player and union contracts. Ned met me this evening at the ancient Franklin Field. I appreciated having someone to enjoy the game with during my quick trip to Philly.

The second half of my Thursday-Saturday, Big East/PAC 10 doubleheader included not only the addition of the Stanford Cardinal to The Goal, but also my first trip to Boston College's Alumni Stadium. The trip gave me a chance to catch up with my good friend Jack Hessler, a former sales manager for one of my major vinyl manufacturers, Vernon Plastics in Haverhill, Massachusetts, when I was Purchasing Manager at Myron Manufacturing. We no longer did business together having both left our former companies. We made it a point though of staying in touch to at least exchange a "Merry Christmas!" every year.

I met him at his place in Foxboro on the way to catch a train to Boston's South Station to connect on the "T" to Chestnut Hill. I looked forward to a *bonus* of sorts at this game. I'd get to see Boston College's senior tight end Frank Misurelli, a former player from our local high school, Lenape Valley Regional, play today. I'd seen him play football and basketball at LVR.

Jack and I boarded the train in a comfortable, double-decker car equipped with skylights to travel directly to Boston, or so we thought. The train pulled into Sharon, Massachusetts, where we abruptly sat, and sat, and sat, and... sat! An announcement finally came through. Power lines had fallen on the tracks ahead of us and all trains along the line were delayed. The railroad people had no idea how long this could take. Great! They had no idea that I had to be at this game to see Stanford, my 74th team! Did they know they could now owe me an all-expense paid trip to Palo Alto? Kidding! Only I thought that, of course.

I sat stewing and cursing the idea that mass transit could actually work in the U.S. In the meantime, arrangements supposedly took shape for buses to pick us up at the previous station to transport us to South Street. When? Time was running out to be at Alumni Stadium for the 3:30 kickoff!

Hundreds of train riders lined up in the empty parking garage. Things did not look good. The line was long, and if buses showed up sporadically, this could be a long wait. I had no idea how long it would take for a bus to get to South Station. Of course my selfish first thought was if I couldn't see at least part of the first quarter, was I going to be able to count Stanford toward my Goal? Finally, four buses came barreling into the garage and pulled up along our sidewalk. One came close to where Jack and I stood, and we were two of the first to get on the standing-only bus. We stood toward the back of as they packed in as many riders as possible.

What a long, strange trip it was

We rolled on to I-93 and sped along at 65 mph. You never see strap-hangers cruising along the interstates, but here we were. I still had no idea how we were even going to be close to see the first quarter no less the opening kickoff. Suddenly, a muffled shout came from the front of the crowded bus over the sound of a diesel engine. "Anybody back there going to the BC game?" As luck would have it, somebody up front also had a fixation to get to Alumni Stadium. I figured there must be a bunch on board with the same plan.

"Two back here!" I answered. A message was relayed back to us to stay on board after everyone else got off at South Station. The driver agreed to drive us to BC's Alumni Stadium directly. What luck! We still didn't know if we'd be there for kickoff, but at least we wouldn't have to wait for a rail connection. The bus doors opened at South Station and people filed out. In the end, there weren't a bunch of Boston College fans left on board clamoring to get to the game—just Jack, me, and two other guys. Luckily for us the other two guys got on last and were able to convince the driver. He just happened to live in the Chestnut Hill neighborhood and agreed to drive us there.

As bad as our luck had turned earlier, it got really good to make up for it. We rumbled past Fenway Park. We barreled along up hills and through nice, residential neighborhoods. Our new, best bus driver pulled right up to the main gate of Alumni Stadium. The four of us got off with profuse thanks. Jack and I got to our seats to watch the opening kick-off with seconds to spare. Sometimes things just fall into place even after things don't start out right. Thank you, Mr. Boston Transit Authority bus driver from Chestnut Hill. The game turned out to be well worth his extra effort for us. First impression once seated: that Stanford mascot has got to be the worst in all of college sports!

Into the woods

In the first half, Frank Misurelli caught a pass for 34 yards on a touchdown drive, but that prancing, Stanford tree! Stanford took a 27-17 lead on Michael Craven's 33-yard interception return heading into the fourth period. Bring on the lumberjacks! BC running back Derrick Knight scored after a fumble recovery on a nine-yard scamper to cut the tree's lead down to three points. A little while later, Sando Sciortino's field goal tied the score. With 1:35 left to play, BC took over from its own 35. In four plays, the Eagles took it to Stanford's 12. With 36 seconds left, Knight took it through the middle for a touchdown and the final 34-27 margin in favor of 2-0 BC. Alumni Stadium erupted. *"Timber!"* The Eagles soared over the fallen Trees.

Jack and I returned via the T to South Station and made our return to Foxboro without incident. We got to the game with great last-minute heroics by our unknown bus driver. The Eagles beat the Cardinal the same way. Again, thank you for your outstanding effort, Mr. Bus Driver! I couldn't have officially recorded team #74 that day without you.

Blind-sided Block of a Lifetime

South Bend, Indiana - Fast forward to Stanford at Notre Dame, 2016: Bill Serafin, Les Di Vite, Steve Ciesla, and I trekked 650 miles from Jersey to South Bend for this October 14 confrontation. Great time in South Bend to start. On Friday night we attended the pep rally in the Convocation Center and partied at the Linebacker Inn. On Saturday, we parked in a prime tailgate lot within close walking distance to Notre Dame Stadium. We took a tour of the Stadium, got pictures with some cute Fighting Irish cheerleaders, attended pre-game Mass, witnessed the tradition of the Irish Guard being harassed by drunken alumni, attended the band pep rally, and marched behind them to the stadium. I won a bet made by Bill when I was the first who ran into somebody I knew, my company Solvay's plant manager from Charleston, South Carolina. We did all things Irish before the 7 pm kickoff. Another fan we met described the visit on campus "like Disney World for Catholics."

We finally headed into the game to sit in our field level seats in the end zone under Touchdown Jesus - most I'd ever paid for a regular season ticket in 35 years of college football. Where we sat, I noted the TV camera platform slightly off to our right. Until the cameraman with his equipment climbed on top, we had no idea we had gotten great seats with the obstructed view behind the television cameraman's platform. The pedestal with a person on the platform blocking two-thirds the width of the field should be unacceptable for any fan paying the high price charged. Evidently, the administration knows this. They just don't inform the fans they sell those seats to. They post no obstructed view message on these tickets nor offer a reduced price. Yet, unprompted ushers throughout the game continually offered those of us with this obstructed view better seats after other fans departed.

When Steve and I were initially approached, I remarked to the genteel, older usher, "Hey, why don't they get that camera guy out of the way so we can all see?" We both knew the answer – national television ratings. He rolled his eyes. Surely, he'd heard this before. The camera platform blocks the view of about 100 ticket buyers, 10 rows up and ten seats across. You'd figure Notre Dame could give ticket-paying fans some kind of a break. Eventually the usher moved Steve and I up about ten rows for a better view midway in the fourth quarter. Too little, too late as far as I was concerned. Bill and Les, seated right in front of us, got relocated down to Row One, seated basically unblocked as well now.

With the Irish leading 10-9, on a second and six at the Notre Dame seven right in front of them, Irish Safety Nico Fertitta made a jarring tackle of Stanford running back Bryce Love, subbing for injured Christian McCaffrey. He knocked the ball loose before Love crossed the goal line. The ball bounced toward the end line. Les saw Irish linebacker Nyles Morgan attempt to scoop it up instead of falling on it ("*Steve, if that had been one of us back in high school, Coach Molitoris would have had us doing fumble drills all week long.*").

Instead, the ball continued to roll, and Les, Bill and the entire front row swore an ND player recovered the ball. By the time the twisted pile of bodies unraveled, Stanford wide receiver J.J. Arcega Whiteside came up with it from under the pile for the Stanford score. Bill said he thought that the Irish player with the ball may have had his leg out of bounds when he

NOW THAT'S WHAT I CALL SERVICE! / BLIND-SIDE BLOCK

seemingly recovered it. After further review, the call could not be disputed. The Cardinal now claimed a 15-10 lead. They lined up for two to extend their lead to seven.

All of Stanford's action before the play indicated they were going right. The Irish defense stacked up to that side before the snap. Cardinal quarterback Ryan Burns showed action right, but adeptly pitched left to Love who ran to that side unscathed for the seven-point lead. Final score: Stanford 17 Notre Dame 10. The Irish went on to 4-8 record that season under Brian Kelly. Aside from the uncalled-for obstruction blocking my view, I was disappointed that we didn't get to see Christian McCaffery play. Now that I think of it, even if he did, we might not have been able to see him play much any way.

Great seats, hey Buddy! Our view at Stanford vs. Notre Dame, 2016.

I still like to see the Irish win. Against most foes, I root for them. I've seen the Irish win 16 of 23 games attended. Most games I attended came at neutral sites and three under the Golden Dome. I contacted the Notre Dame ticket office a few days later to voice my complaint. I was told I could have asked for another seat before the game. I responded, "To where? For four of us? It was a sell-out!" I got nowhere with a rah-rah, "Go Irish" send-off. Followed up firing off an e-mail higher up in the school administration, but as expected, I heard nothing back. Goes to show, Notre Dame was content to take the money despite our blocked view. I'll root for the Irish again when I see them play on the road, but I don't ever plan to attend another game back in South Bend.

It's great to have friends in the right places

Berkeley, California – Fast Forward to Stanford at Cal, 2016: During the summer of 2016, Laurie and I (she's only *St. Laurie* during football season) vacationed in San Francisco. We had the great pleasure and a fun time meeting up with Karen Croft, a friend of ours through Jimmy Lewis when they worked together years before in New York City. During our vacation, we ended up having lunch one day with Karen and then staying for drinks that eventually turned into dinner! No problem for Karen, the restaurant was in the Flat Iron building she worked in downtown. We had a tremendous time.

Of course, at some point, with Karen being a legacy, alumnus, and fan of Stanford University, our conversation turned to Cardinal football. Karen mentioned the possibility of getting me tickets to see the Cardinal (regretfully no longer "Indians" according to her and her late father's perspectives) play in a future game. As reported prior, I already had Stanford at Notre Dame on my schedule for this season. No problem. Karen got back to me.

She got me two tickets for the Cal-Stanford game in November. Love her! I arranged to get back out to San Fran. Of course, always looking to attend two games with one airline ticket, I found out that in a later start,

Air Force played at San Jose State. Only about an hour from Berkeley, I planned Cal and San Jose State home games both for the first time!

I met Karen for dinner Friday night at our favorite San Francisco restaurant once again, and we had a great dinner and fun conversation. I assumed that even though she gave me two tickets that if I couldn't get anybody else to join me, she would come. Turned out that her disdain for Stanford's arrival went far beyond The Big Game. As much as she loves Stanford through and through, she told me she just absolutely refuses to set foot on the Cal-Berkeley campus. Talk about a heated, hateful rivalry!

Christian McCaffery showed up ready to play this time. Like Notre Dame, I had an end zone seat, but a higher one with nobody's butt in my way. On the very first Golden Bear play from scrimmage, Davis Webb connected with his wide-out Chad Hansen on a slant pattern over the middle. Cal ignited with a 70-yard catch and run to score. Cal Head Coach Sonny Dykes figured short kickoffs were better than long McCaffery returns. He stuck with that special team strategy the entire game, but the Cardinal always started with great field position any way. Tied before the half ended, Stanford's Conrad Ukropina delivered a 40-yard field goal to take their first lead of the game, 17-14.

In their 50-yard line seats behind their team, Cal's student body deserved credit for staying throughout this rivalry game despite cold, wet, rainy weather, and the odds of Cal winning. Their Bears came in with a record of 4-6, 2-5. Stanford came in at 8-3, 4-3. Halftime entertainment included Cal's student card section flashing multi-colored placards. Even on the video board directly in front of me, their messages were unreadable. As far as I could tell, they may have been pizza ads featuring a lot of toppings. Cal's Marching Band sounded awesome. They performed a great tribute to the rock band, *"Queen."* They played *"Bohemian Rhapsody"* and *"We are the Champions."* The latter did not inspire their football team to play like that in the second half.

Stanford RB Christian McCaffrey (5) pauses right before he bursts for a 90-yard touchdown romp against the California Golden Bears in The Big Game of 2017.

Bears down, not out

The third period started with the Bears punting and the Stanford Cardinal getting the ball deep in its territory this time. From the ten, the quick-footed, turn-on-a-dime McCaffrey hovered, looked for his blocking, darted left, raced past one defender, and burst forward untouched for a 90-yard touchdown run. California got three points back with a 43-yard field goal. McCaffrey rolled now, and Stanford Head Coach David Shaw's offense took advantage. McCaffrey piled up more yards. He finished the next drive with an 11-yard touchdown run. Before the period ended, Tre Watson scored his second touchdown for the Bears. Cal climbed back within range, 31-24.

Despite a few impressive numbers, Cal quarterback Webb misfired often today on short, west coast offense style passes. In the final period, McCaffrey finished off a drive with a one-yard run to go up, 38-24. The

Stanford Cardinal seemingly put the game away to take "The Axe" trophy back to Palo Alto when Ryan Chryst put enough air under the ball to his receiver Trenton Irwin. He made a beautiful over the shoulder catch in the end zone for a 30-yard score. Stanford extended its lead, 45-24.

The Bears fell short as "the Champions" their band's music alluded to at halftime. Webb followed with a 16-yard scoring pass to Hansen who wrestled the ball away from a Stanford Cardinal defender. Their subsequent onsides kick attempt failed, and the Cardinal proceeded to run out the clock to close the score, 45-31.

Stanford let Christian McCaffrey loose to win. Thanks to Karen, I got to see this performance. He rushed for 284 yards and three touchdowns in the second half to win at California Memorial Stadium in "The Big Game." A constant, cold, steady rain could not slow him down. For me, the cold, damp, dreary weather canceled my plan to San Jose for the Air Force game afterward. With clothes to dry out, a 4 a.m. wake up call to fly out, and heavy traffic in the dark ahead, I aborted the mission. Glad I did. Hopefully, next time. This particular game alone was well worth the entire effort.

I still have to go back to Palo Alto to see a Stanford home game. Bucket List! Even if they host Cal, I hope Karen will join me this time. Maybe, San Jose State will be playing home that day as well.

Maryland 45 - (75) Eastern Michigan 3

Byrd Stadium, College Park, Maryland, September 21, 2002

Time and Now Tide / The D-3 Battle of Sherwood Forest!

(76) Texas Christian at Army, October 12, 2002

West Point, New York - The Texas Christian Horned Frogs arrived on the banks of the Hudson during a hard-driving, wind-swept, rain storm. Our tailgate plans got washed out, but St. Laurie, cousin Frank Scarpa, his former wife Jessie, Dave Headden, and Charlie Roberts all showed up to brave the elements. A driving rainstorm could not stop us from seeing the game in its entirety because we all knew it wouldn't count toward the The Goal!

   Fumbles back and forth led to scores resulting in 32-27 TCU lead late in the third. But suddenly, we had a bigger problem than did the Army football team. A warning blared with the volume turned up over Michie Stadium's public address system, *"Attention all drivers parked by the South Docks! The Hudson has come up over its banks! Please move your cars from that location immediately!"* Guess where we parked?

   Immediately? The fourth quarter was just beginning. It's a good, close game, and TCU can't count as the 76th team in the annals of history until time expires in the fourth quarter. I looked to cold, wet St. Laurie. She seemed to be looking for an excuse to leave a very good game. Taking the keys, she promised to meet us after the game. She left to catch the shuttle bus down to the South Docks. I figured if we didn't meet her in the Thayer parking lot right after the game, we'd probably catch up with her somewhere downstream - like Hoboken, New Jersey! Okay, she gets points for this as *Saint Laurie*.

Of course, after she and many others left for the South Docks, Dave, Charlie, and I moved from our end zone seats to better sideline seats. We prepared to watch what we'd hope to be a down-to-the-wire battle. The rain subsided a bit, but the changing weather seemed to aid the Horned Frogs. A one-yard run by Reggie Holts and a 62-yard scoring jaunt by Donta Hobbs added to a 46-27 TCU victory.

Meanwhile, thanks to St. Laurie, the van was saved from the rising Hudson floodwaters at West Point. She met us in a lot near Thayer Hall. We took off our wet gear, had a few beers under the tailgate, and then headed home. Let the games continue - 76 down and 41 more to go! *"Time and tide wait for no man."* That's because St. Laurie intervened to save the van from the rising waters of the Hudson. Even a rising the tide could not hinder me. I added another team to The Goal.

Fort Worth, Texas - Fast Forward to a TCU game on an excursion to Texas in the future: Two-hundred miles from my daughter Alex in the Austin area, a TCU home game, or a Baylor home game, or a Texas A&M home game could possibly become reality if one of them, or if Texas State schedules a Thursday night home game. That would allow me to visit Alex to attend a TXST game and one of these other campuses for the first time. I think it will come down to an improved TXST Bobcat program over the next few years picking up a Thursday night slot for a prime-time Sun Belt football showdown. I look forward to that happening.

Why Frank Rafferty always tells me, "You're out of control!"

Lake Forest, Illinois - Fast Forward to a D-3 game, 2013: I discussed the possibility of attending a TCU game ten years ago, it didn't happen. However, I met with a new sales rep of a potential contract manufacturer in 2014 who I considered to develop as an alternative source. We eventually got around to discuss my college football adventures. Not only a sports fan, John Jury had just dropped his daughter off for her freshman year at TCU. I told him that I had seen them play already, but not at home.

John decided to test me. He said, "I'll bet you've never seen my school play!" John figured he was coming way out of left field for me. I'd say he did, but I was ready to make the tag at the plate. He said, "*St. Norbert!*" I had to smile. I froze the conversation putting my finger in the air. St. Norbert is an asterisk in my history. He sat back and waited to hear this about his Green Knights from De Pere, Wisconsin, his Alma mater of about 2,000 students among my adventures. It just so happened I had seen them play the previous season, but I did not record the game officially in the annals of my history.

That particular weekend, I put college football on hold, but I did make note of one possibility if time became available. Laurie, Alex, and I headed to The Great Lakes Naval Training Center north of Chicago to attend Eric's ceremony for completion of basic training. We were all so proud of him. Not only did he rise to the grade of Seaman 1/C during training, but he led his company out on parade as Chief. It was a memorable day! The son who had taken many trips with me to various college campuses, played football, baseball, putted the shot, and swam his senior year found his calling in the US Navy.

After the ceremony, we took him out to lunch, his first meal outside the training center since he enlisted in September. He was bushed, and had an early wakeup the next morning to fly from Chicago for further training in Pensacola, Florida. We made dinner plans for the evening. All he wanted to do now was go back to our hotel and take a nap. To get back to my response to John Jury, Plan B then went into action.

Oh here's to Lake Forest

Nearby, the Foresters of Lake Forest College (7-2, 6-2) hosted John's Green Knights (8-2, 8-1) in a D-3 Midwest Conference battle. Foresters vs. Green Knights sounded like the Battle of Sherwood Forest! I found the Lake Forest campus in this quaint neighborhood surrounded by trees and beautifully built homes in styles from decades ago. The Farwell Field crowd displayed passionate energy. Since I had no real plan to be there, I stood at the end of the field and snapped some pictures. I just absorbed the action on the field. The Foresters dominated to the final whistle and triumphed, 31-3. I left as the celebration started.

Despite their loss, St. Norbert made the D-3 playoffs. The bad news for the Knights came when they found their opening game came against No. 1 seeded Wisconsin-Whitewater. Current Kansas Head Coach Lance Leipold's Warhawks ousted the Green Knights, 31-7. In the Stagg Bowl for the D-3 title, Whitewater wasted No. 2 Mt. Union, 52-14.

So, to John's astonishment, this Jersey guy stumbled across a game played by his St. Norbert Green Knights. Someday hopefully, I'll stumble around in Texas to catch his daughter's TCU Horned Frogs play a game at Amon G. Carter Stadium.

Angel in the Desert / Why to Wyoming?

(77) Wyoming at (78) Nevada-Las Vegas, November 2, 2002

Las Vegas, Nevada – Not big gamblers, St. Laurie and I had never visited Las Vegas, but we always wanted to. Checking out possible games to see in 2002, I said, "Honey, I've got enough frequent flyer miles saved up and can get a good deal on a hotel. My mother can come and watch the kids. Why don't we plan a long weekend in Vegas?"

"Why, so we can see a football game?" Ah, she knows me so well! But she had always wanted to go to Vegas, so she was willing to tolerate a few hours of my favorite pastime in order to hit *"The Strip."* With Wyoming in town to play UNLV, I could kill two teams with one ticket though I didn't buy any in advance.

My research indicated we wouldn't need a rental car. We arrived at the Holiday Inn within a short distance of The Strip. Our hotel offered limo service to and from the airport. UNLV's Sam Boyd Stadium wasn't far from where we stayed—or so I thought. I also found public bus transportation could take us close by the stadium—again, so I thought. On Friday night, we hit The Strip. We went to Caesar's Palace where I could play a few college tickets using my "expertise." We felt excited to be here. Game time was 5 p.m. on Saturday, so we did more touring and a little bit of gambling the next morning to shed some of our hard-earned money. In the afternoon, we ate dinner early at a steak place near a bus stop on the way out to Sam Boyd Stadium.

My problem: I was calculating!

We caught the public transit bus. By my calculations from the Vegas map in my road atlas, I was sure where we could get off to walk a short distance. I pointed out the Thurgood Avenue sign to the bus driver to be sure it led to Sam Boyd. She looked at me and just nodded. Things were going well – so I thought. We'd have plenty of time to get there to buy tickets, have a few beers, and settle into our seats. We started to walk down Thurgood with housing developments of fairly new concrete homes on both sides surrounded by concrete walls. The road turned. No stadium came into sight, but it couldn't be that far. It must be behind one of these developments, so I thought. Ahead of us lay an expanse of homes and buildings set in a valley. Where the heck was this stadium?

Eventually, a gray-haired resident came through the entrance of one of the concrete complexes and walked toward us. I asked him if he knew where the heck Sam Boyd Stadium was. He turned and pointed out to the distant valley ahead of us.

"You see that bright red building right in the middle there? That's Sam Boyd Stadium." He had to be kidding! It had to be five miles away. It didn't look that far in the atlas. Maybe I got off the bus at the wrong street. Maybe I didn't realize that the map of Nevada wasn't the same scale as smallish New Jersey. The scale must have been off! I thought it would be much closer. St. Laurie smirked, sighed, and shook her head. She already complained her feet were starting to hurt. I tried to figure out if I could bend my own rules to be sure this game would count if I didn't end up there until the second quarter.

Dead man walking...

We tramped on. Not only was I not going to hear the end of this, no way we were going to get there on time for the opening kickoff on foot! I picked up the pace with my saintly wife trailing behind. Time and pride were now on the line. Unexpectedly, a white mini-van, or I should say a *white knight*, pulled up from behind heading in our direction. A dark-haired, mustachioed guy hollered at us from the shoulder on the opposite side of the street. "Hey, you need tickets for the game?" I couldn't believe it! This was some kind of positive sign that someone upstairs wanted me to accomplish this Goal. St. Laurie must have said a prayer, and God sent us an Angel! On a more worldly level, my professional, negotiating skills kicked in right away. "I'll make a deal with you," I said. "You give us a ride to the stadium, and I'll buy your tickets at face value."

"Get in!" We climbed in. St. Laurie sat in the back next to the baby in the seat. He said, "My wife couldn't make it! Only five miles away, but I have to watch the kids so I can't go to the game. They're good seats in the end zone right behind the goal post. It's a good stadium to watch a game in." If this wasn't divine intervention, I didn't know what was. I couldn't thank this guy enough.

We bought the tickets, and he dropped us off at the main gate. We walked through the parking lot and to our seats. The teams ran onto the field as we sat. St. Laurie's feet didn't hurt anymore. I saved some face, got good seats, had a great story to tell, and the two teams could officially count toward The Goal. It couldn't get any better than this. Of course, it could turn out to be a great ball game, but that would be asking for too much. At this point, who cared? I was saved!

Another Miracle?

As for the game, it turned out to be an offensive showcase. UNLV led 35-21 . . . at the half. In the third, Wyoming put up the only seven on the board to trail 35-28 heading into the final period. UNLV scored again to go up by fourteen. Wyoming made it closer in the fourth quarter (and it was getting downright cold . . . isn't this the desert?) retaliating with a touchdown, but missed the extra point.

With 2:27 left in the game from their fourteen, Wyoming took over again. During the drive, quarterback Corey Bramlett converted a pass on fourth and five from his own 33 into a first down with a 14-yard completion to Dustin Pleasant. With no time left on the clock, Bramlett connected with Scottie Vines in the end zone below us to close the score, 42-40. And yes, with a little Vegas luck, Bramlett ran it in for the two-point conversion.

Overtime! *Jackpot!*

Even St. Laurie commented, "This is really a great game! It was worth the trip!" *Two* miracles in one night were just totally beyond my comprehension. On top of this, *I* was cold. I couldn't imagine how *she* tolerated the falling temperature.

Wyoming got the ball first in OT and chose to play on our end of Sam Boyd. They scored on a run on the fourth play. This could have been the ultimate game if not for the next play. Freshman Scott Parker missed the extra point - wide left! On the Rebel's first offensive play, Jason Thompson passed to fullback Steve Costa for a 25-yard score. Dillon Pieffer did not miss the extra point for UNLV. The Rebels triumphed in a game that even thrilled St. Laurie, 49-48!

We saw two teams with losing records (UNLV 4-5, Wyoming 2-7) each play in their most exciting game of the season. Of course, after the game, it was now dark and cold. We had no idea how we were going to get back to our hotel. No buses could be found. Walking was out of the question. A limo driver approached us. For $75, he would take us back. Seventy-five bucks? I hesitated and thought to check other options, but with St. Laurie's immediate *blessing*, it was a good deal. After the ordeal to get to the game, we couldn't believe how quickly he got us back. It was surely the best $75 we spent all weekend in Las Vegas.

I'll never forget the time the Angel in the Desert rescued me from two fatal blows—missing a game and lifelong humiliation! Moreover, I knew now that someone watching over me wanted me to get this done even more than St. Laurie did!

Boonton Bombers

Laramie, Wyoming - Fast Forward to a Wyoming home game eventually: I tell you right now, a Wyoming Cowboy game at War Memorial Stadium is a top priority for me after Alex's wedding in 2023. Maybe 2025 for this one at the latest. The primary tie that we who attended Boonton High School back in New Jersey have to historical football greatness is our fellow BHS alumnus, the late Wyoming and Miami Dolphin running back Jim Kiick. Kiick played in three Super Bowls with the Dolphins. In 1972, he played for the only undefeated (17-0) Super Bowl champ in the history of the NFL. He and fullback Larry Csonka became known together as *"Butch Cassidy and the Sundance Kid,"* named after characters in the block-buster movie of 1969.

Kiick was ten years older than me. Many friends had brothers or other family members who knew him well. Closest I ever came to know him was at a presentation he gave at BHS to the entire student body after winning that first Super Bowl. He and I both played for the same high school coach, Joe Molitoris. When I was seven or eight, I attended a Bomber game with my dad when Kiick played. My father first reminded me of this when we watched the 1966 Sun Bowl on television. Wyoming (10-1) defeated Florida State (6-5), 28-20. Kiick won MVP honors carrying 25 times for 135 yards and two touchdowns while making four pass receptions for 42 yards.

In the 90s, the retired Miami Dolphin and I both went to Johnny's Tavern in Boonton for a traditional get-together the night before the big Thanksgiving Day rivalry against Parsippany High School. Each year, the winner took home "The Shoe," an actual bronzed high-top football shoe mounted on a pedestal. By about 8 pm, the place packed so tightly you could hardly lift your arm to drink a beer. Jim's buddies kept him pre-occupied in one corner of the bar, so there was no chance to meet him that evening. The Wyoming Athletics Hall of Fame inducted him in 1996. I plan to get out there to check it out.

Great thing, I already have a friend lined up to join me in Laramie. Gary Groner and I worked together back in the early 90s at AlliedSignal, now Honeywell, in Morristown, NJ. Gary, who specialized in procuring energy, graduated from Wyoming and moved back there since. It should be a great time when we pull this together. I'd prefer to find a way to do two games out there, but I'll cross that bridge when I come to it. The only other campus that's convenient to Laramie comes by way of Colorado State in Fort Collins, Colorado - 65 miles away. I really look forward to seeing a game at Wyoming.

As for Vegas, out of nowhere Laurie recently said that we should consider going back. I have no problem with that. Since I started thinking about my Bucket List, I'd like to attend The Battle of Nevada for the Fremont Cannon played between the UNLV Running Rebels and the Nevada Wolfpack. She knows I'll finagle a way to attend another UNLV game, but I already had a vision for this. We're probably not ready to plan this until after Alex's wedding any way.

The winner of the rivalry takes home The Fremont Cannon, a replica of a howitzer transported by explorer and former governor of Nevada, John C. Fremont. The replica is recognized as the heaviest and most expensive rivalry trophy in all of college football. One probable issue for our planning purposes is that they play this game most often traditionally on Thanksgiving weekends. On the other hand, in Vegas, they now play it at Allegiant Stadium downtown - near The Strip. If we can work this out, I can go to the game, and she can go play slots. I'm sure we'll come up with some happy medium here. Timing is everything!

Connecticut 63 - (79) Kent State 21
Memorial Stadium, Storrs, Connecticut, November 9, 2002

End runs and Enron / Record-setting trip

(80) Hawaii at (81) Rice, November 16, 2002

Houston, Texas - Back in 2000, after I analyzed how many IA teams I'd seen and the possibility of seeing the rest, I brazenly approached St. Laurie with a bold idea: we'd finish The Goal together with the final game in Hawaii to see the Rainbow Warriors play in Aloha Stadium! We honeymooned there, and we'd both love to go back. As The Goal progressed though, reality set in. The cost to go back was one thing, but on the other hand, I knew there was no way St. Laurie would take a fall vacation to Hawaii with the kids at school nor winding down into the holiday season - no way we could pull this off.

In the meantime, I contacted my former Juniata College roommate, Todd Kulp. He graduated from Central Bucks West HS in Doylestown, Pennsylvania, a high school football powerhouse. Todd never played a down of football. He dabbled in business and politics. He planned a presidential, political campaign on campus at Juniata. One night, he invited me to go to the airport with him to pick up the main speaker, Pat Paulsen, the *"Rowan and Martin's Laugh-in"* comedian-turned-presidential candidate. Besides seeing President Gerald Ford, Bill Clinton, and most recently Donald Trump at Army-Navy games, that's the closest I've come to meeting someone with presidential aspirations. Come to think of it, Nikki Haley spoke at Alex's University of South Carolina Commencement, not exactly like I was sitting in the same car with Pat Paulsen.

After graduation from Juniata, Todd attended the University of Texas to earn his MBA and settled permanently in the Lone Star State. I contacted him there when I saw a double-dip of new teams: Hawaii at Rice. Of course, St. Laurie asked what happened to finishing The Goal in Hawaii. I told her the Goal may be achievable earlier than expected and that we'd never be able to break away to Hawaii while the kids were in school. "*Excuses! Excuses!*" she replied. She knew more than I that the reason I gave rang true.

I met Todd for dinner with a bunch of his co-workers at a Houston restaurant Friday night before the game. We drank and they shared typical office, war stories. I didn't know the characters personally, but I could relate to many similar circumstances where I worked. They worked for an oil rig platform company—one of the biggest builders of such in the world. Todd worked in Finance. When he and I talked one on one to catch up later on, he told me how his career path led through scandalous Enron where unscrupulous accounting practices led to bankruptcy in 2001 and in jail time for its shady management.

He had worked with the main culprits convicted – Jeffrey Skilling, Anthony Fastow, and Kenneth Lay - but he departed long before all the allegations took place. He sensed trouble early and conferred his words of wisdom that told him to move on. He said, "I've worked for mean people who are smart, and for dumb people who are nice, but I promised myself never to work for *mean* people who are *dumb* again!" Words to live by – Todd avoided a bad situation and moved on to better things, supposedly.

Talk about dumb

The next day we went out for Mexican lunch and went back to his place to watch games. We loafed. We weren't far from Rice Stadium. USA Today indicated the game kicked off at 3 pm. However, I didn't realize all the starting times were set in the Eastern Time zone! Thinking we had plenty of time to check things out before the game, we showed up shortly before two. The game was about to start! Kickoff commenced at 2 pm

CST. Luckily, we didn't have to battle a large crowd. Only 19,174 showed up. We got there in a nick of time.

This game presented a couple of firsts. This marked my first all-WAC game and my first game in football-crazed Texas. Not the most traditional of football programs in the Lone Star, but the Rice game offered some points of interest. For instance, the game program boasted of Rice's propensity to lead the nation in player graduation rates. Thirty-one players graduated the previous spring and earned Rice the Academic Achievement Award presented by USA Today and the NCAA. Also, Rice Stadium hosted Super Bowl VIII. I envisioned fellow Boonton High alum Jim Kiick and fullback Larry Csonka punishing defenders once again that day as the Dolphins defeated the Vikings, 24-7.

Remember George Carlin sports score monologue: ... "Rice 27 - Macaroni 2 for 29..."

Rice enjoyed a 14-10 lead at halftime. At the intermission, I realized I came all the way out from Jersey to see a performance by "the MOB" - the Soprano-free Marching Owl Band, that is. They looked more like an Ivy League band dressed in dark blazers, ties, sunglasses, and baseball caps than the big, traditional, marching brass bands of the South. They sounded much better than the Ivies though. They played *real* instruments. They didn't beat on plastic pumpkin heads or scrape antique washboards among other household devices or articles of clothing or anything else they found in some fraternity or sorority hall. At Columbia in New York City, their band's favorite chant was "beat the traffic!"

The second half showed off Hawaii's offensive firepower programmed by Head Coach June Jones and led by eventual, record-setting quarterback Timmy Chang. Chang spread passes effectively among receivers to rack up 369 passing yards. Two consecutive drives in the third resulted in touchdown passes overcoming the Warriors' deficit to take a 23-14 lead. Rice's Marcus Battle took his only handoff of the game and ran for a 60-yard score that pulled Rice to within, 23-21. The Warriors converted a 21-yard field goal to conclude the third quarter scoring.

With 7:50 left in the game, the Warriors took a 33-21 lead on Thero Mitchell's three-yard run. Rice steadfastly stuck to the ground game under former Air Force coach Ken Hatfield with quarterback Kyle Herm at the controls until the final minutes of play. However, Herm's replacement, Greg Henderson, tossed a 54-yard pass to Battle to cut the Rainbows' lead, 33-28. Subsequent Owl drives stalled though, and Hawaii enjoyed a long, happy flight home. They celebrated their fifth consecutive win to go 8-2 overall and 7-1 in the WAC. For Rice, it was their season finale to finish 4-7 and 1-5 in the conference. Maybe they should have gotten the ball more often to Marcus Battle today and all season long. Like anyone could appreciate my hindsight.

Career moves

As for Todd's end run on Enron, he got out of there and now worked for Transocean Deepwater Horizon, the world's largest offshore drilling contractor, based in Houston. In April 2010, everyone became familiar with Transocean Deepwater Horizon. Its oil rig wellhead exploded in the Gulf of Mexico off Louisiana leaking 210 million gallons of oil into the gulf. I hope my future end run to take St. Laurie to Hawaii is more successful than Todd's end run around his former employer. Todd's had an interesting career. Last time I spoke to him about ten years ago, he was already retired. Probably good for him and any other potential employer!

FBS teams can't travel any farther than this in college football

Amherst, Massachusetts - Fast forward to Hawaii at UMass, 2017: Since the Rainbow Warriors jumped on to my slate earlier than anticipated at Rice, I caught them stateside several times. In 2013, Navy hosted Head Coach Ken Niumatalolo's (former Bow quarterback) Alma mater in a 42-28 win. In 2022, the Bows, as reported in my first trip to Utah State in a Mountain West match-up, lost in Logan, 51-31. Before that though, their most memorable game played on my slate came five years earlier. To open the 2017 season for both teams in August, Hawaii traversed to the furthest FBS team of all to play – the University of Massachusetts. Some would probably argue Boston College is farther, but a two-hour drive from Boston's Logan Airport heading west adds to the overall distance. Surprisingly, they actually drew some Rainbow Warrior fans to Amherst.

Going into the final period, the Minutemen led, 28-21. The UMass offense played conservatively and lost its steam. A wobbly, Hawaii punt hit the UMass return man square in the chest, and the Warriors recovered at the UMass 15. Hawaii quarterback Dru Brown zipped his next pass to Marcus Armstrong-Brown who kept both feet in-bounds near the pylon to re-knot the score at 28-all. Despite UMass pessimism in the stands, returner Andy Isabella took the ensuing kick all the way to Hawaii's 46. On a fourth and one at the U of H 21, Marquis Young broke through the left side of the line all the way for a touchdown. His burst put UMass out in front, 35-28, but 11:41 still remained on the clock.

Hawaii started from their 41. They converted a fourth and one at the 50 for a first. On a critical fourth and three, Brown connected with a wide-open receiver John Ursua for a first down at the 14. "Stupid!" yelled my Rhode Island friend Mike Ford with his son Colby at his first D-IA football game. The UMass defense buckled down and held the Bows to a 35-yard field to cut the lead to 35-31 with 5:23 left. Minutemen fans lamented to me and my Rhode Island friends that after their two-touchdown lead, Head Coach Mark Whipple's play calling became too conservative. We agreed. Hawaii forced a punt after a UMass three-and-out. They took over from their 26. A pass to John Urusa (12 catches, 272 yards) put the Bows at the seven. "Stupid!" reiterated Mike. We all saw who Brown's go-to guy was, and UMass left him too open, again.

With 48 seconds to be played in regulation, the Rainbow "road" Warriors of Hawaii came up all "sevens." On third and seven at the UMass seven-yard line, Dru Brown threw a seven-yard scoring pass to jersey number seven, Metuisela 'Unga for a great comeback victory, 38-35. The final pass won it all. I've still got a game in Hawaii on my Bucket List.

And why not?

I have not approached St. Laurie yet, and probably not until after this book is published. Kids have moved on now. Can we go back to Hawaii? Too soon to ask with Alex's wedding next year. However, the Rainbow Warriors (now coached by former QB Timmy Chang) host Oregon on August 24, 2024. We will celebrate our 35th anniversary in August 2024, but she's got this attitude of "been there, done that." Come on! It's *Hawaii*, and our 35th anniversary. Never attended a game in Hawaii though we've gone there already. Hopefully I get some credit to go. Aloha!

Rice joined the American Athletic this year. So, if the Owls ever take football more seriously to consider them for a second look, maybe I'll see them play. Navy and UAB as hosts give me possibilities to see Rice get cooked again. Like George Carlin insinuated in his monologue, maybe I can find a better bargain if Macaroni plays these other teams instead.

Hawaii QB Dru Brown unleashes a pass against UMass in their win a long way from Honolulu.

Shipshewanna, Indiana / Punt, Leach, Punt

(82) Washington State at Notre Dame, September 6, 2003

South Bend, Indiana – Of course, the Washington State Cougars play far from New Jersey. What chance existed that they'd ever come out east to play? When I saw them slated to open in South Bend against Notre Dame, the gears started turning. How could I work this out? Don Di Vite, Les's brother, told me once that the lubricant distribution company he worked for in central Jersey advertised heavily in some big-time, national college-football game programs. Previously, Don managed to get all of us tickets to the Big East basketball tournament and NCAA opening-round games at The Meadowlands.

When I asked him about the possibilities of working out ND-WSU tickets in South Bend, he knew he couldn't go, but he contacted some people to come up with tickets for Les and me. Bingo! We booked a long weekend and a ten-hour drive to see the Irish host the Cougars to notch the newest team for a notch in my belt play at one of the most revered venues in all of college football. Call it the luck of my Irish ancestors. This marked the first time these two would face each other on the gridiron.

By the time we got tickets, hotel rooms around South Bend were no longer available. Searching the internet, I came up with a discount hotel deal in Shipshewanna, Indiana, 42 miles east of South Bend. We left early Friday morning anticipating the slight possibility of getting to Notre Dame in time for the traditional Friday night Irish pep rally. We arrived a little later than anticipated and drove directly to our hotel. Despite the distance from South Bend, it turned out to be a pretty good place to stay.

Had we brought our wives, they probably could have enjoyed the place with its shops, flea markets, and restaurants. We learned the Amish thrived in this town beyond Lancaster, Pennsylvania. Buggies pulled by trotting horses moved hastily along the main roads. Friendly people on board waved to us to welcome us to their tourist town. Hungry, we decided to delay South Bend and have dinner right down the street at the Blue Gate Restaurant. It offered great prices for all-you-can eat Amish dinners. For dessert, we ate home-made Amish pies. More Amish than Irish, nothing in town indicated that we were within a one-hour drive of the most prominent of schools in college football. Instead, banners welcomed a rodeo to town! Les and I needed a fix of Irish spirit after dinner, so we drove west to South Bend.

We thought we'd catch something happening on campus, but aside from women's soccer, nothing else stirred. Soccer did nothing for us. We drove around until we came to some bustling spot on a corner. The parking lot was packed and the lights shined at the *Linebacker Inn*—just what we were looking for! Like the lot, the joint was packed and hopping. For a three-buck cover charge, you get at least get one, cold beer. All the beers served there came nice and ice-cold. ND fans partied loud and celebrated the anticipation of another successful season under Coach Ty Willingham. His second at South Bend, they talked a lot about Irish football. The spirit of Notre Dame football filled the air!

Cougar fans come with pre-game protection plan

A group of Washington State fans came in. Some were so big we were sure they played for the Cougars in recent years. Being the Cougars first venture to Notre Dame, they had no idea what to expect. So, they probably brought along some protection—like last year's offensive line. Rock music blared on the jukebox while fans danced where they could find room. About every fourth song though, it transitioned from party music to *"The

Notre Dame Victory March!" Of course, all the Irish fans joined in on the song. Les and I definitely found the right place to get in on a little Friday night, Irish spirit. We didn't stay until closing as we had to shuttle back to Shipshewanna to come back to enjoy more Irish pre-game festivities the next morning.

On Saturday, we headed to South Bend to savor more Notre Dame pre-game traditions. We toured the Convocation Center with all the Irish stuff to buy, see, and experience. Former running back Allen Pinkett joined other former Irish football captains to sign autographs. We took our pictures in a rotunda where you stand in the middle of a surrounding photograph of a kick-off between the Irish and Stanford. I bought Eric a gold towel inscribed with the famous, Irish, locker-room inscription, *"Play like a champion today!"* I think it's a great message about living life daily. It still hangs now in my office/museum/ "shrine" here in Tennessee.

We grabbed sausage sandwiches before heading over to listen to the Band of the Fighting Irish getting the fans primed before the game. At the final Kickoff Classic played the previous season, Frank Rafferty, Les, and I watched the Irish defeat Maryland, 22-0. Frank's biggest disappointment—Notre Dame didn't bring the band! I called Frank on his cell phone so he could hear it live. I didn't want let the subway-Irish fan miss out on this. The Irish band led the parade to Notre Dame Stadium.

In 1980, when I visited Notre Dame Stadium to witness the start of "The Bold Experiment," the venerable venue held 59,075. Now keeping in line with the growth, popularity, and growing budgetary demands, the stadium held 80,795. ND's famous stadium ranked now as the 15th largest in the country. If they could add more seats, they'd continue to fill them. Les and I found our section in the south end zone. We kept walking down the steps with our eyes on *"Touchdown Jesus!"* right before us. The seats Don got us were in row 6 just to the left of the goal post. They provided prime views for some significant plays to be seen (much better than the similar seats in the opposite end zone in Notre Dame Stadium behind the TV platform).

Unfortunately for the Irish, they bumbled, stumbled, and fumbled during the first half, and the hard-hitting Cougars took advantage taking a 19-3 halftime lead. During the halftime festivities, Notre Dame introduced former team captains from throughout their historic decades. In the locker room, Tyrone Willingham was surely performing his rendition of a Knute Rockne pep talk! If ever the Irish offense needed a fire lit under it, this was the time.

A die-hard Irish fan from Ontario, Canada we met wondered aloud if the Irish offense had even practiced since last season. Throughout the game, Carlyle Holiday's passes were floaters ripe for the picking. Despite 21 completions, Holiday garnered only 134 yards through the air. Many thrown were of the "dangerous," pick-six variety.

All the halftime inspiration took a while to work evidently, and it wasn't until late in the third quarter, trailing 19-9, that ND started rolling. A fumble gave them field position to close with Holiday's pass to Raheem McKnight, 19-16. Holiday was injured on Notre Dame's next possession. Freshman Brady Quinn entered the game to the delighted fanfare of the Fighting Irish faithful.

Despite Holiday's supposed, quick recovery, Willingham left Quinn in for the entire series. Julius Jones scampered the final 22 yards around right end to pay-dirt for the first Fighting Irish lead of the day, 23-19, with 5:03 left in the game. They added a field goal, but they left too much time on the clock for WAZU to score. The Cougars scored with a minute left on a stunning, diving, bobbling catch by receiver Sammy Moore to our right in our end zone. The Cougars tied it up, 26-26. Overtime at ND…perfect season opener to attend in South Bend.

Getting in their kicks

The Cougars selected our end of the stadium away from the Fighting Irish band and student section. State's Drew Dunning misfired with one of his patented line drive kicks that went wide left from the 34-yard line. The Irish took over. From our prime seats, Nick Setta's kick started wide right, but curved in through the uprights! The Irish started 1-0 after an exciting, hard-fought, comeback game, 29-26, under a bright, blue September sky in South Bend, Indiana. Games like this kept me pursuing this crazy Goal week after week. Not only did I watch my 83rd team, we attended a great college football game, my fourth in overtime! Les and I attended Mass at Notre Dame Cathedral with a thousand others right after the game. Hours later, we drove back to Shipshewanna. We may have to go back there some day to check out the rodeo.

New Brunswick, NJ - Fast Forward to Washington State at Rutgers, 2015: Twelve years after deciding to catch the Washington State Cougars at a game between their home state and north Jersey, they actually showed up at The Birthplace of College Football. Facing the pass-happy Cougars, coached by venerable, memorable, and recently deceased Head Coach Mike "I refuse to punt" Leach, the combination of that strategy against RU's secondary decimated by scandalous crimes, made for a thrilling battle to the finish.

Leach's reputation didn't precede him at RU

On the first play of the final period, Rutgers quarterback Chris Laviano connected to the right side to tight end Mike Flanagan to get within two. He followed up with a pass for the two-point conversion to Leonte Caroo who came open late crossing the back of the end zone. The score deadlocked now, 20-20. Washington State's next drive resulted in a 37-yard field goal by the strong-legged Erik Powell. On the drive, RU burned its third and final time-out. The Cougars' three-point margin did not last long. Scarlet Knight kickoff returner Janarion Grant found blockers and a seam, and cruised down the left sideline for a 100-yard return. The home crowd celebrated its first lead, 27-23. Plenty of time remained, however, with 12:30 remaining for both teams to continue to light up the scoreboard.

The Cougars had three time-outs to burn. Luke Falk hit Gabe Marks with an out pass for 23 yards to recapture the lead, 30-27. Marks' grab looked short of the goal line as his foot hit the pylon, but the play stood. State kicked the ball short to avoid Grant, and RU still started from the 48. On the series, Cougar Peyton Pueller stripped the ball and Isaac Dotson recovered at their 32. State drove to RU's 39. On fourth and six, Leach handed the Knights a gift as Falk's pass failed incomplete. Rutgers got the ball with great field position. One RU fan nearby screamed, *"The Washington State coach is an imbecile."* The teams exchanged punts – yes, with a 4th and six from his own 24, even Leach decided not to go for a first down.

He might as well have though. Janarion Grant received the punt and took it 55 yards for a 34-30 Rutgers lead. With 1:31 remaining and two time-outs left for Washington State, everyone in High Point Solutions Stadium among the 45,536 fans still remaining knew that Rutgers had scored with too much time left on the clock. Falk went to work again.

Wazu down to the wire on the road again

His short passing game eventually converted on a fourth and five at Rutgers' 38 on a 12-yard pass to Robert Lewis to keep the drive alive. After 59 minutes of poor defense, costly penalties, turnovers, explosive special teams play, no RU pass rush, and coaching wonders and blunders, Washington State quarterback Luke Falk tossed an eight-yard touchdown pass to River Cracraft with thirteen seconds left. Rutgers attempted a rugby-like comeback on the final kickoff that almost resulted in a safety before the final ball carrier flipped the ball forward for a penalty. No time remained on the clock. The Cougars took their first victory of 2015 back to Pullman, Washington, 37-34.

What a game! The Cougars' finished with a 9-4 record marking Mike Leach's turn-around season in Pullman. They went on to defeat the Miami Hurricanes in the Sun Bowl, 20-14. He coached there through the 2019 season before leaving to take over at Mississippi State. Regretfully, he passed away before bowl season in 2022. I would have enjoyed motoring down to Starkville again to watch him coach. Always entertaining! As reported earlier, someday I will figure a way to attend a game at Washington State.

Still Rockin' State Stifles Mike Leach

(83) Texas Tech at North Carolina State, September 20, 2003

Raleigh, North Carolina – The Red Raiders ventured east so I flew down to Raleigh to stay with transplanted Penn Stater, Joe Massimilla, John's brother. Last time we left Joe, now a dad with two young sons, he swore at Greg Hardman and me for our snoring contest in his apartment back at State College. Joe had plans with his boys this particular day. However, Bill and Katyna Esoda, good friends of his a few doors down, saved me their extra ticket for the Texas Tech game. They invited me to join them to see my next addition take on their beloved Wolfpack.

Phil Rivers started at quarterback for NC State and had an arsenal of offensive weapons. Red Raider Head Coach Mike Leach (12 years before the follow-up Washington State vs. Rutgers game in the previous chapter) never learned the meaning of "off tackle" or "end around" or "field goal" or "punt." Maybe "draw play." His quarterback B.J. Symonds arrived in Raleigh as the nation's total offense leader. In 2002, NC State triumphed over Tech, 51-48. I hoped for a similar score this year in Raleigh.

Bill and Katyna picked me up at Joe's. We headed to Carter-Finley Stadium where I savored lasting impressions of a great time there in 1998. Would this experience be as good? First, Bill and Katyna presented me with a red NC State golf shirt to wear to the game! Next, I learned that State takes care of its fans. On a scorching-hot day for a noon kickoff, each seat came with a scarlet *Howl Towel*, a cardboard fan on a stick, and two discount coupons for Coca-Cola products. Somebody already polished off a dozen four-ounce bottles of Southern Comfort strewn under the seats in front of us. No full ones remained. I checked. Regretfully, I understood that they weren't offered as part of the promotional package.

Bigger and Better

Major renovations and expansion had taken place since my visit five years earlier. The enclosed stadium made the atmosphere even more raucous than the energetic night I remembered against Syracuse. What a great place to watch a game! I looked forward to watching Head Coach Chuck Amato coach the Wolfpack that afternoon. The native of Easton, PA played football and wrestled as an ACC champ for NC State in the mid-60s.

Despite major yardage racked up by Tech in the first half, State dominated, 21-0. The Wolfpack throttled its Big 12 foe with a balanced offense, a flexible defense, and aggressive special teams play. The high-powered but scoreless Red Raider offense managed to move from its own 20 to State's 8-yard line with 25 seconds left. However, a 25-yard field goal by PK Keith *Toogood* - no good!

Bill and Katyna beat the stadium crowd out before halftime. They took a short walk back to their tailgate to serve lunch to members of the hungry, NC State swimming team. I stood in long lines on the way out of the seating area on this hot, sun-drenched Saturday. At least I found some shade out from under the sweltering heat!

State running back T.A. McClendon rambled for 67 yards on one play in the first series of the third quarter to put the ball at the Tech one. Josh Brown went in on the next play to put a nail in the Raider coffin to lead, 28-0. One of Tech's patented long drives finally paid off as the next 80-yard drive ended in a 3-yard run by Johnnie Mack. Though trailing 28-7 in the third, there was still a feeling that with a few breaks, the Red Raiders could get right back in this game with its high-powered offense.

Bang! NC State fumbled on the kick-off return. Tech seemed poised to click at the Pack 22. A heavy rush by State pushed Tech back into a fourth and twelve-yard situation. Symonds set up in the pocket, broke loose, rushed up field, passed the first down marker, and fumbled! A block in the back after the recovery gave State the ball at its own six. This seemed to be the final nail necessary to seal the Red Raiders coffin, but the Wolf Pack came up with a few more. A 37-yard pass to Jerricho Cotchery and a pass interference call in the end zone keyed Josh Brown's second touchdown from two yards out. The Pack controlled, 35-7, late in the third period.

Both teams scored touchdowns on long drives in the fourth. The Pack continued to score just like the previous season's shoot-out. Tech padded stats with its first team offense and used the clock against second and third team defenders to make the score seem somewhat respectable. Despite 586 passing yards by slinging B.J. Symonds, who fired the ball 63 times, Rivers finished more efficiently. He completed 18 of 22 for 257 yards in a 49-21 NC State victory.

Over all, it was an old-fashioned ass-whooping with some miscalculated coaching decisions by Tech's Mike Leach. He deferred some easy first-half field goals to put points on the board and build momentum for his team. Instead, the Raiders came up empty, but that was their style. State's defense rose to the occasion in tough situations.

I tailgated with the Esodas and friends after the game. NC State proved again to have a fun, partying, football atmosphere despite their stronger reputation as an ACC basketball power. In the Esoda's tradition, they asked me sign the underside of their tailgate canopy as did all their guests. I scribed: "Collegefootballfan.com: Texas Tech #84, but NC State rocks!" I look forward to going back there. It's another repeat on the Bucket List.

Boston College 53 - (84) Ball State 29
Alumni Stadium, Chestnut Hill, Massachusetts, September 27, 2003

Boston College indoor practice facility to which No. 1 Alum Bob "Pops" LeBlanc and his fellow Eagle Alumni contributed.

Am I really here? / Bowl Selections and Perceptions

(85) UL-Monroe at (86) UL-Lafayette, October 11, 2003

Lafayette, Louisiana - As John McGrath aptly pointed out in his article about my adventures, "*College Football's Superfan,*" in the 2005 edition of <u>Lindy's</u> pre-season publications: "Sometimes it's heaven, watching college football games between big-time heavyweights. And sometimes you make a U-turn and drive a few miles down a highway, and find out it's even better."[1] That's basically what happened when I determined it was too big a risk to travel to Dallas in 2003 for the Red River Shootout. Initially, I proposed to attend the perennial war waged at the Texas State Fairgrounds between Texas and Oklahoma that weekend.

My former Juniata roommate and Texas MBA, Todd Kulp, tried to get tickets, but to no avail. Rather than take a chance and not find a ticket or go pay some outrageous scalper price, I decided to hold my cards. I searched for the next "best" match-up that weekend. No other *glamorous* match-ups benefiting The Goal were scheduled. So, to come up with two new teams to meet my criteria, logistical analysis helped determine my final decision. I accumulated significant frequent flier miles. So, I determined my best strategy. I opted for a game between two teams yet to be added who were quite a distance. Both teams Identified would help me reach The Goal - perfect for my purpose, UL- Monroe at UL-Lafayette. My internet search indicated that some of the highest airfares from Newark's Liberty Airport to other parts of the country included flights to Louisiana.

On a previous business trip to Lafayette, I recalled seeing signs to UL-Lafayette, home of the Ragin' Cajuns. Not far from my hotel, it was close to the airport. A free airline ticket, no need for a rental car, a cheap hotel, and some good old Cajun' cooking nearby finalized my decision. I planned to see a match-up between two of the worst college football teams this side of the new millennium.

The week before, in a game I referred to on my site as the *"Battle at the Bottom of the Barrel,"* ESPN.com coined it as its *"Pillow Fight of the Week."* Undaunted, I flew to Lafayette, Louisiana to see the Ragin' Cajuns (0-6) host the Indians of UL-Monroe (0-6). They played not only for the basement of the Sun Belt Conference, but the outcome would determine the worst team in all of Division-IA college football!

Cajun Country cooks!

What's not to love about Louisiana? People there start with *Mardi Gras* in New Orleans and party throughout the state for the rest of the year. They even have Margarita drive-thrus! Walking up to the visitor's side of Cajun Field about 40 minutes prior to kick-off was like walking into a ghost town. On the home side though, I found a lively parking lot. A rock band entertained hosting hundreds of Cajun tailgate homecoming parties.

In the middle sat a Budweiser beer wagon, an oasis of refreshment after a three-mile hike with no immediate tailgate plans. A Ragin' Cajun cook-off took place for Homecoming festivities. They know how to eat, drink, and party all year long in Louisiana. The Ragin' Cajun Marching Band performed and then marched into Cajun Field before I bought a ticket on the home side. However, I could choose to sit anywhere I wanted to among a homecoming crowd of 13,540.

After the Monroe Indians completed a pass on the first play from scrimmage, I laughed, shook my head, and said, "I can't believe I'm really *here!*" Instead of two 0-6 teams, I could have been watching Texas play Oklahoma. As for this setting, the personality of today's game took shape all around me. Ragin Cajun quarterback Eric Rekieta heard the calls. No doubt, he read the facetious signs, "Rekieta for Heisman!"

After an early Monroe touchdown, the two teams demonstrated why they were ranked at the very bottom of IA football. During the next six series, both teams generally went backwards. Poor blocking, delays of game, and motion penalties prevailed. Both teams generally began each series with a first and 15 or more. Even the electric scoreboard operator at Cajun Field felt frustration or insinuated sarcasm. The result of a Monroe punt from the six-yard line on fourth and long prompted the scoreboard message, "Nice play!" That's as good as it got early in this game.

By the end of the first half, No. 116 UL-M led No. 117 UL-L, 28-14. During halftime, Lafayette-Louisiana (formerly SW Louisiana) introduced a distinguished alumnus - Cy Young Award Winner and former NY Yankee Ron "Gator" Guidry, "Louisiana Lightning." I wondered if Guidry was somehow paying attention to the Yankee-Red Sox playoff game going on while attending his alma mater's homecoming festivities. Hmmm? Two 0-6 college teams or a "classic" Major League playoff series in one of the biggest rivalries in professional sports? Tough call for Gator?

UL-L tied the score with a one-yard run following a long pass by "Heisman candidate" Rekieta to Fred Stamps on a 64-yard pass. The Ragin' Cajuns challenged in the second half. Monroe took back the lead, 35-28, when substitute quarterback Dan DaPrato ran 45 yards to set up a one-yard plunge by Jason Schule.

Around that time, the loudest cheer of the day came from the combined stands of fans. Over the PA system, it was announced LSU was on the short end of the score against Florida. Louisianans couldn't have been happier at Cajun Field! Call it jealousy or lack of respect, but pure Ragin' Cajun and "Injun" hatred stirred in Louisiana for the SEC Tigers. Two girls wore shirts that read, "If you don't support the Cajuns, move to Baton Rouge!"

Wake me up. Somebody, pinch me, please!

After several non-scoring series for both teams, Monroe scored again to go up 42-28 on Kevin Payne's two-yard touchdown run. It wasn't over!

Rekieta retaliated leading a pair of scoring drives culminating with passes to tight end Josh Joerg and to Bill Sampy. Game tied 42-42 with 5:23 left. "I can't believe I'm really *here*!" At that point, a young, UL-Lafayette coed ran down behind me from the exhilarated, student section so she could hear. She conversed on her cell phone with someone evidently on the way to pick her up. She intensely shouted into her phone. "It's the fourth quarter. We just scored. It's 42-42. There's 4:17 left. This is serious! I have a *dollar* on this game!" That's the kind of fan loyalty that makes college football a great game.

On a third and 14 on their ensuing series, the Indians ran a double reverse option pass to Mack Vincent. He hauled it in at the Lafayette 34. With 1:46 left, Tyler Kuecker (pronounced "kicker") booted a 31-yarder which gave the Indians the game-winner, 45-42. Wow! What an exciting finish to this game between the two worst teams in D-IA after a very shaky start. The 1-6 Indians congratulated their vanquished, winless foe. They knelt to pray with them, and then sprinted to their contingency of fans who celebrated like it was the national championship. LSU be damned! "I can't believe I'm *really here*!"

Despite the ineptitudes on both sides rated as the two worst by ESPN.com the prior week, it was a hard-fought, exciting, memorable game. Played between equally talented teams played in a spirited, competitive game, it was an exhilarating Cajun homecoming despite their loss. My timing worked out better than I could ever imagine. The annual Red River Shoot-out between Texas and Oklahoma ended in a Sooner rout, 65-13. That couldn't compare to this in excitement and intensity! Great timing for me.

Though at the lower end of the spectrum, this game allowed me to add two new teams. Even better, I didn't have to see either 0-6 team get blown out by better teams. Instead, I got to enjoy a surprisingly remarkable 45-42 fight to the finish. Rekieta ended up with 474 passing yards and four touchdown passes, but eventually, no Heisman. As I said all along that day, "I can't believe I'm really *here*!" However, I'm glad I was! "*What better way to spend an autumn afternoon?*" UT vs OU remains on the Bucket

List for a future showdown. Hopefully, it will be as competitive as this clash.

San Marcos, Texas - Fast Forward to Louisiana at Texas State (TXST), 2020: As mentioned, my daughter Alex became my prime Texas connection. Primarily, it all starts with her fiancé Zach. He's now Director of Business Development at TXST, basically fund-raising for the Bobcat athletic programs. As a member of the Sun Belt Conference, the Bobcats play both the Louisiana Ragin' Cajuns, formerly UL-Lafayette, and UL-Monroe, former Indians, now Warhawks, annually in the West Division.

With our donations to support his Bobcats, Zach sets St. Laurie and I up nicely when we visit the Austin area for a football weekend. Thanks to Zach and to Texas State football regarding 2020. When many venues did not allow many, if any fans, to attend games, St. Laurie and I got to attend one in San Marcos. This turned out to be one of my only three games during that Covid-wrecked season. The Bobcats hosted the Ragin Cajuns for my first game of 2020, the day after Halloween.

On a perfect evening for football under a full Halloween moon, it started with a lot of bumps in the night at Bobcat Stadium. The Cajuns quickly swiped two Bobcat passes. They turned both into 14 points for an early lead. Instead of allowing a romp after starting the game with a 14-point deficit, Texas State answered with 21 points of their own. The Cajuns tied it up on quarterback Levi Lewis's 12-yard touchdown run.

With 2:26 to go in the half, Lewis's passes and Trey Ragas's runs put the Cajuns in the end zone in six plays. TXST took over with a minute left. However, Brady McBride threw his third interception of the half, second by Cajun defensive back Eric Garror. With seven ticks left, Lewis connected with Kyren Lacy for a one-yard score. The Ragin Cajun's led, 34-21, going into halftime.

Forget the "new" normal!

With Covid-19 bringing us into the world of abnormality, it really hit even more at halftime. A pre-recorded show was featured on two Bobcat Stadium video boards located on angles at each end of the horseshoe-shaped stadium. The recordings just don't do justice for the experience of attending a live, energetic college football halftime show. The Texas State University Strutter's Precision Dance Team, 111-strong, sat relegated in the enclosed end zone all dressed up with no place to go along with 7,500 others estimated to be in attendance. All sat and watched their pre-recorded performance. What a letdown for students and Bobcat fans. Fans couldn't wait for good, old normalcy to return.

To start the second half, the visitors extended their lead, 37-21, with a 42-yard field goal. The home team closed the gap, 37-27, with a run from 10 yards out. The two-point conversion failed. The Bobcat D forced a Cajun punt to potentially make the game more interesting, but the offense sputtered. In the fourth, Louisiana relied on their running game to eat up the clock. Ragas rushed for a seven-yard TD, his third of the game. Bobcat Brock Sturges ran for his second score of the day from 18 yards out. TXST's onsides attempt landed safely in the grasp of the Louisiana hands team. The visitors from Cajun country prevailed, 44-34.

Good news and better news for the Cajuns who ran their record to 10-1 in 2020. Good news, they defeated 7-5 UTSA in the First Responder "Bowl" in Dallas, 31-24 (Bowl/Consolation game?). Better news? The momentum carried them into 2021 to go 13-1 defeating Appalachian State in the Sun Belt Championship game and Marshall (7-6) in the New Orleans "Bowl" (consolation?).

Lynchburg, Virginia - Fast Forward to Louisiana at Liberty, 2021: After losing their opener at Texas, the Ragin' Cajuns ran the table against their Sun Belt foes. In addition, St. Laurie and I stopped on our way back to NJ for Thanksgiving to see the Cajuns soundly defeat a good Liberty team in Lynchburg, Virginia, 42-14. Bad news, however, came later when the Florida Gators recognized the Ragin' Cajuns' success and absconded with Head Coach Billy Napier to lead them against SEC foes in the future.

As for UL-Monroe, they remain a one-time gamer in my history book right now. Maybe they'll meet at a Texas State game we'll attend eventually. If they ever hit a winning stride, maybe I'll catch them against some other tough Sun Belt foe whether on the road or at home.

Bowl Selections: pair strengths against perceptions

Louisiana (12-1) deserved a better bowl challenge than Marshall (7-5) in the 2021 New Orleans Bowl. Louisiana demonstrated the potential as a current Group of Five team to be as good, if not better, than many teams considered to be "Power Five." For the "better," a new selection strategy would not only to enhance bowl game competition to conjure up more interesting head-to-head match-ups, but to also challenge perceived differences between programs in the Group of Five compared to the Power Five. Of course, this counters media network misconceptions that supports Power Five monopolization. Rather than contract teams annually from two different conferences to guarantee what teams/conferences gain the most dollars, pair teams randomly after every season through a Selection Committee based on more objective measurements.

Levi Lewis (1) outgunned Liberty's Malik Willis in No. 16 Louisiana's 42-14 win at Lynchburg, Virginia on their way to 13-1 in 2021.

[1] John McGrath, "College Football's Superfan," Lindy's 2005 Pre-season (2005): p. 20.

Toe beats Heels by a Foot / Big Ugly: A Case of NIL Enticements

(87) Arizona State at North Carolina, October 18, 2003

Chapel Hill, NC - I drove further than usual to catch my last remaining PAC-10 team because I didn't have to fly. The Arizona State Sun Devils traveled east to face the North Carolina Tar Heels. The rematch of the previous year's UNC 38-35 victory in the desert provided me with an opportunity to see a game played in Chapel Hill for the first time.

During my drive, it sounded like followers of 1-5 North Carolina had already written off football season. A local radio sports program on a station referred to the *"Voice of the Tar Heels"* already talked basketball. There was cause for excitement though because Roy Williams was on his way from Kansas to take over the Tar Heel basketball program. However, the sportscaster lost control of his senses when he dedicated a song saying, *"'Love Train'* - with no love to the Wildcats!" *Wildcats*? I knew what he meant. Someone needed to remind him that today's football game was against the *Arizona State Sun Devils*! A basketball game versus the *Arizona Wildcats* would follow a few months from now.

The game started off competitively, but the officiating crew created controversies from the start with horrible calls, no calls, and even a "re-call!" Questionable calls mounted, mostly against the visitors. ASU tallied 16 flags for 153 yards while Carolina had only three for 22. Visiting teams normally warranted crews from their conferences, but supposedly because of distance, an ACC crew officiated - hard to believe in this day and age. One example of a bad call came on a UNC possession. The refs flagged quarterback Darian Durant for intentional grounding. He clearly ran beyond the tackle box and threw to a receiver in an area when he tossed it out of bounds. Everyone at Kenan understood the rule except for the refs. After a long-winded discussion amongst this bumbling crew, the umpire waved off the flag and hollered, "No foul!" In unison, you heard the UNC crowd respond, "*No s—t!*"

The score stood deadlocked 14-14 in the second period until ASU's Jess Ainsworth booted a 21-yard field goal. The Sun Devils recovered a misplayed punt at the Tar Heel 12 with 1:38 left before halftime. One first down, one offside penalty, and six time-outs later, Ainsworth booted a 24-yarder to extend the ASU lead, 20-14.

Trailing 27-17 later in the game, one Tar Heel fan blurted out, "Bring on basketball season!" His football team didn't give up though. On the next play, Durant completed a 63-yard scoring pass to Jawarski Pollock. Now the Heels trailed, 27-24. To start the final period, Arizona State missed a 32-yard field goal, and UNC took over from its 20. With the aid of a questionable interference call, the Heels had first and ten at the ASU 20. On the final play of the 15-play series, Durant showed good patience as he rolled to his right and waited a split second to connect with Jacques Lewis out of the backfield at the right goal line pylon for a 1-yard score. Carolina took the lead, 31-27, with 7:43 remaining. Game not over.

The teams traded punts until Sun Devil Daryl Lightfoot returned a punt 28 yards to put his team on their 39 with only 36 seconds to play. A 42-yard pass to Derek Hagan put the Sun Devils at the five with six ticks left. Andrew Walter spiked the ball to reset the clock at three. With no time remaining, Walter fired to Skyler Fulton who dragged his toe about one foot in-bounds at the back of the end zone for the game-winning score, 33-31! The Wildcats, er…Sun Devils, sprinted en masse to their cheering fans on the far end of the field where the State contingent started their chant, "A-S-U! A-S-U! A-S-U!" The Heels fell with no time left. They hung their heads. Their fans fell silent, and together, UNC's collective thoughts turned: "Bring on basketball season." This turned out to be the second of seven consecutive games I'd attend where the final score was determined on the last play of the game! A record for me, but probably in anybody else's book, too.

A Case of NIL Bidding

Tempe, Arizona - Fast forward to a game at Arizona State in the future in a conference to be determined later: I hope to see the Sun Devils play for a second time eventually - either home or away. Regarding freshman Jaden Rashada, as of spring 2023, he's at Arizona State taking reps at quarterback under new Head Coach Kenny Dillingham who looks to rebuild off a 3-9 season. If Jaden's as good as reported, I hope to see the Sun Devils play again while he's at Arizona State. The Rashada family went through a whirlwind of issues regarding the new Name, Image, and Likeness (NIL) policy initiated by the NCAA. However, the recruitment of Jaden demonstrates the confusion and turmoil presented by recruiting factions regarding this new NIL policy. This case is analyzed in Essay I of this book, "Vision of the Future" under section 5, "Who's controlling all the mayhem?" His family did everything right through the entire ordeal. According to reports from different sources, the Rashada family did not discuss any NIL agreements before Jaden committed to Arizona State.[1]

Connecticut 38 - (88) Akron 37
Rentschler Field, East Hartford, Connecticut, October 25, 2003

Maryland 23 - (89) Northern Illinois 20
Byrd Stadium, College Park, Maryland. September 4, 2004

[1] Ryan Bologna, Clutch Points, "Full details of Jaden Rashada's termination of $13.85 million deal", February 6, 2023

Dumped on!

(90) Western Michigan at Virginia Tech, September 11, 2004

Blacksburg, Virginia - The Hokies home opener began as a solemn occasion. Virginia Tech's Corps of Cadets (ROTC) honored alumnus Lt. Tim Price, a 2001 graduate, who lost his life in action in Iraq only a few days prior to this game played on 9/11. The huge Hokie crowd observed a moment of silence to his memory. It gives one pause to reflect that the Americans over there come from all walks of life from all around this country to put their lives on the line for peace and freedom against terrorism. The somber occasion was marked by its Corps of Cadets marching on before the game with musical accompaniment by its drum and bugle corps, the "Highty Tighties." It ended on a high note with the awesome display of a loud and majestic flyover of a B-52H Stratofortess.

Flanker Eddie Royal scored on the Hokies first play from scrimmage on an 11-yard reverse. Cedric Humes rumbled in from the 21 for the next score. Tailback Justin Hamilton punched it in from one, and Bryan Randall threw his first of two touchdown passes in the game to Royal on a 35-yarder. It was "only" 28-0 at the half. WMU's offense was anemic. Their defense wasn't so hot either. Tech freshman quarterback Sean Glennon threw for two scores after replacing Randall. I was committed to stay, of course. Getting bored while sitting in seat No. 1 at the end of a row in the south end zone witnessing decimation, excitement loomed, but it wasn't on the field.

Making the best of a mess!

PLOP! A platter of nachos landed directly into my lap—cheese, salsa, peppers, beans, chili sauce, and chopped meat! A genteel grandmother on the way down the stairs with a snack for her grandkids was jostled by some VA Tech ROTC chopping on his way up. He bumped into her arm, and she disposed of her hot platter into my lap. She apologized profusely, and offered the wad of napkins she had. Luckily, the tasty dish only got as far as my left leg and missed the new pair of binoculars dangling from my neck. I cleaned up my shorts as best I could, but it put a further damper on any note-taking in what was a boring game any way.

The accident initiated a conversation with one Hokie fan. We watched the rest of the game together, a happy victory for him after four straight losses, and a disappointment to soiled-and-spoiled me. Spoiled primarily because I'd seen so many good games during the previous season. This was a letdown after a long drive to Blacksburg. How much can be said about a team beaten by the widest margin of victory I'd ever seen? Virginia Tech dominated WMU on offense, on defense, on special teams, with second teams, and every imaginable way. The Hokies busted these Broncos, 63-0!

The carnage continued as the nacho cheese and chili sauce dried on my shorts during the fourth period. Western Michigan became the 90th team toward The Goal, and the streak of good, close games seen since the previous September came to an end. A clunker was due. This was it. To get to this crazy Goal, sometimes somebody has to get dumped on. However, I never expected it to be me!

Kalamazoo, Michigan - Fast Forward, maybe? Too cold for night games in November anywhere in Michigan, so probably not.

Penn State 37 - (91) Central Florida 13
Beaver Stadium, State College, Pennsylvania, September 18, 2004

Fast Forward to 2020- Football just wasn't the same during Covid-19 when I at least got to see Cincinnati battle with Central Florida in Orlando.

Undefeated and BCS-bound - Not! / ♫♪Liberty! Liberty! Liberty! ... Over-time! ♪♫

(92) Arkansas at Auburn, October 16, 2004

Auburn, Alabama - The Razorbacks remained one of two SEC teams' unseen. This year Arkansas, maybe next year, Mississippi State. I contacted Charlie Murren to see if he had an "in" this season to attend the Arkansas-Auburn game. Boy! Did Charlie have an *"in"*.

Every family wants their kids to achieve beyond what they've done. I remember my first trips to Auburn to stay with Charlie at his Magnolia dorm. Back then, Lynda, his future wife, worked in one of the school's cafeterias. Now, their two daughters attended Auburn. Laura, a freshman, didn't live in a dorm much unlike Charlie's, but as far as convenience, she had a great location allowing us to tailgate close to Jordan-Hare Stadium right in front of her apartment. Charlie backed his pick-up loaded down with tailgate trimmings and furnishings right up the front door of Laura's first-floor apartment, convenient with running water and a private bathroom, to set up our tailgate.

Megan, a junior, outdid her mom as far as college employment. Majoring in journalism, she worked for the P.R. staff of the Auburn Tiger football program. She worked the press box during games charting and distributing stats to the working press. Basically, she worked for Tommy Tuberville, knew all the players, kept game stats, and even wrote a featured article in that day's edition of *Auburn Football Illustrated*. Talk about an "in!" It only got better.

We arrived at Auburn early to meet with Megan before the game. Once we set up the tailgate on Laura's front lawn, Charlie and I ambled over to Jordan-Hare. Charlie was as excited as I was and proud, too! Megan arranged to meet with us before the game to take us on a tour of the stadium press box. This was big! After 25 years of attending games, this was our first opportunity to view the field from the perch of pundits.

A Friend in High Places

Megan greeted us with hugs and press passes. We took the elevator up to press row. She showed us how the press lives compared to us true fans among the huddled masses. We passed a bunch of the media guys seated at tables enjoying a free buffet in a lounge well-protected from the elements. We checked out their covered, unobstructed view of the entire playing field. Tables provided plenty of elbow room. Wiring for electronic hook-ups stood ready for their observations for the entire sports world to read and hear. We strolled by a radio booth and popped into the CBS-TV broadcast booth. Vern Lundquist and Todd Blackledge hadn't arrived yet, but Charlie and I were ready to fill in just in case.

The game itself featured a number of players who would soon be watched by NFL writers, too. The home team struck quickly on a reverse flea-flicker 1:10 into the game. Jason Campbell hooked up with Davin Arrmashodu for a 67-yard score. The Tigers extended the lead, 10-0, on John Vaughn's 27-yard field goal. Auburn made it 17-0 before the quarter ended on a 30-yard scoring strike from Campbell to tight end Courtney Taylor. The Tigers drove 53 yards on their next possession culminated by Ronnie Brown's one-yard plunge. Carnell "Cadillac" Williams did the damage next time as he took it over from two yards after another long Tiger scoring drive. Houston Nutt's Razorbacks finished the half with an 80-yard scoring drive. Matt Jones tossed a 19-yard TD pass to Chris Baker. Auburn led in a 30-13 rout at the half.

With future Washington Redskin quarterback Jason Campbell calling signals, the fourth-ranked Auburn Tigers went on to a 38-20 win. Backs Ronnie Brown (Dolphins) and Carnell "Cadillac" Williams (Buccaneers) ran for 103 and 75 yards respectively. Each recorded a score. Matt Jones, the Arkansas quarterback and only returning starter on offense for the Hogs, got selected as a wide receiver by the Jacksonville Jaguars. Megan provided me with my own personal stat sheet fresh from press row. I had all the stats I needed for this week's Game Review on www.collegefootballfan.com.

The final of 38-20 wasn't as close as it sounds. Campbell watched from the sidelines by the fourth. However, even though this turned out to be one of 13 wins for Auburn against no defeats, the big news for the season was that the Tigers got left out of the BCS championship game - a game that was supposed to end all the controversies regarding the national title. It didn't! USC whipped Oklahoma for the national championship, 55-19. Auburn defeated VA Tech in the Sugar Bowl, 16-13, to remain another undefeated team at the end of a season at No. 2.

Give me Liberty Bowl, and give us overtime!

Memphis, TN - Fast forward to Arkansas vs. Kansas in the Liberty Bowl, 2022: When the Bowl announced the Jayhawks would meet the Razorbacks in Memphis, I jumped at the chance to see KU finally play for only the second time since 1993. As I noted earlier, I wanted to see Kansas Head Coach Lance Leipold win his seventh game of the season. I called Rick Selak, the Auburn friend who insulted this Mets fan when he called me a Yankee so many years ago down at that "little village on the Plains." Rick lived right outside of Memphis for many years now. He was game. He looked forward to a night out, and he had a vested interest. His daughter and his money graduated from the University of Arkansas!

Arkansas led Kansas by 25 with four minutes left in the third. The Jayhawks stormed back:

- An 86-yard drive capped by a two-yard run;
- A 36-yard field goal;

- A fumble recovery resulting in a 10-yard touchdown pass by Jalon Daniels;
- An onsides kick recovered, followed by a 21-yard scoring pass;
- And a successful pass for two points tied the score at the end of regulation, 38-38.

In the first two overtimes, both teams tallied 15 points. Next, on their first two-point conversion attempt, the Razorbacks scored in the third OT on a run by Rashad Dubinion. For Kansas, running back Jason Bean flipped an errant option pass despite appearing to have room ahead to run the ball in himself. Tough break to end a fantastic game. The Razorbacks took the bowl victory, 55-53. At the end of regulation in front of an enthusiastic crowd of 52,847 pretty evenly divided between both schools, all I could say was, "Wow!" Rick conferred, "That about sums it up!"

Regarding my future with Arkansas, Reynolds Razorback Stadium remains one of two SEC stadiums I've yet to attend (until Oklahoma joins anyway). So, a game there definitely looms on my Bucket List in the next few years.

Arkansas 24 - (93) Mississippi State 21
Davis Wade Stadium, Starkville, Mississippi, November 20, 2004

Didn't get a good night's sleep? / Broncos Bust Hokies, but not BCS.

(94) Boise State at Georgia, September 3, 2005

Athens, Georgia - I looked forward to 2005 with great anticipation. Over 14 weekends, the schedule I planned offered me opportunities to add 12 new teams I hadn't seen yet. It also included several new venues including a significant one at which to open the season. Charlie Murren III came through again. My unexpected trip to see Mississippi State the previous year completed the SEC for me. So instead of heading out to an Auburn game, Charlie came up with tickets through one of his managers at work.

Gary Smith, a Georgia grad and season ticket holder, came up with six tickets for UGA's opener to allow us to see the next team toward The Goal, the Boise State Broncos. Not only for me, but for Charlie and Lynda and their son Danny who lived about 30 miles away from Athens, it presented the first chance to see a game "between the hedges" at historic Sanford Stadium. The second largest campus venue I got to visit at this point. It also turned out to definitely be the loudest!

What a great start to the season for me personally. Both schools ranked in everybody's Top 25 preseason polls. The hometown Dawgs returned experienced and deep at key positions. Boise State boasted a high-powered offense led by Heisman hopeful, quarterback Jared Zabransky. On top of the great match-up and new venue to start the season, Eric now age 10, joined me for his first trip to fly to a game with me. He couldn't wait!

The next day, Charlie and Lynda set up one of their great tailgate spreads as usual. We settled in a parking lot under shade trees at the corner of Lumpkin and Dougherty in Athens. We took seats in the upper deck to watch warm-ups and pre-game festivities. The stadium reverberated already. We got ready to watch a very competitive game.

One of those days, Jared?

On his first pass from scrimmage, Zabransky rolled right. He threw an interception right into the hands of middle linebacker Tony Taylor. Two minutes and three seconds into the "contest," Georgia QB D.J. Shockley completed the short 37-yard drive with a 14-yard touchdown run. Unchallenged, Zabransky's next pass ended up in the hands of linebacker Dannel Ellerbe. The Dawgs started at BSU's 38. Shockley zipped the ball to split end Kenneth Harris for a 40-yard score. Zabransky fumbled at the UGA 20 on his next series to thwart any offensive threat by the Broncos in the first quarter. On the next offensive series, he overthrew a pass directly into the waiting hands of rover back Tra Battle. He who took it to the Boise 41.

Zabransky faced little or no pressure on any of his errant passes. Brandon Coutu put up three from the 43 yards out for a 17-0 Georgia lead. Free Safety Greg Blue would be the next recipient of a misguided Bronco pass. Danny Murren noted that Zabransky could only complete passes to the players in *red* Bulldog jerseys! Later, in the shotgun formation, the snap hit an unwitting Zabransky in the shoulder pad. The Dawgs recovered his fumble at the Boise 20 with :48 remaining in the half. Eric blurted, "This is sad!" Boy, was he right! Georgia's Danny Ware snuck out of the backfield on the next play for a 20-yard scoring strike from Shockley. Georgia took a 24-0 lead before the half.

Boise Coach Dan Hawkins finally pulled Zabransky. What a horrible 2005 debut for a player who had such a brilliant sophomore season. He loomed as a potential Heisman candidate. This game ended that conjecture. Sorry to say that I cannot remember a poorer individual performance. All I could think of were those clever *Holiday Inn* commercials: "Didn't get a good night's sleep?" Low lights of Zabransky's performance this day would be perfect for one of those ads.

The first-half score sent Charlie and Lynda off to explore downtown Athens for the rest of the game. Gary, Georgia grad, fan, and host, stuck around with Eric and me. The shoppers didn't miss anything. UGA was up 45-7 after three quarters, and it ended up 48-13. The game was a sour disappointment. We witnessed an unexpected clunker to start the season.

A Better Boise Beginning

Landover, Maryland - Fast forward to Boise State vs. Virginia Tech at FEDEX Field, 2010: Though the opener for both teams, this duel looked to be key for No. 3 Boise State's challenge to win the BCS. For No. 10 Virginia Tech, the game in Landover, five hours away from Blacksburg in the suburbs of D.C., was basically a home game. Since the 2006 season when the Broncos pulled their big 43-42 upset against the Oklahoma Sooners in the Fiesta Bowl, Head Coach Chris Petersen's team rolled on to a record of 50-4 heading into 2010. Key returnees included quarterback Kellen Moore with over 7,000 passing yards and 64 touchdown passes the last two seasons. With a 26-1 record, he returned for his junior season. The Broncos came to D.C. riding a 14-game winning streak from the previous undefeated season.

BSU opened this season heavily favored to win the Western Athletic once again. The Hokies presented their biggest challenge for the upcoming season. On this Labor Day evening at FEDEX in the second half, Virginia Polytechnic Institute recovered a Boise State fumble. They then proceeded 31 yards to take a 21-20 lead. State responded immediately. On a third and one, D.J. Harper broke loose on a 71-yard touchdown gallop. The PAT failed. Before the end of the third on fourth and four, Tech's Tyrod Taylor connected with Jarrett Boykin for a 28-yard scoring pass. Their two-point pass failed, but the Hokies led, 28-27.

To start the final period, Boise drove, but a 30-yard field goal attempt misfired. Tech responded with a drive resulting in Chris Hazley's 34-yard marker to extend their lead, 30-26. Both teams exchanged punts. A return of 25 yards by Boise's Mitch Burroughs put the Broncos on their 44. Three passes to three different receivers placed BSU at Tech's 13. With 1:09 left, Moore connected with Austin Pettis to regain the lead, 33-30. Three incompletes by Tech and a Boise sack gave BSU the ball back to run out the clock.

It looked like the Broncos had a clear path ahead to an undefeated season and a legitimate shot at the Bowl Championship Series title game. It looked that way ten games into the season. The Broncos visited the 10-1 Nevada Wolfpack, however, and came up short, 34-31. Both won their remaining games and bowls, but with eight teams left with zero or one loss each at the end of the regular season, 14-0 Auburn defeated 12-1 Oregon in the BCS title game.

Of course, there's no doubt that my Bucket List has to include Boise State's Albertson's Stadium "Smurf turf." There are no real nearby venues to tie this to for a second game, but I think it will be worth the trip to attend a good game there eventually.

(95) New Mexico 45 - (96) Missouri 35
Memorial Stadium, Columbia, Missouri, September 10, 2005

(97) Baylor 20 Army 10
Michie Stadium, West Point, NY, September 17, 2005

No. 5 Baylor's defensive charge in their 29-20 win against Texas State in 2021.

(98) Iowa State 28 Army 21
Michie Stadium, West Point, NY, September 23, 2005

UNJ-Durham Fans? / My Two Utes Games

(99) Utah at North Carolina, October 1, 2005

Chapel Hill, NC - Like Arizona State the year before, the Utah Utes ventured east to Chapel Hill to put them within the limits of my eight-hour driving range. This time, St. Laurie came along to visit with my good friend and former work colleague, Mary Jean Shannon, who was a Quality Control Manager while we worked at AlliedSignal. She and husband Bruce, along with their kids Taylor and Grace, now lived in Cary, not far from Chapel Hill. M.J. and I teamed up together on many business projects. She and Bruce "bled orange." They met at UT in Knoxville, and their kids will have no choice (Update: Grace followed her parents to become a Volunteer. Taylor took to the sky to become a pilot and soar with the Embry-Riddle Eagles).

I always held PSU's bowl wins versus Tennessee over Mary Jean's head when I had to keep her in check at work. It had been about five years since we last worked together, but we kept in touch about kids and football, particularly about my Goal and her Vols! She and Bruce had other plans that Saturday. However, they welcomed us to come down to stay Friday night. They made a great dinner for us while Taylor and Grace proudly performed their renditions of *"Rocky Top!"*

Say what?

On Saturday morning, St. Laurie and I parted, looking forward to visiting the Shannon's again some time. We headed to the game where I found convenient parking at the Chapel Hill Museum. A student we met on Franklin Street was nice enough to give us a personal tour of the campus on our way over to the stadium. When it came up in conversation that we were from New Jersey, he looked me square in the eye. Seriously he asked, "Oh, so you're *Duke* fans?" Puzzled, I told him no, and as a matter of fact to the contrary, we were Navy fans.

Navy played Duke at Durham that afternoon. I had initially hoped that I could have made this a double-header Saturday. If both games didn't share the same kickoff time, we'd be seeing that game as well and rooting for the Mids. However, my priority was to watch UNC host my 99th team, Utah. Duke fans? Surprisingly, he explained Carolina fans consider Duke "the University of New Jersey at Durham." According to him, so many Duke students from our home state matriculate there. I knew many students from Jersey went there, but I'd never heard that reference before. We got tickets in the upper deck from a Tar Heel fan we enjoyed the game with.

Utah visited Chapel Hill just one year after its greatest football season ever, a 12-0 finish and a final No. 4 ranking. The Utes trounced UNC in Salt Lake the previous year, 46-14. They recorded 699 yards in total offense. I hoped this year's game would be more competitive, especially with coaching and quarterback changes at Utah. After 2004, Head Coach Urban Meyer left for Florida, and QB Alex Smith was drafted by the San Francisco 49ers.

Utah was definitely not the same team this year. In fact, they gave up a 95-yard kickoff return to start the game! A pretty slow first half followed, and UNC led 10-7. What a difference a year makes. After allowing the Utes to dominate on offense in last season's loss, Carolina's defense stepped up and forced *five* turnovers. Carolina led 17-14 when Barrington Edwards went in from one to extend the Tar Heel lead. Utah's Dan Beardall converted a 35-yard field goal to whittle the margin to 24-17.

Utah took the ball back on their 44 to start a drive for at least a tie, but on third and fourteen, LB Tommy Richardson recovered Brian Johnson's fumble at the Heels' 19. Gaining only one yard, UNC punter Dave Woolridge held the Utes in check again by holding them to no return yards by hanging them high to force fair catches. Utah's Quinto Ganther fumbled on the ensuing drive. Seven plays later, UNC wide-out Jesse Holley caught a tipped pass from Matt Baker on the right side. He sped across and up the left side to the end zone for six. The home team took a 31-17 lead and the previous year's embarrassment was avenged. Fumble recoveries by linebacker Tommy Richardson and big pass plays from Matt Baker in the final period sealed the win for the Heels. Even if I was a Duke fan, I'd be impressed!

One of the biggest cheers at Kenan came late in the game when the scoreboard indicated that Navy beat Duke, 28-21. Even though the Duke U. football program had been down for many years, it's still UNC's primary rival. Inflamed by the two schools' basketball traditions and a mere nine miles between campuses, they despise each other greatly.

Utes on both coasts

Fast forward to Utah at UCLA at the Rose Bowl in September 2006: Utah's second game for me was a bonus stop. I had seen both the Utes and the UCLA Bruins play already. My primary goal for this west coast trip featured a Thursday night battle between U. of Texas-El Paso at San Diego State. Both appeared as first-time teams to be added! Conveniently, the Utes and Bruins met in Pasadena for me to attend on Saturday. After it was over, the Ute's stood 0-2 still in the annals of my history.

As for former Quality Control Manager, Mary Jean, who I enjoyed the opportunity to work with and still remain friends with, has done very well in her career. She is now President and Managing Director of an international chemical company, Bozzetto, Inc., located in Greensboro, NC. We await attending a Penn State vs. Tennessee game in the future together if and when that happens again. Maybe even a game in Knoxville.

(100) Ohio U. 34 - (101) Buffalo 20
U. of Buffalo Stadium, Amherst, NY, October 29, 2005

Out on the Nut Farm / Finding my Way to San Jose.

(102) San Jose at (103) Fresno State, November 5, 2005

Fresno, California - My future brother-in-law, Frank Lorito, not only lived in the same town as I did now, but we also grew up in the same town, Boonton. We traded stories about events and people we both knew having lived in both small towns. Frank's sister, Marie, who I didn't know, graduated from Boonton High School my freshman year. From Frank, I learned Marie moved out to Fresno, California 30 years earlier with her husband, Sam Chimienti, and they started an almond farm. The wheels of my mind started turning, "If Frank's going to marry my sister..."

Somebody had to start new family ties

It got better! Marie's son Frankie just graduated from Fresno State. Best yet, my new-to-be-cousin Frankie had season tickets for Bulldog football! His Uncle Frank had *never* visited his sister and her family in Fresno. Basically, this was because he feared flying. I volunteered to help Frank overcome his fear of flying. He could do it by visiting his sister in California. To show him the kind of brother-in-law I would be, I'd help by going to Fresno with him, especially if we could work out something in the fall, and particularly on the weekend of November 5. He was way overdue to get out there. I'd keep it open just for him. That's just the kind of guy I am.

By the way, it also just happened that the Fresno State Bulldogs hosted the San Jose State Spartans that Saturday. These two teams would probably never make it out to Jersey, much less the east coast. Since I'd seen neither team play, this seemed like the perfect opportunity to add these two teams to get this thing done, and I could get acquainted with my extended family. *Finally*, Frank realized how much he missed his sister. We were on our way, but on separate flights. He "toughed" it out on his own. Proud of him, he flew solo. However, I would still get out there to show my support. He arrived in Fresno a day before I did.

Learning about Life on the Nut Farm

The Chimienti homestead sat like an oasis in the middle of flat fertile farmland. A few hundred acres of almond trees, a swimming pool, and vineyards surrounded it. Sam converted most of his farmland to grow almond trees to meet the demands of the growing market. Frank and I toured the land with him to see the intricate irrigation system and see first-hand the methods to get rid of pesky ground squirrels. It reminded me of Bill Murray's war with the groundhog in *"Caddyshack."* Picking off the little varmints with a rifle firing down rows of almond trees seemed the most challenging. New technology, similar to Murray's in the movie, took a lot of the challenge away.

We stopped in Sam's workshop, filled with equipment for planting, maintaining, and harvesting almonds and citrus. He told us how he knew nothing about farming when he moved out from Jersey 30 years before. When he started growing almonds, he faced other challenges. At first, he used to shake the branches of trees with sticks while the nuts fell on to mats lying below. He realized that this wasn't going to work if he ever wanted to turn almonds into cash. He invested in machines with long steel bars with cushions on the end that wrapped around the almond tree trunks. The arms vibrated at high speeds shaking off all the nuts so quickly that the trees sent up thick clouds of white smoke.

Frank and I witnessed a dose of difficulty farmers face when Sam stopped by his office to check his mail. He received a letter doubling the cost of his beehives needed for pollination of the almond trees. Bees were inexplicably dying off by the millions throughout the country, reducing supply and raising costs for farmers, but also threatening the longevity and supply of certain food crops. Frank and I were getting an education out on the nut farm. As a matter of fact, Sam helped us to better understand the distinctive regions of the state of California. He broke it down. He explained, "Fruits in the north, flakes in the south, and nuts in the middle!" The trip turned out to be a truly educational experience as well as a chance to meet my extended Chimienti family and experience a tailgate party at a Fresno State football game.

Air time

A few days prior to departure, my site Collegefootballfan.com, took on more hits and e-mails than usual. A Fresno fan who managed a Bulldog website made note of my history and upcoming trip out to Fresno. Thanks to his mention, radio station KMJ580's *Dog Talk Show* contacted me to set up an interview before Saturday night's game. They'd call me on my cell while tailgating with my long-lost Chimienti cousins and their Bulldog friends. It turned out to be a larger tailgate than I expected.

It's a good thing I convinced Frank to get out and visit his sister. Despite living and farming in Fresno for 30 years and sending a son to Fresno State, Sam and Marie had never been to a Fresno State football game! They hadn't realized what they were missing. Cousin Frankie invited us all to party with some of his fraternity brothers at *Zuber Realty's* tailgate party. They had a large area cordoned off next to a company truck that brought in all the tables, chairs, grills, and buffet supplies needed for a large gathering.

Servers piled up chili, rice, beans, and other good stuff on our plates from the Mexican-style buffet. It was first-class all the way! Margaritas and pitchers of beer were available for all us Fresno fans, old and new. Frankie's buddies were intrigued by my Goal. I was having a good time until I had to excuse myself for my KMJ580 moment of fame.

Frank, Marie, Frankie, and others crammed into cars nearby to tune in.

The call came through. I was on the air! The hosts asked typical questions about who I'd seen, what teams remained, how I got to this game, and some of my travel experiences. Near the end, when one of them thought they would trap me into some form of shame, I caught him off-guard! "So, basically what you do is travel around the country, go to games, and eat for free!"

"And drink!" I unabashedly replied. When I get together with friends, old or new, near or far, it's a party, especially at a football game! I'm not allowed to carry a cooler on a plane, but I make the effort to pick up beer or bring something else with me. At least I get around to visiting friends, old and new, who I rarely get the chance to be with otherwise in these times when everyone is constantly busy working, raising families, and moving to far-off places. Going to games around the country gave me memorable experiences to do this on many great occasions to places I would never get to visit otherwise.

Fresno Head Coach Pat Hill and I think alike: "Anybody, anytime, anywhere!"

I figured this match-up would be a blowout unless the Bulldogs took the Spartans lightly, and they had good reason to. Co-WAC leader Boise State would visit Fresno the following Thursday. Two Saturdays after this game, the Bulldogs would travel to the L.A. Coliseum to match up against the No.1 Trojans of USC, part of Coach Pat Hill's mantra, "Anybody, anytime, anywhere!" Kind of like my football adventure now that I was traveling more often around this great country to attend games much farther away.

The No. 22-ranked Fresno State Bulldogs did not, after all, look past their "defenseless" WAC rival to its next two games. Spartan tailback Al Guidry broke off a 30-yard touchdown run to avert a Bulldog shut-out. FSU proceeded to bash the San Jose State Spartans, 45-7. FSU's Paul Pinegar threw for 368 yards and three scores and ran for another. Wendell Mathis rushed for 105 yards. For SJSU, Yonus Davis ran for 136 yards. For me, it was the second time I'd seen a team coached by Dick Tomey, hailed for building Arizona's Desert Swarm defense, get its butt kicked.

In the "Want to get away game," Penn State blasted his Arizona Wildcats, 41-7, in the Pigskin Classic of 1999 in State College. Recall that half an hour after time expired, a Boeing 737 rose above the tree line northeast of the stadium, got altitude, took a sharp turn in the direction of Tucson, Arizona to high-tail it quickly out of central Pennsylvania. Directly overhead, I couldn't see what airline it was, but their quick departure reminded me of one airline's ad campaign seen on TV a few years later – "Want to get away?"

Still finding my way to San Jose

New Brunswick, NJ - Fast forward Fresno at Rutgers, 2008: Turned out I was wrong about Fresno's future travel plans. The Bulldogs came to Jersey to open the 2008 season against Rutgers in New Brunswick. I'm definitely glad I didn't wait until then. I thoroughly enjoyed experiencing a Bulldog game while visiting my extended family out on the nut farm! At Rutgers, Fresno won again, 24-7.

Also in 2012, 10-2 San Jose came out to play 8-4 Bowling Green in the Military Bowl at RFK Stadium in D.C. I bought tickets for Eric and me, but a bad cold sidelined me to the couch for a few days. The four-hour drive and the cold weather just wouldn't agree with me. Wish we could have gone. SJSU defeated BGSU, 29-20. Better game than the next big game I saved myself for. I recovered to fly down to the much-anticipated BCS Championship in Miami on January 7. There, Eric and I got to see Alabama embarrass Notre Dame, 42-14.

As mentioned previously, I want to see a game in Palo Alto with my friend and stalwart Stanford alumnus, Karen Croft. San Jose lies 20 miles away. It would be great to combine a match-up out there after seeing a Stanford game and heading over to see a game between the Spartans and whoever they play.

Army 38 - (104) Arkansas State 10
Michie Stadium, West Point, NY, November 19, 2005

Connecticut 15 - (105) South Florida 10
Rentschler Field, E. Hartford, Connecticut, November 26, 2005

South Florida cheerleaders duck below TV camera on their way back into Lincoln Financial Field at game against Temple in 2016. Their No. 19 Bulls lost to the Owls, 46-30.

Mr. San Diego State! Aztec to the End / UTEP joins C-USA

(106) Texas-El Paso at (107) San Diego State, August 31, 2006

San Diego, California - Several years before the 2006 season, I read a *Sports Illustrated* article about a San Diego State fan by the name of Tom Ables who had attended almost every Aztec game since 1946! I decided that if I ever went out there to watch the Aztecs play, I would have to meet him. SDSU seldom ventured out to play games on the east coast. They mostly play from Hawaii to the Rocky Mountains and sometimes foray into the Midwest. When the 2006 SDSU slate became final, the Aztecs announced their season home-opener against Texas-El Paso. Perfect! I needed both teams.

    I contacted San Diego State by e-mail to see if I could get in touch with their greatest fan when I came out to see them play. They forwarded my message to Tom and he contacted me the very next day. He enjoyed hearing about my quest to see every team play. He also said that he had 22 season tickets for his family, and if any weren't being used, my brother Chris and I were invited as his guests.

    Of course, going to a Thursday night opener in California also opened up the opportunity for me to attend a game on Saturday. As I would be staying with Chris in Long Beach, I could join him and Jill, a UCLA grad, along with their kids Emily and Nick, who'd never been to a Bruins game at the Rose Bowl before. On Saturday, UCLA would host Utah for my left-coast weekend double-header.

With Tom Ables, Live and in-person!

In San Diego, Chris and I kicked off the season having the honor and privilege of sitting with Tom. This evening, he cheered his Aztecs on in-person for his 646th time. We shared great conversation exchanging stories while rooting for Tom's Aztecs. Among our tales, I'd seen games coached by legends such as Paul "Bear" Bryant, Joe Paterno, Bobby Bowden, and Harold "Tubby" Raymond. Tom's history went back even further. In one of his early SDSU games covering for the school paper as a student, his team played the University of the Pacific, coached by none other than Amos Alonzo Stagg. Talk about a great connection to college football history! Tom still wrote articles for the program *Aztec Game Day*.

Under *"Looking Back"* in this game's edition, he gave a history of all the head coaching debuts at San Diego State. Chuck Long, former Oklahoma offensive coordinator and former Iowa Hawkeye quarterback I'd seen in action against Penn State, made his head coaching debut for the Aztecs in this game. In an editor's note, it stated Tom had seen 645 games in 61 seasons. He missed a trip to Cal Poly in 1964. His son Ken told me, Tom was sick that weekend. His doctor told him to stay home. Whenever he told the story about missing that game he always added: "and I don't think I was that sick; I should have gone to the game." Since then, however, he's attended 475 Aztec games in a row! He missed a previous 1951 trek to the Pineapple Bowl in Hawaii because he couldn't afford it.

Denny Fallon, president of the SDSU Alumni Association and rabid Aztec fan, of course, stopped by to welcome my brother and me. He presented me with "vintage" Aztec sportswear featuring "Monty," as in Montezuma, the Aztec chieftain.

During halftime, we conversed with Tom about some of the stadiums where I'd like to attend games in the future. He provided us with his insights to the ones he'd been to: Wisconsin's Camp Randall— "Great atmosphere!" Ohio State's Ohio Stadium— "Loved the stadium and the fans there." After a 16-13 loss, the Buckeye fans gave his Aztecs a standing ovation. The Big House at Michigan—unimpressed. His wife, Nancy, veteran of 411 games as of this date, says that the one place she will not go back to is Laramie, Wyoming. "Too cold!"

Tom told how the Aztecs almost didn't make it to the game there on October 6, 1984. The team traveled through a blizzard. Wyoming pushed for a no-show forfeit while the Aztecs were traveling through treacherous weather. SDSU showed up an hour late. They played and went on to defeat the Cowboys, 24-21. Tom described the Aztecs field goal as "going straight into the jaws of the blizzard" to break a 21-21 tie just as time ran out to end the game (pre-OT regulations).

Tom's 646th; my 294th

As for action on the field this evening, UTEP was led by quarterback Jordan Palmer, brother of former USC star, Carson. He led them to a 14-3 lead at the half. Tyler Campbell, son of Pro Hall of Famer Earl, returned the ball for SDSU to start the second half. In the third period, things didn't look good for the Aztecs trailing, 27-3. Then, a quarterback switch and a couple of big plays by the Aztec defense helped SDSU challenge. With 4:38 remaining, the Miners were up, 34-24, but there was no sign of quitting from Tom's Aztecs.

Starting the next drive, the replacement quarterback, Darren Mougey, completed four straight passes to bring State to the UTEP 10. The Aztecs settled for Garrett Palmer's 34-yard field goal. With 1:59 left in the game trailing 34-27, their onside kick went out of bounds. The Miners took over, but the suspense didn't end there. UTEP Coach Mike Price decided to hand off to a runner three times rather than take a knee to avoid risking a fumble back to the Aztecs. I busted Tom, "Didn't Price ever hear of The Miracle at the Meadowlands?" He smiled and said, "Herman Edwards played for San Diego State!"

No miracle occurred at Qualcomm today as time expired for a final of 34-27 in favor of the Miners. SDSU fans told me they often have to look for a silver lining. Tom Ables said he was proud that his team never quit. He had every right to feel that way. Take that from a guy who just attended his 646th Aztec game.

In 2010, Tom, accompanied by his son Ken, went back to Laramie, Wyoming without his wife Nancy (her choice evidently), to attend his 700th Aztec game. A week later at halftime against Colorado State at Qualcomm, San Diego State presented Tom, with Nancy at his side, the ball from the Wyoming game commemorating his record. He proudly displays it in his office at the company he owns, Venture, where he still worked daily. By the end of the season, Tom was up to game 705 and planning for the 2011 San Diego State season. I hoped to catch up with him again some time.

My brother Chris and I meet Mr. San Diego State, Tom Ables, at the Aztec-UTEP Miner game.

Traveling Tom

State College, Pennsylvania - Fast forward to San Diego State at Penn State, 2015: The history here is not so much the game between the Nittany Lions and the Aztecs. The real highlight came catching up with Tom nine years after meeting him the first time. At the age of 89, with the help of his son Ken, he followed his Aztecs all the way out to Beaver Stadium in Happy Valley. With his cane, he stood and watched from the SDSU sideline. Talk about dedication! And also, the fact that the San Diego State football program did whatever they could to maintain his venerable presence as part of their team.

Before our Penn State reunion, in 2010, Eric and I stopped at his office in San Diego when we traveled out there for the Holiday Bowl. His business, Venture, maintained camera equipment for horse racing tracks in California. As a WWII Navy vet, he'd get a kick out of knowing today that the 15-year-old in his office then, now serves as a Chief Petty Officer in the Navy.

No competition here: One team for Tom! All for me!

Regarding the Penn State-San Diego State clash, Tom was attending his 761st SDSU game. He led me by a whopping 271 games this day, my 490th. Today, he traveled over 2,500 miles for his 591st SDSU game in a row since his regrettable miss in 1964! As for the action at Beaver Stadium that sunny, windy afternoon, it started out competitively.

In the second period, Aztec quarterback Max Smith fired to Mikah Holder in back of the end zone for a great catch to give the visitors a 14-13 advantage. The Aztec defense then blocked a 55-yard PSU field goal attempt. Forcing the Lions to punt, the SDSU returner fumbled and Chris Goodwin recovered for the Lions at SDSU's 27. At the 13, Christian Hackenberg hit running back Mark Allen in the left flat, and he crossed the goal line for a 20-14 lead with 1:03 left in the second. PSU forced a fumble that was recovered by Nittany Lion defensive tackle Anthony Zettel. Penn State took advantage. Hackenberg threw his third scoring pass from 11 yards to Godwin for a 27-14 halftime lead.

In the third, Donnell Pumphrey brought SDSU to within 27-21 on a one-yard run. In the final period, Penn State's 323-lb defensive tackle Austin Johnson picked up a fumble and rambled, somewhat slowly, for a 71-yard touchdown. The Lions built a 13-point cushion with 13:44 remaining. PSU kicker Joey Julius's 26-yard field goal finalized the days' scoring, the Nittany Lions made their valley happy, 37-21, to improve to 3-1. For the Aztecs with Tom, they returned home miserably at 1-3.

Funny thing though, the season was early. Penn State finished their season at 7-6 losing five of their last seven games - four to superior Big Ten opponents before losing in the TaxSlayer Bowl to Georgia.

For San Diego State with their greatest fan along the sidelines, they totally turned their 2015 season around. They won all eight Mountain West games to face Air Force at Qualcomm for the conference championship. Their 27-24 victory propelled them to the Hawaii Bowl where they blasted Cincinnati, 42-7. Due to an ear infection, however, unable to fly, Tom stayed home. He watched his Aztecs play on TV for the first time ever! He was disheartened. His record attendance streak ended at 600 with the win over Air Force. In retrospect, their momentum catapulted the program during the next two seasons to eleven and ten wins, respectively. Aztec success had Tom fired up.

This loss couldn't dishearten the Aztec's No. 1 fan

I spoke to Tom before the 2016 season. Excitement stirred within him because he couldn't wait to follow his Aztecs to Mobile, Alabama for their game against South Alabama. The previous season, the Aztecs had lost to them, 34-27, the week before their loss to Penn State. Tom wasn't focused on this trip for a grudge match though. The thrill he anticipated on top of going to the game came from his opportunity to revisit his proud past. This dedicated WWII Navy vet could not wait to visit his retired ship on which he served, the Battleship USS Alabama, BB-60. The ship resides now in Mobile Bay at Battleship Memorial Park.

At the game, Tom was introduced during a timeout and received a long ovation from the fans. A Jaguar cheerleader came over and shook his hand. As he walked off the field after the game, fans called out to him. His son Ken reminisced when they visited the Alabama in 2011 after the New Orleans Bowl: "We drove from New Orleans to Mobile. We stopped for something to eat in Mississippi near the Alabama border. Offhand, Tom mentioned to the cashier that we were going to visit his old ship. She said she had been on the Alabama, her son had done a sleep over on the Alabama, but had never met anyone who had served on the Alabama." Like this woman, the South Alabama fans appreciated a visit by one of the sailors who actually served aboard their historic, floating monument.

I spoke with Tom again afterward. What a thrill it was for him to have gone back. He rehashed proud memories of his service aboard and with the other sailors he served with. He cherished walking on board the deck of the ship he served 70 years before. His team went into that game on a 13-game winning streak, but fell to the South Alabama Jaguars, 42-26. Disappointed, of course, but thankfully Tom got to relish great memories aboard his ship to diminish the loss that weekend.

After that, SDSU rebounded with six straight victories. They lost their last two regular season Mountain West games, but their 6-2 conference record earned their way back into the MWC championship game. Of all places in December, they headed to Laramie, Wyoming. Not only was it not a place Tom's wife Nancy would go to, but only two weeks before, the Aztecs visited Laramie and fell to the Cowboys, 34-33. Not this time. Instead, they came away with a 27-24 win for the conference championship. For that victory, they headed to the Las Vegas Bowl where they defeated the 9-3 Houston Cougars, 34-10.

The Aztecs vaulted to No. 25. The bowl win inspired Tom to update his book, *Go Aztecs!* for a fourth edition to proudly proclaim San Diego State's second straight 11-win season. He also wanted to recognize running back D.J. Pumphrey's NCAA-record rushing performance.[1] In 2016, Pumphrey rushed for 2,018 yards. During the Las Vegas Bowl win, he surpassed the record set by Ron Dayne of Wisconsin for the all-time NCAA Division I FBS lead in career rushing yards with 6,405. Sportswriters challenge the validity of the record, however, due to the NCAA's omission of bowl statistics accumulated by players prior to 2002.[2]

Aztec to the end

The Aztecs started off hot once again for 2017. They reeled off six straight wins including triumphs over PAC-12 foes Arizona State and Stanford. Before the Aztecs played their next game against Boise State the following Saturday night at SDCCU Stadium, Tom announced on a pregame video posted on his Twitter account that he was attending his 788th SDSU football game.[3] His Aztecs fell to the Broncos that night, 31-14. On October 17, the following Monday morning at Scripps Mercy Hospital, the same place Tom Ables came into the world 91 years before, he suddenly passed away.

In addition to 788 Aztec football games, Tom attended more than 1,000 SDSU basketball games over seven decades.[4] I called his son Ken when the Aztec basketball team won their game to go on to this year's Final Four, and how much Tom would have loved that! I'm sure he enjoyed it from above. In 1993, the Aztec Hall of Fame inducted Tom as an honorary member. He and his wife Nancy had celebrated their 69th wedding anniversary the summer before he passed. I have to say I enjoyed having gotten to know him, though for a short time and mostly from afar, during this long journey of my own. May I enjoy my journey as much as he did his.

My next call to his son Ken will be to get back out to see the Aztecs in a game at their new Snapdragon Stadium. It opened in 2022 adjacent to where Qualcomm/Jack Murphy/SDCCU Stadium originally stood. You know that's on my Bucket List! In addition, I have to work my way down to Mobile, Alabama, about a seven-hour drive for me now. Along with a visit to Battleship Memorial Park to visit Tom's memory, the USS Alabama, I'll work in a South Alabama Jaguar game at Hancock -Whitney Stadium. Definitely classifies as a personal weekend, tailgate doubleheader!

FIFTY YEARS OF TAILGATE TALES:

Great to meet with Tom and his son Ken when San Diego State played Penn State at Beaver Stadium in 2015. Mike Ford stands with me to my left for his first game in State College.

[1] Dan Greenspan, Dan, "San Diego State's Pumphrey sets NCAA Career Rushing Record. ABC News. Associated Press. December 17, 2016.

[2] Alex Kirshner, Alex. "Blame the NCAA for Donnel Pumphrey breaking Ron Dayne's Record with fewer yards'" SB Nation. December 18, 2016.

[3] Kirk Kenney, "Aztecs Super Fan Tom Ables dies," The San Diego Union-Tribune, October 17, 2016.

[4] Ibid

Hey, Ralphie...Girl? /"Prime Time."

(108) Colorado State vs. (109) Colorado, September 9, 2006

Denver, Colorado - In 2005, when Lindy's pre-season football publication did a nice article about my pursuit of The Goal, an illustration depicted me as "Super Fan" in a funny cartoon checking off my list. The list accurately depicted teams I had and had not seen. The article gave me some new notoriety. My Web site www.collegefootballfan.com picked up more hits, and I received more e-mails.

One in particular came from Dave Plati, Sports Information Director at the University of Colorado. Dave noticed that I'd never seen his Golden Buffaloes nor the Colorado State Rams play. He extended an invitation to me and St. Laurie to attend the 2005 game known as the Rocky Mountain Showdown between the two rivals. Played annually, this particular year they played at Denver's Invesco Field at Mile High Stadium. I had to decline his benevolent offer. I had already committed to add Boise State against the Georgia Bulldogs that day.

Dave left the invitation open for a future encounter. I penned in the intrastate rivalry for 2006. With air miles saved up, I took St. Laurie on our first visit to Boulder, Colorado. Dave sent me a media guide, parking pass, complimentary tickets, and a sideline pass to meet and even run on the field with Ralphie IV. Colorado's famed bison charges on to the football field leading the team before each game. I couldn't thank Dave enough for this great opportunity!

On Friday, my wife and I toured the beautiful, Boulder campus. We visited brown-bricked Folsom Stadium, the bookstore, and other facilities. The campus seemed quaint for a big university. We didn't catch up with Dave since he was busy with media activities that day. However, one of the nice things that he did that I didn't know about was to inform the media of my attendance. A blurb in the papers mentioned me and The Goal before I visited Colorado. CSTV contacted me for an interview to be held supposedly during halftime. I couldn't imagine my mug on TV being interviewed at a college football game!

Pre-game warm-up

St. Laurie and I arrived early at Invesco Park and found our seats in the front row at the 20-yard line to the left of the CU bench. Wearing my blue Collegefootballfan.com jersey given to me by St. Laurie for Christmas the year before (the front of my jersey has the number "119" on front for all the current teams in IA football. Above the number, it reads, "SEE THEM ALL"). I was greeted by several fans who had read the article which at the time I knew nothing about. Several shook hands with me and stated that it was something that they would love to do. They wished me luck. Comments like theirs inspired me to write this book to share these stories with fans like them.

With sideline passes, St. Laurie and I passed though security checks leading down through Invesco to the playing field level. We walked along the end zone to the Colorado sideline. We ventured over to meet Ralphie IV and her handlers and took some pictures. Ralphie stared at my blue jersey, probably trying to figure out how I fit in among all the black, gold, and green. I'm glad I didn't wear my red one. Would she have charged?

St. Laurie and I got to talk to one of her handlers, Taylor "Bubba" Leary. The political science major started his second season "escorting" Ralphie IV on to the field. Handlers try out every year. Taylor planned to do so again his senior year. They were already training Ralphie V for 2007, as Ralphie IV in her tenth season, started to get a little too mean and ornery in her old age. You could see her swinging her horns close to the nearest handlers when she ran out in the second half. The training entails running her down the length of the field and right into her trailer.

Taylor said Ralphie appreciates the run just to get away from the maddening crowd. Females are chosen as mascots because they are smaller than the bulls. As big as Ralphie is though, the lone Colorado State Ram handler got tripped and dragged a little by the CSU Ram mascot toward the end of the game. Mascot handlers evidently take some knocks on the field during the season, too.

Just being along the sideline on the field near players running drills thrilled me to be there right before a big game. Today, I got to absorb the atmosphere surrounding the field with all the game preparation going on before us. I spied a couple of CU staffers nearby to ask how I might be able to catch up with Dave Plati to thank him. He was up in the press box.

They had read about me, and we talked for a while before one of them said, "By the way, my wife would love your jersey. When I first read it, it looks like it says, 'SEE THE MALL.'" I requested "SEE 'EM ALL." However, K&N *Sporting Goods*, owned by Frank who loves the Notre Dame marching band and his wife Patty, couldn't come up with an apostrophe for a contraction. That frustrated me originally, but now I grew more concerned that people might think I'm a living ad for 119 shopping malls!

I was invited to run out on the field with Ralphie IV and her handlers, but I got cold feet mainly because I didn't feel right about running out in front of all those CU fans that'd never gotten a chance to do this. Here I was, only a first-timer at a CU game, and at the big intrastate rivalry. Did I deserve to do this? Now that I've accomplished The Goal though, I would do it if I had the chance again.

In on the action, sort of

At the Colorado State three, with Bernard Jackson as the unexpected starting quarterback for the Buffs, he started right and reversed left to score six. State responded with a 27-yard pass from Caleb Hanie to Johnny Walker to get to the Buffs' three. Hanie optioned right from there to take it in standing up. The two teams played to a 7-7 first-quarter tie. Kicks and punts really travel high and far at Mile High. CU's Matt Di Lallo boomed a 71-yard punt to put CSU back on their 15. On that series, State fumbled and corner Terrence Wheatley recovered for the Buffaloes on the Ram 26.

The Rams would not yield, however, and CU's All-America place kicker and team captain, Mason Crosby, put three on the board from 41 yards out. Hanie was on target to Walker and Brett Willis to lead his offense down to the Colorado three. With play action, he connected with TE Kory Sperry. At the end of the first half, the Rams held a 14-10 edge.

Post-halftime entertainment – me!

At the beginning of the third quarter, CSTV's sideline reporter, Ann Marie, came over to invite me down for an interview about The Goal. With my pre-game sideline pass to meet Ralphie, I worked my way back up to the main concourse, through security to elevators to take me down to the playing field. I found my way to the entrance to the field at about the 50 right behind the CU bench. Things had gotten intense there. I was only a few feet behind the CU defense huddled with their coaches. There was pad-pounding and shouting going on. It felt great to be near the action. The intensity of big-time, college football electrified me!

I spotted Ann Marie about 20 yards to my right and went to meet her. The game continued. The crowd roared. Fans focused intensely on the action—definitely a great perspective for a first-timer on the field in front of 65,701. Ann Marie introduced me to the camera crew and told me what she would ask. We worked our way toward the north end zone to our left as the Buffs drove that way. I walked past St. Laurie. She could only laugh. Ann Marie and I stood together waiting for a break in the action. Meantime, she asked me to check her teeth for chocolate stains. No! She passed inspection. It struck me that she has very nice teeth.

Colorado's Mason Crosby missed a field goal. The red camera light suddenly flashed at us! Ann Marie quickly introduced me to CSTV Land as a "True college football fan" whose Goal was to see all 119 teams play. She hit me with her first question, "Why do you want to do this?" I could see we were going to be pressed for time, so I left my three-page speech in my pocket. I told her I had always enjoyed college football, loved the

HEY, RALPHIE...GIRL? / "PRIME TIME."

action on the field, and got caught up in the spirit of the games like the one here.

"How many teams does this game make?" I told her that these were No. 108 and No. 109 with ten teams left to see after this contest.

"What teams are left?" she asked. As I was about to answer, she held up her hand as she listened to her headset. Action was continuing on the field behind us, but I didn't know what was going on. The red light went back on. She asked again.

"Oklahoma. Oklahoma State, Kansas State, and a few Sun Belt teams," I said. "I'll finish up next year with Idaho and Nevada." Presumably pressed for time, I refrained from telling her about my upcoming double-header with Tulsa at Navy and Florida International at Maryland. With a close game at hand, I figured everyone watching was anxious to get back to the action on the field. I'm sure I could have gotten more time if a blowout was taking place, but that's not something I'd want, especially after traveling 1,600 miles. I always root for a close, memorable game.

She signed off, and I thanked her for my two minutes of television fame. I told her that maybe I would see her at some other game in the future. I proceeded back to my front row seat. With coverage to 70 million households, someone must have seen it on CSTV. Back home though, I knew most were watching Notre Dame play Penn State. The third quarter ended with Colorado State still leading, 14-10. And they still did in the fourth . . . game over. Hey, I got on TV! Maybe someday I can meet Ralphie V!

Regarding the Maryland weekend I held back from Ann Marie, not waiting to hear *"Navy Blue and Gold"* after Tulsa defeated Navy in OT, I beat a substantial part of the crowd to the buses to satellite parking to head on to College Park. A couple of fans on the bus recognized me from my brief interview during the Colorado-CSU game on CSTV. Someone had actually seen me! Nolan and his wife, Nebraska grads, talked about having a similar goal to get to all the stadiums. We compared college football anecdotes. Good luck to them on their quest. It's not easy seeing all the teams no less a game at every 1-A venue. Maybe I'll see them at a game in the future. In the meantime, I headed off to Byrd Stadium!

Back to Boulder

Boulder, Colorado - Colorado vs. USC at Folsom Field, 2015: In the case of Colorado University, I managed a weekend double-header to see them in November 2015 on a Friday night. The next day, I headed to Colorado Springs to see Air Force host Utah State. This shows you the method to my madness! I met up with Sports Information Director Dave Plati once again to attend this Colorado game on press row, and this time at the Golden Buffaloes home field. Anticipating cold weather this time of year, I thought I made the correct assumption to watch from the enclosed area. The weather turned out to be more summer-like than expected. I always preferred the outdoor seating, but between possible cold weather and assuring I would meet up with Dave, tonight I observed from the press box.

Before the game, I also got to meet the new Ralphie! By now, however, a great college football tradition had met its demise. Honored guests running out with Ralphie before the game by were no longer allowed due to liability issues. Just as well. In my case, my sprinting capability slowed now to a brisk walk. The TV guys couldn't risk losing precious, commercial time anyway.

Despite losing starting quarterback Sefo Liufau to a leg injury late in the first period, Colorado led the favored USC Trojans by as much as 17-3 in the first half. CU freshman replacement Cade Apsay started adequately in Liufau's place, but struggled later in the game. At Denver Metro Airport earlier that day, locals laughed telling arriving USC fans that their team risked little threat from the Colorado Buffaloes. Third-year Head Coach Mike McIntyre seemed to be making some positive progress. According to Saturday's <u>Denver Post</u>, Colorado Athletic Director Rick George confirmed McIntyre would be back next season despite 10-24, 2-22 overall and conference records.

McIntyre, however, committed a *faux pas* of his own making right before the first half ended. The Trojans attempted a 46-yard field goal and the

Buffs blocked it – all for nothing! McIntyre called time-out just before the ball was snapped! It's pot luck, a big risk. He gave the Trojans a second chance. They converted as time expired. Had the block stood it would have been demoralizing for the Trojans. Instead, they gained momentum despite trailing still, 17-6. Hindsight, but rather than relying on luck, put some faith in the ability of the players. Easier said than done, of course.

Snowboarding? What happened to music and dance teams?
As for halftime, I was somewhat disappointed that the USC Trojan Marching Band did not perform after Colorado's Marching Band. Instead, after CU's band performance, for the first time ever, I watched snowboarding as halftime entertainment. A short, snow slope with a rail from the end zone stands to my right was rigged up to watch young winter athletes purposely fall on their butts.

My disappointment came because I couldn't get a better view of the USC *Song Girls Dance Team*! Talk about a great college football tradition. They performed in my obstructed view down at my far left along the sideline during the game. I had hoped to enjoy a prime view at halftime from Row 2 in Press Row above the 45-yard line. In person, I'd never seen their dance routines. There are some college football traditions that are *must-see's* whether you're a fan of a particular team or not! No more pre-game jaunts with Ralphie! Now I couldn't see *USC's Song Girls*! Snow-boarding?

Speaking of eyes in the sky, according to Dave Plati, we sat among 19 pro scouts in the press box evaluating Cody Kessler. Along with several other successful USC quarterbacks, pro career results preclude Southern Cal from being known as "Quarterback U." Maybe that's a reason now that so many successful high school quarterbacks from California seek opportunities to play for out-of-state programs.

In the third, Kessler threw a four-yard pass to Jahleel Pinner to cut the CU lead, 17-13. Christian Powell's fumble gave the ball back to USC. Trojan Antwan Woods recovery at the Colorado 34 resulted in Kessler's next scoring strike to Taylor McNamara for a 20-17 USC lead.

Colorado attempted a 52-yard field goal, but Adoree 'Jackson blocked it and recovered at Colorado's 35. Two plays later, Kessler threw a 36-yard pass to Juju Smith-Schuster to extend the lead, 27-17. Apsay could not get the Buffs driving again. CU's defense held the Trojans in check and forced a punt from its nine. Colorado returned the punt 45 yards to the four and two were tacked on for a late hit out of bounds. Apsay connected with George Frazier from the one to climb back, 27-24.

The Buffs halted the next Trojan drive and took over from their 21. Apsay's fourth down pass fell incomplete with 1:22 left. The Trojans offense ran the clock down to preserve a tougher than expected win. The Buffaloes remain 0-2 and still looking for a win in the annals of my history. How will they do now under new Head Coach Deion Sanders taking over the struggling program?

"Prime-time?"

Can incoming Head Coach Deion Sanders answer the call to turn this Buffalo program around? Over my long observations over six decades following college football games in person, the three keys to successful coaching include recruiting, player development, and strategy, planned before and executed during a game. No doubt Sanders has the charisma, personality, and reputation to attain some of the best talent around. However, up until now coaching only an FCS program, he's had the upper hand recruiting against other Historically Black Colleges and Universities (HBCUs) he's played the last two years. He leaves Jackson State with an impressive 23-3 record. Both years, his JSU Tigers won the Southwest Athletic Conference (SWAC) title.

However, among his three losses, one came against the only FBS team he played, UL-Monroe, 12-7. The Warhawks had a 4-8 record in the Sun Belt when they met in 2021. The other two losses came against champions of the Mid-Eastern Athletic Conference (MEAC), South Carolina State (7-5) and North Carolina Central (10-2) in the Cricket Celebration Bowl. I've followed HBCU team results over the past few years. The scores against teams at the FBS level have been consistently non-competitive.

Talent transfer

During 2022, in 17 combined games played between SWAC and MEAC schools (both FCS conferences) against FBS schools, they lost every game by an average score of 55-10. Over previous years, results have been similar. In 1978, Sam *"The Bam"* Cunningham showed Alabama's Paul Bear Bryant that African-Americans could compete at the highest level of college football back when the USC running back ran roughshod over The Bear's Crimson Tide. The major IA programs, especially in the South, took notice and started recruiting football talent they had ignored until then.

In essence, Sam Cunningham opened the door for more of the best African-American football players to play at the Division IA level. The HBCUs, in general, don't get the level of talent they used to get before the 1980s. I grew up watching great players in the NFL/AFL days come from legendary Head Coach Eddie Robinson's Grambling program – Buck Buchanan, Willie Davis, Willie Brown, and Charlie Joiner. All are enshrined in the Pro Football Hall of Fame. Wide receiver Otis Taylor graduated from Prairie View to play for the KC Chiefs back in 1965. Defensive tackle John Mendenhall from Grambling performed as a stalwart for the NY Giants for 13 seasons starting in 1972. The late, outstanding Walter Payton was drafted out of Jackson State in 1975. Amazing linebacker Harry Carson from South Carolina State was selected by the Giants in '76 and excelled during a Hall of Fame career for 12 seasons. Super Bowl quarterback Doug Williams embarked on his NFL career drafted out of Grambling in 1978. Hall of Fame wide receiver Jerry Rice played for Mississippi Valley State from 1981-1985. The list goes on.

In the days before the internet, social media, and growing saturation by national TV coverage, talents these players displayed in high school weren't exposed to the general public like they are today. After 1978, players as talented as these highlighted started filling out more rosters in the SEC and Southwestern Conference where they had never been recruited before. In 1985, Deion Sanders didn't go to play for an HBCU program. He went to play at Florida State under Bobby Bowden. There, he gained his notoriety as a two-time consensus All-American cornerback in 1987 and 1988. The Seminoles landed ranked at No. 2 and No. 3 in those seasons in the final AP Top 25. FSU's biggest obstacle to No. 1 came from the Miami Hurricanes who defeated them both seasons. In those days, the Canes were putting more players, mostly African Americans, in the pros than any other programs. In previous decades, players with these talents filled the rosters of D-2 HBCUs.

He can recruit, but can he coach?

The Atlanta Falcons drafted Sanders at No. 5 to start his illustrious professional career. The point is that Deion Sander's aura from his notoriety as a great pro player had enough influence to recruit Travis Hunter and others away from FBS programs to Jackson State. Since the early 80's, HBCU programs could rarely do the same. Now at Colorado, Sander's recruiting competition, set aside the NIL and transfer portal policies as they now stand, will come from more comparable FBS teams he's going to be playing against at the next level. He has much to prove.

First of all, he can't recruit all the top talent. Successful PAC-12 programs like Oregon, Utah, and Washington already have solid FBS recruiting reputations and strategies in place. Same can be said of Big XII programs when Colorado returns to play against some former comparable foes. For Sander's new school, he can definitely improve recruiting, but it will not make his Buffaloes as superior as his recruiting for Jackson State against the HBCUs he's played the last few years. Next, consider his player development and game strategies.

With the superior talent he's recruited among HBCU programs, it's difficult to assess his player development skills. Did he rely solely on superior talent he recruited, or did he improve their skills? Being a talent on the playing field that he was, does not always translate into effective teaching skills. As far as coaching strategies? Again, his recruiting prowess may have been his greatest strength. In the two championship losses in the Celebrations Classics, his superior talent didn't win out. Was he out-coached in these situations? We'll see if that's brought to light this upcoming season and the next.

As far as seeing his Buffaloes play again, I'll have to wait for now. The expectations around Boulder have led to a season-ticket sell-out already. Maybe his Buffs will be among the visitors I can schedule among the realigned Big XII. In addition, will Deion still be coaching in a few years? That will depend on him capturing very short-term success. His success will depend on his player development, his game-coaching, and leadership skills he'll have to demonstrate against comparable FBS competition.

As for CSU

Murfreesboro, Tennessee - Fast Forward to Colorado State at MTSU in the future: For the CSU Golden Rams, this game still stands today as their only performance in my history. Someday, I might get out to Fort Collins to see a contest at Canvas Stadium, most likely if it coincides with a trip to see the Wyoming Cowboys. The two campuses are about an hour apart. Bucket List possibility.

(110) Tulsa 24 Navy 23 (OT)
Navy-Marine Corps Memorial, Annapolis, Maryland, September 23, 2006

Maryland 14 - (111) Florida International 10
Byrd Stadium, College Park, Maryland, September 23, 2006

Honorary Pony on The Boulevard / Pony Express to PAC-12?

Tulsa at (112) Southern Methodist, November 18, 2006

Dallas, Texas - Originally, I planned to see Southern Methodist University at East Carolina trying to hook up with my old Syracuse buddy Bernie Olszyk in 2006. He relocated to Williamsburg, Virginia in anticipation of his approaching retirement. However, plans changed that week as Bernardo's work duties called him away. I didn't feel like going all the way to Greenville, North Carolina by myself. Did I panic? Of course not! I re-checked the SMU schedule and noted a golden opportunity I initially didn't recognize.

The Mustangs hosted the Tulsa Golden Hurricane at 2 p.m. on November 18. Not only that, but 40 miles north in Denton, Texas, the Mean Green of North Texas State hosted Howard Schnellenberger's Florida Atlantic Owls that evening. This presented must-see football action. That Saturday in Texas offered the chance to add *three* new teams in one day! I booked a flight, a couple of cheap hotels, and I headed to the Lone Star State for what I referred to on my site as "Texas Two-Step to See Three!"

Late Saturday morning, I headed over to SMU to check out the campus and the pre-game happenings. For a quick getaway heading north to Denton on I-35 North after the game, I found a side street off campus figuring it looked like a direct route. I could see lights and flags over Gerard

J. Ford Stadium a few blocks from where I parked. Some construction blocked a direct path, so I walked along a street that led to the middle of campus. I ventured to an intersection of a tree-lined street with a wide, green-grass median. No traffic passed by, but people gathered on both sides of the street to tailgate.

Not taking it so hard on the Boulevard

I turned left toward the stadium when I spotted a beer wagon with a freshly- tapped CO_2 system. What timing! No line formed yet, so I ventured over. Beers were $5 a pop. Oh well, I figured I'd get one and see what else "The Boulevard" of the SMU campus had to offer. I fell into the perfect trap! Brian Bischoff of the SMU Mustang Club approached me. His club offered $5 beers, but if I chose to join the Mustang Club for a nominal fee, I could get all the beer and wings I could handle, two tickets to the game, and a ticket for this evening's basketball home-opener against Dayton.

He made me an offer I couldn't refuse! With Matt Doherty, formerly of Notre Dame and UNC, now the new head basketball coach at SMU, the last part of the offer was tempting, but my mission already lay ahead of me this evening. For $25, I couldn't have found a better deal for a ticket and a tailgate party to boot!

Brian introduced me to other club members, Chip Hiemenz '06, Jamie, and Jeremy among others. Chip worked for SMU's office of Development and Alumni Affairs. The beer wagon was equipped with three TV monitors to keep up with action around the country. In front of the Natorium across the street, the *PitPops* provided music. I met Jerad Romo, quarterback of last year's Mustangs. He led them past the No. 11 ranked TCU for the Horned Frogs only loss in an 11-1 season - SMU's first win over a ranked team in many years. All nice guys, the fan turn-out disappointed these die-hards following a tough homecoming loss to Houston. For their sakes, I hoped that the Ponies would get their bowl after their long, dry spell following the NCAA's Death Penalty in 1986.

Figuring beers cost five bucks each, I drank my $25 worth before the game to be sure my two tickets were free! The game hadn't started yet, I ate wings, and I wouldn't be driving for at least four more hours after watching a game. Life on The Boulevard is great on Saturdays before games. The guys enjoyed hearing about my exploits. I enjoyed getting updates about the SMU program. Before I headed over to Gerard J. Ford Stadium, I thanked them for their great hospitality. They gave me directions to get to Denton quickly, and they recommended watching the Mean Green from a beer pavilion at Fouts Field. They also forewarned me about a particular annoyance I would find there.

"Tulsa Time"

Tulsa scored just about every time it had the ball in the first half. SMU drives stalled about every time. It was 24-7 in favor of Tulsa at the half, but having seen two similar leads dissipate in recent games at Rutgers and at Princeton, I sensed this game was far from over. While the SMU band played *"She'll Be Comin' Round the Mountain"*, not the most stirring of fight songs, at the end of the half, I went to check out SMU's Heritage Hall.

There are tributes to the late Heisman winner Doak Walker and to the 11-0-1 1982 team's 7-3 Cotton Bowl win over Pitt - four years before the NCAA sanctioned the Mustangs with the first *death penalty*. Two more wins this year would end twenty-two years of bowl-less frustration for my new, fellow Pony Club members. Hopes were already fading though after one half of play against Tulsa.

SMU followers dispersed in the second half. Many fans deemed the Ponies done. But a pair of field goals and a touchdown, sans PAT, brought SMU within reach, 24-19. With off tackle play action, SMU quarterback Justin Willis faked a hand-off and carried around the right side for a six-yard touchdown run. Perfectly set-up, Willis ran the draw to perfection on the two-point conversion. SMU took a 27-24 lead with 12:46 left.

The Mustang defense stuffed the Tulsa offense in the second half allowing only 80 yards. They forced another punt. SMU drove to the Golden Hurricane 14. Willis fired a long lateral to wide-out Blake Warren on his left. He picked up two beautiful blocks and went into the end zone to extend SMU's lead, 34-24. Over four minutes remained. The Ponies held on. I listened to the public address and the final cheers of the remaining SMU faithful as I approached my rental car to start my search for Highway 35. Great game! On to Denton! *One* new team down, and *two* to go!

As for my Pony Club brethren, SMU lost the following week to the Rice Owls to finish the season at 6-6. The 7-6 Owls earned the bid to the New Orleans Bowl. Pony Club bowl frustration continued on The Boulevard until 2009. June Jones was hired from Hawaii to take over the program and returned with his new team to Honolulu for the Hawaii Bowl. There, the 'Stangs drubbed Nevada, 45-10. It wasn't quite the Cotton Bowl win of 1982, but after a long, dry spell of 27 years, the Pony Club could celebrate a post-season win. It couldn't be better for a nicer bunch of guys.

Sea-dog and Pony Shows

Annapolis, Maryland - Fast forward to SMU vs. Navy games, 2010 and 2019: No longer a dues-paying honorary member of the Pony Club for a day back in 2006, I went back to my "roots" at Navy to see the Mustangs face the Mids at Navy-Marine Corp Memorial Stadium twice. The final outcomes resulted in similar fashion. In 2010, my now brother-in-law Frank Lorito and I watched SMU and Navy fight to a draw with two minutes left, 21-21. At the 1:55 mark, Navy's linebacker Tyler Simmons picked off Kyle Padron's pass at SMU's 19 to return to the 13. Seventeen seconds later, Navy fullback Alex Teich scored on a four-yard run. At the Navy 41, the Mustang drive ended as time expired for Navy's 28-21 win. The Mids finished this season at 9-4, and the Ponies, 7-7.

Maybe last conference showdown

In 2019, my friend Paul Fraley, Brother Knight and former softball teammate, joined me for this SMU-USNA battle. Early in the last quarter, the Mids took a 26-21 lead with a 13-yard scoring pass. Head Coach Ken Niumatalolo called for the two-point conversion. Slotback C.J. Williams made an outstanding, leaping, horizontal catch. He fell flat on his back into the end zone to put USNA up by seven. The Mustangs came right back. Shane Buechele connected with Rashee Rice for a 61-yard scoring pass to even the score.

Navy responded with their strength. Quarterback Malcolm Perry broke loose for a 70-yard sprint with six minutes left to play. The Mid defense shut down the high-powered Mustang passing game averaging 328 passing yards per game and totaling 28 touchdown passes. Buechele engineered a drive for a third and four at the Midshipman 12. His first attempt to James Proche landed incomplete. On fourth down, his pass to Proche was nicely broken up by defender Cameron Kinley.

The Ponies still had two time-outs remaining with 2:35 left in the game. Navy converted one first down, and on fourth and two from the 31, SMU spent their final time-out. Ken Niumatatolo left his offense on the field to go for it. With cheers echoing throughout Navy-Marine Corps Memorial Stadium, SMU jumped offsides. A flag flew simultaneously with a protest from Head Coach Sonny Dyke's staff along the adjacent SMU sideline. With another Navy first down to run out the clock, game over. The Mids beat the Ponies once again in the final minute, 35-28.

It looks like SMU and Navy will no longer battle as American Athletic foes. With California and Stanford located on the Pacific Coast, college football defies geographical logic making them and SMU members of what is currently called the Atlantic Coast Conference. As for the AAC, Army may be a possibility for membership to replace the Mustangs. Makes sense. It's tough to plan a schedule now as an Independent, and if you remain as such with all the realignments, that may become tougher for Army to do. Assuredly, it keeps the Army-Navy rivalry intact. There's no reason for the AAC and Army-West Point not to come to an agreement.

Not so Green, and not that Mean / On to AAC

(113) Florida Atlantic at (114) North Texas State, November 18, 2006

Denton, Texas – After leaving the SMU win over Dallas in the late afternoon, I got to Fouts Field of North Texas State mid-way through the first period. Walking into North Texas State's stadium and seeing rows of empty, aluminum bleacher seats, the scene reminded me of my trip to see Ohio U. play at Buffalo the previous season to add team Nos. 100 and 101. As I took my seat, The Mean Green of North Texas, in black uniforms with green helmets, scored on a three-yard run by freshman Evan Robertson.

What the SMU guys had warned me about, my second impression came to light. Screeching eagle cries over the loudspeaker are *annoying*! They played screeches after scores, on defensive third downs, on offensive third downs, after big plays, after turnovers, time-outs, whatever—the screeches and the *AC-DC* bell gongs can be put to rest. Their announced crowd of 9,806 displayed no reactions at all.

Things got interesting eventually, but not on the field. As the first quarter expired, some real head-knocking commenced along the sideline. Florida Atlantic's Owl mascot mixed it up with North Texas State's Eagle mascot. The Owl literally knocked the Eagle's head off, revealing the small head of some ticked-off college kid. Eventually, the headless Eagle had to retaliate. At first, the best he could do was twist the Owl's head around 180 degrees.

He eventually knocked it off. Before the cockfight escalated, "cooler," non-detachable heads intervened. In other sidelines news, I moved to another seat to get a better view of Mean Green's *Dance Team* performing in front of the band. It was a great move on my part. It turned out to be a much better view of the prime action along the sideline!

Mean Green needs to "find itself"

As for the action on the field, the annoying sound effects continued until cannon fire ended the half. FAU took a 17-10 lead into the locker room. NTSU Mean Green? Black uniforms? Eagle mascot? Eagle screeches? Bells? Cannons? I'm not sure what North Texas wanted to be. NTSU mustered two field goals by Denis Hopovac in the second half to get within one point. FAU free safety Taheem Acevedo picked off a Mean Green pass in the end zone in the first half. He then sealed the victory with another in his own territory to thwart Mean Green's final drive of the game. Without giving a hoot, Howard Schnellenberger's Owls spoiled all that screaming eagle noise-making to hold on to a 17-16 win. The Green didn't display much "Mean." Of all green creatures, the Frankenstein monster makes the most sense as the Mean Green mascot. Scar on head, bolts in neck, fierce growl, a ball and chain attached to leg, no Owl's going to knock his head off.

I was satisfied after a long day, but I wanted to catch the Ohio State-Michigan highlights back at the local hotel. On a day when most of college football nation witnessed No. 1 Ohio State's exciting 41-38 victory over No. 2 Michigan, I was thrilled to have attended two close, hard-fought football games. Not particularly played by the best, but played by student-athletes giving their best. That's what college football is supposed to be about. Watching that Mean Green Dance Team was very worthwhile, too! My much anticipated excursion lived up to expectations and beyond. I couldn't have asked for much more except to stop that screeching eagle recording. Eventually, I attended an Ohio State–Michigan game, but regrettably for my purposes, the Buckeyes dominated, 42-14.

C-USA to American Athletic to Big XII

Fast forward for Florida Atlantic and North Texas games in the future: This was the only time I watched both of these teams play. FAU and North Texas along with Charlotte, Rice, UAB, and UTSA joined the American Athletic. They somewhat fill the void of Central Florida, Cincinnati, and Houston going to the Big XII, doing the same for Texas and Oklahoma fleeing that conference. The three teams leaving the AAC helped held a cusp of hope the AAC could transform into the sixth "Power" conference. They held their own during regular seasons and bowls playing Power Five programs. Cincinnati even made it to the CFP in 2021. With SMU now exiting for the ACC, the American Athletic looks like a football conference made up of spare parts.

It's the Final Countdown!

(115) Kansas State at Auburn, September 1, 2007

Auburn, Alabama - Kansas State remained one of my five teams left to achieve The Goal! The Wildcats initially fell on Fresno State's schedule as the season home opener for the Bulldogs. I contemplated flying out to the Nut Farm again with or without Frank Lorito. Later, the game got rescheduled to November 24, Thanksgiving weekend! That wouldn't work. My Goal came down to planning for five remaining teams to be seen, but the original schedules announced worked against me. The other four teams paired off against one another on October 27—Oklahoma State at Oklahoma and Idaho at Nevada-Reno.

I sought alternative plans. On October 13, Fresno would play at Idaho. For TV scheduling, Nevada would play at Boise on Sunday night, October 14. I'd never traveled to Idaho before, and the trip would entail two unique venues. I looked forward to the possibility. The IU Vandals host games in their 16,000-seat indoor arena, the Kibbie Dome. Boise's Bronco Stadium is famous for its blue "Smurf" turf. I always wanted to go there.

The Saturday-Sunday schedule gave me time to drive the 300-mile difference. I booked a flight. Several weeks later, Oklahoma and Oklahoma State announced they would start their new Thanksgiving weekend rivalry a year earlier than originally planned. The price to fly to Oklahoma on the big holiday weekend was unfathomable. Plus, it wouldn't be appreciated by certain family members that I may miss our traditional Thanksgiving weekend together. I catch enough grief for taking in a local playoff game

IT'S THE FINAL COUNTDOWN!

somewhere in New England on the following Saturday afternoon.

Called *my* audible; *"Idaho!"* - not "Omaha!"

I had to re-plan. The airline added a change fee for my formerly free, mileage-plus tickets. I rescheduled my Idaho plans to head to Reno to see Idaho play Nevada on October 27. Luckily, the latest TV schedules offered an unexpected opportunity to reschedule the two teams in Oklahoma for a Friday-Saturday combination. I learned through the years that imagination, patience, persistence, and luck allowed me to pursue this dream quicker than I ever thought possible taking into consideration my financial and personal limitations.

What about Kansas State? Should I consider a trip to see them play at Oklahoma State? That would mean an additional trip on another weekend to Oklahoma, but between work, personal plans, and other games on my slate, I couldn't be sure if 2007 could be the year I could finally finish this off. Then, the luck set in. Of all the teams Kansas State scheduled to open at - Auburn! *"Hello, Charlie? If you can get us four tickets, St. Laurie and I would like to come down and visit you and Lynda on the Plains at Auburn!"*

Who better to start the final year of achieving this crazy Goal with? Charlie had been there since the beginning. He invited me down to see Auburn play Georgia in 1979 and Iron Bowls in '80 and '81. Added the Gators at AU. We attended games at The Meadowlands, at Richmond, at West Virginia; we even saw Rutgers play at Princeton! On top of those, there were the games against Ole Miss and Arkansas in recent years down at Auburn. This couldn't be better!

With my long-time Auburn connections Lynda and Charlie Murren at the Music City Bowl in Nashville won by Auburn, 63-14, over Purdue in 2018.

Perfect together, again

After a nice visit with our usual Auburn host and hostess, we watched the home team enjoy a 6-3 halftime lead. The Auburn Marching Band performed while we got to wander the Nelson Club Level of Jordan-Hare that hosted 86,439 college football fans this evening.

In the third period, KSU played with a different, albeit unexpected, offensive strategy. Four reverse options eventually brought the Wildcats to the Tiger 25. Chicanery paid off finally on a reverse end-around pass from wide receiver Jordy Nelson to a wide-open James Patton in the right corner of the end zone, the first touchdown of the game. Wildcats up, 10-6. On K-State's subsequent drive, the deception stopped, but a Brooks Rossman field goal made the score, 13-6.

Later in the period, Auburn's Robert Dunn took advantage of poor

IT'S THE FINAL COUNTDOWN!

K-State punt coverage speeding up the middle about twenty yards and breaking a few tackles for a 57-yard return to the Wildcats' 15. Wes Bynum kicked in a 31-yard field goal to cut the Kansas State lead, 13-9, heading into the fourth.

Auburn trailed with 2:01 left in the game. On play-action, wide open tight end Gabe McKenzie caught Brandon Cox's pass deep in the left corner of the end zone. The Tigers finally led, 16-13. State came out throwing. Auburn rushed hard. On second down, Quentin Groves sacked Josh Freeman from behind, forcing a fumble. Tiger Antonio Coleman picked up the ball and ran 34 yards into the end zone untouched. He put the game away, 23-13, with 1:09 left. Auburn celebrated a tough, but sloppy, win. Thanks to Charlie and Lynda, the 115th team toward the Goal was the seventh I added over the years on trips whenever I visited them at Auburn. It would have been tough to do without my Auburn connection. Now, I focused on my personal "Final Four."

0-2 KSU, but I'll make an exception here

Austin, Texas - Fast forward to Kansas State at Texas, 2019: Texas kicker Cameron Dicker launched a successful 26-yard field goal as time expired. The Longhorns upended No. 20 Big XII rival Kansas State for a 27-24 victory. It kept the Longhorns slim hopes alive for a Big 12 championship showdown. For the third week in a row, I attended a game where the final play of the game resulted in the winning score. Navy downed Tulane with a field goal, 41-38, and Dartmouth put Harvard away, 9-6, with a tipped "Hail Mary" pass for the winning score. My daughter, Alex, had just moved down to the Austin area. We met some other college fans from around the country before the game for an energetic, festive pregame experience.

Normally my *Fast Forwards* include a victory for the featured, chronologically-numbered team in each tale. Granted, this became only my second game with Kansas State and on the road no less. They're 0-2, but that's all I can offer. They were both, however, hard-fought, last-minute losses. A game in Manhattan, Kansas combined with one now in Lawrence someday will be on my radar screen. Seeing either team play against Colorado coached by Deion Sanders might be a great option.

The real significance here is that Alex had only moved to Austin the week before last with her big mutt, Simba, from her apartment in Philadelphia. As mentioned before, she's now my primary Texas connection, of course! With her fiancé Zach employed at Texas State, that's where their local college football priority lies. However, the move has given me opportunities to see the Longhorns and eventually a few other new venues not far from the Austin City Limits.

Charlie Murren, on far right, invited me to Auburn-Penn State tailgate in 2022. Our history dating back to games since 1978 will continue when Auburn visits Vandy in Nashville.

Will-Call / Terrible Trio – CFP, Sooners and The Heisman

(116) Oklahoma at Tulsa, September 21, 2007

Tulsa, Oklahoma - So how did my plans work out to see Oklahoma and Oklahoma State without seeing their game against one another on Thanksgiving weekend? Even better, without taking two separate trips to see them play somewhere in Big XII territory. As luck would have it, TV moved the Oklahoma at Tulsa game to a Friday night. The next day, 70 miles west of Tulsa, the Oklahoma State Cowboys would host Mike Leach's pass-happy Red Raiders of Texas Tech in Stillwater!

A couple of years back, my brother Chris out in Long Beach, California told me that if I ever wanted to see a game played at Tulsa, he had a good friend who played for them back in the '60s. He had season tickets, too! "Hello, Chris?" He put me in touch with his friend, Joe Pistoia, a native Brooklynite. Joe played wide receiver for Tulsa a few years after All-American Howard Twilley back in the 60s. Now, Joe's son, Tyler, played this season as a red-shirt freshman for the Golden Hurricane. Joe had a ticket for me to meet him at Skelly Field in Chapman Stadium. My "Final Four" now became clear: Oklahoma (1) at Tulsa, Texas Tech at Oklahoma State (2), and Idaho (3) at Nevada (4).

Before the OU-Tulsa game, I got to experience some local culture at *Ed's Hurricane Lounge* on 11th Street right across the street from the stadium. Beers cost $2 a bottle, ESPN graced two TV screens, and the ceiling was adorned with more styles of women's brassieres than a *Victoria Secret's* boutique. I assumed paying customers donated them. A cloud of tobacco smoke hung heavy in the air among the bras. You rarely found that in the northeast any more – the smoke, I meant.

Picking up beer before meeting up with Joe, his wife Joyce, and some of Joe's Tulsa acquaintances for tailgating, I learned that the state of Oklahoma had some different laws regarding alcohol then. You couldn't buy *cold* beer in a liquor store unless it's *"3.2 beer"*! I hadn't even heard that term used since 1975 in Annapolis, Maryland. You can't buy ice at the liquor store either! Despite ads all over the store for *Rolling Rock* beer, they couldn't sell it now because it recently became an Anheuser-Busch product. I didn't understand their laws. I bought two twelve-packs of warm beer on a very hot day without ice for tailgating.

Joe and Joyce Pistoia met me outside the stadium parking lot. We walked to meet their friends at a pre-arranged tailgate spot. Joyce, Tyler's step-mom, bought wine from a local liquor store. I showed up to tailgate with my warm beer. We bought bags of ice from some guys who sold them from the back of a golf cart on an afternoon when the temperature soared into the 90s. You could find the ice guys easily by following the leaking water trail the melting ice bags left behind.

Joe introduced me to John Dobbs, our host for the pregame get-together. He played ball at Tulsa with Joe. His father was Glen Dobbs, star Hurricane tailback in the 40s who returned to become one of Tulsa's most successful head coaches. Glen was elected to the College Football Hall of Fame in 1980. Dobbs' wide-open passing attack lured Joe to play for Tulsa. However, Coach Dobbs stayed only one more year before his successor took over. He de-emphasized the passing attack, much to Joe's chagrin. The transfer rules aren't what they are today. He stayed, and Tulsa finished 1-9 that season.

Joe, Joyce, and I stopped for a burger at the Tulsa Alumni Association tent. From there, Joe left us to take part in a Tulsa tradition where former players go into the locker room to seek out the player wearing the same jersey number each donned as a Hurricane player. Joe confided that they look each other in the eye, shake hands, and the former player wishes the current player luck before the game. As number 25, Joe met up with starting running back Tarrion Adams. Tarrion would carry nine times for 43 yards and grab three passes for 16 against the Sooners.

Joe's piece in infamous college football history

Joe reminisced when he played for the 1968 Tulsa team that they trailed the Houston Cougars at the half in the Astrodome, 24-0. The entire Golden Hurricane team suffered badly with a flu bug. Some starters didn't make the trip. Players suffered so much in the locker-room that Coach Dobbs offered to forfeit at halftime because most of his players were too sick to even stand, let alone play. The NCAA responded there would be severe consequences if Tulsa didn't come out for the second half.

So, weakened and apathetic, Tulsa returned to play the second half. Houston scored the last ten possessions they had the ball. Houston Head Coach Bill Yeoman's veer offense posted 27 points in the third period. Unloading his bench in the fourth, 49 points more were scored by some players who never played another down all season. One such player was Ricky Skaggs, the country music recording star who I've seen host the Grand ol' Opry at the Ryman Theater since I've moved to Tennessee. Tulsa lost the game, 100-6! One hundred points in a game - 79 in one half is even harder to imagine. Those Tulsa players had to be lifeless.

Surprise guests

As a guest of Tyler's, a ticket awaited me at the will-call window with Joe and Joyce's tickets. We walked together to pick them up. Waiting on line, we were met by another blonde woman. Joe pulled me aside. He mentioned that he and Joyce would be sitting below while I'd be sitting in seats farther up with this other woman, Janet. I was a little confused as to what was going on. Janet knew them, and suddenly showed up out of the blue. She had no idea who I was either. We weren't formally introduced. Finally in a somewhat uncomfortable conversation in our seats, I eventually said I was "Joe's friend's brother." She asked, "What's your brother's name?" I replied, "Chris Koreivo." She replied, "Oh! Emily's dad!" Her daughter attended Wilson High in Long Beach with my niece. Now we both got it! Things became clearer to both of us. I can be thick at times, but I finally realized that Janet was Tyler's mother. She had just flown into Tulsa last-minute to see the game on her way back from Pittsburgh on a business trip. Turned out she's president of a printing business that happened to do a lot of business with the University of Southern California. My first thought turned to seeing the USC Trojans play at the L.A. Coliseum someday.

Pistoia flu-bug: 1968 to 2007

Janet, like Joe and Joyce, was very concerned about Tyler. He rested in bed all day with a bad sore throat and swollen glands. He felt very weak. They advised him to see a doctor, but he wanted to see how he felt before the game. With parents in town to see him suit up in his Tulsa uniform, I couldn't imagine him not making some kind of effort to get out on that playing field, even just to warm up. Janet and I saw him run on the field with the Golden Hurricane. She felt relieved, but still a little concerned.

Paul Smith's 15-yard scoring strike to Jesse Meyer gave Tulsa an early lead, and the home crowd chanted *"Tulsa"* and *"Hurricane"* back and forth across Skelly Field during this unusual Friday night game. When the Sooners got to the Tulsa 29, the 'Cane defense stacked up the middle and Allen Patrick took advantage, running around right end for OU's first score to tie, 7-7. Sam Bradford's touchdown pass to Juaquin Iglesias and DeMarco Murray's four-yard run quieted the home crowd at that point. Tulsa came back to make it 21-14 on Smith's second touchdown pass to Brannon Marion from the 48.

The stout Sooner defense figured out the Hurricane offense for the rest of the game. If Smith rolled one direction, he always reversed field and threw from the other side. They OU defense learned to "stay at home," and forced turnovers quickly. Their stops resulted in two more scores for a 35-14 halftime lead.

Tulsa scored in the third, but eleven seconds later, OU's DeMarco

Murray returned the ensuing kickoff 81 yards to extend the Sooner lead, 42-21. Things didn't improve for Tulsa offensively or defensively. OU romped, 66-21.

After the game, I finally got to meet my true "Tulsa connection". Talk about swollen glands! Tyler had to be hurting. He was cordial through our introduction, but he could barely speak. He didn't disappoint any of us despite not feeling well. I had hoped to get to see him play again, but during his four years of eligibility, he only saw limited action in a couple of games.

Give him credit though, as a walk-on he stuck it out for four years and earned his degree. While there, the Golden Hurricane won the GMAC Bowl in both his redshirt freshman and sophomore years. His team won the Hawaii Bowl against Hawaii his senior season. Tulsa's record was 36-17 during Tyler's career. I was honored to be able to get a ticket from an actual squad member of a D-I team at the "Will-call" window! Planned my future phone call though: "Hello, Janet? How about that USC game at the Coliseum? UCLA or Notre Dame will do. Maybe even Stanford."

Sooners later

Atlanta, Georgia - Fast forward to four Oklahoma bowl games, 2007-2019: First, let me say that I never got to use Janet as a California connection. My brother Chris and his wife eventually divorced, he moved back to Jersey, and I fended for myself. As previously reminisced, I made it out to the LA Coliseum on my own. Among Fresno, Stanford, and San Diego State, I've done very well with various California connections while living back east.

As for Oklahoma, after walloping Tulsa in this regular season game, my experiences with the Sooners all turned out to be "wallopings." In three of the four though, they turned out to be the "wallopees." This same season, they out-matched Big East Champ UConn (8-5) in my only Fiesta Bowl recorded previously. OU won, 48-20, in a dull, spirit-less game led by OU's Heisman-winning quarterback Sam Bradford. After that, it was all downhill in bowl games for Oklahoma Sooner football with Heisman

Trophy winning quarterbacks under Lincoln Riley previously reported in my Southern Cal chapter, "'Wunderbride' and 'Wunderkind,'" before he moved on to take over the Trojan program.

High hopes for my CFP future

I haven't seen a game in Norman, Oklahoma yet. With them now heading into the SEC, my daughter Alex and good old Charlie Murren will be expecting phone calls when South Carolina or Auburn head there to play the Sooners. Norman, Oklahoma is on the Bucket List.

Every time I purchased a CFP semi-final ticket, Oklahoma showed up and got beat bad. If OU makes the CFP (and Penn State's doesn't), I won't buy tickets in advance. Besides, only one more four-team CFP format will be played. The championship game itself? One year, I'm going to have to break down and get one, and recently, I just caught a big break.

The city of Nashville approved $2.1 billion funding for a new domed stadium downtown. They want the College Football Playoff Championship, the Super Bowl, the Final Four, the SEC Championship, the World Cup, and who knows what else? I definitely want the CFP ticket, even if the Trojans or Sooners show up! For me, no airfare and no hotel necessary - just very short drive. If for some reason I can't get a ticket, maybe I'll think about renting out my house for the weekend for a fee to cover my Bucket List.

Shoot-out at OK State!

Texas Tech at (117) Oklahoma State, September 22, 2007

Stillwater, Oklahoma – Oklahoma State's pre-game, radio show featured Cowboy fans questioning quarterback Bobby Reid's fortitude for not playing well in previous losses to Georgia and Troy. Preseason reports rated him highly. I initially anticipated a high-scoring, competitive game when I booked it to see State host Texas Tech (3-0). However, the Cowboy loss to Troy State the previous week seemed to indicate a lesser game than expected. The loss of their starter Bobby Reid replaced by one-time starter, Zac Robinson, combined with a porous defense against Mike Leach's pass-happy, offensive, scoring machine disappointed me. I may have traveled all the way to Stillwater to watch a blow-out. Aside from that, the OSU ticket I purchased in advance through the ticket office assured me my ticket cost the most I had ever paid anywhere in the country as of this date. At $80 a ticket, I'd better see something special. The Cowboys weren't a powerhouse in recent years, just a middle-of-the-road Big XII team.

T. Boone Pickens Stadium was still under construction. Plans called for expansion to 60,000 seats. To fill it, they'll evidently have to start selling tickets at lower prices. This game didn't sell out like I was led to believe. I'll say this though; the seats and aisles offer more room and comfort than many other college stadiums I've visited.

Before the game, I stopped for beers, shade, and score updates at the Stonewall Tavern, just a stone's throw from T.B.P. Stadium. Once inside the stadium, my ticket thankfully placed me in the shade of the south stands. Four rows from the top, refreshing shade provided a cooling effect. OSU parents sitting next to me received cell phone calls from their kids sitting across from us about the agonizingly hot sun. Hand fans given away could be seen flapping vigorously throughout the student section. Kids sat in the sun-drenched, 90-degree temperatures. The action on the field got so hot, however, that fans would eventually forget the sweltering heat in Stillwater!

Cowboy and Red Raider guns come out blazing!

Just like a rodeo, a chute opened and the Oklahoma State Cowboys (1-2) burst out on to the field before the game. The first half turned out to be an offensive free-for-all. The two teams combined for nine touchdowns. Tech's Graham Harrell threw three of his first half scoring passes to Mike Crabtree. The other found Eric Morris. Shannon Woods scored on a 6-yard run. State kept pace with three rushing touchdowns – Dantrell Savage on a four-yarder, Kendall Hunter on a 42-yard run, and the sub-quarterback Zac Robinson raced in from 48 yards away. He also tossed a short score to Dez Bryant. Bullet, the beautiful, black stallion that carries a Cowpoke with the OSU flag, raced out over the Pro-turf after every Cowboy score. At the half, the Texas Tech Red Raiders led, 35-28.

Overloading the backfield to the left, Robinson faked a dive left to his tailback, and reverse-rolled to the right. He finished a 68-yard scoring drive with an 11-yard run to tie the score, 35-35. After combining for 63 points in the first half, it looked like neither would score again until the Cowboys tied it with 1:15 remaining in the third. The announcer informed the crowd that both teams had already combined for over 1,000 yards before the third period ended. The Cowboys and Raiders reloaded for a shoot-out to settle this Big XII showdown.

Early fourth-quarter possessions stalled. Would the defenses dominate the balance of the game and force this game into overtime? Answer: a 33-yard pass from Robinson to Jeremy Broadway gave the Cowboys the lead. Harrell hooked up with Danny Amendola for a 41-yard Red Raider score to tie. Could either team play defense now? Alex Trlica put up the first field goal of the game that put Tech on top by three. OSU retaliated with seven points on a 55-yard pass play from Robinson to Brandon Pettigrew for another tenuous Cowboy lead, 49-45. Tech needed six.

Not over 'til...

Tenuous, you ask? Before the first half ended, Mike Leach's Raiders needed only 15 seconds to drive 86 yards to score a touchdown! Not only did 1:28 remain in the battle with the ball on their 28, but Tech had two time-outs left. A 40-yard pass took them almost instantly to Oklahoma State's 18. After a short run and two incomplete passes, the Cowboy defense held the Raiders to a fourth down at the fifteen.

With one bullet left in the chamber, Harrell dropped back in the pocket and fired toward his favorite target. Crabtree sprinted over the middle into the end zone. Free safety Ricky Price may have slightly touched the ball, but either way, the ball glanced off the freshman receiver's shoulder pad. Misfire! Tech's final offensive threat fell to the turf! The Raiders used their two time-outs. Over the last 00:19, Robinson took a knee three times to run out the clock. Bullet had finished his laps for the day. The Cowboys successfully defended T.B.P. Stadium from the Red Raiders. They overcame their early season struggles against these well-armed Raiders. The combined total of the 49-45 Cowboy victory stood as the third highest score I'd seen among all my FBS games over the years at that time. Another fight to the finish.

The two offenses combined for 94 points and 1,328 total yards. Robinson aptly replaced Bobby Reid in only his second start completing 16 of 32 for 211 yards and two touchdowns. He ran for 116 yards and two scores. Harrell performed better than expected in Mike Leach's offense with 46 completions among 67 attempts for 646 yards and five TDs. The total yardage amounted to the fourth highest ever in Football Bowl Division game history.

Too bad I didn't get a press pass for two reasons

For one, the most expensive game ticket I ever purchased, but it paid off in a thrilling shoot-out that went down to the last minute of play! The second though, not a member of the press, I missed Coach Mike Gundy's well-documented, tirade about being "a man" after the game in defense of his now *former* quarterback Bobby Reid. I'll never forget this shoot-out for what it was! I'm glad I could be there. It turned out to be worth paying the full price for *this* ticket. From the other sideline, I can say that the late Head Coach Mike Leach coached some thrilling offensive game plans on my schedule.

Fast forward to Oklahoma State somewhere at a game in the future: As for future Oklahoma State Cowboy contests, with Big XII membership updates, I'll be looking for some opportunities to see them play at possible campuses like Texas Tech or Baylor when I'm in the Lone Star State. With Cincinnati now in the Big XII, they might offer possibilities against these Cowboys in Ohio. Timing isn't always *everything* in these cases. I'm still looking for the most competitive match-ups every week. Not that it always works out that way, but more often than not, I selected a lot of great, competitive gridiron clashes to attend over all these many years!

Perfect Ending! A Future Rivalry / A Step Back / Note: Sorry if I confuse you*

(~~118~~) Idaho at (118) Nevada, October 27, 2007

Reno, Nevada – At this time, 119 teams made up the Football Bowl Subdivision and I was able to make it out to Reno, Nevada. I couldn't believe that this crazy Goal could ever be achieved as quickly as it was (seven years to add 61 teams). Several months earlier through my website, I had been contacted by a Nevada Wolfpack fan, Paul Andrew. Paul invited me to tailgate with him and a bunch of dedicated Nevada fans. He informed me that the Pack didn't have a huge football following, so they would be easy to find. He gave me his cell number, and we talked several times before I headed out. I looked forward to partying with his fellow Wolfpack tailgaters since none of my stalwarts over the years could afford to make it out for my grand finale.

Entering the Twilight Zone

On the flight into Reno on Friday, I noticed a few strange things. First, the heavy, smoky haze from ongoing forest fires in California blanketed much of Nevada. I hoped all my acquaintances back in California were fine, and I made several calls. Thankfully, no major problems. Secondly, I noticed no typical activity taking place around schools on a Friday morning. Parking lots were empty and a school bus depot looked full. I took the shuttle to stay at the *Sands Hotel and Casino* which the locals consider part of "old Reno." Once settled, I checked out the sports lines for the college games I'd be interested in. It's my primary gambling entertainment I enjoy while in Nevada.

That afternoon, I toured the University of Nevada campus. Few people were there. The basketball team scrimmaged in the main arena on campus. The school bookstore was closed. On a Friday before a game day, little on campus stirred. No students walked to classes. Nobody hung out at the student center. No vehicles rolled in or out for the weekend. I know Paul told me that the Wolfpack didn't have a great fan following, but I wondered if Nevada-Reno even had any students! Heading off campus, I stopped by *The Ritz Bar and Grill* on the edge.

Chloe, a nice-looking bartender who served me and her one other customer, filled me in. I happened to show up on *Nevada Day*! Schools, the state government, the university, and some businesses all closed for the annual holiday. They still celebrate Nevada's statehood by shutting down. We hoisted a few shots along with Mike the cook to celebrate. He made great burgers. Chloe gave me information about some of the local celebrations and on some of the casinos. She even checked out my website while I was there. At least I had found the right place for beer and burgers near campus.

I watched *Game Day* Saturday morning at 7 a.m. At 9 a.m. while drinking Bloody Mary's at the *Silver Legacy Casino*, I watched games played in the east. Not used to that so early where I lived. I played several game tickets, but I left at halftime for most games already started on TV - doing pretty well - to meet Paul at the tailgate party hosted by his buddy, Steve. On the way up Virginia Avenue for my first tailgate party at Nevada, I picked up cold beer. Not like Oklahoma! Found Paul, and there I met a great bunch of Wolfpack fans. I had exited the Twi-light Zone.

From The Twi-light Zone to Halloween in Reno

Paul introduced me to a couple of dozen people. They grilled, we drank, we ate, and we shared a lot of football stories. Paul's Dad played for Cal back in the early '50s. In the Homecoming edition of Nevada's game magazine, *Pack Edge*, Paul had written an article entitled, *"The Battle Born Rivalry."* It highlighted some interesting games in the Nevada-UNLV rivalry played since 1969. He insisted that when I return to Reno, that's the game to go to.

With a capacity of 29,964, Mackay Stadium sells out for the *"Battle of the Fremont Cannon"* when UNLV comes to town every other year. Winner takes home the cannon. Reno probably has plenty of UNLV alum managing the growing Casino business downtown. Paul told me Boise and Fresno in the top-heavy Western Athletic Conference bring in the other big crowds at Mackay.

I noted Nevada had lot of construction under way on campus. Paul told me much of the funding comes through state gambling taxes. Tuition is free for in-state students who maintain good grades. He told me," Don't worry! Whatever you lose in Reno, just remember that you're helping my kids through school!" That's funny, with Atlantic City and all the lotteries in Jersey, someone in our state government has to explain to me why NJ kids don't get the same benefit. We headed over to Mackay. I bought an extra ticket from some women on the way in. I sat with Paul and his buddies, Todd and Phil. On the 20-yard line we sat right next to the Nevada band. Paul's son played in the Wolfpack band. As a prelude to Halloween, it seemed appropriate that a team of *Vandals* kicked off to the *Wolfpack*!

Why I don't bet often.

The Pack took an early, commanding, comfortable, 17-0 lead. It looked like Nevada was on the verge of a big win in the first period, but their faithful remained pessimistic. They'd seen the Pack do this too often before. They still enjoyed the lead at halftime, 17-7, holding the Vandals to only 79 yards. The Wolfpack Marching Band celebrated Halloween with local kids in costumes at the intermission.

On a third and nine at Nevada's 18, Idaho quarterback Nathan Enderle fired a pass to Eric Greenwood to cut the score early in the third period, 17-14. Nevada extended the lead, 24-14, when Luke Lippincott took it in from the two. Nevada forced a Vandal punt and took over on its own 15. Freshman quarterback Colin Kaepernick's 23-yard pass to Kyle Sammons put Nevada at the Idaho 28-yard line. His next pass fluttered into the end zone, but Marko Mitchell came back to get it with a diving catch for a score and widened the margin, 31-14. The Pack fans cheered, but it disappointed me. I had taken Idaho and the 16-1/2 points at the casino! I figured I may have to make this game interesting. Besides, what else are you supposed to do when you visit Reno?

Idaho's Deonte Jackson, who came into this game as the nation's eleventh leading rusher, scored from the two to close the gap back to ten, 31-21. I was ahead. Lippincott's run from deep in the Pistol for 11 yards around the right side gave the Pack a 37-21 lead. The Pack fans were ecstatic as I cringed awaiting a 17-point Nevada win. Brett Jaekle missed the extra point! I was happy – for a while. I found later that another team on my ticket lost. To think though that a missed extra-point in this game could make or break winning or losing money. Oh, well! That's why I never bet – unless I visit Nevada!

That was the final score . . . 37-21. The final score of the final game of my Goal! I had seen all 119 teams, but another opportunity loomed on the horizon. Western Kentucky planned to join the FBS in 2009. I planned to see them play as Team #120 when they became an official FBS team. I had to keep up so I could be sure that I could always say that I'd seen 'em all. For now, I was on top of college football fandom!

Summed up in one sentence

Without prompting from me, my new football friend in Nevada came up with a perfect ending to punctuate this story to see my 119th and final team. Talking about this particular game to finish The Goal before kick-off, several tailgaters asked me why I "saved" this game for last. Sarcastically, I had told them that I saved the best for last. They chuckled and shook their heads knowing the two teams we were about to watch better than I did.

I mentioned though that I had opted out of attending Penn State-Ohio State today for Nevada and Idaho instead - been there, done that! More importantly, I *needed* to see these two teams play. I could have gone to State College, but I didn't want to wait to go to Idaho next year or to wait two years to get back to Reno. Astounded, Paul responded, *"You gave up going to see Penn State play Ohio State to come to* **this** *game?* **YOU ARE THE FAN!"**

He summed up The Goal perfectly. It took some extra effort and creativity to see 'em all. I enjoyed every minute, every mile, every game, and every memory I still have of this fun endeavor. I hope they last. Perfect summation, thanks to Paul!

Smart step down

Moscow, Idaho - Fast Forward for Idaho back to the FCS: Give credit to the University of Idaho for pulling the plug on playing FBS football. They tried it, they struggled on the field, they most likely struggled on the financial side, so why not tone it down and play other programs with similar identities? For the Idaho Vandals, the FCS move made much more sense. I know a few other programs that should consider this "downsizing" strategy from FBS to FCS for all the same reasons. There's no shame in such a move. The school administrations just have to face reality.

Reno, Nevada – Fast Forward to a future "Battle of the Fremont Cannon" - As for Nevada, this marks their only game in my history. As I mentioned in my UNLV chapter, and as Paul suggested when I met him back in Reno, my best opportunity to see the Wolfpack and the Rebels play would be against each other in the Battle Born Rivalry for the Fremont Cannon. Either at Reno or in Vegas, I just have to try to work this around a Thanksgiving weekend most likely. Bucket List if the timing becomes convenient.

*Referring to "Perfect Ending" here

A note of clarification. You see the University of Idaho and Nevada team numbers were both recorded as Team 118 in this chapter. Convenient timing. My next-to-last team dropped admirably back into the FCS as reported. My next Tale highlights Western Kentucky when they joined the FBS. They replaced Nevada as team 119 and Nevada slid into No. 118

position when Idaho left the FBS. So once again, without breaking stride, as the late, great broadcaster Lindsay Nelson used to interject during Sunday morning Notre Dame highlights during the 60s and early 70s when game action became insignificant, *"We move on to further action..."*

Hilltoppers rocky-topped! Whew!

Western Kentucky (119) at Tennessee, September 5, 2009

Knoxville, Tennessee – Western Kentucky shed its transitional status and now joined FBS membership as a full-fledged member of the struggling Sun Belt Conference. If I still wanted to say that I'd seen 'em all, I figured I'd catch them early and take advantage to watch a game at a new venue. My plan was in place when I saw the chance to get a ticket to an opener at Neyland Stadium. Of course, with the Labor Day weekend, I made the most of it, so I headed down to Raleigh to catch up with Joe Massimilla and attended the Thursday night game between the NC State Wolfpack and Steve Spurrier's South Carolina Gamecocks. USC prevailed in a surprising defensive struggle, 7-3. I headed west to Knoxville from there.

I'm sure the scenery was beautiful, but driving up and down through a curvy, mountainous I-40 West doesn't leave one much pause to enjoy the sights. You have to focus on who's driving slowly ahead of you and who's barreling down from behind. That was my first time through the Appalachians in western North Carolina. I was glad to get to Knoxville. I was even happier to find *Woodruff's Bar and Grill* on Gay Street for Happy Hour that night. Thankfully, it lasted until 10 pm.

The next morning, I walked streets named Phil Fulmer Avenue, Johnny Majors Way, and Peyton Manning Pass. The Vol Walk near Neyland was packed. The Volunteer marching band entertained on the Silverstein Building steps and then belted out *"Rocky Top Tennessee"* as the team strolled down the path engulfed by a sea of orange. It wasn't until later on that day I could appreciate that the UT band knew more than just one song. The debut of Lane Kiffin brought 98,761 to UT's opener. It was difficult to maneuver near Neyland to hunt for a ticket. I eventually bought an extra from a nice family of Tennessee fans. We sat 17 rows up from the 15-yard line on the WKU sideline. The two grandparents were taking their 8-year-old grandson, David, *and me* to our first Tennessee home game.

Anyone know the Hilltoppers' song?
   WKU's defense competed with UT in the first quarter thwarting the first two drives with an interception and a fumble recovery, but the Hilltopper offense was anemic against the quick, hard-hitting Tennessee defense. Western Kentucky played the Tennessee Volunteers to a 0-0 stalemate by the end of the first quarter. I just knew that Tennessee could not be held down by the newest team in D-I, and once they scored, the floodgate would open. Every first down, every score, every turnover, and every WKU punt was celebrated to the tune of *"Good ol' Rocky Top!"* The Vols raced to 28-0 lead by the end of the second quarter. The band entertained at halftime and finished its performance with their fight song, of course!
   In the third, Montario Hardesty scored on a one-play drive from the WKU 43 to extend the lead. *"Good ol' Rocky Top!"* The visitors finally scored on a 66-yard drive capped by Bobby Rainey's 19-yard TD run to put Western on the board to trail now, 35-7. It was all Tennessee in the fourth though as Jonathan Crompton connected again with Stocker from the six and then with freshman Marsalis Teague from the five. On first downs – *"Good ol' Rocky Top!"* David Oku, another frosh, ran it in from the two and from the one to finish the next two Tennessee drives and make the final score, 63-7. I was *Rocky-Topped out!* Tennessee out-gained WKU 657 to 83 yards and never punted. WKU's Jeremy Moore did an excellent job on his nine punts averaging 44.8 and allowing only 35 return yards. That's the best I could say about the Hilltoppers' inauguration into FBS football.

Take the Lane out of Knoxville

The Hilltoppers won no games all season. UT finished 6-6 and Lane Kiffin fled town back to Southern California leaving teams of NCAA investigators in his jet stream. He replaced his former mentor Pete Carroll who left L.A. for the pros leaving behind some questions about his USC program as well. It doesn't seem right that the NFL should be an escape hatch for college coaches in violation of college football standards.

"Rocky Top" made me appreciate the fact that Penn State's Blue Band has a repertoire of at least ten different school songs. One tune, especially after nine touchdowns, first downs, time-outs, second downs, official time-outs, etc., etc., can get monotonous. Enough with the *"Whews!"* Even David's Grandmother, a UT season ticket holder, leaned over to me at one point and asked, "Are you sick of *'Rocky Top'* yet?" I told her I had been warned. They need to learn a few other tunes down in Knoxville. I'm glad to say I retired to the Music City instead! I'm about a one-hour drive away from Bowling Green, Kentucky where I've seen a fledging WKU football team play several times already. Not their song, but here's an idea: *"Good old Hilly Top - Hilly Top, Kentucky!"*

FIFTY YEARS OF TAILGATE TALES:

Big Red, Western Kentucky's mascot roams the stadium turf in Bowling Green.

Reason for this Season / USA - Full Speed Ahead

(120) University of Texas San Antonio at (121) South Alabama, September 1, 2012

Mobile, Alabama - I looked forward to the 2012 season for three reasons. I already had two guaranteed seats to this season's BCS Championship game. Three years prior to see three Orange Bowls in a row guaranteed me to go to this year's BCS Championship game at Sun Life Stadium in Miami Lakes. Already, I etched in No. 1 versus No. 2 to decide the national title on the field of play on my 2012 schedule. Secondly, four new teams officially joined the FBS, and my plan kept pace to still "seen 'em all!" The third reason I looked forward to this football season did not have to do with college ball. As a matter of fact, it presented somewhat of an obstacle for my desired goal.

My son, Eric, would be playing his senior season of high school football at Lenape Valley Regional in Stanhope, NJ. A perennially strong program coming off an 8-2 season with losses to two Group II State champs, Eric would be starting at offensive tackle for the well-oiled Wing-T offense run by Head Coach Don Smolyn, already a New Jersey Sports Hall of Fame member. As one senior at the previous season's football banquet said in his farewell speech, Lenape Valley epitomized *"Friday Night Lights"* in New Jersey. As far as our area's dedication and enthusiasm supporting the high school football program, the players viewed it that way. Luckily for me, for the first time, every regular season LVRHS game was to be contested on a Friday night.

My Saturday college habit had a clear path with none of Eric's scheduled games conflicting into early November. The big issue for me arose later. A prime concern for me would not be where or against whom, but when? They might play on a Saturday or two. One November Saturday afternoon in question would conflict with my plan as No. 124 from far away happened to venture within convenient driving distance. There was no question where I would be if Eric and his "band of brothers" played a game that day. I would just have to wait if Lenape moved on through their playoffs.

Not a Golden or a Miami, but an Isaac

I planned the start of my 2012 season perfectly. Three games over Labor Day weekend couldn't be better. Eric's season would not start until the following Saturday. Among the three games I planned to see, my centerpiece was what most fans would consider the least favored – between FBS newcomers UT San Antonio and South Alabama. They would open in Mobile, Alabama on Thursday night; on Saturday night, I'd meet my buddy Charlie Murren with his family and friends at the Georgia Dome where their beloved Auburn would battle Clemson; and on Monday evening, I'd see Georgia Tech play at Virginia Tech in an opener between two promising ACC title contenders.

For me, the most anticipated featured the two newbies. Don't believe me? Hurricane Isaac ripped through the Gulf Coast a few nights before my trip got started. The postponement between the Roadrunners and the Jaguars changed from Thursday night to Saturday afternoon. Because of Isaac, travel cancellations jeopardized getting to this one. First, I called Charlie to see if he could get someone else to join his tailgate at the Auburn-Clemson game on Saturday. He had no problem getting someone else to go see two teams of Tigers go at it in Atlanta. He understood my objective to "see 'em all!"

Rather than go down to Mobile on Thursday from Roanoke, Virginia, I rebooked my flight to Friday. I booked from Roanoke because I planned my original third game on Monday night at Virginia Tech's Lane Stadium nearby. Easier and cheaper than flying to multiple cities until I lost my free flight based on frequent flier miles. This was hassle enough until I got on the plane in Roanoke to Mobile, Alabama via Charlotte, NC.

After a seven-hour drive to Roanoke, the flight delayed 40 minutes, then another 15. As we sat by the gate waiting to push back, the hydraulics on the main hatch failed. The door finally shut manually with a loud, metallic slam! The stewardess kept re-checking the hatch. We were about to taxi until the pilot reported lights indicated something amiss with the luggage compartment hatch. More worried about luggage than passengers? He announced the plane was unsafe for our 50-minute flight to Charlotte.

Ain't no stopping me now

This was the last scheduled flight out of Roanoke. No connections to Mobile until morning. The people working for the airline were very helpful. They booked local hotel rooms and cabs for me and the other stranded passengers. Roger at the service desk worked with me getting a connecting flight to Mobile next day. He couldn't get me there in time for the 1 pm kickoff through Charlotte, so finally, he booked me an earlier flight to Pensacola, 64 miles from Mobile. I would make it by noon latest. Great! Two things though– I had to get up for the return cab at 4 am. It was close to 11 pm already. Second, I reserved a car in Mobile, and my return flight was booked out of there as well. Another hassle.

My plan for a happy occasion enjoying the start of a new season using vacation time and discounted travel fares was falling apart. This seemed more like one of my typical business trips. At this point, I figured to forget about it. On to the game! I arrived at Ladd-Peebles on Saturday an hour before kickoff.

Under intense sunshine in an area exposed to high winds and the rain of Hurricane Isaac earlier in the week, the two teams clashed for an entertaining game in front of 17,144 fans. Many sought the comforts of shade and air-conditioning before this contest was over. I sweated out the entire game hoping for an exciting finish.

Let's get this season started

The South Alabama Jaguars got off to a quick 7-0 lead. Late in the second, UTSA kicker Sean Ianno booted a 32-yarder for a 20-7 Roadrunner lead. USA drove from their 35 down to UTSA's two-yard line. Jag quarterback C.J. Bennet rolled right to connect with back Desmond Jones with :20 remaining in the half to cut the Roadrunner lead, 20-14, at the intermission. I probably chose the right game to see them both compete in this year. Like most fans at halftime, I found shade under the stadium stands. Beers sold for $3.50, a bargain compared to prices at most venues.

I stayed out under the scorching sun in humid, 90-degree temperatures. Now, I understood why they originally scheduled this game on Thursday night! I also realized why they rescheduled this game for Saturday afternoon instead evening. With both Alabama and Auburn slated to play in separate games during prime time, only the small contingent of UTSA fans, family members of USA players, and one college football fan from New Jersey with a unique goal to accomplish would have been in attendance. More so, nobody else in Alabama would tune into this game on TV at that time.

South Alabama closed the score to within three in the third. Sloppy play and stupid penalties marked the quick quarter. Heat seemed to break down the discipline for both sides. South Alabama cornerback Tyrell Pearson stepped in front of UTSA's intended receiver and ran it back to the Roadrunner seven. "USA! USA! USA!" chanted the home crowd. A one-yard run put the University of South Alabama in the lead, 24-20.

On a fourth and five at USA's 35, UTSA went for broke in the left corner of the end zone to rebound for a 27-24 Roadrunner lead. On USA's next possession when jostled by his running back, the Jag quarterback fumbled a handoff and Roadrunner Jason Neill recovered at the USA 21. The visitors seemed ready to put the game away, but USA held them to a 21-yard field goal to stay within reach at 30-24. The clock stopped with 6:35 remaining. I pondered if UTSA Head Coach Larry Coker considered going for six on fourth and goal at the three instead, but that's why I don't coach!

Two series later, a UTSA punt was returned by South Alabama to the Roadrunner 35. With 2:46, Bennet connected with Jereme' Jones on a 34-yard touchdown pass, and his Jaguars took a 31-30 lead with the extra point. On the ensuing return, UTSA brought the ball to their 31. A personal foul after the play against South Alabama brought it out to the 46. On fourth down with 16 seconds remaining, Ianno booted a 52-yard field goal. UTSA celebrated their first win of the new season and first FBS win, 33-31! Four South Alabama turnovers and a costly penalty late in the game weighed heavily against the home team in the final outcome.

This loss was the first opening day loss suffered by USA after their four years of FCS football. The Jaguar record was now 23-5 under their only head coach, Joey Jones, a former Alabama wide receiver who played for Bear Bryant. The balance of their inaugural FBS season was not quite up to par with their building years though, only a 2-11 season.

UTSA, under former Miami Hurricane Head Coach Larry Coker finished their second season ever at 8-4, 3-3 in the Western Athletic Conference. Four wins came over non-FBS teams. Game costs at South Alabama were nominal. Parking - $10 on a local neighborhood lawn; 40-yard line seat, $15; program, $5; and beers, $3.50. Low-cost entertainment, but darn that Hurricane Isaac for screwing up my original plans. I missed another game, lost free FF miles, and shelled out some extra money for a rental car!

On Monday, I made it to Blacksburg to see Virginia Tech defeat Georgia Tech in OT, 20-17. It kicked off mediocre seasons for both. Happily, for me, the centerpiece of my original plan turned out to be a good one featuring an exciting game between the two newest members of the FBS. I looked forward to seeing both play again.

Murfreesboro, TN - Fast forward to Texas-San Antonio at Middle Tennessee, 2022: With my move to Tennessee being so close to Murfreesboro, I got to see the Roadrunners again in C-USA action against the Middle Tennessee Blue Raiders. Under Head Coach Jeff Traylor, the UTSA offense scored early and often. With quarterback Frank Harris's prolific day running and scoring (27 completions, 414 yards, two scoring passes, two rushing scores, but three interceptions), the Road Runners scored on their first five of six possessions. The scoring drives went for 75, 74, 75, 73, and 79 yards respectively for a 31-20 lead at halftime.

Harris dazzled until three picks killed the Road Runner momentum, and Middle Tennessee rebounded to trail, 38-30, late in the game. It took a defensive stand and a 45-yard scoring drive with 1:32 left to seal a victory for UTSA, 45-30. They finished with an 11-3 record losing to 12-2 Troy in the Cure Bowl. Regretfully, as written earlier, UTSA didn't get to compete in a bowl against a Power Five school.

Mobile, Alabama - South Alabama at Hancock-Whitney Stadium, in the future: I'll probably see UTSA eventually play in an American Athletic contest in the next few years. As mentioned in my previous San Diego State chapter about tying a South Alabama game to a visit to Tom Ables' battleship, the USS Alabama in Mobile, definitely a future Bucket List adventure.

To be Big Time, or not Big-Time? / Back to the FCS?

Indiana at (122) Massachusetts, September 8, 2012

Foxboro, Massachusetts – The Indiana Hoosiers primarily dwell near the bottom of the Big Ten in football every season. As the first Power Five conference team to visit UMass in their inaugural FBS season, I had hoped that this would actually be a chance for the Minutemen to win one of the few games they could. I always hope to see a competitive game. To add the Minutemen as the 122nd FBS team to my quest, I ventured to Gillette Stadium, the home of the New England Patriots.

Despite with their historical ineptitude, the Hoosiers arrived in Foxboro with a 1-0 record after a 24-17 win over FCS Indiana State. The previous year, the Hoosiers finished 1-11 with the only win against FCS South Carolina State. It seemed like the Minutemen invited the right competitor for their FBS home opener. Hopefully, they learned and made adjustments from their 37-0 loss at FBS Connecticut nine days earlier. Maybe not.Maybe. Then again, maybe not.

Comedian Bill Cosby was on hand to help with their first home, coin-toss. What followed after wasn't funny – for UMass football nor metaphorically for the comic's, life-long reputation. IU took a 7-0 lead on its second possession with a 50-yard touchdown run. UMass looked like it was up to the challenge. It answered with its first ever FBS touchdown on a 16-yard run by quarterback Mike Wegzyn. At the start of the next IU series, an observant Minuteman fan observed, "Indiana has some quick players." Well, welcome to the big time! And just think, this was lowly Indiana opening his eyes. UMass decided to leave the Colonial Athletic Association for the next level and this is what it got.

Leading 21-6 early in the second period, the Hoosiers moved down close to the Minutemen goal before signal-caller Tre Roberson went down into the line. He stayed down holding his left leg. The medical staff immediately summoned the ambulance. They applied an air cast, and he was transported to a local hospital. Indiana settled for a 19-yard field goal to extend the lead, 24-6. From there, the game just got worse for the Minutemen. IU scored at will, even with their second team pocket passer. At the half, the Hoosiers advanced to a 38-6 lead. Boring!

Slick road ahead for the Minutemen

As the second half began, rain started, slow at first, but then harder. UMass was done playing, and their fans were done watching. I checked them off as FBS team No. 122, and I make that assessment begrudgingly. The Hoosiers showed the Minutemen that they have a steep climb ahead of them to compete at the highest level of college football. The lowly Hoosiers whipped them handily at Gillette Stadium, 45-6. The game was not even as close as the final score indicates.

My feeling after the game surmised that UMass owed me one. Their Head Coach Charley Molnar seemed to have had a somewhat lackluster football career to say the least. For someone coaching at this level, his season records as a college player (D-2 Lock Haven State) and as assistant coach were all well below .500 from 1984-2005. In 2006, he started coaching under Brian Kelly at Central Michigan, then Cincinnati, and then Notre Dame on winning teams. Even the game program noted that his overall record as an assistant stood at 132-186-3. Then it noted his record for the last six seasons at 59-20, evidently on the coat tails of Brian Kelly. UMass selected him as their first head coach. He lasted two seasons. Poor choice realized evidently.

Amherst, Massachusetts - Fast Forward to Liberty U. at UMass, 2018:

After their Indiana embarrassment in their FBS opener, UMass owed me. I kept an eye on them to see if they ever offered a chance to make this up to me. Eventually, re-hiring former Head Coach Mark Whipple who coached the Minutemen to the 1988 IAA National Championship, the program improved ever so slightly. I caught their greatest game ever as an FBS team when I added the Liberty Flames as a new latest FBS program. Their clash turned out to be my highlight game for both of these teams in my FBS history.

Texas State – only a beginning / TXST Bobcat Connection

(123) Texas State at Navy, November 17, 2012

Annapolis, Maryland– Before reporting on this game to sustain my goal to see 'em all, let me go back to that obstacle I mentioned before the 2012 season began, Eric's senior football season. Super Storm Sandy damaged to the roof of the high school and canceled classes for two weeks. Most the games in New Jersey north of Atlantic City were postponed pushing back the playoff schedule one full week. On Friday November 9, the Patriots played under the lights at No. 4 Bernards (9-0). The winner was seeded to most likely play at No. 1 Madison the following Saturday afternoon. In a heartbreaking loss for our Patriots, Bernards scored the winning touchdown in the last minute of play, 26-20. Disappointingly, the Patriot season came to an end. I definitely would have gone to that game the following Saturday.

Got to look at the bright side

My "silver lining" of sorts resulted in the opportunity to add Texas State as my 123rd team. The Bobcats were scheduled to play Navy in Annapolis. At least I wouldn't have to wait until 2013 to figure how I'd attend a Bobcat game. Proud of my son, he made second team All-Conference offensive tackle. The Lenape Valley Patriot offense established the school's seasonal rushing record. As a matter of fact, every starting lineman and running back on his team made first or second all-conference. More importantly, I could tell the teamwork, sacrifice, and hard work playing LVR football helped him to grow as a young man. Eric decided on his own to enlist in the US Navy after graduation.

Speaking of Navy, I trekked to Annapolis Friday night with three guys to add Texas State to continue to "see 'em all!" Dave Headden and Frank Scarpa both were attending a Navy game in Annapolis for the first time. Frank Lorito had been with me there on a couple occasions. He looked forward to going back. As I've always said, every college football fan should see at least one game at West Point and one game at Annapolis. We enjoyed a unique tailgate experience as we parked in a nearby backyard. The official parking lots around the stadium were sold-out.

Tight squeeze

We parked in a backyard on nearby Locust Avenue behind some friendly, family's house where they allowed us to tailgate. We moved up slightly a few feet from their back fence to allow us to set up a table and chairs to hang out in their back yard. People next door did the same with their backyard. However, they parked the yard so tightly though that as one customer started to leave his car, he awoke a woman in an adjacent car. Hearing his car door close, she climbed up through her sun roof and yelled, "I'm trapped in my car! I can't open the doors!" So much for that neighbor's plan. Cars had to be rearranged eventually.

Today, we didn't expect a defensive battle. Only last week, both teams lost in high-scoring affairs. Navy fell to Troy, 41-31. Texas State fell to No. 20 Louisiana Tech, 62-55. Surprise! The first half ended with an unexpectedly low score of 7-0 with Navy leading. They kicked off to start the second half, and Texas State gave up the ball right away when John O'Boyle's hit on returner Jafus Gaines caused a fumble. James Britton recovered on the TXST 16. One play and 14 seconds into the half, Noah Copeland ran it over the goal line for a 14-0 Navy lead. Finally, State retaliated with a 36-yard kick and trailed at the end of the third, 14-3.

Navy's next drive culminated in Slotback Gee Gee Greene's six-yard sweep left for a 21-3 lead. After a return out to State's 38, Shaun Rutherford heaved a pass to Isaiah Battle for a one-play, 62-yard Bobcat touchdown drive and closed the gap with 12:43 left, 21-10. Bobcat Head Coach Dennis Franchione called for some trickery. Texas State kicker Will Johnson recovered his onside kick dribbling down field to give TXST possession at their 46. On a fourth down play, the Bobcat drive to the Navy 34 came up short. After two exchanges, Texas State drove down to the Navy three as time expired.

We attended a competitive game along with 31,000 others to see the latest of four entrants into the FBS field beaten by the Mids, 21-10. Navy rushed for 407 yards as a team led by fullback Noah Copeland who tallied 110 yards and two touchdowns. USNA defeated the team that sealed my effort to officially say once again, I'd "seen 'em all!"

After the game, we had a few beers and shared football adventures with some friends tailgating in the stadium parking lot. Of course, the evening didn't end there: dinner at Buddy's Crabs and Ribs downtown while we watched Kansas State and Oregon both get knocked off as teams No. 1 and No. 2; walked over to the Annapolis Cigar Company on Main Street; bought cigars; in the back lounge, puffed away, watched more football, drank Don Julio Tequila; and observed the entertainment of others who only knew one song playing with their lone guitar. Found a board game called "Crap or Fact" and played until closing. The guys all wanted to come back next season. This tradition of going to Annapolis for great tailgating and football has continued every year since. A traditional future mainstay annually on the Bucket List.

San Marcos, Texas - Fast Forward to Texas State vs. Louisiana, 2020: I never thought that a Texas football adventure would bring me to Bobcat Stadium in San Marcos to see the TXST Bobcats play before ever seeing games at places like Texas Stadium, A&M's Kyle Field, or even to Waco to see Baylor play. As fate would have it, my daughter Alex moved to Philly in her final year of her Master's program for Occupational Therapy (OT) at Misericordia University in Dallas, PA.

Dog-gone! Off to Texas!

With her dog, Simba, he met a Husky named Dixon while at a dog park in the City of Brotherly Love. Dixon belonged to Zach, a Penn State grad then working toward a Sports Management degree at Temple. Alex and Zach started dating. He accepted a position as Business Development Director at Texas State. She found the OT market to be very tight in the northeast with all the therapeutic-degreed candidates from so many programs. In the state of Texas, with only four schools offering similar curriculum, she found more employment opportunities available there that interested her. After interviews over the phone, she and Simba relocated to Austin, Texas. The rest is history. Alex and Zach get married next April. So, as mentioned in previous chapters, my Texas connection is set!

Regarding Texas State football, great opportunity for St. Laurie and I to go any time. We visit our daughter and her three boys, Simba, Zach, and Dixon. A place to stay as we've become designated dog-sitters in return. Great club seats at Bobcat Stadium. Great pre-game tailgates in the stadium. Downtown Austin. The Strutters Dance Team. Post-game entertainment in stadium. Nice fans. Nice people. But, an 0-4 Texas State Bobcats football team in the annals of my history!

In 2020, a good thing – the Bobcats hosted one of three games I attended during COVID restrictions. However, they lost to No. 19 Louisiana (10-1), 44-34, and in 2021, lost to No. 5 Baylor (12-2), 29-20. Again, the Ragin' Cajuns (6-7) won in 2022, 41-13. The Bobcat's record for those three years, 10-26.

After that last loss we attended, Texas State infused new coaching blood hiring new Head Coach G.J. Kinne. As both player and coach since he transferred from Texas to Tulsa back in 2008, he's bounced around a lot. Once established as the key signal-caller with the Golden Hurricane in 2009, he threw for 9,472 yards and 81 touchdowns for a 23-15 record. He must at least have thrown some practice passes to my Tulsa will-call guy, Tyler Pistoia. Go Bobcats!

FIFTY YEARS OF TAILGATE TALES:

My daughter Alex and I at Kansas State vs. Texas game in 2019.

These are the Good, Old Days / As the Tide Turns

Marshall at (124) Old Dominion, October 4, 2014

Norfolk, Virginia - I looked to accomplish two significant milestones this weekend. I added Old Dominion University, a first-year FBS member, as my 124th. Foreman Field at S.B. Ballard Stadium became my 49th FBS venue, my 123rd stadium overall. Best of all, St. Laurie and I got to spend the weekend and the game with our son, Eric. Now a Seaman 1/C stationed at Norfolk Naval Base, his billet provided this new football opportunity. Most of our weekend turned out great. As far as seeing a quality FBS game as hoped for, reality fell far short. Exciting games came later that evening on television. My goal to "see 'em all" still means having to take the good, along with the bad and sometimes the ugly. I'd categorize this one as *very ugly*. It transpired totally unexpected though. ODU seemed to be on a roll entering the new next level. It was good to get out with Eric once again no matter what the outcome of the game.

I anticipated a shootout. So did some Marshall fans sitting right in front of us based on the scoring prowess of both teams so far this season. Instead, The Thundering Herd, expected to finish unbeaten and win Conference-USA, demonstrated dominant power over the new FBS Monarchs (3-3, 1-2). Marshall proved not only to be superior in experience, quickness, and size, but possessed superior coaching capabilities under Doc Holliday, too. The Monarchs under Bobby Wilder since 2009 boasted a record of

46-14 indicating they probably could compete.

In this game, however, Old Dominion never wavered from their original strategy. Utilizing the same offense, the same formations, they never re-adjusted to anything even after the Herd jumped out to a 28-0 lead in the first 15 minutes.

The key to the Thundering Herd offense was the powerful running of fullback Devon Johnson (20 carries/198 yards/three touchdowns). He was the best fullback I'd seen anywhere in a long time. Marshall fans told us, "Watch him. He's a horse." A plow horse for sure. The epitome of what a fullback playing for "The Thundering Herd" should be. Devon was *The Thunder* in the herd. Johnson banged, punished, pulled, crushed, and carried Monarch defenders' multiple times with second and third efforts. He never let up. The Monarchs eventually put up seven with 36 ticks left in the first half to trail, 35-7. At that point, Eric asked a question similar to one at the Penn State-Louisiana Tech in the 67-7 blow-out 14 years earlier, "How long are we going to stay for this one?"

Déjà vu'! 14 years later.

At halftime, I told Eric and St. Laurie that I'd like stay until the end of the third. They questioned, why? I figured Wilder and his staff were going to the locker room to make adjustments to prevent the slaughter. Though I try to stay to the end of a game the first time I add a new team, I thought back to Louisiana Tech at Penn State back in 2000 when Eric was five-years old. To start the third, Johnson blasted through the line for 46 yards and followed with a seven-yard touchdown run.

I said to Eric, "This is like watching the varsity scrimmage the JVs." He quickly responded, "More like the varsity against the freshman." He was right. The other Herd running back, Remi Watson, scored his second in the third on Marshall's second series of the half. That was it. The heck with waiting for the third to end. I checked off Old Dominion as my 124th team. Most of the ODU fans were already gone. Eric owned a pickup truck now and did the driving today. No flat tire! We found a Buffalo Wild Wings in Virginia Beach and caught up on more interesting action on all their big screens.

We didn't miss much after we left. Marshall put in second-teamers, water boys, some tough looking female cheerleaders, and according to St. Laurie, some alumni they pulled out of the stands (not really). Undefeated Marshall manhandled the Monarchs from beginning to end, 56-14. It doesn't get worse than this.

Gone, but not forgotten

After ODU shanked a punt on its first possession, quarterback Rakeem Cato went to Marshall's most powerful weapon, fullback Devon Johnson, to run up the middle for 35 yards. He polished off the 59-yard drive with a two-yard touchdown. I figured Devon Johnson, a junior, would be playing for somebody on Sundays in the next few years, and dominating. Another Derrick Henry, for sure!

In 2016, he went undrafted. Unbelievable! Carolina signed him as a free agent, but let him go in 2017. On November 6, 2018 at age 25, he passed away of causes not known to this day. So tragic. He looked like a sure-fire, pro fullback. Healthy as a horse, seemingly. So sorry for him and his family, and so disappointed to never see him play football again.

Another Newbie in Norfolk

Norfolk, Virginia - Fast forward Charlotte at Old Dominion, 2015: ODU welcoming this year's newcomer, the Charlotte 49ers, into the FBS would hopefully make for a much more entertaining and competitive game. The winner would mark the first win ever for either program in ConferenceUSA. Hopefully, a battle would rage before me and my buddy Bernie Olszyk, subbing for Eric while on duty this weekend.

Charlotte ran a no-huddle offense successfully in the first half, but slowed down the tempo in the second half to come up empty on the scoreboard in the third period. Monarch David Washington caught a pass early from his wide receiver position. After the first series, he replaced original starting quarterback Shuler Bentley. Either way, both Monarch quarterbacks had stronger arms than what I'd seen the previous season.

Surprisingly to Bernie and to me, last year's Monarch signal-caller, Taylor Heinicke, who had not impressed against Marshall, made the Minnesota Viking roster.

Charlotte kept ODU's defense off balance with their no-huddle offense in the first half. Charlotte quarterback Lee McNeil moved the team through the air while his alternate Matt Johnson picked up 42 yards on the ground running read options. The 49er offense seemed to work well with a two-quarterback strategy. They led, 24-12, at the half.

Old Dominion scored the only ten points in the third quarter. Washington threw a pass tipped to Marquis Little. He took it for a 33-yard score. A 49er field goal attempt was blocked and Marvin Branch returned it to the Charlotte 37. Chris Kirtley converted on a 45-yard field goal. Not sure why the 49ers dismissed the no-huddle strategy in the second half even though they retained a 24-22 lead into the last period.

A year later, this ODU game didn't disappoint

The 49ers got back on a scoring track. They finished a 79-yard drive with Kalif Phillips going over from the one to widen the lead, 31-22. They wanted that first big conference win. Old Dominion's ensuing comeback attempt sputtered with a missed field goal from 35 yards. Luck turned their way quickly though when Andrew Buie fumbled the ball on the Niners first play. Shadow Williams recovered at the Charlotte 17. Washington's ensuing 15-yard pass into the end zone caught by Zach Pascal put ODU within two again. Charlotte punted after a three-and-out. With the clock running down, the Monarch's rushing attempt on a fake punt came up short.

Charlotte settled for Blake Brewer's 20-yard field goal to lead by five. Starting from the 25, Washington connected with Pascal for a 33-yard pass to the Charlotte 42. On third and seven, Washington ran to the 29 for the first. On two consecutive runs brought the ball to the ODU eleven. From there, Washington hooked up with Pascal in the end zone again to grab a one-point lead. A two-point conversion pass to Jonathan Duhart gave the Monarchs a 37-34 lead with 2:18 left.

Bernie and I wondered if the home team left too much time on the clock. Charlotte moved the ball to the Monarch 44, but on a fourth and 13, McNeil's pass attempt to T.J. Ford bounced incomplete. The Monarchs ran out the clock and took their first ConferenceUSA win for either team in their short histories. It turned out to be an entertaining game with an exciting finish. Monarch quarterback David Washington came up big with 365 passing yards and four touchdown tosses. Charlotte definitely displayed the gutsiest performance among all the teams I attended in recent years for their first FBS encounter. Seeing them play a struggling, second-year program in ODU helped, but the Monarchs definitely showed improvement in one season. The tide in Norfolk started to turn for Old Dominion.

For now, having seen the last of all 128 FBS teams, again I could claim precisely, "seen 'em all." It doesn't get any better than seeing two evenly matched teams play down to the wire no matter what their records or their ranking at this level of play. Update: Both teams move on to the American Athletic.

Sad note: My good friend Bernie "Bernardo" Olszyk passed away from lymphoma that suddenly snuck up on him in the spring of 2023. We shared a lot of great memories working together on business projects for our companies, as Brother Knights of Columbus, and as a friend sharing several fun experiences at football games together over the years. He was a great supporter of this book and a key contributor to some of the stories - especially at Syracuse. It was best to know him mostly as a great friend.

Fight Fire with Fire, and "Ice" with "Ice"

Georgia State (125) at Appalachian State (126), November 1, 2014

Boone, North Carolina - The fourth period started typically for the Georgia State Panthers. Back-up quarterback Ronnie Bell tried to take it in on a third and goal at the three. However, Appalachian State defensive tackle Deuce Robinson forced him to fumble at the five. Mountaineer running back Ricky Ferguson covered the next 95 yards on four carries for the Mountaineers highlighted by his 84-yard sprint down to the GSU seven. He took his fourth carry the final four yards for a TD and ASU's 44-0 lead.

A little over eleven minutes remained. Joe Massimilla looked at me and said, "Up to you." Similar to when I added Old Dominion earlier this season and Louisiana Tech many years before to add them the annals of my history, I utilized the *"Blow-out waiver."* In this case, the apathy factor along with the freezing, as opposed to sweltering, temperature got considered into the process.

We headed out of Kidd Brewer Stadium and didn't miss a thing. We'd seen the final score of the day by Appalachian over Georgia State along with a never-seen before highlight play. I'd been up since 4 a.m. to catch my flight to Raleigh to meet up with Joe. We were hungry and had a three-hour drive ahead of us.I had to catch an 8:30 am flight home the next day. The Mountaineers and Panthers were both now in the fold.

In swirling, cold, gusting wet snow, 3,332 feet above sea level, the Appalachian State Mountaineers humiliated the Georgia State Panthers,

44-0, in a Sun Belt Conference contest between two first-year FBS football programs. ASU's Marcus Cox rushed for 250 yards and three scores. Ferguson rushed for 123 yards and a TD. They combined for the second straight week rushing over 100 yards each. Georgia State totaled eight yards on the ground as snow swirled throughout the game. The Panthers entered the game averaging 316 passing yards per game. Quarterbacks Nick Arbuckle and Ronnie Bell only combined for nine completions of 17 attempts for 54 yards and an interception.

In the second half as snow started to stick to the Pro-turf, maintenance workers removed what they could off the yard markers with leaf blowers during TV time-outs. By this time, who was watching this game on ESPN3 any longer? Joe Massimilla's son, Sam, a sophomore at ASU majoring in music education, played trumpet with the Marching Mountaineers to meet the criteria of the ASU Music Department. We came well prepared with extra layers of clothes and rain gear to withstand the elements to remain for Sam's halftime performance. Many long-time, faithful Appy fans and the ASU marching band left the cold slaughter at the end of halftime before Joe and I did.

A play call like no other

To give one example though of the ASU dominance over GSU to start their FBS histories, I share this one particular game situation. *Hilarious!* Joe and I witnessed what should be a top "ESPN classic football folly" forever.

After a 10-yard Georgia State punt into the swirling, gusty winds of Kidd-Brewer Stadium, ASU drove from the GSU 38 to the 17-yard line. Head Coach Scott Satterfield used all three remaining time-outs to try to get into the end zone leading, 20-0. With three seconds left on the clock, ASU PK Bentlee Critcher came in to extend the score from 30 yards away. Figuring he still had his three time-outs to burn, Panther Head Coach Trent Miles decided he'd use them all to "ice" ASU on the attempt on this freezing cold day. Crescendos of "boos" met each of his time-outs. He prolonged only the agony of those of us sitting in cold, wet, snow-covered aluminum bleachers.

After his third consecutive and final time-out, the Panther sideline jumped up and down in unison. To add to the "intimidation," they directed taunts, screams, curses, whatever toward Critcher. Set up for the final chance for the attempt, Critcher suddenly went in motion running toward the GSU sideline. The left side of the Panther D reacted that way with no time-outs left to call. The jumping Panthers on the side suddenly froze to a standstill and stared in confusion. The long snapper hiked directly back to the holder, Simms McElfresh. He stood up, caught the football, and ran untouched through a huge gap on the right side of the line for a 13-yard touchdown to extend the halftime lead, 27-0.

Don't go away mad, just go away

The result was met by cheers and laughter from the Appalachian State crowd. The Panthers jogged silently to their locker room behind the goal post after the extra point. Joe and I agreed the entire sequence should be on of ESPN's Top 10 plays of the day. We'd probably never see anything like it again. Appy was assessed a 15-yard penalty for excessive celebration on the second half kickoff. It was definitely worth it for the freezing home team and for the frozen fans in attendance. They witnessed an early exclamation point on the Mountaineers 44-0 win.

A good call here, too

Boone, NC - Fast Forward to Coastal Carolina at Appy State in, 2021: Luckily, I avoided a very non-competitive 52-20 blow-out by Coastal Carolina over Arkansas State on Thursday night, October 7, to attend a potential thriller instead. On Wednesday night, October 21, the same Coastal Carolina Chanticleers, the next team added to my quest, headed to Boone to play the ASU Mountaineers before a very excited and enthusiastic packed house of 31,061 at Kidd Brewer Stadium.

Former Appy State two-time All-American offensive lineman Shawn Clark took over ASU coaching duties in 2020. His first Mountaineer team won nine games and the Myrtle Beach Bowl. For this evening's contest, his team sported a 5-2 record after dismally falling hard to 4-1 Louisiana in their previous clash, 41-13. Scott Satterfield had left for temptations of supposed "greener" pastures to Louisville of the ACC after guiding ASU to four bowl games and three Sun Belt Championships.

Bouncing back and forth in Boone

The 13th-ranked Chanticleers of CCU got off to a fast and dominating start with Grayson McCall at quarterback. After the dismal Mountaineer loss to the Ragin Cajuns a week ago, things looked bleak for the home team down 14-0 at the end of the first quarter. ASU climbed back to within seven followed by a perfect, one-hop onsides kick by kicker Michael Hughes. Milan Tucker recovered to start ASU with a prize possession at Coastal's 48. The Mountaineers wasted no time when quarterback Chase Brice connected with Malik Williams on a streak for a 47-yard score to tie. The undefeated Chants had rarely been challenged midway through this season.

A sack of McCall halted their next possession at Appalachian's 33. Massimo Biscardi made good with a 50-yard field goal. Next, CCU recovered a Mountaineer fumble on a pass play to take over at the ASU 29. As the half ended, Biscardi made good again from 47 for a CCU 20-14 lead.

The energetic crowd cheered their Mountaineers to start the second half. Their defense forced a Chanticleer punt. Momentum and the home crowd's energy built off that stop. Brice connected with Corey Sutton for a 28-yard scoring pass to take the lead, 21-20. The Chants' offense got back in gear. They moved the ball 83 yards on nine plays. Shemari Jones' run capped the drive from the one, CCU up by six. The Mountaineer offense stayed on track relying on its ground game. Camerun Peoples eventually shot through the right side of his line rambling 43 yards to tie the score. A misplayed snap on the extra point resulted in a failed two-point conversion. The score remained dead-locked at 27 going into the fourth quarter.

Late in the period, Appalachian State held Coastal on their 26, highlighted by a hard tackle for a loss and heavy pressure on McCall. A heavy rush hurried a third down incompletion forcing a punt. The Mountaineers took possession from their 38. Brice connected with Williams on consecutive passes of 16 and 19 yards to get down to the Coastal 25. From there, ASU stayed on the ground. CCU used its remaining time-outs. In the waning minute, an ASU runner stopped short of the goal line taking a knee to avoid a touchdown pending a kickoff back to Coastal with time remaining. Head Coach Shawn Clark's staff managed the game clock well late in this game.

The offense centered the ball between the uprights. With 0:03 left, ASU called time out. Staton put the finishing touch on this Mountaineers upset score, 30-27, with his game-winning 24-yard kick. The ASU celebration began! The student body stormed the field as the previously undefeated Chants (6-1, 2-1) exited the field with heads hanging. No shame, just great disappointment. Tonight, college football was played at its best!

Watch out for Sun Belt football!

The Mountaineers won the Sun Belt East title with a record of 7-1 over the Chanticleers who finished 6-2. ASU fell once again to West Champ Louisiana in the SBC championship, 24-16. The Ragin Cajuns finished the season ranked No. 16 in the AP poll.

Every season, Sun Belt football only gets better. In particular, seeing these Appalachian and Coastal programs both play each other again makes for a traditionally great game. As for Georgia State, they've seen some improvements since that initial 1-11 debacle back in 2014. Under Head Coach Shawn Elliott, they've come up with four winning seasons and taken victories in three of four post-season games during his six seasons there. Hopefully, I can catch them in a meaningful game at their Center Parc Credit Union Stadium if not someplace else in the improving Sun Belt Conference.

FIGHT FIRE WITH FIRE, AND "ICE" WITH "ICE"

Appalachian State on November 1, 2014

Navy 52 – (127) Georgia Southern 19
Navy-Marine Corps Memorial, Annapolis, Maryland, November 15, 2014

Old Dominion 37 Charlotte (128) 34
S.B. Ballard Stadium, Norfolk, Virginia, November 17, 2015

Battle of the Interims / Legacy of Joe Moglia

Georgia Southern at Coastal Carolina (129), December 2, 2017

Conway, South Carolina – No need to spend a couple of days in Myrtle Beach during early December. However, the departure flight of my very affordable Saturday round trip from Atlantic City to Myrtle Beach to add Coastal Carolina made this opportunity very convenient. Especially with two South Jersey family connections.

   The night before, I drove to my cousin Cathy's house in Pt. Pleasant, NJ to stay over and catch an early flight next morning about an hour away in Atlantic City. There, I parked in the lot of the airport's fire station where my nephew and Air Force Reservist Brian is now Fire Chief. He dropped me over at the main terminal. I'd return late that evening to AC from Myrtle Beach and then drive home for over three hours that night. This game "featured" 2-9 Georgia Southern at 2-9 Coastal Carolina. Do I love this sport or what?

   On the flight to Myrtle Beach, I sat with two other dedicated college football fans, Larry and Pat, high school football coaches from Delaware. They also headed down to attend this clash between Sun Belt squads. Larry played for Delaware back in the '70s, and Pat played for Ursinus, a D-3 nemesis of the Alma mater dear, Juniata. Both played for current CCU Head Coach Joe Moglia early in his career. They maintained a close relationship with him ever since. A little background in order here: Joe

Moglia coached high school and college football successfully for 16 years. In 1984, he made a career change by entering the MBA training program for Merrill Lynch. After graduation, he became their most productive asset manager leading to a major career move. He then became CEO for the investment service, TD Ameritrade. TDA featured those entertaining, talking baby commercials.

For seven years, he led that firm to great success increasing its clients' wealth to over $10 billion, a 500 percent return. From there, he became Chairman of the Board for TDA. After great success in business, here returned to coaching college football in 2009. Moglia served as executive advisor to the Nebraska Cornhusker football program helping administer two Big 12 North championships. He left to take over the Coastal Carolina Chanticleer program in 2012. Since he became head coach at Coastal, his teams racked up a record of 51-15.

Something's not right here

Larry and Pat filled me in on something that I hadn't heard about. Moglia sidelined himself right from the start of this season due to an irritable lung infection. That explained my surprise regarding Coastal's poorer than expected record at 2-9 in this, their first season of FBS football. In my game today, two Sun Belt bottom feeders played without the head coaches they started their seasons with. Before kickoff on the Brooks Stadium video board, Moglia's recorded message confirmed what Larry and Pat told me.

He informed the Coastal Carolina fandom that his life was not in danger. However, breathing problems had to be addressed. He emphasized that he did this now to assure his health for the long-term. In the future, he planned to continue as head coach of the Chanticleers for many years to come. In the meantime, he had appointed his offensive coordinator, Jamey Chadwell, up until last year the head coach of a successful Charleston Southern program in the FCS, as his interim replacement. Moglia planned to return to the sideline next season at full strength.

As for the Georgia Southern Eagles, after an 0-6 start to this season, the school's administration released Head Coach Tyson Summers. His record included a loss to FCS New Hampshire and one at struggling UMASS. He had taken over for Willie Fritz who I saw coach the Eagles in 2014 against Navy. He stayed at GSU only two seasons before he departed to Tulane. The Coastal Carolina school administration had seen enough of Summers. Not used to losing, they also wanted to ramp up now joining the FBS. Interim Chad Lunsford replaced Summers since mid-season.

Interim vs. Interim

The teams battled into the third quarter. To start the third, Southern's Miles Campbell returned the kick out to Coastal's 48. The Eagles finished a scoring drive with an eight-yard pass from Shai Werts to tight end Ellis Richardson to take a 17-14 lead. GSU forced a CCU punt from its 43. The turning point of the game occurred when Coastal fullback Osharmar Abercrombie took the snap directly in punt formation. He powered for 19 yards for a first down to maintain possession. Quarterback Kilton Anderson connected with Malcolm Williams for a 37-yard pass to regain the lead, 21-17. Next series, the Chants forced the Eagles to punt from their 27. On the legs of Abercrombie, a 41-yard burst brought the Chants to the one. Abercrombie finished off what he started to extend the home team's lead, 28-17.

The score stabilized in the fourth primarily due to CCU's defensive efforts. The Chant's stopped Werts on downs at their 37. Two series later, cornerback Preston Carey picked off a Werts pass at his 24. The Chanticleer D halted GSU's final drive at their 29 on fourth down with 1:29 left to play. They preserved their third victory of the season. Werts, a redshirt freshman, led his team in passing for 57 yards, for rushing with 108 yards, and even in receiving yards, one catch for 30 yards. A rarity, despite the low number in the passing game and losing, I don't recall anybody ever laying claim to lead in all three categories. If a quarterback leads a team in receiving, unless it's running the triple option, it probably indicates a loss.

Both teams showed potential, but have lots of work cut out ahead as other teams in the Sun Belt conference were making great strides toward improvement. Both teams finished for the season. As Pat and Larry told me, if Moglia was feeling better, the Chant's would be out practicing that evening. Like most other programs, these staffs headed back out on the recruiting trail right after this tussle. Their seasons ended later than most in the first weekend of December.

As for Georgia Southern, there was probably a meeting with Lunsford and the rest of the coaches right away to determine their status in the short-term. They needed to continue recruiting while planning to announce who their next Head Coach would be. Georgia Southern eventually announced Chad Lunsford as their new head coach heading into 2018. He would coach the Eagles to a 25-14 record including two wins in three bowl games. After a 1-3 start in 2021, Georgia Southern pulled out the plug and replaced him. Now coaching tight ends at Florida Atlantic, Clay Helton, fired coach from Southern Cal, now runs the GSU football program.

Darn! Say it ain't so, Joe!

As for Joe Moglia, he returned to the sideline for the Chanticleers in 2018. He retained Jamey Chadwell as his offensive coordinator. They finished 5-7 losing their last four games. Despite a contract through 2021, in January 2019, Joe Moglia announced "in the best interest of the program to do so", he stepped down. He handed the position over to Jamey Chadwell.[1]

In September 2021, the university announced that Joe Moglia would make a large financial gift to Coastal Carolina. CCU President Michael T. Benson further announced that the combined academic and athletic facility to be designed would be named The Joe Moglia Center.[2]

Fast Forward to future Coastal Carolina games: As previously recorded, I attended a great game, though lost by CCU at Appalachian State in 2021. Under Jamey Chadwell over the last three seasons, the Chants won 31 games. The third season took a turn for the worst when Grayson McCall went down to injury before losing their last three games. With his proven success, Chadwell moves on in 2023 to replace Hugh Freeze at Liberty who took over at Auburn.

McCall originally entered the transfer portal, but has reneged since. Tim Beck who takes the reins from Chadwell, has spent the past 12 years at other major programs as offensive coordinator. The last, where he contributed to NC State's success, gave Beck some leverage to convince McCall to remain with the Chanticleers beyond 2022.

[1] Ladd, Aaron. "Moglia stepping down as CCU's head football coach after seven seasons." WMBF-TV. Retrieved 19 January 2019.

[2] Blondin, Alan. "Former football coach makes a large donation to CCU to build new athletic facilities." The Sun News. Retrieved 8 September 2021

Battle of Independents

Liberty U. (130) at UMass, November 3, 2018

Amherst, Massachusetts– In reverence to Virginia Governor Patrick Henry, when he defended his resolution to raise militia in 1775 to prepare for the eventual war he envisioned to win independence from the British, he declared, *"I know not what course others may take; but as for me, give me liberty or give me death!"* In my much humbler desire to add Liberty University from Lynchburg, Virginia as my 130th FBS team, my paraphrased title here indicates that as long as I added Liberty to my cause, I didn't care which of these two teams won. As long as these Independents with records of 4-3 (Liberty) and 3-6 (UMASS) came to play, I just hoped to see a well-played game! Even Liberty's record came into question with a seven-point win over FCS Idaho State at home two weeks before.

Bombs bursting in air

On a blustery day that got colder as the sun went down after a 3:30 pm kickoff, the two offenses heated up the first half. A high-scoring game was anticipated. The scores of previous games played by both these teams indicated both could score a lot more points, but not because of potent offenses, but because of their porous defenses. For the Minutemen, Ross Comis threw two bombs that went to Andy Isabella for 89 and 61-yard scores. Comis ran one in from the seven. For Liberty, Stephen Calvert threw a 15-yard score to Antonio Gandy-Golden for the first score by Liberty. Frankie Hickson scored on an 11-yard run in the second period.

What followed was a supposed rarity.

Calvert tossed a bomb into the end zone from the 50. UMASS defensive back Lee Moses picked it off in the end zone and returned it to the 15. However, he fumbled, and Liberty's Khaleb Coleman scooped it to return for a 21-yard score. What's funny here is for me to consider this a "supposed rarity." Just the previous Saturday, I watched William and Mary score the same way reversing an interception into a fumble recovery returned for a touchdown against Rhode Island. With Alex Roberts's 21-yard field goal, Liberty forged ahead, 24-21. However, as time expired in the first half, Cooper Garcia converted a 28-yard three-pointer for UMass to complete a seven-play, 58-yard drive. It ended the half all even, 24-24.

The 10,388 in attendance at Homecoming in McGuirk Stadium could not have envisioned what was to follow a great halftime show. Things did not go either team's way early in the third after the high-scoring first half. Threatening to end a possession with another long bomb, Calvert went deep to the end zone. There, defensive back Isaiah Rodgers, who at 5'9" got taken advantage of on several plays by much taller Gandy-Golden, made a nice over the shoulder running interception. He raced across to the opposite side of the end zone, and returned it out to his 35. Marquis Young completed the ensuing 65-yard scoring drive with a four-yard run for a brief Minuteman lead, 31-24, with 3:00 left in the third.

A Battle of Independents

To start the fourth, the game did not go UMass's way. Liberty scored three touchdowns within 3:14. Gandy-Golden caught a 14-yard pass to tie the score. With a 38-yard run, Hickson set up a one-yard score by Boyd. Young fumbled the ball away on UMass's next possession. Liberty LB Solomon Ajayi returned it to the Minutemen four. Frank Boyd took it in again to extend the lead for the Flames, 45-31.

November 2018: UMass tailgating prior to game against Liberty. Beautiful day before freezing temperatures set in after sundown.

The sun had set, the wind picked up, the temperature dropped. The clock showed 11:01 remained. Liberty had turned momentum its way. Many UMass fans could not bear to watch any longer. They slowly began to abandon McGuirk. One longtime, die-hard sitting to my left the entire game, wrapped in a blanket, passed me on the way out, looked me in the eye, and said, "I've had enough." I could understand to a point, of course, but I persevered. Luckily, I also came by myself so no one could force my hand to leave before time expired.

Like many others who showed up on a sunny, but windy afternoon, I did not come prepared with heavier clothing for the cold, bone-chilling evening. It was freezing! However, I didn't drive three and a half hours to Amherst to miss the last 11 minutes of any game with a 14-point margin. Too much time remained for both not to score against the other. I knew that this would not be the final score. A two touchdown-margin?

FIFTY YEARS OF TAILGATE TALES:

Overtime? I wondered.

Liberty kicked off for a touch back. Seventy-five yards later with 6:42 left, Comis finished the UMass drive with a six-yard score after faking a dive hand-off and taking it in himself. On third and two, a bad snap by the Liberty center sent the Flames back on their 34 with a fourth and 11. Gimpy, Isabella fielded the punt. The Minutemen possessed the ball again on their 25 with 2:57 left. After losing four yards on a sack and five-yards for illegal motion, UMass got back to the 31. Fourth and four! Comis hooked up with Sadiq Palmer for a 15-yard gain and a new set of downs.

Young carried the ball four times on the next five plays. On the final carry, he ran it in from the nine with 25 seconds left. Garcia connected on the PAT to knot it, 45-45. Overtime!

- First OT – Liberty scored on Boyd's five-yard run. Comis responded with a seven-yard touchdown pass to Samuel Emilus. With both PATs good, 52-52.
- Second OT – For UMass first, Comis connected quickly with Emilus for a 23-yard TD pass. PAT good. Liberty ran the ball seven straight times with Hickson going in from the two. PAT good, 59-59. Give me Liberty!
- Third OT – "I wanna go home!!!" yelled a 20-something UMass stalwart a few rows down. He got his happy wish. LB Jarell Addo intercepted Calvert in the end zone. Just like the first half as time expired, Cooper Garcia kicked a 22-yard field goal for the Minutemens' fourth victory of the 2018 season, 62-59. Give us Minutemen! The final score set collegefootballfan.com's single game scoring record.

The weather turned bitter-cold for people wearing sweatshirts and windbreakers. I gladly got out of windy, freezing McGuirk, jumped into my car, turned the heat on high, and headed, not home, but luckily to my sister's house less than two hours away in Cumberland, RI.

In my fifth game seeing UMass struggle…I mean compete…at the FBS level, this was the first win I attended. As written in their chapter, *"To be Big Time, or not Big-Time?"* I suggested UMass go back and play FCS football. Still do!

The total of 121 points scored eclipsed my Collegefootballfan.com record of 111 total points that resulted in two-OT game back in 1998 won by Army over Louisville at West Point, 59-52. However, Louisville's win over Wake Forest by the exact same score a year later in 2019, slightly outshone this one. No overtimes in that one between Deacs and Cardinals. Look for more details about this game and other records I've witnessed on my blog, **www.collegefootballfan.com.**

Conflict of Convenience

Lynchburg, Virginia - Fast forward to Louisiana at Liberty, 2021: St. Laurie and I ventured back to New Jersey in November 2021 to enjoy a long Thanksgiving holiday week having moved to Tennessee. Rather than drive the full 13 hours straight through, I convinced her we could break the trip in half. Conveniently, we left Saturday to stay that night in Lynchburg, Virginia, home of Liberty University. On the beautiful campus nestled in the middle of nowhere, the Flames (7-4) hosted the No. 23 Louisiana Ragin Cajuns (10-1). Perfect timing to attend a game there for the first time.

After a slow start, the Ragin Cajuns built a lead and the Flames came within reach. Louisiana started the fourth at the Flames' 26. Two plays in, Levi Lewis tossed a two-yard TD pass to 6'4" Neal Johnson to extend their lead, 35-14. Hugh Freeze's Flames drove to the Louisiana 28. Desperate now in fourth down territory, a six-yard sack resulted with the Cajuns taking over on their 34. With momentum going their way, the Cajuns just bullied the Flames down field with backs Montrell Johnson and then Emani Bailey fighting their way to the goal line.

With 2:26 left, Bailey took it over from two. To seal the deal, the Cajuns picked off their third interception of the half off Malik Wills. They started to celebrate their 10th straight victory all the way back to Lafayette, Louisiana to the tune of 42-14. To defeat LU in our presence, Cajun QB

Levi Lewis threw three touchdown taking advantage of his tall receiving corps near the end zone. Louisiana sacked Malik Willis seven times, four by linebacker Chauncey Manac. Willis was very unimpressive with 162 yards, two touchdowns, and two picks. Despite this performance, the Tennessee Titans selected Willis in the third round of the 2022 draft. Granted, I witnessed only one Liberty game with Willis at quarterback, but I believe scouts should analyze losses like this one closely as a priority in their decision-making processes.

After 2022, Liberty abandoned its status as an Independent and joins ConferenceUSA. Jamey Chadwell, former head coach of Coastal Carolina, joined the Flames as their new mentor.

In Year One, James Madison University fought their way into the FBS with an 8-3 record.

BATTLE OF INDEPENDENTS

Louisville 34 - (131) James Madison 10

Cardinal Stadium, Louisville, Kentucky, November 5, 2022

It's not over! Fast forward to...

Jacksonville State (132), Sam Houston State (133) and Kennesaw State (134)

Jacksonville, Alabama – "By hook or by crook," as the old saying goes. No. 132 Jacksonville State Gamecocks opens their first FBS season in 2023. In the case of the No. 133 Sam Houston Bearkats, it's as if this entire adventure will have gone full circle no matter when or wherever I see the Bearkats play.

However, that only happens based on one particular factor - their current head coach. Back in 2000, when I analyzed my history up until that point, I decided to pursue this lofty adventure tracing it back to the first game I attended after my graduation from Juniata. On September 8, 1979, I traveled to Kingston, Rhode Island. My sister Mary Kay, attended the University of Rhode Island at that time. I planned to visit with the idea of seeing the Rhode Island Rams play against a very good small school, the University of Delaware.

As one of the top programs in those days, Harold "Tubby" Raymond coached the Fighting Blue Hens of Delaware. In the game to open the 1979 season and the first of over 600 games for me, UD defeated URI, 49-14. The Blue Hens went on to win the D-2 national championship that year. Quarterback Scott Brunner got drafted by the New York Giants after this season. Among other starters for that team, at middle linebacker played K.C. Keeler, a junior from Emmaus, Pennsylvania. Over the years, I followed the Delaware program, one of my favorites among lower division teams.

In the case of Keeler, it became easy to track his future progress as a head college football coach. From 1993 to 2001, he led Rowan University, formerly Glassboro State in New Jersey, to an 88-21-1 record. I saw his team play three times including a 55-0 rout of Ursinus in the 1999 D-3 playoffs. He led the Profs to the Amos Alonzo Stagg Bowl five times for the D-3 championship, but never won it. I attended his debut at Delaware in 2002. To open the season, his Hall of Fame Head Coach, the legendary Harold "Tubby" Raymond ceremoniously handed the program over to him. Raymond won 300 games at UD before he retired. The Blue Hens defeated FCS Georgia Southern in their opener that evening, 22-19.

Keeler spent 11 seasons at UD finishing with a record of 86-52. His Blue Hens won the D-IAA title in 2003 defeating Colgate in the final. In 2007 and 2010, they came up short in the finals against Appalachian State and Eastern Washington respectively. Along the latter quest, I attended two UD wins against Lehigh and Georgia Southern on the way to the championship game. His teams won five and lost two among the games I saw his Hens play. In a 2006 loss, I went to see a Juniata friend's son, Jon Hermann, start at center for UD. In a shoot-out, with Joe Flacco playing quarterback for the Fightin' Blue Hens, Delaware fell to Towson, 49-35.

Since 2014, Keeler's been head coach for Sam Houston State sporting a record of 85-27. In 2020, his Bearkats won the FCS championship over South Dakota State, 23-21. The following season they finished 11-1 and in the transition season of 2022, 5-4. What will be interesting to me with Keeler's entry into the FBS will be his penchant for picking up transfers since his days going as far back as Rowan. With players like Joe Flacco dropping down to the next level wherever he coached, they didn't have to sit out a season to transfer. If anybody has a game plan for the transfer portal, it's K.C. Keeler. On the other hand, everybody's doing it now. The process is becoming messier, however, with the NIL policy and transfer portals combined.

From Game No. 1 to Game No.???

FIFTY YEARS OF TAILGATE TALES:

Forty-four years ago, in the first game of my unique college football history, Keeler started at middle linebacker for a national champion. Today, he's coaching a successful program heading into the FBS level with a career coaching record of 259-100-1. Will he match his mentor Tubby Raymond's record of 300 wins? I look forward to eventually seeing him coach again marking this as a full circle in this life-long adventure.

As for the No. 134 Kennesaw State Owls, they don't join the FBS until 2024. They are a three-hour drive from me now and joining ConferenceUSA. I'll see them play somewhere in the future to once again claim, "seen 'em all!"

I love this game, its traditions, the fun, the excitement, the intensity, the teamwork, the efforts, the dedicated coaches, and all the people who root so hard for their respective teams! In recent years, corruption, crimes, and scandals have marred this great game. I think and hope that solutions will be found to correct most of those problems. It is truly a great and unique American tradition. I'm glad and fortunate to have lived to enjoy this surreal adventure and to write about these fun and memorable experiences to share with so many others. I look forward to continue doing this for many years to come. In the future, please follow my future adventures on my blog:

www.collegefootballfan.com.

—- S.J.K.

IT'S NOT OVER! FAST FORWARD TO...

Thanksgiving Saturday 2022 at Texas State with my family: Me, St. Laurie, Eric, Alex and Zach

II

Essay I

My research and analysis regarding the future of college football has me concerned that the future focuses way too far on ways just to increase revenues. No doubt, money is necessary to fund this great American sport, but focus is being lost on other values that college football has provided for those who play the game and for those who cheer their teams on with great passion to revel in this great sport. I don't want to see players nor fans lose their passions derived from college football.

Vision of the Future

I've performed due diligence by doing research on line and talking to people, but the things that really concern me are not things people involved in college football administrations are willing to discuss. Instead, I'm more concerned about particular cases regarding issues people do not want to answer questions about or refuse to talk about at all - especially regarding relationships between schools and collectives. Compliance between these two parties has to do more with adherence to state laws, not about the Dos and Don't s of NCAA NIL policies.

As I've compiled and examined a list of issues, I came up with proposals to offer solutions for improvement, but as I've started to view these issues collectively, I envision an evolution with many of them combined contributing to a new order of college football. These changes won't include all the teams of the Football Bowl Subdivision today, but primarily an elite group that can separate themselves from how we currently understand college football. Yet the ones that will implement these changes can and will still impact other programs that would not be part of it. I break down potential moves in an order of things that can happen, and basically, they've already started. They can create a totally different college football model that will evolve over a short period of time, maybe only a few years from now.

Their goal is basic, for schools to make more money. The initial reason will be to fund their athletic programs, but in the long term, with the amounts of revenue to be made, they could allocate monies for other unclear desires as well. Football is big business in this country, and schools not only see this, but they already have capabilities in place to benefit from it even more. Nebraska Athletic Director Trev Alberts came out with a statement recently that sums up my initial findings here, but I believe what he says is only the tip of the iceberg. Regarding realignments, he stated, "It's more likely than not that there will be continued periods of angst. I believe that the next go-around — that's my basic conclusion — will be far more disruptive than anything we're currently engaged in. We need to prepare ourselves mentally for that." [1] In addition, what he projected further is what I see as the real impactful influence on the future of college football: "Alberts believes that the future of college football may need to be separated from the rest of the sports, since football drives all of college athletics despite it having different needs."[2] This is where it all starts - with the need to increase revenues to support all college athletics. Here are ten steps below that can attain what the schools ultimately want to in order to maximize revenues desired for their goals:

1.) **Conference realignments** bring together 40-48 universities to leverage negotiations to maximize revenues nationally with sports television networks.
2.) Among these, they will form two to four **Super-conferences** for regular season games among the best teams in college football. Playoff formats will be proposed.
3.) Regarding **Television contracts**, college football already owns exclusive rights to Saturday television coverage. It already fills air time Tuesday-Friday which the NFL also does at times, too. College football's current standing with the networks and a future format proposal will allow them to negotiate more prime time coverage as needed.
4.) A totally separate **Administrative Organization** just for football among the 40-48 schools will be started and they will leave the NCAA. With new state laws prohibiting the NCAA from interfering with the Name, Image and Likeness (NILs) policy implemented in July 2021,

Basketball will remain under the NCAA as many more schools play the sport and the NCAA Tournament is the organization's largest money-maker which the 40-48 will still want to be part of.

5.) **Name, Image and Likeness contracts** will be allowed as pay for play incentives in this organization. Football with its pay for play incentives will start to separate itself from amateur athletics supported by the NCAA.

6.) **Collectives** will come under the schools' auspices as administrative arms allowed to collect donations to build more resources to pay football players.

7.) **Recruiting practices** will continue to attract high school players, but they will also offer incentives such as NILs to players of schools remaining at college programs outside of the 40-48. Some are already approaching players from other NCAA programs through collectives, who under NCAA Do's and Don't s, they are currently not subject to. Only schools and student-athletes are named as parties within guidelines that need to conform to these NCAA rules.

8.) **Transfer portals** will remain, but to retain their team quality standards among members more consistently, the only time-frame window to allow transfer will come after the championship is concluded after the first semester. No window will be open to transfer after spring practices. Transferring will become a free-for-all of collegiate free agents.

9.) **Unionization by players** will take place to reap more of the rewards for them from the television contracts. It will be a friendly relationship between the players and the owners (i.e., the new organization, the two-four conferences, and the individual schools). The players will become employees of the schools. After graduation or other separation, players can stay at the school as employees to play football in order to continue to raise revenues for the schools. To maintain the standard of the product they market on the field, schools will be able to keep the star players they want under contract. The revenues brought in continue to finance the school athletic

department and any other needs the schools so desire, so they want to retain the best of the best. With TV money, NILs, donations from alum, sponsors, merchandising and other financial resources, schools can offer significant amounts of money to their revenue-sharing employees.

10.) **Waivers** for extra years to play for these college teams will no longer be necessary as they become full-time employees. College football will now compete with pro football for talent. Players can stay as employees of the university or consider offers from the pros. The strengths that colleges possess are built-in fan bases – students living on campuses near stadiums - and large alumni populations buying tickets to games and donating money. The NFL may have to consider doing what it would never do otherwise. Like professional baseball and hockey, they may start drafting out of high schools to develop players at their own cost. College football still has benefits to offer players free educations and to play in front of big crowds to compete with offers from the pros who may consider a minor league system of their own. However that would be too costly and too late.

This is a model of possibilities I envision if the major schools want to go forward to benefit from their desired monetary gains. There may be some obstacles ahead, but the combined schools with vast political ties are probably powerful enough to overcome them. They can also leverage their basketball memberships to take football out of the NCAA.

Below, I provide due diligence I've researched and analyzed, but there are still some underlying factors that haven't been exposed yet. On the other hand, due to federal anti-trust laws and IRS regulations, how and when does federal legislation in these matters react to state laws? Schools compete and recruit across state lines. It seems only a matter of time before national legislation gets involved. Remember, this is all about and only about money. Think about how high the cost of college educations are already. Institutions of higher academia want more. They are morphing into profit centers.

1.) NCAA lack of control is in the hands of its members

Conference realignments, formations of super-conferences, media contracts, NIL compliance, transfer portals, and improving standards for some but not all their student-athletes to compete as equally as possible for a championship may be policies endorsed by the NCAA. When it comes to controls and meeting standards, however, schools and conferences control what has to be done with little monitoring or guidance by the NCAA which they are all members of. Decisions made seem to be put into place without clear guidance and minimal control. Without either, such policies tend to result in confusion when various members among the organization interpret rules differently and gain support from state legislators to circumvent legal powers the NCAA currently has. The NCAA seems to have limited resources to monitor what all their members are doing. It has little power. It can only wield what its membership allows.

2.) Conference realignments

Destroying any balance of power based on TV revenues looks to be a major threat to weakening competitiveness among 134 FBS football programs. Only some will benefit, not all. National alliances increase costs of travel and impact times spent by student-athletes traveling and competing coast to coast in the future. Eventually if this is the case, splitting the FBS into two subdivisions makes sense. Start analysis with "Power Five" vs. "Group of Five" but based on budgets, TV revenues, and geography. Terminate inter-divisional play and re-establish the determination of division championships.

Some FBS teams need to go back to FCS

Smartly and for the right reasons, Idaho did it. After playing in the Big West, the Sun Belt, the Western Athletic, as an Independent, and back in the Sun Belt again from 1996 to 2017, at best, Idaho most often topped out at mediocrity. In 12 of 21 seasons, they won four games or less. Reality is that it couldn't compete in the FBS financially. Entering Big Sky play in 2022, they went 7-5 overall, 6-2 in conference. They defeated their in-state arch-rival, Idaho State in their season finale and made the FCS playoffs. It's in a better position to maximize it profits by cutting costs and growing its revenues.

Message to UMASS administration: take a lesson from Idaho. Playing in the Colonial Athletic where geographically, academically, and budget-wise, the football program can play and recruit against equivalent competition. There's no shame. Restore school spirit, pride, and a winning atmosphere to Amherst on fall Saturdays. Some other current FBS teams should and probably will follow after conferences realign.

3.) Super conferences

Eventually, major college football is consolidating down to 40-48 teams from coast to coast from what we now call the SEC, Big Ten, and possibly the Big XII with remnants from among the ACC and PAC-12. Include Notre Dame, of course. Controlling most major media markets and prime college football markets, with all that TV money, they'll leverage among their members to become "super-conferences" and basically form a quasi-professional football league. TV networks will take care of most financing - along with state tax dollars, student tuitions, alumni donations, endowments, school merchandising and NIL money from many contributors to recruit players to play for their teams. As the NCAA will not oversee this new league, look for the television networks to assume more control than they have today.

A winning formulation

Will the power conference members, the "haves," stop scheduling contests against the "have nots?" Surely from this perspective, they'll have to. Playing games amongst the 40-48 programs serves the monetary purpose better. The following scenario presents the case for the short-term, or if the 40-48 cannot divest themselves from the NCAA.

Under the current structure of FBS football, the SEC decided already how they will leave enough open dates to pad their 2023 non-conference schedules so they can market their .500 or better records into guaranteed bowl revenue. In the past four of five years in 58 games against non-conference Power Five schools during the regular season (none played in 2020), the SEC won 60% (35-23) of those games, the majority played at home. Against Group of Fives and the FCS over that same period, the SEC has won 92% (152-14), basically all home games. Now more Power Five non-conference games should be scheduled among each other in the future to better challenge and assess the true strengths of these schools.

Consider the 40-48 teams with a new playoff format that will now probably dominate the media in the post-season. From the best of the best, they'll select at least the Top 32 teams and have a five-weekend national tournament through December every year. Who's going to need bowl games? They can do this in sponsor name only while playing at campus sites in early rounds to assure maximum stadium capacities. The television networks will eat this up.

Improve fan attendance

Average attendance per game among FBS members declined every year from 2014 to 2021 (2020 numbers excluded) from 44,603 down to 39,848, lowest figure since 1981.[3] And understand, college football, unlike the pros, does not deduct "no-shows" from their announced attendance totals.[4] In 2022, average attendance jumped up 5% to 41,840. A blip? Can growth be sustained? Several attributes considered for last season's increase include: digital tickets, the affluence of college fans, alcohol sales in stadiums, and the fact that teams with six of the largest stadiums qualified for major bowls.

According to SEC commissioner Greg Sankey, he believes, "It's not the game that's more experiential. It's the day and the weekend [that is] college football. There's always been a component of what happens around the game that's unique to college football."[5] From my 50 years of attending games, outside of the alcohol sales inside more stadiums, I don't see major changes adding to game experiences at most venues. Like the commissioner says, the experiential factor has always been there, and they're fantastic! The existence of festivities and traditions surrounding college football has continually grown over the last century. The addition of weekday night games, however, initiate negative impact on game experiences and reduce attendance, but that's primarily impacted Group of Five programs. They're scheduled specifically for television just like all the new bowl games initiated in recent years . In 2023, they're claiming the elimination of time-outs after a first down will improve the experience of watching a game. Fans say eliminating more media time-outs would be even better.

"Even the highest-resourced athletic department marketing division *can't count on winning* to sell tickets."[6] Agreed! Teams may sell season tickets, but fans don't show up to all the games, especially those against perceived, inferior competitors. It's predetermined every season that several home games are one-sided. Even students on campus will leave games at the half to start their victory parties early.

To quote the late, great NFL coach and fellow Juniata College alum, Chuck Knox: in pro football, a team's "highest duty is just that – to make a city (in his case Buffalo) feel good about itself."[7] In the case of college football, substitute "city" with college or university. How can this be done? Using the cliché, "leveling the playing field," is what most college football fans would want to see when they attend a game. If the best play among these 40-48, every schedule should be very competitive.

Avoiding play among inferior competitors should now fill the stadiums with comparable competition visiting every week and in the largest stadiums of the most highly populated student communities. More of those no-show seats among this group should now be filled.

4.) Television contracts

The goal of major college football persists to focus primarily on building conferences of superior teams that draw from major media markets already established. This is how college athletic programs command "big bucks." As I stated in the Introduction of this book, "Most changes primarily pursue monetary aspects. Necessary, but they should not be foremost." That's the real struggle to keep college football for what it truly came into existence for. Let the pros be pros, and let college be colleges, but financially, the schools see what professional football can command and they want more of that as well.

5.) Name, Image and Likeness (NIL) policy

The NCAA still does not allow "pay for play." Gray areas exist, but most gravely, there are already instances where players committed to programs already are being made offers to enter the transfer portal to leave and play for more NIL money elsewhere. The purpose of NILs goes above and beyond what was primarily for legitimate individuals or business entities to support players needing basic financial assistance. NILs now give student-athletes the potential to market themselves in an industry that primarily offered them free educations - a deal a lot of non-athletic scholarship families would love to have. However, already financial incentives are being offered to recruit potential student athletes to come to play a sport. Didn't the NCAA think this was going to open up some challenges to their "pay for play" regulations? Nothing seems to be in place to stop incentives from being offered now.

The real Ugly – lack of controls for NILs and collectives

During the ACC media conference this past summer, Wake Forest Head Coach Dave Clawson confirmed some examples of competitive inducements offered to some of his Demon Deacon football players. Six to eight of them were approached by other programs with lucrative endorsement deals ranging between from $150,000 to around $500,000. Proudly, Clawson said of his players, "They let us know after the fact. None of them came to me and said, 'Coach, I have this offer to go here. What can the collective do?' They didn't try to leverage, negotiate. But when you get the firsthand examples of it, of 'This school offered me this much to go there at this time,' those are very real things." [8] In addition, during ACC media days, North Carolina's Mack Brown stated, "You add

(NIL) and transfer portal and the collision of the two and tampering, those are things that make it more difficult to be a head coach." [9] Clawson did not identify any specific schools or collectives, but only mentioned that none were fellow members of the ACC. [10]

What is Prohibited Under the NIL Rules?

Pay-for-play is prohibited under NCAA policy, but what else cannot be done in regards to NILs?

Although it differs by state and school, in general, athletes are prohibited from:

- Receiving any performance-based incentives.
- Receiving compensation from a school or college for their NIL.
- Receiving compensation for athletic participation or achievement.
- Profiting from certain categories of goods (alcohol, casinos, tobacco, etc.)
- Using school logos to benefit their NIL (in most cases, unless the school says otherwise).
- Being coerced or incentivized to attend a certain school based on their NIL agreement.[11]

Though these prohibitions specify "school or college" and "athletes," they make no mention of "collectives." That party needs to be clarified as participants conforming to these regulations, otherwise it seems to make it the responsibilities of the schools not to approach the athletes, but collectives do that for the schools. The language seems useless by stating "Receiving" is prohibitive, when it says nothing about anyone "Offering" incentives or only "compensation from a school or college" to be prohibited. If collectives are not bound by these rules, what prevents them from offering deals to offer athletes incentives on their behalf to leave other schools? Collectives are outside entities from school administrations. What they do seems to conflict with NCAA guidelines for schools and athletes.

I've reached out to various sources looking to get clarification on the adherence of collectives to these rules, but my suspicions have become more aroused as no one seems willing to talk about this. What's not stopping the contacts now as several coaches have reported recently? Who's contacting the players directly? Schools aren't supposed to, but collectives can. Who monitors these incentives being offered and how do they do this? I'm told school compliance officers don't monitor interactions between collectives and student-athletes. They only monitor that the collectives abide by state laws. Is anyone with knowledge of supposedly illicit offers obligated to report this? Evidently not. Coaches hear about violations from their players, but no one is reporting any violations directly to the NCAA, yet.

It seems like this can lead to a lot of finger-pointing, bad blood, and legal battles among FBS football members if accusations can be made. Coaches have enough to focus on regarding games no less the recruiting wars. Eventually, if these are violations of NIL regulations, they can go on indefinitely as no one will want risk reporting them as a "whistle-blower." According to how the NCAA Dos and Don'ts of the NIL are written as shown here, it's illegal to receive them, but it's legal by organizations other than NCAA members, to offer them. That seems like a lot of responsibility on the wrong parties.

It may come down to this

The NCAA shut down the SMU football program in 1987 with a death penalty shutting down their football program from playing for two years. Not until 2009 did SMU play in a bowl game again as a member of ConferenceUSA. Only in recent years have they won more games than lost, and finally played more competitively in the American Athletic.

What the NCAA punished SMU for then ("pay for play"), it now inadvertently seems to encourage through the NIL policy by allowing schools to contact players through collectives. Schools are already reporting other teams trying to recruit their athletes away from them.

Worst of all, either loose or no rules exist to control this or to punish parties who break the rules

Who's controlling all of this mayhem?

An extreme case involved four-star, quarterback recruit Jaden Rashada. To be clear, this information does not insinuate that the recruit did anything wrong here. Rashada just happens to be the one this happened to and it was reported in the media.

Rashada's "dream school" to join after his successful high school career at IMG Academy was reportedly the University of Florida.[12] Second-year Florida Head Coach Billy Napier anticipated his commitment. Enticed by an NIL offer of $9.5 MILLION by the University of Miami Hurricanes, Rashada withdrew his letter of intent to accept an NIL offer to play for Miami. By the way, but did anyone at Miami, or will any other school, check to be sure there's not another Nevin Shapiro (see the chapter "How about those Hurricanes?") lurking within their so-called collectives?

Note this arrangement has nothing to do with earning money to "play football." After a player commits to a program, it makes sense for a corresponding collective to arrange an NIL deal, but a player can't receive compensation in the recruiting process. A collective representing the University of Florida, remember under no official jurisdiction of the university itself, next approached young Jaden and offered an NIL package of $13.85 MILLION to lure him back from Miami.

Before going further regarding consideration, Jaden Rashada, assume his parents, and probably some other acquaintances who provided legal advice, backed out of the contract before committing to anything proposed by either collective mentioned. People applying just common sense could read right through this contractual language that stated: *"Collective in its sole and absolute discretion can terminate without penalty of further obligation,"* according to The Athletic. [13] With that, this proposed agreement is literally not worth the paper it was written on. It goes to show either the ignorance, the audacity, or the underhandedness of people offering these young players incentives to offer their services to a school that they somehow portend to represent. At *any* time for *any* reason the collective party decides to terminate, it can. Who would sign this? Maybe a young person without any legal representation would.

The collective offered to pay Jaden $250,000 monthly during his freshman year.[14] Here's the consideration the Florida collective requested: 1.) reside in Gainesville, Florida, 2.) make branded Twitter and Instagram posts once a month, 3.) participate in eight engagements with fans per year, and 4.) autograph 15 pieces of merchandise each year. [15]

Unless this NIL policy gets some definitive control, it could be the ruin of college football as amateur athletics. Too much focus on money starts turning college football into a professional entity.

More clarifications

To fill in some pieces of missing information, in a very timely article by Ross Dellenger of Sports Illustrated, he adeptly identifies obstacles and issues coming from new state laws preventing the NCAA from implementing controls.[16] I had hoped there would be solutions provided to avoid one huge mistake here, but in Dellenger's in-depth summary, it seems a very tangled web lies ahead.

Said "Mississippi State president Mark Keenum, the longest-serving president in the league (SEC). 'What NIL has become is universities going out through their foundations and collectives and raising dollars to give to athletes. They're just paying them to come play and there is no limit on that.' "[17] A key question posed in the article is how will the Internal Revenue Service (IRS) respond? As presented previously, some non-profits offered benefits as tax write-offs to fans as charity funds to student-athletes, and the IRS banned this practice.

Some states' new laws "feature language to permit a school's non-profit fundraising arm" (formerly known as foundations) "to provide NIL deals, and prohibits the NCAA or any other enforcement arm (i.e., the SEC) from penalizing a school in the state for following the law."[18] Foundations at most schools were developed primarily as fundraising programs that fund coaching salaries, scholarships, and athletic facilities upgrades. Collectives were established separately outside of school jurisdictions to raise funds for athletes given through the uncontrolled NIL policy.[19] These state laws now draw these entities closer together risking their players' status to change from student-athletes to employees.

Texas A&M athletic director Ross Bjork defends such moves like this: "We're just trying to do all we can to support our athletes," he says. "There is no national standard. It's all local standards, so that's what we've done. We've adapted to our local environment."[20] He says, "Do <u>all we can</u> to support our athletes." Shouldn't schools do all they can to support <u>all their athletes</u>? The first equity issue brought up entails Title IX, addressing higher payments to men than to women. However, much notoriety featured the two female basketball twins, Haley and Hanna Cavinder at Miami, and the top-paid NCAA athlete, gymnast Olivia Dunne of LSU. These female student-athletes made millions. Consider all the teammates of highly-paid players, both men and women. There's no equal pay anywhere here for everybody's name, image, and likeness.

Bjork himself says, "The average compensation for a Power 5 football player from a collective ranges widely, usually around $10,000 to $50,000 annually, but "about five players per roster are making more than $100,000 on average."[21] More than $100, 000 annually? The contracts offered to some of these NIL stars total more than $250,000 per month.

To be honest, regretfully the one thing that could happen to prevent excessive abuse of compensation offers will be the ultimate Death Penalty for some major violators. Beforehand though, the very weak NCAA needs to rein in some major loopholes.

Dazed, confused, and now even more concerned

On the other hand, ESPN.com reported, "Record-setting UTSA QB Frank Harris to return for seventh season". [22] I understand red-shirt seasons and that all players received an extra year to play because of the 2020 Covid season. Many qualified for a sixth season, but seven? The article states: "Now, with UTSA headed to the AAC next season, coach Jeff Traylor lobbied his fans to ante up the name, image, and likeness money to keep Harris in San Antonio after the C-USA title game."[23] This is confusing. A head coach is soliciting funds for the NIL collective which is not part of the school.

Then, Traylor is quoted again, "I'd really make it hard for him to leave. He's fun to watch. That's the best money you could ever spend."[24] What's that got to do with the Name, Image, and Likeness policy? Traylor addressed his fan base directly to solicit NIL money for Harris to play for UTSA another season. Basically, he wanted to keep Harris from not only transferring, but from going to play professionally. [25] I can understand his feelings as a coach who needs to win to keep his career moving forward. It starts with coaches. They all need to win to keep their jobs or move on to the next, more rewarding one. However, this smacks of competing with money to keep Harris from playing professional football. Isn't this pay for play? What's this got to do with a name, an image, or a likeness?

To me, it indicates colleges are now even competing with the NFL for players by offering money. Does this step turn college football into professional football? Will games still be played by "student- athletes" on college campuses? It doesn't make sense that it can if this continues.

6.) Collectives

Currently, "collectives" to raise funds are being formed outside the administration of major college athletic programs. In particular, collectives focus on raising funds for the newly implemented Name, Image, and Likeness (NIL) policy available to attract student-athletes. NILs have been in place for non-student-athletes before the NCAA allowed these in July 2021. Some college football players like former Alabama QB Bryce Young could command NIL value without going through a collective. He signed directly with CAA, an agency, to negotiate NIL deals directly for him.[26] Georgia tight end Brock Bower, first-team All-SEC, first-team All-American and the John Mackey Award winner as the nation's top tight end in 2022, refused a deal with Georgia's Classic City Collective. Instead, he also signed on with an agent to represent him independently for advertising and sponsorship negotiations.[27] More power to both of them.

Individual states now set regulations for NILs. In Missouri, a high school athlete who signs only with an in-state college, can earn compensation for an NIL before enrolling at the school. At Texas A&M, contributors will earn priority points for athletic donations. In Arkansas, college athletes make appearances through a non-profit organization owned to raise funds for athletic programs.[28] Legal means challenge fair recruiting practices among state schools. These new state laws bring NIL programs under their state school administrations and prohibit the NCAA and conferences' authority to enforce.[29]

Collectives 2023

I reached out to develop a better understanding of collective interactions within the current process to avoid scenarios regarding "pay for play." I confided in one Vice President at a collective for student athletes where he manages the relationships for some Power Five programs. He confirmed collectives are third parties connecting fans to student athletes (brands); three ways this is done: through donors, fan memberships (ex: monthly contributions), and the development of commercial relationships with student-athletes; collectives work in compliance with school staffs of NCAA members to build communication within guidelines (i.e., state laws); they manage access between student-athletes and fans (ex: autograph sessions and social media).

He commented that collectives work under retainer contracts and engagement contracts with schools they represent to promote these relationships. He said some non-profits offered benefits as tax write-offs to fans as charity funds to student-athletes. Recently, the IRS banned this practice. He mentioned an underhanded tactic where an NIL agent from another organization offered a student-athlete 30 credits short of a degree a five-figure salary to transfer to a lesser qualified academic school from a highly-ranked academic institution. This inducement is illegal. It demonstrates how some students under current situations are being exploited – basically taking short-term benefits as opposed to considering long-term, educational benefits. However, it's still the student's choice. It seems that the NCAA will need to closely monitor such tactics if it can. Another contact, an assistant coach within a mid-major FBS program who requested to remain anonymous, stated that this is a massive undertaking for the NCAA. It has neither the manpower nor the business/legal acumen to enforce this effectively.

My collective contact also pointed out that NIL money will not be equivalent among all schools. Collectives provide 75-80% of the NIL money. So, the bigger the alumni associations/fan bases, the bigger schools have an advantage over schools with smaller followings. One can surmise, "the rich get richer." He suggests the NCAA hold summits among athletes, schools, collectives, donors, and others involved be held to improve clarification of these guidelines.

Regarding Name, Image, and Likeness agreements, the NIL industry already existed as a multi-billion-dollar business before being offered to college athletes. Actors, musicians, pro athletes, and social media personalities connect through agencies with companies for brand endorsements and commercial opportunities already. Social media's development over recent years has developed players' capabilities to brand themselves. They develop large followings before they even determine what college to play for. Again, this has been going on for years now through the introduction of social media. It's become a way of the social media world.

The entire process is not without infallibility. Early on, issues will be addressed to streamline the process as much as possible. My one question remains if the NCAA is going to be able to allow this without some form of federal intervention involved to address potential issues. States are already drawing their lines in the sand with laws prohibiting NCAA interaction, and states have a lot of financial strength when it comes to universities within their jurisdictions to adhere to state laws in lieu of the NCAA's.

In June 2021, the Supreme Court's decision in NCAA v. Alston only concluded the NCAA could not restrict education-related benefits. However, Justice Brett Kavanaugh warned, "...NCAA's business model of using unpaid student athletes to generate billions of dollars in revenue for the colleges raises serious questions under the antitrust laws… The NCAA's business model would be flatly illegal in almost any other industry in America," he wrote.[30] The decision rendered "pay for play" illegal as the NCAA's primary tool to sustain a strong position regarding its involvement to support amateur athletics. The Supreme Court decision seems to leave room open to possible market violations and to future debate.

As July 1, 2021 drew near regarding a decision regarding NILs for college athletes, new companies entered the soon to be booming NIL market, offering products and services to both schools and athletes. The 150 NIL platforms already in existence encountered many new competitors. What processes are in place to assure all approaching these markets are abiding by NCAA rules since these organizations are separate entities from the schools?

Besides laws approaching pay for play of college athletes, what's preventing the Nevin Shapiro's of the world from becoming an integral part of these collectives? Since collectives are not affiliated directly with school administrations, who knows what incentives will be offered to 18-year-old student-athletes and their families? Collectives need to meet compliance guidelines not only regarding state laws, but also NCAA standards monitored by authorized agencies. Loosely monitored adherence to rules will keep exposed schools from participating in amateur sports as we know them today if not monitored properly.

7.) Recruiting practices

Already hit on NIL money being offered to players of other programs and bidding wars for high school talent. Supposedly new rules are being put in place. Also, coaches are limited in talks with players from other programs, but how will anyone monitor players recruiting other players? With social media, cell phones, interactions forging friendships at high school football camps, networking during college recruiting processes, players keep in touch knowing who's unhappy, who wants to move, who's leaving, and who's available before their head coaches know. They can eventually pass the word along. Makes sense, and it can't be stopped.

Recruiting has always been a behind-the-scenes process. It seems like it can continue now through an even broader network.

8.) Transfer portals

The NCAA determined to limit the windows when players can move on through the transfer portals. The first window is open for 45 days from Dec. 5 until Jan. 18. The second runs in the spring from May 1-15. However, in retrospect, does it make sense to open that portal right after spring football practice sessions end? Coaches work their teams to develop and prepare them for the following season. They determine needs and skills and then position players on the depth chart to get ready for summer practices.

After recent spring practices, some teams saw mass exoduses of players transferring. In some cases, surely some disgruntled players left thinking they had no future to move up. Whatever happened to "the old college try?" Shamefully, society seems to be losing that healthy, standard value. As a coach with players leaving, it seems like they just wasted a lot of time preparing players to be essential for next season's roster, or even beyond. All players don't develop at the same pace. Is this the best time for opening up the transfer portal after the time dedicated to train, evaluate and put together a team? It now seems, come summer sessions, team-building starts all over again for some coaching staffs to evaluate players to find out who can do what.

Portal Traps

In regards to player success entering transfer portals, "the grass isn't always greener on the other side," but in many cases, the other side doesn't even exist. As of January 2023, according to statistics reported by the NCAA on their dashboard "Transfer Portal Data: Division I Student-Athlete Transfer Trends," data indicates 4,121 FBS players entered the portal in 2020 and 2021. Among FBS players, 54% (2,323) who entered the portal enrolled at a new school, but 41% (1,798) still awaited options to play elsewhere, transferred to non-NCAA schools, or ceased playing football. Considering that there are basically 85 players on each FBS roster, the number of players who didn't re-enroll totaled enough players to make 21 full FBS rosters. That's a lot of former scholar-athletes who had money for education possibly unable to be playing college football any longer. Only 36% (1,097) of FCS players who entered the transfer portal during the two-year period found opportunities to play at another NCAA program including D-2 or D-3 schools where there are fewer athletic scholarships available.

Short-term thinking can hurt some long-term plans for student-athletes. The number for FCS transfer success may be indicative of the different talent levels between the two highest existing subdivisions. As good as an FCS player may be at that level, many don't meet the standards of the FBS level.

Sad reality for many who could have continued to compete to play where they were, no other programs had interest in providing a new opportunity. Players may have been discontent where they were, but maybe the original program never found the value expected. Maybe no other programs see it either. Perhaps the player's potential, or even worse, maybe the player's effort wasn't there to begin with.

The transfer portal needs to be addressed

Thankfully, the NCAA announced as to when players can exit a program in the future. It was unfair to teams and coaching staffs for players to leave on such short notice. This move contradicts major intangibles college football should be about – loyalty, commitment, and teamwork. It's also shameful, dishonest, unsportsmanlike, and eventually should be illegal if another program entices a player to leave their existing school. College football is big business. If players' goals are to make money from it, there should be valid contracts between them and their schools. If this is the way it's going to be, it's time for NCAA policy-makers to wake up. Already, there are incidents, like it or not, that pay for play incites players to leave their current team to play for another. This is "pay for play" and NIL offers can be used as significant lures.

He who offers the carrot, should get the stick

During the 2023 American Athletic media conferences, new Alabama-Birmingham Head Coach Trent Dilfer went on record exposing the true issue regarding transfer portals combined with the NIL incentives. Some football programs through collectives approach players of other FBS programs to enter the transfer portal to accept proposed NIL incentives. Though Dilfer won't say what programs these are, he states he has evidence to prove it.[31] It's one thing for a collective to offer a player an NIL package after an athlete commits to play for a specific team, but the intention was not for collectives to entice players away from other programs with NIL incentives and enter the transfer portal to play for their program. If this is the case, it will only tend to open up ongoing bidding wars among schools to encourage the best active players to transfer to the highest bidders. No doubt it can be said it's great financially for the athletes, but how can this then not be considered pay for play? That's the NCAA purpose - to maintain its domain only over amateur athletics.

Dilfer, a former college and Super Bowl quarterback, rightly and strongly proposes saying, "There has got to be a mechanism in place, where the player personnel director of said school will never work in college football again if he coerces somebody from another team [into the portal with NIL promises] and it is proven."[32] This exposes the weakness of the NCAA's foresight regarding conflicts their new NIL policy can create. Dilfer's suggestion may be the strongest deterrent to such violations. The person or persons involved between the university and the collective as well as the respective university should understand the consequences of a strong and damaging penalty.

No other deterrence can be as strong as seen historically by the consequences of a "death penalty." Any collective involved should also be banned from any further contact with any university regarding NIL representation. However, the NCAA needs to develop clear rules, restrictions, and penalties for violators regarding abuses in regards to

NILs coercing player transfers through portals. With collectives outside the realm of academic institutions, it's unclear who the "player personnel directors of said schools" are. And as found, compliance officers only need to assure collectives abide by state laws. If they are in accordance with state laws, what crime has been committed?

Are we trying to spell "Team" now as "Teim?"

As far as who can transfer and how, there appears to be a start. A new rule will limit waivers for a second transfer starting in the 2023-2024 season.[33] Players applying for waivers will have to meet specific guidelines. Exemptions will be made for physical injuries or mental health concerns. However, these two potentially undermine that spirit. A player can now state, "I got injured. I want to transfer." How does that justify entering the transfer portal? Maybe if the university doesn't help in the recovery process, that could be an issue, but that would have to be validated.

As for mental health, that could expose totally different scenarios. If a coach benches a player for lack of performance, or if another player steps up, can a player claim his benching caused a mental health issue? Consider the case where Jalen Hurts got benched for Tua Tagovailoa against Georgia in the 2017 CFP championship game. Based on Tagovailoa's performance in the comeback win and evidently competition in spring practice, he started for Alabama the next season. Hurts spent that season on the bench after leading the Crimson Tide's drive to the title game.

To Hurts' credit, he didn't publicly sulk, and he complied with the decision ready to step in for the starter if and when necessary. No doubt a tough situation for the quarterback who led Alabama to the 2017 CFP championship game. He displayed admirable fortitude. When he had the opportunity to play again at Oklahoma after earning a degree at Alabama, Hurts transferred as a graduate student. Would another player under the proposed transfer process deem this to be a mental health issue to request a waiver because he suffered depression by getting benched and no longer playing? Does the NCAA give that player a pass, or do they eloquently reply, "Suck it up," before the internet explodes with comments for both sides of either response?

Watch out for transfer portal waivers

Loopholes still exist in the transfer portal processes. This year, over 2,000 student-athletes applied for waivers into the transfer portal. One hundred and twenty were quarterbacks. Not many were told "no." To deter this free movement, a player now has to graduate from one of his first two schools. If not, he has to sit out a year of eligibility.[34] It's a start, but nothing prevents a player from applying for an exemption.

A player may apply for a waiver, but who's to say that the real reason for the request isn't because another school offered some NIL incentive? One can claim "mental health," but will the NCAA actually be able to investigate this and prove there is an enticement here instead to confirm and provide a certifiable "no?" And as Trent Dilfer proposes, those exposed initiating such deception should be banned from ever working in collegiate sports again. More fine-tuning will be necessary regarding waivers as loopholes. Certainly, this process will come under further scrutiny.

What the game of football means

To me, football means the total opposite to the ways of thinking of many becoming avid Fantasy Football participants. I don't ever foresee my love for this game ever changing to be involved from that aspect. A great part probably has to do with playing in high school and efforts to overcome the obstacles like transfer rules and knee injuries I came up against in college to be part of a team. I root for teams and the players on it as a whole. I can't pull for individuals and their stats on separate teams competing against various teams for the same ultimate team championship. I want my team to win. This fantasy aspect has nothing to do with the goal of a team winning. To be honest again, it's only about money. To each their own. I use mine to continue on this adventure, but the point is that this thinking focuses on individualism, not teamwork. That's just against my nature. The team wins, we all win.

Fantasy Football is not as prevalent in college football as pro football at this time, but it totally contradicts what the game itself is about - the ultimate team sport. It's about eleven players on each side blocking and tackling and doing it well. The beauty of it comes in how all eleven perform their assignments with all their combined heart, mind, and strength with different and specialized skills to make them all successful by defeating the eleven guys on the field across from them. I am an advocate of what General George S. Patton's monologue in the movie *"Patton"* states because it echoes lessons learned on the gridiron that can be utilized for a lifetime: "Now an Army" (or a country, or a school, or a company, or a family, or all of society for that matter) "is a team - it lives, eats, sleeps, fights as a team. This individuality stuff is a bunch of crap." What a member of any of these entities does is supposed to be for the good of the team, not primarily for individual accolades.

Football always epitomized the truest form of a team sport. The ultimate goal of any team is to cross the goal line to win. When the team wins, individual rewards and accolades should be secondary after the results of successful teamwork. That's what is being lost in this new order of college football. It seems now that no matter how the team finishes, the priority now is to look to go somewhere else. That's fine in pro football where athletes make a living, but college football needs to focus on values educating the 98% of its players who don't become professional athletes.

9.) Unionization

My anonymous FBS coaching source pointed out that this is the worst-case scenario for the college athletes. Unionization works best in the NFL more than for other major sports leagues against ownership, but with the diversity in college football from starting quarterbacks to underclass bench warmers, collective bargaining for benefits would be almost impossible. Generally, each player's status changes over three to four years. Plus, as NCAA members or some other organization to be developed to manage these super-conferences, the schools would be bargaining with their employees and enforcing their rules. How can 18-20-year-olds rotating to play every three to five years, at most, among 134 college football programs across the country organize long-term to leverage any strength to negotiate with the NCAA, their respective conferences, and individual schools (the three "owners" in this scenario) that survive indefinitely. They also hold abundant, financial reserves.

The National Labor Relations Board (NLRB) has already set forth actions to legally recognize college football and basketball players at the University of Southern Cal as employees of the university, the PAC-12, and the NCAA. The NLRB initiated actions in December 2022.[35] The claim was filed on behalf of USC athletes by the National College Players Association (NCPA), a support group that has led prior campaigns to attain various benefits for college athletes. This could become a test case if employee status is granted to Trojan athletes.

Previously, the NLRB's effort to unionize Northwestern's student-athletes in 2015 failed. However, because the NCAA has instituted new rules since, allowing athletes to receive compensation from third parties (i.e., collectives), they raised legal questions addressed by the Supreme Court in June 2021.[36] As always per its primary existence, the NCAA emphasized that amateurism was essential for its business. In a sign indicative to changing perceptions, "Justice Brett Kavanaugh said college athletes could find a more, fair path toward sharing in the revenue they help to create by establishing some kind of collective bargaining group."[37] Players should beware, however, that this is not their strongest position. Under current regulations, through NILs, revenues will vary among individual players potentially year to year. They will profit better and possibly for the duration of their college playing careers rather than some ongoing collective bargaining strategy. Under this new model with changes I envision, this can all be changed in a new order.

10.) Waivers

As mentioned earlier, wholesale changes among the 40-48 teams may address these unionized shortcomings by making players employees instead of students. Football players may be able to stay longer than the traditional four years to attain a college education. With waivers, some have matriculated for up to seven years and already earned degrees. Colleges will now see the benefit of hiring players as employees instead.

[1] Daniel Chavkin, August 15, 2023, Sports Illustrated, "Nebraska AD Trev Alberts Warns Next Conference Moves Will Be 'Far More Disruptive,'" Retrieved 22 August 2023.

[2] Ibid.
 [3] Dennis Dodd, CBSSports.com, "College football attendance rose in 2022 with largest year-over-year increase since 1982." Mar 8, 2023
 [4] Nels Popp, Jason Simmons, Stephen L. Shapiro, and Nick Wantanabe, "Predicting Ticket Holder No-Shows: Examining Differences Between Reported and Actual Attendance at College Football Games," fitpublishing.com. March 23, 2023.
 [5] Ibid.
 [6] Ibid.
 [7] Chuck Knox and Bill Plaschke, Hard Knox: The Life of an NFL Coach, 1988, page 201.
 [8] Aaron Beard, AP Sports Writer, AP Associated press, "Wake Forest's Dave Clawson says multiple players returned despite tampering by other schools," 7/27/2023.

[9] Ibid.
 [10] Ibid.
 [11] Nick Zoroya (November 8, 2022), "NCAA NIL Rules Guide: The Do's & Don'ts of NIL." laxallstars.com. Retrieved 31 July 2023.

[12] Ryan Bologna, Clutch Points, "Full details of Jaden Rashada's termination of $13.85 million deal", February 6, 2023.
 [13] Ibid.
 [14] John Buhler, Fansided.com, "Ill-fated Jaden Rashada Florida NIL

contract details revealed," Feb 3, 2023.

[15] Ibid

[16] Ross Dellenger, Sports Illustrated, "Inside the NIL Battle That Is Splintering the SEC: 'We're All Money Laundering'", May 30, 2023.

[17] Ibid.

[18] Ibid.

[19] Ibid.

[20] Ibid.

[21] Ibid.

[22] Dave Wilson, ESPN Staff Writer, "Record Setting UTSA QB Frank Harris to return for 7th Season". ESPN.com. December 7, 2022.

[23] Ibid

[24] Ibid

[25] Ibid

[26] Samantha Greenberg, Sports Agent Blog, July 7, 2021, "Bryce Young Signs with CAA For NIL Representation." Retrieved August 15, 2023.

[27] Dan Wetzel, YahooSports.com, July 18, 2023, "Brock Bowers' selfless NIL move shows Georgia still has big picture in mind while chasing 3-peat." Retrieved 16 August 2023.

[28] Ross Dellenger, Sports Illustrated, 5/30/2023. "Inside the NIL Battle That Is Splintering the SEC: 'We're All Money Laundering.'" Retrieved May 30, 2023.

[29] Ibid.

[30] *Melissa Quinn (June 21, 2021).* CBS News *"Supreme Court rules for student-athletes in battle over NCAA limits on certain benefits. Retrieved June 21, 2021.*

[31] Daniel Bates. "Trent Dilfer Wants College Football Coaches Banned for Life If They Break One Rule," The Spun. July 26, 2023.

[32] Ibid.

[33] James Parks. "NCAA makes changes to college football transfer

portal", CFB-HQ on Fox Nation. January 12, 2023.

[34] Ibid.

[35] Dan Murphy, ESPN Staff writer, "NLRB to pursue unlawful labor practices against USC, PAC-12, NCAA", December 15, 2022.

[36]Ibid.

[37]Ibid.

III

Essay II

Based on my passion and knowledge of this game for fifty years, I address issues here, some more critical than others, to make this game more competitive among the existing 134 Football Bowl Subdivision football programs. In my analysis, other needs should be addressed with solutions I'd like to propose. As a dedicated fanatic of college football as depicted through my life-long journey, my greatest desire is to see this sport improve for long-term, sustainable success for players and for fans.

For the Love of the Game

With the research and analysis presented herein, my goal is to help fans realize possible detriments facing college football's future. I consider that these issues represent some, for lack of a better term, the "Ugly," of college football. With the analysis of individual issues, I present some solutions that I think can make this game even better, meaning proposing changes as stated to "level the playing field" so more teams currently in the FBS can compete for the national championship.

With that in mind, look beyond the scope of any one particular team. Every fan has a favorite or favorites, or an iconic state university, or a beloved Alma mater. All fans root for their favorites to be the best, or even more, they always want to see them challenge to play to the best of their capabilities, and that's the way it should be. However, without comparable resources starting out on equal footing, or on a so-called "level playing field," where all teams can strive for the same ultimate goal to win a national championship, there seems be less purpose and little desire to play all these games among the 134 currently competing for that same goal.

If college football remains status quo which no one believes regarding its future, or a faction of the game we know today remains under the current guidelines of the NCAA, these are changes proposed for considerations to make the college football fairer for all FBS members to compete for the same national championship.

1.) Bowl games vs. "Consolation" games

Let's categorize post-season games into what they really are. Some games should be considered rewards for very good seasons. Of 12 regular-season games played, a minimum of nine wins against FBS competition should qualify as "bowl eligible" - not six. Let's face it, if it wasn't for all the air-time available on television, most of today's "bowl" games wouldn't exist for what all bowl games used to be - rewards for excellent seasons. Most now exist to fill in air time for television programming to build revenue when men are home during the holidays with not much else to watch on television. I enjoy seeing more football games televised during the holiday season. However, a distinction should be made between awards for good seasons and for games played primarily for entertainment. That's what the "E" in ESPN stands for.

Now, teams even with sub-.500 records get invited to bowl games. Reality, these are "consolation" games. I hate to hear that a schedule is determined as "tough" because a particular team plays ten teams who played in a bowl game the previous season. The term "bowl game" is a misnomer. About 75% of all FBS teams – not just the Top 20 to 30 - play in so-called bowl games! Most are contracted into guaranteed contests with a minimum 6-6 record. And generally, one win comes against an FCS team that can't even qualify for bowl eligibility. Below is a proposal regarding "Post-season games for all." That's what college football is moving towards any way. As the conventional saying goes for today's youth, "Everybody gets a trophy." How can college football separate great from good seasons, and the mediocre and the bad? Going forward, reward just the great achievers with "bowl bids." At least, call post-season games between teams with eight wins or fewer "consolation games."

Bowl Committee Selections: pair strengths and eradicate perceptions

It was disappointing this past season to see UT San Antonio (11-2) and Troy (11-2) square off against each other in the Cure Bowl. Both teams met after winning their respective Group of Five conferences (C-USA and Sun Belt). Troy won a competitive Cure Bowl game between them, 18-12.

One had to lose another game diluting the perceived quality of "Group" school reputations in the Top 25. Instead, had a playoff for just the Group of Five been formatted, both teams deserved to be ranked highly in that respective scenario with the potential to meet for a national title. Instead, UTSA lost a competitive game to Troy and got jumped over by Power Five teams in less competitive bowls. It leaves a misconception that UTSA is not as strong as mediocre Power Five programs. UTSA dropped out of the Top 25 while Troy climbed five spots from No. 25 to No. 19.

In reality, under existing circumstances, Troy and UTSA both deserved to play against teams with superior "Power Five" perceptions. Eventually opportunities like this can knock down the barriers between the subjective titles of Power Fives and Group of Five. How else are these two factions currently categorized objectively? Teams like Vanderbilt, Mississippi State, Rutgers, Indiana, Washington State, California, Duke, and Iowa State rarely crack the Top 25 in football, but they get consideration as Power Fives. Group of Five programs like Boise State, San Diego State, Cincinnati, Navy, BYU, Memphis, and Central Florida have more combined Top 25 finishes over the past ten years than these programs. These programs have held their own against these Powers head-to-head competitions as well.

Regarding bowl selections and "consolation games:" after first selecting the twelve College Football Playoff (CFP) teams, and then seeding them accordingly in the finalized playoff format, a Bowl Selection Committee for the non-College Football Playoff games could be established to match teams to align all other bowl and consolation games as competitively as possible. The twelve-team playoff format has already been announced starting for the 2024 season. The CFP tournament will consist of the six highest-ranked conference champions and the remaining six highest-ranked teams. The four highest-ranked conference champions will get first-round byes. In first round pairings, the higher seeds among the other eight teams will host the lower seeds on campus or at a site of their choice.[1]

Following the finalized playoff pairings, the proposed bowl selection committee should analyze the final regular season results of all remaining, eligible post-season teams. Under a new system proposed below based on "Power Points" I propose, or some other improved tool for strengthening objectivity of schedule metrics, pair teams up to play based on equitable power points to rank teams accordingly. At the least, authorize a committee matching teams with similar records despite what conferences they belong to.

In particular, however, the committee should pair Group of Five schools with the best records in games against Power Five schools. Mix more Group teams against Power teams to establish more comparisons between the two factions. If not, this provides even more reason to divide the Power schools and the Group schools. Categorize them into two separate divisions playing for two separate and equal subdivision national championships. To start, as an example, call one "FBS-Power" and the other "FBS-Group," or FBS-I and FBS-II.

Consider post-season variables

At the end of 2022 instead of playing one another, as examples, UTSA and Troy could have played against LSU and Florida State respectively. These two matchups would be very worthwhile to watch. Likewise, fans and the media just take these perceptions for granted. Florida State (9-3) struggled against 6-6 Oklahoma in their bowl after the Sooners lost three of their last four games. LSU annihilated Purdue 63-7 after Boilermaker quarterback Aidan O'Connell and others opted out. A selection committee could take these late-season factors into consideration and instead pair LSU against a more deserving 11-2 Group team intact with a starting signal-caller planning to return next season. Why not have paired the Seminoles against a proven UTSA or Troy with eleven wins? Let the lower ranked Power Fives compete against one another based on their lesser records. In this case, they could have pitted Oklahoma (7-5) against Purdue (8-4) instead of against FSU (9-3) and LSU (9-4) respectively. The Group schools in this situation at least deserve a shot with talent intact to face Power schools they don't get to play during the regular season.

Maybe it will be a different story in the future if Troy and UTSA would play in the 12-team format as conference champions. Hopefully that can happen eventually, but more likely they will be blocked based on their perceived "strength of schedule" if not among the top six conference champs. The Power Fives (soon to be four?) will basically fill five of those seeds. One Group team will get the other championship bid as did Tulane among the CFP bowls last year. When it comes to the remaining six teams, however, they'll most likely come from among the Power Five. Below these top teams, once analyzed further down the rankings, that level playing field between the Group teams and the Power teams is closer than perceived. Pairing such non-CFP bowl games between more of these two categories will encourage future recruits to consider such Group programs in their decision-making processes.

Disprove perception, expose reality

This offers the most effective method of leveling the playing field to allow more from the Group of Five show their equality by playing more Power Five teams, and not primarily comparing them to just those at the very top (examples: Alabama, Georgia, Clemson, Michigan, Ohio State, Oklahoma, USC, etc.) who basically already dominate among other Power Fives. "Powers" with records of 6-6, 7-5, or even 8-4 proved they couldn't match up with the cream of the top Power Fives as they only become eligible to play in bowls with a minimum of six wins.

Last season, the Group defeated the Powers in three of five post-season games: Air Force beat Baylor, Fresno State defeated Washington State, and Tulane was the big winner over USC in the Cotton Bowl. Two Mountain Wests and an American Athletic won games against the Big Twelve and two PAC-12. The Military Bowl annually pits the American Athletic against the ACC. Since this format started six years ago, the conference records are 3-3. How would the middle of the pack among the Big Ten and SEC perform against more of the best among the Group of Five? Or are they hesitant and unwilling to be exposed as non-Powers? Let's see how these teams match-up against the best among the Group of Five. Maybe it will give those lesser-thought of Group teams more viability that they are or aren't on the same level as the top Power Fives.

2.) Graduate studies

Senior players now graduate and transfer to graduate schools at other football-playing universities. Why not just offer graduate degrees in Football now? When one semester of football is all these student-athletes can basically play after graduation, are they really earning a second degree? Not too many graduate programs can be completed in two semesters no less the one when they will play during football season. Are they really getting anything other than a Master's in Football? Professional Football is big business now. Why can't qualified college graduates pursue a career in that field? Schools offer graduate degrees now in Sports Management and in Coaching for employment by professional sports organizations. Be open and honest about it – grad studies for players in their desired career paths.

The point is the graduate school transfer portal doesn't seem very academically oriented for a serious student pursuing a post-graduate degree. The reality is that they applied for grad school primarily to play football. Does it seem right for graduate schools to act in these cases as a vehicle to basically benefit the football program? If it is, be open about it. Especially since the player's already earned a four-year degree qualifying him for graduate studies.

3.) Post-season games for all teams

Refer to "consolation" games above. Allow every team to at least a voluntarily play in a post-season contest. Schools can determine among admin, budgets, coaches, and players if they want the opportunity or not. The overall health of all teams with non-winning records may be consideration for not participating in a post-season contest. Next, let a selection committee pit teams with comparable records play one another.

Flip a coin for home team or work out a neutral site together. Even the weakest teams will get the benefit of more post-season practice like the good teams and the mediocre teams currently get for playing in "bowl" games. Bunch these with the rest of the other glorified, "consolation" games. Around 75% of FBS teams participate in post-season play. Why prevent the others? Imagine two winless teams playing for their only win of the season. That will draw some interest among fans and the media hype. Recruiting time-frames should be reassessed in conjunction with the end of the season, of course.

4.) Proposed playoff formats

Below under "Strength of Schedules," I include proposals regarding point systems to evaluate teams more objectively as opposed to utilizing current, subjective input. That's a proposed start. Otherwise, class recruit rankings, questionable strength of schedules, media manipulation, and preconceived prejudices all get jumbled around to come up with the twelve top teams. There's no concern about coming up with the top six now that the initial format automatically invites six conference champions. There are more fair and equitable ways to determine the best of the Top 12 for the CFP than through "political processes" and trades made for votes ("I'll vote for yours if you vote for mine").

5.) Revenue sharing

Television money should at least be shared equally among all schools under common network contracts. Bowl revenues from contracts are already shared equally among conference members. NIL money and even any funding from the NFL should be equally shared by all 134 FBS teams. There are no controls now to monitor this, but this policy can be considered by the NCAA. The need to reassess whatever controls are necessary to take care of this should be a top priority. The NFL does this already to make small team media markets play on equal footing financially with the large team markets. Colleges pose different issues with endowments and donations as examples, but that's probably the best way to assess Power Five teams from Group of Five teams. Consideration for two divisions based on money available.

One lesson that college football should learn from pro football

As NFL revenue sharing equalizes small markets like Green Bay and Pittsburgh against the big market franchises in New York and Los Angeles, financially every team wins by sharing comparable earnings to finance equivalent payrolls. Colleges could share the wealth of available revenues instead of hoarding as individual schools can do now. On the field of play, wins and losses may shift, but why should wins and losses derive primarily from unfair competitive financial advantages that exist today? It's called monopolization in free markets. There are laws that prevent this. Individual university endowments are means around this currently, but equal allocations could be considered.

In 2020, the NCAA represented one of the world's most powerful trade associations not subject to special federal oversight. It's made up of public and private universities earning $13 billion annually hosting collegiate athletic events. Thirty-eight institutions generated over $100 million in annual athletic revenue. The University of Texas totaled revenues in excess of more than $200 million.[2]

Profits from college sports are used differently by members of the NCAA. Some invest revenues to pay administrators, athletic directors, and coaches very high salaries for their perceived value to lead sports teams. Alabama paid Head Coach Nick Saban $8.3 million per year. Michigan paid five football coaches on staff around $1 million per year. These numbers far exceed the pay of many coaches considered leaders of comparable FBS competition.[3] In reality, how can the Colorado States, UConn's, and New Mexico States of the FBS compete on the same gridiron based lower football revenues? Yet that's some of the teams the well-compensated ones schedule to play every year.

Is revenue sharing realistic among for the NCAA?

Probably the only way for this to start is for federal legislation to supersede new NIL laws imposed by individual states. How else will the playing field ever be level? If implemented, I initially propose the NCAA forms an internal NIL agency office. All parties interested in contributing funds to use student-athletes names, images, and likenesses would deposit funds into an NIL reserve of the contributor's choice for a particular sport – football, men's basketball, women's basketball, women's gymnastics, softball, baseball, etc. – and for the level of play – FBS or FCS for football as an example.

From each fund, eligible student-athletes would get an equal stipend from the allocations to each category. The funds would first be applied one or two ways to be considered. First, if it's that much money, cover the cost of athletes' educations. If $13.85 MILLION can be provided by one collective for one player,[4] why can't all 85 players in the Florida program, as an example, benefit? If divided equally among all, that comes to $170,000 per player. Take out taxes and use the money to pay for their tuitions. Whatever is left, each player uses for spending money.

To take this option a step further to level the funding among all members for all athletes, it would depend on the benevolence of all contributors to contribute through a centralized organization, namely the NCAA. If $13.85 MILLION can be provided by one collective for one player at one school, how much NIL money can be generated by all 134 FBS programs? Miami's $9.5 MILLION[5] added to this coffer gives all 11,390 players another $834 each. How much can other collectives offer has yet to be determined. To avoid incremental stipends for all 134 schools to offer different amounts based on what each school can raise, for an estimated 11,390 football players (134 teams X 85 players) at the FBS level every year, that's $2,050 raised for each FBS player from these two schools alone. What's in it for collectives? Fair play, competitive games. Most money contributed now intends to give Alma Mater U. the edge.

The NCAA agency can assign athletes requested to use for the benefit of their names, likenesses, and images. I still don't understand where that value comes from other than for these individuals playing a sport. The agency would need to monitor where the revenue sources come from. It would assure legality of all sources and transactions. They would also have to monitor that the schools are staying within the finances allocated through the agency. Definitely, there would have to be some monitoring to assure students don't get overwhelmed making such obligations surrendering too much time for school obligations. The NCAA could use some of the money to hire more resources to monitor allocations of revenues.

Not an easy task at all, but the risk of the Death Penalty should be made known. Look at the price SMU paid for violations over 30 years ago. Schools and collectives alike need to know what is legal and illegal, or else they risk shutting down athletic programs to sit out a few years which have resulted in severe losses when implemented in the past.

My suggestions will be considered as pie-in-the-sky to some, but let's face it, NIL funds wouldn't be available to any players if it weren't for all the players they're competing against. They all have names, images and likenesses, too. They're also seen every week on television.

College football needs to overcome major, pending detriments before they get worse. If not, reality is that the rich get richer. The competition on the field becomes more diluted, and at what point does fan interest level off? Student-athletes were always honored members of the entire student body. With the changes in the sport taking place today, athletes are moving closer to becoming hired mercenaries. Will the school populations continue to support that?

6.) Scheduling manipulation

Recruit the best talent available, but avoid playing comparable competition as much as possible to rack up wins. And develop support to indicate you play a tough schedule because the paid media sells everybody that your conference competition is better than any others. Every year, no less, and only based on total wins not considering the level of competition. Their prerogative is to sell air time to build an audience for games on their networks whether the teams playing are competitive with one another or not. Again, consider a Point System based on the values of each opponent played during the current season. States around the country rank high schools like this already to determine playoffs.

Jim Harbaugh is not Bobby Bowden

If you read about my respect for the late Florida State Head Coach Bobby Bowden, you will understand my perspective of Michigan's Jim Harbaugh here. Here's a coach that boasts taking world-wide sorties to recruit the best players from around the globe. He brags of it. The media covers it. Fine. But if such efforts are made to recruit to get the best of the best talent, then why don't you stack your team up against comparable competition? Why schedule opponents in or nearest among ESPN's Bottom Ten?

Last season Michigan opened against Colorado State (3-9), Hawaii (3-9), and UConn (surprisingly 6-7). To start in 2023, of 134 FBS football programs, Harbaugh's blue-chip recruits take on #71 East Carolina, # 121 Nevada-Las Vegas, and # 119 Bowling Green. That's like the LA Dodgers playing minor league teams at the AA league level if you consider all the top players in professional baseball. Below in "Strength of Schedules; Power Points," I will critique the very flawed methodology used to determine these ratings in the preseason. On the other hand, based on last year's results, these three 2023 ratings seem acceptable from a 30,000-foot perspective.

First of all, none of these six teams Michigan plays compete in a Power Five conference. Power Fives typically rate tops for recruiting the best talent. These opponents scheduled fall far short in comparison. All travel to Michigan to play in front of crowds of over 100,000 partisan, Big Blue fans. They'll show up just to enjoy a lop-sided score. It's kind of like paying money to watch your favorite team practice. Why bother? Party, of course, and then celebrate!

When Harbaugh started with Michigan after his four years coaching in the pros, they played one or two non-conference games annually against Notre Dame, Florida, and a few PAC-12 schools. His record against Power Five non-conference teams coaching at Michigan and previously at Stanford over eleven seasons stands at 10-7. Not bad, but evidently, Harbaugh realized he could eliminate the risk of losing against any opponents he didn't have to play within the Big Ten Conference. And yet, Michigan ranks highly among the top recruiting programs in the nation.

Sad state of mind for college football in general. Most programs trend this way. When they expand to a 12-team format in 2024, hopefully this will create a solution to avoiding these schedule-padding practices to create more competitive regular season games among Power Five schools. The problem is basically every Power program does this now. Better inter-conference games will also offer better points of comparison during the course of a season for rankings. As mentioned already, college football needs to become more competitive for fans of more schools in the future, not fewer. Demonstrate prowess on the field, not on perceived recruiting capabilities.

"Bring us your quarterback!"

I started that mantra attending 22 Kick-off Classic contests. A returning starting quarterback is a key to start any season. An inexperienced signal-caller is just at the beginning of his learning curve. You know who loves to see a returning quarterbacks begin a new season? Ticket-buying fans looking for an exciting opening game between two teams. You know who hates this? Head coaches looking for an opening win against another Power Five opponent. So, what do they do? They schedule games against a pretty good program who they know will definitely lose an experienced, seasoned quarterback from the previous season or two. Check out Nick Saban at Alabama. He's the master of this practice. The media also tends to over-hype such early matchups.

No more Jackson, no more Jones...

In 2016 and 2017, upstart Louisville won 9 and 8 games respectively. With Heisman Trophy winner Lamar Jackson under center, the Cardinals scored 553 and 495 points in consecutive seasons. A program on the rise – not really. Perennial power Alabama under Saban scheduled Louisville at a "neutral" site, Orlando, Florida, for both teams' season openers in 2018. However, Jackson was in Baltimore playing for the NFL Ravens by then. Alabama came off a 13-1 national championship with not one, but two quarterbacks who had led Bama to CFP championship games – Tua Tagovailoa and Jalen Hurts. Bama wins this game easily, 51-14. The Cardinals lost more than just their QB from 2017. They finished 2-10 in 2018.

Repeat 2019. Alabama hosts Duke for both teams' openers at another "neutral site," Atlanta. Funny thing is that Bama fans had cheered the Tide there ten times since 2010. That included the SEC Championship win over Georgia the previous year. The following season, Tagovailoa returns as the starter for the 14-1 No. 2 Tide of 2018. Duke finished 8-5 the previous year with signal-caller Daniel Jones leading the offense for 382 points. Formidable foe? Maybe if the Tide played the New York Giants. They drafted Jones in the first round back in April. Not surprisingly, Bama won the opener under these circumstances, 42-3. The Tide went home with a win over Duke who'd finish 5-7.

Bama pushed back an opener at Penn State two years when the Lions had no returning quarterback in 2010. Freshman Rob Bolden started. Here's more proof of this strategy - watch for this in 2024. I'm writing this "on the wall." In 2023, Western Kentucky quarterback Austin Reed returns after leading the nation in passing yardage as did his predecessor Bailey Zappe. An experienced and healthy Reed will probably exceed this mark at WKU in his final season there as a graduate student.

The Hilltoppers will probably have a strong, successful season with a good record and bowl game, based on a high-scoring, successful offense with Reed under center. On paper, the Hilltoppers come off a successful record in 2024. Bama opens at home then against Western Kentucky to welcome a brand-new, Hilltopper quarterback. Saban's smart. To pollsters, a win is a win. These early season wins accelerate quick starts to the top. That's the intent here.

One good thing about the transfer portal - a wary opponent's roster can surprisingly be upgraded if such a game is scheduled for this reason.

Either way, the Hilltoppers will introduce a new quarterback with no experience in the Western Kentucky offensive scheme. Whoever it is will probably be at the start of a learning curve.

7.) Strength of schedules; use Power Points

Change strength of schedule ratings based on objective reality. Can anyone agree about the strength of schedules (SOS) in pre-season publications? Or with what talking heads on television insist are clear to everyone regarding which teams play the toughest slates of all? An article on the website, FBS Schedules, by Kevin Kelley published on February 20, 2023 entitled, "College football strength of schedule: 2023 Win/Loss method" clarifies, but also confirms how inept and inaccurate this methodology is for use during any season.[6] To use the current method he presents leaves a lot of shortcomings. When analyzed, it doesn't make any sense. Funny, but when it comes to rankings and bowl bids, strength of schedule seems to take the lead as the hottest topic. It needs to reflect up-to-date, objective reality.

Kelley states in the article, *"The win/loss method is exactly as it sounds — it's based on wins and losses. In order to look ahead before any games are played, the win/loss method is based solely on a team's opponents' win/loss record from the previous season."* [7] The previous season? That makes no sense.Especially in this new era where the portal transfer is wide open and the NIL is being used to attract the best talent not only from high schools, but also to attract and disperse talent of their competitors for immediate playing time. None of these teams will field the same rosters from the previous year, and that's no longer based on who graduated and what underclassmen will step in.

On top of this, the won/lost records of teams played calculated don't take into account the level of play each teams' competitors played against. There are games scheduled among Power Five programs, the Group of Five who generally don't compete well recruiting-wise for the highest talent overall, and the FCS with fewer scholarships and less TV revenue to invest in recruiting than the FBS teams. According to Rivals.com, a website dedicated to evaluating football talent recruited annually by all FBS schools, of the top 50 teams they ranked in 2022, all but one came from among Power Five teams - Memphis ranked 47th overall. Of teams ranked from 51-100 in the Rival.com poll, 29 Group of Five schools ranked among these. How do FCS schools compare to the FBS teams they play? FBS football programs can have a maximum of 85 full-ride athletic scholarships during one season. FCS football programs carry a maximum of 63 total athletic scholarships each season. The number of scholarships offered varies by each school season to season depending on needs and who they recruit.

The Power Five conferences in 2022 consisted of:
·The Atlantic Coast Conference (ACC)
·The Big Ten
·The Big XII
·The Pacific Athletic Conference (PAC-12)
·The Southeastern Conference (SEC)
·And Notre Dame (an Independent)
The Group of Five Conferences in 2022 consisted of:
American Athletic Conference (AAC)
Conference USA (C-USA)
Mid-American Conference (The MAC)
Mountain West Conference (MWC)
The Sun Belt Conference (SBC)
And Independents: Army-West Point, Brigham Young, Connecticut, Liberty, Massachusetts, and New Mexico State

The Football Championship Subdivision (FCS) consisted of 128 teams among 15 conferences. They compete not for Bowl games, but for positions to be seeded in a playoff format consisting of 24 teams to play for the FCS National Championship. This topic further isn't a critique of South Carolina's schedule. Focus spotlights the evident weaknesses of the elements used to determine best schedules from the most objective perspectives possible.

Among the complete strength of schedule rankings with 2022 win/loss records and winning percentage based on each FBS team's 2023 opponents (includes all games played; numbers compiled by Phil Steele); the No. 1 SOS comes out as South Carolina: 103-53 (66.0%).[8] However, consider teams on Carolina's schedule in 2023 and their records of last year. At first glance, it definitely doesn't make any sense. The toughest FBS schedule includes playing two 2022 FCS teams. That entire subdivision plays teams much lower in overall talent. Scoring is based solely on total wins, not the quality of those wins nor the wins of the teams on its schedule.

- Furman, 10-3, an FCS school with no 2022 wins over any FBS program
- Jacksonville State, 9-2, transitions to FBS this year, but all 2022 wins came over FCS schools
- The eight SEC schools on tap for South Carolina in 2023 totaled eight wins over FCS schools
- The two ACC schools on board won games in 2022 over Furman and Florida A&M

Of 103 wins Carolina opponents had in 2022, 29 wins came over teams that cannot compete for bowl games nor for the CFP. Scheduling like is this is not something unique to South Carolina. In the future, all team schedules should be re-evaluated based on relevant and equivalent criteria. Hopefully, these criteria, once exposed and evaluated, will result in better regular season, non-conference games.

Against competition the Gamecocks play in 2023, the cumulative W-L record of Carolina's opponents competing for the FBS championship in 2022, when re-calculated, comes out 81-51 (61.8%). Only these games should be considered in the SOS calculation.

Every program should be evaluated the same way. As mentioned earlier, examples like Michigan are ranked as a top recruiting program annually. They currently avoid scheduling any non-conference Power Five schools. This needs to be addressed when evaluating strengths of schedules as well.

Instead, let's measure this as objectively as possible. Below is a proposal regarding how this can be improved.

Power points

I suggest implementing a power point system similar to what some states currently utilize regarding high school football play-offs. They weight programs based on the amount of eligible male students that can play football in each school. <u>In the case of college football, weight schools based on athletic budgets.</u> Generally, high school teams schedule teams with student populations of comparable size, but schools may have wins against teams categorized at a lower level or a higher level. Each is weighted according to its group. The higher the football playing population, the higher the power point total based on comparably sized teams in their category for playoff evaluation.

In a Power Point system for college football, a loss accumulates "0" points against any team, meaning no "style" points for close losses nor one to a highly ranked opponent. A win, however, earns each team points based on the weighted scale. That scale is based on a team's "power" (in this case, its football budget) multiplied by points they've accumulated in wins over their competition. This can all be set up in some computer algorithm of course. By doing this, ratings can be updated weekly during any season for publication and comparison.

A college football tier-system proposal

In 2020, 38 of 130 NCAA FBS programs earned over $100 million athletic revenue. The University of Texas, topped all with more than $200 million.[9] Let's start there. It can only be assumed weighted points awarded based on these criteria would result in a scale sorting out The Power Five from the Group of Five and further down to the FCS. At some points in the analysis, some mixing may be found with "Group" members among lower "Power" members. Teams will only acquire points for wins, no points get awarded for losses. Once annual financial information is submitted by each FBS member and then evaluated and audited by the

NCAA, each football program can be categorized into a predetermined scale of how these figures are weighted regarding each FBS member.

Of 134 current FBS programs, they can separate into five categories or as many as 10 from top to bottom for points to be awarded to each. From this, points would be assigned based on wins and weighted based on the category of each team defeated. Only points accumulated among other FBS programs would be awarded. No points would be earned for wins against FCS programs since they are not eligible for the FBS championship. Teams are ranked based on the highest total weighted points earned. Financial ratings make the scales as objective as possible. Power points remove subjectivity from the rankings. Teams can base their schedules on how they can accumulate the highest amount of power points possible as opposed to finding the weakest opponents they can play to basically assure non-conference wins against inferior competition.

Beyond Football Budgets

When it comes to determining finances for a tiered-system or for revenue sharing, to be fair, it has to be determined how much money is allocated among the various men's and women's sports within each academic institution. These budgets are allocated among athletic admin staffs, coaching staffs, medical staffs, health and safety, facilities, equipment, uniforms, travel, food services, and many more needs. And among universities, the number of athletic teams in each vary greatly. Taken from a random sample online of athletic departments from various FBS institutions and one FCS university, geographically spread throughout the country, and from all FBS conferences, here's a listing of seventeen schools ranked in order having the most to least number of varsity sports in their athletic programs:

1. Harvard 40
2. Ohio State 37
3. Stanford 35
4. Penn State 29

5. Notre Dame 20
6. Washington 20
7. Texas 19
8. Florida State 18
9. Memphis 18
10. Syracuse 18
11. San Diego State 17
12. Texas A&M 16
13. Toledo 16
14. Alabama 15
15. Colorado 15
16. Louisiana – Monroe 15
17. Kansas State 12

Next time a school insists that it needs an additional home football game to fund all its sports programs, understand who most of that money benefits among all its sports and how allocations among teams differ from school to school.

A fair, equitable FCS solution instead

Some argue that FCS programs need a big money pay-out by playing an FBS program on the road. If FBS programs are willing to support FCS programs, there is another way. Now should all FBS competitors play games only among FBS competitors and FCS limits play only to FCS schools as well, FBS programs can designate revenues from their twelfth FBS game to make a charitable contribution the FCS programs. Channel all those FBS monies raised through the NCAA to distribute the total of donated funds equally among all the FCS programs.

It doesn't make sense to play inter-subdivision games for any reason other than to make monetary contributions. Pay-days for FCS programs that visit FBS venues range between $300,00 to $500,000 per game. Under the current circumstances, the FCS has no better opportunity to make some money other than for a game with little chance to win. Why should they sacrifice a weekend when they could be playing another FCS program for a ranking to get into the common championship playoff with a victory for the highest possible seed instead of almost an almost assured loss for more money?

At the end of the season, final power points rank the order of teams for playoffs, bowl games, and my proposed idea regarding "consolation games" for all. They also allow pairing teams for competitive bowl games and consolations instead of pre-arranged bowls aligned under contracts with specific conferences. It would be interesting to see new match-ups unlikely to be seen on a regular basis.

In summary, this proposal offers two major Strength of Schedule rating improvements based on using Power Points:

1.) Records from a year prior are not indicative of teams' relative strengths or weaknesses during the current year; 2.) If teams are not competing at the same level for the same championship, nor with equivalent finances, stadium capacities, specific team budgets, and other data-based criteria, competitors of the upcoming season should be weighted and not be considered equals within the overall power point equation that they are now. Both considerations can level the proverbial "playing field" of FBS football.

I saw Auburn and Penn State play a home-and-home series the last two years. College football needs more Power Five inter-conference games to determine viable rankings.

8.) TV time-outs

These are not influenced by any teams. As a spectator enjoying being part of the game atmosphere though, nothing kills game momentum more than the volume of TV time-outs. How many smile cams, kiss cams, dance cams, video board games, video advertisements, video races, miscellaneous presentations, and award ceremonies have to be watched? And at home, how many repetitive ads for insurance, mobile phone services, fast food joints, cars and movies do fans watching have to see for over two additional hours for game action that's played for 60 minutes? Most likely, fans just click their remotes to catch action from another game, but wishing not to see the same commercials which often happens.

There's another sports model to follow - from hockey. Play the 15-minute quarters straight through without commercial interruptions, although trailers below the action constantly bombard with ads already. In between the first and second quarters and between the third and fourth quarters, break ten minutes for advertising. Maintain the 20 minutes for half-time along with game analysis. Still, plenty of time to run the current repetitive ads and negotiate for the same money made now. Less time available becomes more costly and should drive the price per minute up anyway. Also, instead of three 30-second time-outs, give both teams three one-minute time-outs in each half. Networks may even be able to add one more full game to its Saturday, national line-up as well.

Handle the injury time-outs the same as today. Will 15-minute periods wear players out more quickly? Another lesson from hockey: if necessary, substitute players more often. Maybe giving more players (i.e. - second-teamers) more actual playing time will cut down on many wanting to leave through the transfer portals due to lack of playing time. Maybe they would feel more like an actual part of the team. Another plus if that's an issue.

Granted, television revenue to support the sport is derived from commercials, but it's at a point now where revenue-making supersedes the primary purpose. We all desire to *"spend what better way to enjoy an autumn afternoon?"* COLLEGE FOOTBALL!

[1] Anonymous, Collegefootballplayoff.com, "College Football Playoff Announces 2024 and 2025 Game Dates", 5/2/2023 11:30:00 AM.

[2] Marc Edelman, Senior Contributor, FORBESBUSINESSSPORTS MONEY: EDITORS'PICK. "Why Congress Would Be Crazy to Grant the NCAA An Antitrust Exemption," May 6, 2020,09:50 am EDT

[3] Ibid.

[4] Ryan Bologna, Clutch Points, "Full details of Jaden Rashada's termination of $13.85 million deal", February 6, 2023.

[5] Ibid.

[6] Kevin Kelley, FBS Schedules: "College football strength of schedule: 2023 Win/Loss method", February 20, 2023.

[7] Ibid.

[8] Ibid

[9] Marc Edelman, Senior Contributor, FORBESBUSINESSSPORTS MONEY: EDITORS'PICK."Why Congress Would Be Crazy to Grant the NCAA An Antitrust Exemption," May 6, 2020, 09:50 am EDT

Afterword

Entering my sixth decade of attending college football games basically every fall weekend, I think I'm qualified to provide my input and insight. As I said right from the start, I have a passion for this great game. Improvements can always be made, but only if it improves the sport in a sense that all teams can become as competitive as possible. It shouldn't allow privileges for the very few who continue to dominate. The privilege comes mostly from the amount of revenue that can be generated due to comparative advantages.

If the playing field can be leveled so all that can start at the same point, we go from there based on the talents, commitment, loyalty and teamwork of coaches and players. If it makes sense that this can't be done equally for 134 different Football Bowl Subdivision programs, let it be decided that there are at least two different factions of teams that want to play by different standards when it comes to playing on a "level field."

I see establishing two separate divisions from the current FBS as a viable alternative. Remove the Super-conference teams from the rest of the NCAA football members and let there be two separate and distinct levels of play for two National Championships with different levels of standards and off-field rules pertaining to finances,recruiting, scheduling, and allocation of resource such as coaching staff sizes. We then have FBS, FCS, D-2, D-3 and Super-conferences.

What has to be considered: are the games only primarily about making money for school-funding needs, or should there be more emphasis on educating players outside of the classroom to be successful as men, as fathers, and as leaders in whatever profession or career-path they choose to do for the rest of their lives? That's the question institutions of higher learning have to answer for themselves and be clear about it.

Bucket List

This adventure is not over! I list below in my summation of tales shared, my many ideas of the "Good" and "Fun" things I hope to do in years ahead pertaining to seeing more college football games. I probably won't get to do all, and I'll probably die while trying. No pun intended, that's just reality. They're listed in alphabetical order. I'll just pick and choose what I want to do when and if I can. Time, budget, convenience, and personal priorities will lead me along the way.

I'll review season to season. I'm basically booked through 2023. A few listed below I've already bumped up into 2023 while writing about this fantastic voyage, incredible journey, or whatever you want to call it. I figure before future seasons, that I won't plan as early as I usually do to give myself more flexibility. However, I will try to consider these as my priorities when I start planning upcoming schedules. Before each season, I'll continue to post my tentative schedules.You will be able to view them as always on my website/blog, **collegefootballfan.com**.

- Add games to be played in remaining 12 states: Arkansas, Hawaii, Idaho, Kansas, Montana, Nebraska, New Mexico, North Dakota, Oregon, South Dakota, Vermont, and Washington (none in Alaska)
- Arizona and Arizona State home games
- Arkansas via Arkansas State for a doubleheader weekend

BUCKET LIST

- Boise State game on Blue "Smurf Turf"
- BYU day game and Utah home game in Salt Lake City
- Central Michigan tailgate in Mt. Pleasant, MI with Meyer family
- Cortaca Bowl: annual rivalry in NY between Cortland State and Ithaca
- D-3 game in Vermont (Norwich, Castleton State, or Middlebury)
- Duke game with some meaning at Wade Wallace Stadium
- Every Army-Navy game for as long as I can
- FCS Championship game
- FCS games in Montana, North Dakota, and South Dakota
- FIU and FAU home games combined on a late fall weekend
- Florida State game at Doak Campbell
- Game 700 in 2024, Navy vs. Notre Dame in The Meadowlands
- Georgia Southern FBS home game
- Georgia State FBS home game
- Hawaii home game (don't tell St. Laurie, it's a surprise)
- Idaho U. at home in Kibbie Dome
- Jacksonville State (#132) FBS home game
- James Madison FBS home game
- Kansas home game under Head Coach Lance Leipold
- Kennesaw State (#134) FBS home game
- LSU home game of significance
- Miami, Ohio game and *The Cradle of Coaches*, by sculptor Kristen Visbal.
- Minnesota game vs Big Ten with the Gopher Tails!
- NC State home game and tailgate
- Nebraska game in Lincoln under Head Coach Matt Rhule
- New Mexico, NMSU home games, or both; tied to UTEP home game
- North Dakota State game in Fargo
- Ohio U. at home and at Akron or Kent for weekday doubleheader
- Oklahoma home game vs. SEC opponent
- Oregon/Washington games for a long weekend
- Penn State in CFP championship
- Red River Showdown – Texas vs. Oklahoma

FIFTY YEARS OF TAILGATE TALES:

- Sam Houston State (#133) FBS game under K.C. Keeler
- San Diego State home game at Snapdragon Stadium
- Seeing games in as many remaining FBS venues as possible
- South Alabama home game and visit to USS Alabama
- Sun Bowl in El Paso
- Tennessee Tailgate with Shannon's and Pirrello's
- The Battle of the Fremont Cannon – UNLV vs. Nevada
- The Grove at Ole Miss for another tailgate!
- Toledo vs. Bowling Green rivalry
- Tulane home game and breakfast at Brennan's
- UAB home game in Protective Stadium
- Wisconsin home game/ Fifth quarter
- Wyoming Cowboy game in Laramie

About the Author, Steve Koreivo

This author lives college football. He's attended 676 college football games since 1972, and he's seen every Football Bowl Subdivision (FBS) team play at least once. He's also attended games played by Football Championship Subdivision (FCS), D-2, and D-3 teams. As he enters retirement after 42 years as a Purchasing professional, his journey continues as reflected in his updated Bucket List. In 2011, he published his first book, Tales from the Tailgate: From the Fan who's seen 'em all!

A native of New Jersey, The Birthplace of College Football, he retired to Middle Tennessee to extend his life-long adventure! Married to "*St. Laurie*" for most of this journey, he took time to write this book to share his 50-year adventure with others. His unique adventure continues! Check out his website www.collegefootballfan.com where he shares his latest adventures and where he shares his insights on the latest in college football in "Steveo's Salvos."

The "Good" and the "Fun":

- 676 college football games attended since 1972 (655 since college graduation in 1979)
- Attended at least one game played by all 131 FBS teams. Adding the next three shortly.
- Attended games in 37 states and D.C. at 171 stadiums among FBS (79),

FCS, D-2, and D-3.
- 22 different Heisman Trophy winners seen in action from Tony Dorsett to Bryce Young.
- 46 bowls: BCS championship, Rose, Sugar, Orange, Cotton, Fiesta, CFP semis, and more.
- HOF Coaches: Bryant, Paterno, Parseghian, Bowden, Osborne, Beamer, Saban…
- Saw thirteen FBS and six lower NCAA division national champions in action since 1979.
- FBS games decided by seven points or less – 206; three or less – 96; by one – 33.
- ArmyNavy (18), Auburn-Alabama (2), Ohio State-Michigan, Pitt-Penn State (6), USC-UCLA, Stanford-Cal, Clemson-South Carolina (2), Rutgers-Princeton, Harvard-Yale (2).

BIBLIOGRAPHY

Adelson, Andrea, October 22, 2013. "University of Miami Scandal." ESPN.com "Nevin Shapiro." Last page edited 21 April 2023.

Anonymous, 5/2/2023 11:30:00 AM. "College Football Playoff Announces 2024 and 2025 Game Dates." Collegefootballplayoff.com. Retrieved 2 August 2023.

Anonymous, 1/23/2008." Todd Marinovich." Biographicon: all the people of the world. Jan. 4-23, 2008. www.biographican.com/history/ldpc4/Todd_Marinovich. Retrieved 1/30/2010.

Anonymous, July 25, 2012. "Illinois Coaches Head to Penn State Campus to Recruit Players." CBS News Chicago. Retrieved June 25, 2023.

Bates, Daniel, July 26, 2023. "Trent Dilfer Wants College Football Coaches Banned for Life If They Break One Rule," The Spun. Retrieved 26 July 2023.

Beard, Aaron, AP Sports Writer, 7/27/2023. "Wake Forest's Dave Clawson says multiple players returned despite tampering by other schools." AP Associated press. Retrieved 27 July 2023.

Blondin, Alan, 9/8/2021. "Former football coach makes a large donation to CCU to build new athletic facilities." The Sun News. Retrieved 30 April 2023

Bologna, Ryan, 2/6/2023. "Full details of Jaden Rashada's termination of $13.85 million deal". Clutch Points. Retrieved April 16, 2023.

Buhler, John, 2/3/2023. "Ill-fated Jaden Rashada Florida NIL contract details revealed." Fansided.com. Retrieved April 16, 2023.

Chavkin, Daniel, 8/15/2023. "Nebraska AD Trev Alberts Warns Next Conference Moves Will Be 'Far More Disruptive.'" Sports Illustrated. Retrieved 22 August 2023.

Dellenger, Ross, 5/30/2023. "Inside the NIL Battle That Is Splintering the SEC: 'We're All Money Laundering.'" Sports Illustrated, Retrieved May 30, 2023.

Edelman, Marc, Senior Contributor, May 6, 2020 "Why Congress Would Be Crazy to Grant the NCAA An Antitrust Exemption." FORBESBUSINESSSPORTSMONEY: EDITORS'PICK. Retrieved 27 June 2023.

Graves, Tyler, June 2, 2023. "SEC announces 8-game Schedule Format, Puts Georgia Rivalry Games in Peril." Dawgs Daily on FanNation. Retrieved June 2, 2023.

Greenberg, Samantha, July 7, 2021. "Bryce Young Signs with CAA For NIL Representation." Sports Agent Blog. Retrieved August 15, 2023.

Greenspan, Dan, 12/17/2016. "San Diego State's Pumphrey Sets NCAA Rushing Record." ABC News. Associated Press. Retrieved April 29, 2023.

Kelley, Kevin, 2/20/2023. "College football strength of schedule: 2023 Win/Loss method." FBS Schedules. Retrieved February 20, 2023.

BIBLIOGRAPHY

Kenney, Kirk, 10/17/2016. "Aztecs Super Fan Tom Ables dies." The San Diego Union-Tribune. Retrieved March 30, 2023.

Kirshner, Alex, 12/18/2016. "Blame the NCAA for Donnel Pumphrey breaking Ron Dayne's Rushing Record with fewer yards." SB Nation. Retrieved December 28, 2016.

Knox, Chuck, and Bill Plaschke. Hard Knox: The Life of an NFL Coach. New York: Harcourt, Brace, Jovanovich Publishers, 1988.

Ladd, Aaron, 1/18/2019. "Moglia stepping down as CCU's head football coach after seven seasons." WMBF News. Retrieved 30 April 2023.

Matula, Thaddeus D., Director, December 11, 2010. "Pony Excess." 30 for 30. Season 1. Episode 30. ESPN Retrieved July 10, 2023.

McGrath, John. "College Football's Superfan," Lindy's 2005 Pre-season (2005): p. 18-20.

Murphy, Dan 12/15/2022. ESPN Staff writer, "NLRB to pursue unlawful labor practices against USC, PAC-12, NCAA." ESPN.com. Retrieved 27 June 2023.

Papanek, John (editor-in-chief). "25 Words (or less)," ESPN The Magazine (29 October 2001): p 32.

Parks, James, January 30, 2023. "New details emerge in car crash that killed Georgia football player, staff member", Fan Nation/College Football HQ, Retrieved July 23, 2023.

Parks, James, January 12, 2023. "NCAA makes changes to college football transfer portal", CFB-HQ on Fox Nation. Retrieved January 12, 2023.

Popp, Nels, Jason Simmons, Stephen L. Shapiro, and Nick Wantanabe, March 23, 2023. "Predicting Ticket Holder No-Shows: Examining Differences Between Reported and Actual Attendance at College Football Games," fitpublishing.com. Retrieved August 1, 2023.

Quinn, Melissa, June 21, 2021. "Supreme Court rules for student-athletes in battle over NCAA limits on certain benefits." CBS News. Retrieved June 21, 2021.

Sager, Mike, "Todd Marinovich: The Man who Never was." Esquire, April 14, 2009.

Solomon, Jon, "UAB football is back, reinstatement announcement set for Monday." http://www.cbssports.com/college-football. Retrieved 23 June 2023..

University Archives' Student Life and Culture Archival Program. "Origin of the University of Illinois Homecoming." http://www.library.csi.cuny.edu/dept/history/lavender/footnote.hmtl. Admin.illinois.edu.2005. Retrieved 3/30/2010.

Vescey, George. "Sports of the Times: Osborne is Finally the Champ," New York Times, January 3, 1995, Section B, page 7.

Wetzel, Dan, July 18, 2023. "Brock Bowers' selfless NIL move shows Georgia still has big picture in mind while chasing 3-peat." YahooSports.com, Retrieved 16 August 2023.

Wilson, Dave, 12/7/2022. ESPN Staff Writer, "Record Setting UTSA QB Frank Harris to return for 7th Season." ESPN.com. Retrieved 15 May 2023.

Wolff, Ted (ed.). "Six years and a flip!" Texas vs. Penn State Official Game

Program, 29 September 1985: p. 25.

Wolff, Ted (ed.). "Wisconsin Band's 'Fifth Quarter' is a vast Polka Party." Garden State Bowl IV Game Program: Tennessee vs. Wisconsin, 13 December 1981: p. 57.

Zoroya, Nick. "NCAA NIL Rules Guide: The Do's & Don'ts of NIL." laxallstars.com.
8 November 2021.

Made in United States
North Haven, CT
04 February 2024